Nancy
Cunard
Perfect
Stranger

Nancy Cunard
Perfect Stranger

By Jane Marcus

**Edited and with an Introduction
and Afterword by Jean Mills**

CLEMSON
UNIVERSITY
PRESS

First Edition, 2020
This paperback edition published 2024

ISBN: 978-1-949979-29-9 (hardback)
ISBN: 978-1-83553-874-6 (paperback)
eISBN: 978-1-949979-30-5 (e-book)

Published by Clemson University Press
in association with Liverpool University Press

For information about Clemson University Press,
please visit our website at www.clemson.edu/press.

Library of Congress Cataloging-in-Publication Data

Names: Marcus, Jane, author. | Mills, Jean (Professor of English) editor.
Title: Nancy Cunard : perfect stranger / by Jane Marcus ; edited and with
an introduction and afterword by Jean Mills.
Description: Clemson : Clemson University Press, 2020. | Includes
bibliographical references and index. | Summary: "In the wake of
inadequate histories of radical writing and activism, Nancy Cunard:
Perfect Stranger rejects stereotypes of Cunard as spoiled heiress and
"sexually dangerous New Woman," offering instead a bold, unapologetic,
evidence-based portrait of a woman and her significant contributions to
twenty-first-century considerations of gender, race, and class"--
Provided by publisher.
Identifiers: LCCN 2020012563 (print) | LCCN 2020012564 (ebook) | ISBN
9781949979299 (hardback) | ISBN 9781949979305 (ebook)
Subjects: LCSH: Cunard, Nancy, 1896-1965. | Authors, English--20th
century--Biography. | Women political activists--England--Biography. |
Women journalists--England--Biography.
Classification: LCC PR6005.U46 Z657 2008 (print) | LCC PR6005.U46 (ebook)
| DDC 821/.912--dc23
LC record available at https://lccn.loc.gov/2020012563
LC ebook record available at https://lccn.loc.gov/2020012564

Typeset in Minion Pro by Carnegie Book Production.
Printed and bound by CPI Group (UK) Ltd, Croydon CR0 4YY.

for Michael

Contents

Figures

Acknowledgments

The reader who wants a chronological narrative of Nancy Cunard's life is referred to the excellent biography by Anne Chisholm, to which I am deeply indebted. Further details and recollections by her friends are provided in Hugh Ford's labor of love, *Nancy Cunard: Brave Poet, Indomitable Rebel 1896–1965*, an invaluable source of material about Cunard's life and work.

Anthony Hobson represents the Cunard Literary Estate and I am grateful for his permission to quote from her work, as well as for his patient responses to many queries and his kind letters giving me access to the Harry Ransom Humanities Research Center (HRHRC) at the University of Texas in Austin, and other collections where Cunard's papers are held. Many of Cunard's papers, surviving diaries, letters, scrapbooks, and typescript drafts of her poems and articles are in the HRHRC. The same library houses an important collection of photographs relating to her life. My personal debt to this library and its helpful and devoted staff is enormous and spread out over more than twenty years, many different projects, and several changes of staff. Let me here express my thanks to Cathy Henderson, curator of manuscripts, and her staff, the staff of the reading room and the photography collection, and most particularly Ken Craven, who took a special interest in Cunard and was especially helpful in finding uncatalogued materials early in this project. I am also grateful for the support of Tom Staley and a grant from the library's Mellon Fellowship to work in the collection. My colleagues

Elizabeth Cullingford and Alan Friedman and Sue and Kurt Heinzelman were unfailingly generous with hospitality and stimulating discussions during my visits. Serving as adviser for Holly McSpadden's M.A. thesis on Cunard and her later Ph.D. kept my interest alive while I was engaged on other projects, and I am grateful to her.

To Michael Pretina and Anne Marie Franco at the Camargo Foundation I owe thanks for the time and space to think out, plan, and begin to write in ideal circumstances in 1996. Some work was done on this project while I was a Fellow at Clare Hall, Cambridge, and I am grateful for their support, especially from Terri Apter and Mary Hamer. I am grateful to Professor Gillian Beer and the fellows as well for their interest in the project. In Cambridge, the friendship and support of Mary Joannou was invaluable. Several chapters were sketched out while my husband and I were guests at the Indian Statistical Institutes in Calcutta, Bangalore, and Delhi in January and February 1997. As always, I thank the Mathematics Department of the University of Strasbourg for hospitality during several summers of writing. The Rockefeller Foundation provided a very productive residency at Bellagio, and the City University of New York's sabbatical leave for 1996–97 as well as several CUNY Research Grants made much of the necessary travel to libraries and collections possible, as well as funding copies of documents and photographs.

Throughout this project my young German colleague Sabine Broeck has been a constant critic and inspiration, challenging and encouraging and keeping me up to the mark. Traci-Ann Williams has been a loyal research assistant and the work of Anna Katsavos, Gay Wachman, Robin Hackett, and Nancy Berke on their dissertations during the writing of this book has provided a strong intellectual context for my work. Lillian Robinson has supported this project from the beginning. She has provided rare books, chaired a meeting at the Modern Language Association on the *Negro* anthology in 1996, and acted as an example of a writer and critic. As a public intellectual whose work means a great deal to women on the left, she has believed in Nancy Cunard and she has believed in me.

I am grateful to the universities, colleagues, and conferences who sponsored talks on Nancy Cunard and responded to my arguments: Celeste Schenck and the American University in Paris; Carolyn Allen and the University of Washington, Seattle; Michael Pretina at the Camargo Foundation, Cassis; Marianne DeKoven and the Modernism's Others session at the 1996 MLA; Lillian Robinson and the panelists at the *Negro* anthology session at the 1996 MLA; the New York Council for the Humanities; Jaime Hovey and Shari Benstock and the "Quer(y)ing Primitivism" panel, MLA, 1995; English, Comparative Literature and Women's Studies, Lee and Annabel Patterson, Yale University; Alan Friedman and the 20th Century British Literature Division, MLA, 1994; Claire Buck and the Modernism Research Seminar, University of North London, 1994; Benita Parry and the Warwick University conference in honor of Edward Said, "The Politics of Identity, Secular Criticism and the Politics of History"; Maud Ellmann and the Cambridge University Seminar on Women, 1994; Sabine Broeck and the Institut fur England-und-Amerikastudien, Frankfurt, 1993; Nancy Miller and the "What Was the Twentieth Century" conference, CUNY, 1992; Mae Henderson and The English Institute, 1992; and William Germano, editor of the English Institute volumes at Routledge. Many of the ideas in this book were first tried out in seminars at the City College of New York, where Dean Martin Tamny supported the seminar with a speakers' series, and at CUNY Graduate Center. To the participants in those lively and politically problematic meetings, especially on questions of race and identity, I am deeply indebted, especially to my colleagues James de Jongh and Michele Wallace. It is a tribute to the spirit of free intellectual inquiry that this course was taught during the heated debates about Afro-centrism and the "free speech" rights of its proponents, which tore the City College of New York apart during this period.

Many individuals and libraries have provided resources and help, answered questions, copied documents, or given support to the project in other ways. First I would like to thank Rick Utick of the CCNY Library who provided seminar participants with a rare copy of the *Negro* anthology for our classes. I hope that all the others are adequately acknowledged here. My thanks to Christine Stansell, Eunice Lipton, Maureen Shanahan, Lisa Marcus, Shelley Fisher Fishkin, Louise Yelin, Josh Gosciak, Marianne Guenot, Louise DeSalvo, Abby Tallmer, Susan Stanford Friedman, Shari Benstock, Karla Jay, Vron Ware, Mary Ann Caws, Margaret Carson, Anne Chisholm, Shaun Carey, Susan Pennybacker, Joe Boone, Linda Evans at the Chicago Historical Society, Desley Deacon, Cheryl Fish, Margaret Higonnet, Molara Ogundipe-Leslie, Ian Patterson, Carla Kaplan, Claire Tylee, and Carolyn Ferrell.

I want to thank the staffs of the Schomburg Library of Black Culture, New York City, the Beinecke Library, Yale University, the Tate Gallery Research Library, the British Library, the Cambridge University Library, the Bodleian Library, and the National Portrait Gallery, London.

Acknowledgments by Jean Mills

I'd like to thank Michael Marcus for his support and belief that I could bring this project to fruition. Thanks, too, for the good conversation and many meals that we have shared (he continues to amaze in the kitchen!) after long days of teaching, while I attempted to retrace Jane's steps in various collections and archives during the course of my research. Thanks to my editor, John Morgenstern, for his expertise (somewhat of a lost art), but especially for sharing in my vision for the book, and to Alison Mero, for her efforts in shepherding this book through the editorial process and a pandemic, no less. I'm indebted to the Jane Marcus Estate and to her family for allowing me to continue my intellectual conversations with Jane in this way; to her friends, peace historian Sandi Cooper and Eleanor Roosevelt biographer, Blanche Wiesen-Cook, for sharing their stories with me about Jane's progress on Cunard; to Leslie Fields for her work and support in helping us establish the Jane Marcus Papers at Mount Holyoke College, S. Hadley, Massachusetts, and for her assistance in helping me navigate the archive for some missing materials; to the Office for the Advancement of Research at John Jay College-CUNY and the Professional Staff Congress for helping fund my research; to the staff at the Harry Ransom Humanities Research Center, especially Elizabeth L. Garver, for her patience and expertise in navigating the collection; to Tom Staley, who took time out of his own writing schedule (and retirement!) to have lunch with me to discuss the project; to Alan Friedman and Elizabeth Cullingford for meeting with me to help track down missing information or gaps in the research and for being willing to reminisce with me about Jane's time teaching at the University of Texas, Austin; to the staff of the Man Ray Estate; to Penelope Small, Curtis Moffat's daughter, for giving us permission to use her father's photo for our cover; to Rachel Kett of the Victoria and Albert Museum; to Lisa Olrich at the National Portrait Gallery; to the staff at Princeton University's Rare Book Collection archives; and to Daniel Trujillo at Artists' Rights Society. My thanks to all of Jane's former students and mentees for their encouragement along the way, including Anne Donlon, J. Ashley Foster, Linda Camarasano, Robin Hackett, and Cori Gabbard; and to my colleagues in Woolf Studies and Peace Studies, especially Charles Andrews, and members of the faculty in the English Department at John Jay College-CUNY for their patience and understanding regarding delays in other projects while I finalized this one.

I am deeply indebted, as ever, to my wife, Martha Lou Haag, for her grace, integrity, and ongoing support of my teaching and writing life; to my step-sons, Maxwell Basch, Audry Basch, and Harrison Basch, and my daughter Abigail Sarah Mills Goldfarb for reminding me that youth is in fact not misspent on the young. *Nox est perpetua una dormienda.*

A Note about the Cover

In the summer of 1978, Jane Marcus and her husband, mathematician Michael Marcus, spent three months traveling through England in a rented VW camper, attending conferences and conducting research in their respective fields. Jane was working on Virginia Woolf and Bloomsbury at the time when she came upon the photography studio of Curtis Moffat quite by accident. She spent the day talking to him about Woolf and her circle, but mostly he spoke to her about Nancy Cunard. The photo on the cover by Moffat is from a series of photographs Cunard sat for in 1925. Before Jane left to conduct further research in Denmark and Poland, Moffat gave her a framed photo of this portrait, slightly cropped, with his embossed studio impression on the matting. I trace the inspiration for her scholarship on Nancy Cunard to this portrait and to these early conversations with Moffat in 1978. The photograph is reproduced here with the kind permission of Moffat's daughter, Penelope Small, and the Victoria and Albert Museum.

Editor's Introduction
Scholarship's Afterlife: The Return of Rage

As Jane Marcus writes in the manuscript that has become *Nancy Cunard: Perfect Stranger*, "I am shaking up the kaleidoscope of modernism here, making other patterns with the same pieces, so that different stories emerge." A distinguished and path-breaking feminist scholar, who was responsible in large part for reshaping our critical understanding of Virginia Woolf as a public intellectual and major literary and political voice of the twentieth century, Jane Marcus began the substantive portions of her research on Nancy Cunard in the early 1990s, working intermittently through the early to mid-2000s until illness interrupted her momentum. She changed direction out of necessity, publishing shorter pieces on Cunard in other publications. "Bonding and Bondage: Nancy Cunard and the Making of the *Negro* Anthology" was published by Routledge in 1995 in *Borders, Boundaries and Frameworks* (Essays from the English Institute), parts of which Marcus intended to include here. Her essay "Laying Down the White Woman's Burden: Michael Arlen's *The Green Hat* and Mulk Raj Anand's *Coolie*" was also intended to be the fifth chapter of this longer study. I've dropped both of these chapters, however, as versions of these were reprinted in her last work, a collection of essays on race, *Hearts of Darkness: White Women Write Race*.[1] Marcus's longer work, her full-length study of the intellectual, political, and cultural life of Nancy Cunard presented here, is all new material, with the exception of the final chapter, "Race on the Wire: Nancy Cunard's War Stories," in Part V.[2] Because this essay is less well known to audiences beyond specific scholarly circles, her former students, and mentees, I've included it here, as it also demonstrates her insights into Nancy Cunard's journalism, an often overlooked aspect of Cunard's critical contributions.

The manuscript remained largely intact but unorganized, and parts of it were unfinished at the time of Marcus's death in 2015. With the support of the Jane Marcus Estate, her archive now housed in the Jane Marcus Papers deeded as a gift in 2016 to Mount Holyoke College in South Hadley, Massachusetts, and a grant from the Office of the Advancement of Research at John Jay College-CUNY, I have spent the last two years organizing the manuscript, performing minor edits, and filling in and updating some of the research. Much of my work on *Perfect Stranger* is concerned with its paratexts, but even these are largely supported by our conversations about Marcus's ideas and direction for the manuscript while she was alive. She had a number of working titles over the course of her research, but I ultimately chose *Nancy Cunard: Perfect Stranger*, excerpting it from Marcus's foregrounding of Cunard as a "perfect stranger" in the early chapters of what I consider to be a provocative, incisive, and fearless portrait of a woman we all thought we knew.

Reputation and Representation

In effect, *Perfect Stranger* does for Nancy Cunard what Marcus did for Virginia Woolf—it reshapes our understanding of a woman whose reputation and role in key historical, political, and cultural moments were either dismissed and attacked, or undervalued. In Cunard's case, Marcus insists we reconsider issues of gender, race, and class in relation to the accusations, stereotypes, and scandals which have dominated, and continue to dominate, our perception of Nancy Cunard in the public record.

In the wake of inadequate histories of radical writing and activism, *Nancy Cunard: Perfect Stranger* is unafraid and unapologetic in addressing and contesting Cunard's reputation and reception as "a sexually dangerous New Woman." Cunard was famously marked by "anonymous," misogynistic, and hostile reviews of her anti-war poem *Parallax* (1925), which accused her of plagiarizing T. S. Eliot's *The Waste Land*. Marcus offers a bold re-reading, a project worth doing, "since the history of Cunard's career as a poet consists simply of the repetition of this accusation." She ultimately links the poem's reception to a "fear of what the woman artist and her sexuality will do to the 'market' for highbrow verse." Marcus crafts a different portrait of Cunard as a poet, urging us to read Eliot's poem as he insisted it be read, as a personal "grouse against life" and "a piece of rhythmical grumbling," and casts Cunard, not instead, but alongside, as one of the "great poet(s) of the Aftermath" of war, a scorched-earth landscape, which, Marcus convincingly argues, "women's poetry is in tune with…"

Although the publication of any book is a small miracle, if not an invitation to be shot at, it seems fitting that an unfinished manuscript about a woman often driven by rage throughout the 1930s by the author of 1988's *Art and Anger: Reading like a Woman* is finding a more generous and capacious reading in 2020. Critical trends and new directions in the field of modernism have created opportunities for these reconsiderations, if not returns to inquiries into how we navigate and negotiate rage. As Urmila Seshagiri recently wrote in *Modernism/Modernity*, the Modernist Studies Association's affiliated journal, and their first issue dedicated to feminism and women modernists, "Feminism is repetitive because patriarchy is undead."[3] Seshagiri was pointing to the gap between a discipline that recognizes that women, feminists, and feminist women fundamentally shaped modernism and modernity and a body of scholarship responding to that subject, which continues to overlook women's roles. These lacunae also led to the establishment of the journal *Feminist Modernist Studies* in 2018, whose inaugural issue outlined the resistance it faced in arguing for its *raison d'être*. As presses, librarians, and other cultural gatekeepers told its founding editors that such a journal would be unnecessary or difficult to categorize, the journal's founder, Cassandra Laity, wrote that the editors "wondered how scholarship on modernism and feminism/gender/sexuality could be simultaneously unnecessary (e.g. already done, fully integrated into modernist studies) and not recognizable as a category of academic study."[4] It was out of this uneasy climate and sense that feminism was acknowledged, sustained, and included in modernist studies and yet at the same time silenced and invisible that the journal aimed to "re-enter a diversely defined modernism through a feminist/gendered lens."[5]

Both Laity and Seshagiri were also writing within the context of a global political turn in 2016 to far-right ideologies, anti-feminist thought, an increase in racist rhetoric and hate crimes, and a nationalism and populism that demanded and invigorated a feminist politics and response. In an age now commonly referred to through hashtags such as the #MeToo generation and #TimesUp, folksonomies such as these devoted to narratives of sexual assault and sexual harassment have replenished themselves in various media, gaining traction to the point where they have become indicators of a feminist zeitgeist, of distinct and transformative changes in public discourse. Contemporary titles such as Soraya Chemaly's *Rage Becomes Her: The Power of Women's Anger* (Simon and Schuster, 2018), Charlene A. Carruthers's *Unapologetic: A Black, Queer and Feminist Mandate for Radical Movements* (Beacon Press, 2018), and Rebecca Traister's *Good and Mad: The Revolutionary Power of Women's Anger* (Simon and Schuster, 2018) are driving a public conversation that intersects with and is supported by new feminist scholarship, theory, and research. Another leading feminist journal, *Signs: The Journal of Women and Culture in Society*, will be publishing a special issue, titled and entirely devoted to rage, in 2021.[6]

It is within this broader context of both scholarly and contemporary cultural debate that Jane Marcus's work on Nancy Cunard has found its audience more than two decades after she began her research. Allowing for the prolepsis often typical in the intellectual histories of feminist thought, there is a degree of irony in the fact that the manuscript often points to the ways in which Cunard poses challenges to feminist readers. "Nancy Cunard did not identify as a feminist," as Marcus reminds us, and *Perfect Stranger* challenges us to grapple with the complexities of representation, whether along gender, class, or racial lines, and their intersections. At one point, Marcus connects Cunard's feminism to her activism and to her class politics. She writes, in Chapter 10 on Cunard and the Spanish Civil War, that "the intense life-long political effort of connecting people and groups to one another, gathering them for intellectual action, publishing and translating radical poems and introducing revolutionary writers to their counterparts from all over the world was, I believe, the feminist element in her anarcho-communism." She also cites race and war, especially World War I, as artistic and intellectual crucibles for Cunard, not gender. But the effects of Cunard's anger, both as a resource and as a means to pathologize and medicalize her, are interrogated throughout the book from a feminist perspective. In relation to her work on the *Negro* anthology, Marcus writes that

> Cunard's anger at injustice was the force that drove her to complete such an enormous task. Anger became the chief aspect of her personality at some points, much to the chagrin of her friends. But it fueled her work for the cause and she was very productive and very effective.

Her long-time friend, the poet and journalist Solita Solano, would agree, writing that "Nancy functioned best in a state of fury."

The ways in which Nancy Cunard navigated and negotiated her rage throughout her life are on display in *Perfect Stranger*, and Marcus's feminist reading of Cunard's example is intersectional and instructive as it raises important questions about how to strategize and make use of the rich storehouses of anger at work on the contemporary political stage. As Margot Kotler so presciently pointed out, it's not so much the feminist credo from the 1970s "the personal is political" that we need to embrace, but "the personal is factual."[7] And it is to that sense of accuracy, objectivity, and truth-seeking, in what is so callously and dangerously sometimes referred to today as a post-truth world, that *Perfect Stranger* insists we dwell to find our catalysts and strategies for change.

She Speaks

If the audience for *Perfect Stranger* has been delayed, its voice, I would argue, is remarkably on time. As in much of the best of her scholarly writing, Marcus's argument is erudite, explicitly stated, and urgent. In addition to an investigation into Cunard's commitment to Black culture with the compilation and publication of the *Negro* anthology as well as the more frequently understudied journalism, both on the Spanish Civil War and extensive writings in the Black press, *Perfect Stranger* showcases Jane Marcus's talent for vitality, provocation, and original thinking on the level of the sentence. She often raises uncomfortable, difficult questions ("Who benefits, we may ask, when Cunard is constructed as a brainless sexual predator and scapegoated as a particularly virulent kind of racist, a white woman who identifies with Black people?" and "Why is it represented as ethically more incorrect to identify with the struggles of the oppressed than to ignore them?"); no matter how we respond, the energy and intellectual intensity of her prose style insists we not look away. "Is it too bold to ask?," "Dare I suggest?," "Might it be possible?," "Who benefits from this erasure?" not only speak to her ability to formulate meaningful, generative questions, but also to her methodology as dialogic and shared.

Ultimately, the aim of this study was, as Marcus notes, to "reframe her life in terms of her work." As she explores Cunard's unique relationship with *Vogue*, for example, as she modeled for its pages and tried to carve out a position there as a columnist, Marcus focuses on the obstacles Cunard faced as a woman and the conflict such an arrangement posed and, more importantly, on the writing that Cunard actually produced. Although the editors "preferred to look at her anorectic face and body in murderous and self-destructive photographs [...]," Marcus writes, "the writing is as vivid and rapid as her letters." Unlike Janet Flanner's "shaped and controlled prose," Cunard "is present in the text in a personal way, telling us with relief that you can drink at the bicycle races [... or that] the food is good at the Boeuf sur le Toit." She follows Cunard's stint at *Vogue* with a more in-depth examination of her extensive journalism, which documents "the suffering refugee, the conscripted soldier, the black prisoner of war," leading Marcus to characterize Cunard as "a pioneer against racism in the daily press."

Bringing Nancy Cunard into the twenty-first century in *Perfect Stranger*, Marcus follows the money metaphor used to undercut Cunard's reputation, a woman from the upper classes politically at odds with her culture, her race, and her class, who nonetheless maintained a role with the literary avant-garde. As she cautions the reader in her Introduction,

> this is not the story of Nancy Cunard as an English heiress of the Anglo-American shipping family. This is not a family romance about the ungrateful daughter of Maud (Burke) Cunard, silver mine heiress from San Francisco who married Sir Bache Cunard and grew up at Nevill Holt...

Refusing to foster and encourage gossip, Marcus articulates a portrait of Cunard that does not suppress the problematic aspects of her work from a feminist, class, and race perspective, but also argues that it is not acceptable to dismiss her considerable contributions on behalf of feminist, class, and anti-racist causes.

In preparing the manuscript for publication, I organized it around the idea of "making," a trope that emerged through Cunard's central achievement, and Marcus's focus in this book, the anthology *Negro*, subtitled "made by Nancy Cunard." As Cunard writes in the foreword to *Negro*, "It was necessary to make this book" in order to document "the struggles and achievements, the persecutions and the revolts against" African-Americans.[8] Cunard as a "maker" also resonates with twenty-first-century forms of address and accreditation, as workers from the technology and business sectors to the arts and humanities now often refer to themselves as "makers" or "creatives," a more broadly conceived, collaborative form of attribution. *Making, fabricating, translating,* and *reporting* are the verb forms which both capture Cunard's life-long activity and activism and drive Marcus's argument from the first chapter to the last.

Outlining the parameters and focus of the book, Part I, "Outlaws: The Making of the Woman Poet as Perfect Stranger," explores Cunard's identity as a poet, which Marcus argues she created "out of the consciousness of her racial identity as white." The "Outlaws" of the title is taken from Cunard's first book of poetry, *Outlaws,* published in 1921. The "perfect stranger" of this part's title as well as the title of the book comes from Cunard's poem "Answer to a Reproof," and the line "I, the perfect stranger." The poem, as Marcus tells us, was her response to Ezra Pound's rejection of her work and her refusal to submit to his criticism. This section investigates Cunard's relationship to exile, outsidership, and the woman poet as intellectual nomad, as she argues that "Outlaws speaks for all the women artists badly mentored by men."

Part II, "Poetry, War, and Primitivism: Making Modern Life," places Cunard in the context of the discourse of primitivism in European modernism, as well as among her friends in the literary avant-garde. Marcus reads Vernon Lee's *Satan the Waster* (1920) against the primitivist dances of death and sacrifice of Diaghilev and Nijinsky and Blaise Cendrars's ballet *La Création du monde* (1923), unpacking modernist responses and engagements with primitivism along gender, race, and class lines. In a recent selection of Cunard's poetry, Sandeep Parmar writes in her introduction of the poem "Letter," which Cunard wrote upon hearing the news of T. S. Eliot's death in 1965, that it is "marvellously coy."[9] In this section, the reader will find a more candid and expansive analysis of both the poem and its reception and meaning in relation to the dynamics of reputation and representation.

Chapter 5, "Girlfriends, Boyfriends, and Bright Young Things," was unfinished, with the first subsection of this chapter, "Girlfriends," ending with an incomplete sentence: "This particular triangle…" I dropped this, rather than trying to recreate it, as the transition to the next section of the chapter seemed to make enough sense that it wasn't a complete departure from points made earlier on. Another part of this chapter, "Three Weeks: How to be an Adventuress," was also eliminated as it was published as part of "Laying Down the White Woman's Burden."[10] The last subsection, "Aragon's Prick, or The Revolution in the Service of Surrealism" was added to this chapter, according to Marcus's own note considering such a move, but with a question mark next to it, as she was working out a variety of possible structures for the book. It now makes up the final section of Part II, as it rounds out Marcus's discussion of gender and the sex dynamics of reputation, and was "meant to suggest the simultaneous sex-obsession and misogyny of the band of elite intellectuals who called themselves Surrealists and communists in Paris in the twenties and thirties."

In addition to Marcus's interrogation of Cunard's relationship to race and the Black racialized self, which is present throughout the book, Part III, "*Grands Hommes:* Fabricating a Father," provides a striking meditation on and investigation into whiteness. Three chapters, two on the novelist George Moore, and one on the novelist and travel writer Norman Douglas, examine themes of purity, cleanliness, and the "erotic maternal of the white woman's breast" in an argument, making a constellation of intriguing connections between the early study for Édouard Manet's famous painting *Le Linge*, which was given to Moore by Manet and then to Nancy Cunard, the models used in the portraits, and Cunard's own struggle over and sense of cultural displacement and homelessness. This part provides, in my view, remarkably fresh insights into women as muses and women's poverty, and an incisive indictment of colonial gauges of successful art making, which will be of interest to scholars working in post-colonialism, critical race theory, and anti-colonial literary/cultural production today.

Marcus's reading of *Negro* in Part IV, "Translating Africa: The *Negro* Anthology," is central to the book, and Marcus argues for *Negro* as Cunard's most significant achievement. She also outlines her reasons for advocating that the book be published anew, unbowdlerized unlike the Hugh Ford edition published in 1969, so that it can be studied and taught, included on syllabi and curricula as "a monumental example of the thirties documentary as a collective work of art." After placing *Negro* within the context of Cunard's other publishing ventures, the beautifully and meticulously hand-set editions of the Hours Press, and the ethnographic Surrealism of its era, Marcus reads the text in relation to a contemporaneous "translation" of Africa by Sylvia Leith-Ross, *African Women: A Study of the Ibo of Nigeria* (Faber, 1939), in order to expose the ways in which myths are made and misogynist, racist narratives advanced, repeated, and accepted.

The final part, "Reporting War: The Journalism," helps us to understand Nancy Cunard as Marcus has drawn her, as an internationalist and public intellectual, whose work not only engaged with the politics of Harlem and the American South, but with an "international and multiracial cross-class culture of protest against fascism in journalism" that was also multilingual. She brought together poets and intellectuals in her *Poems for Spain* and later *Poems for France*, as well as in her manifesto, *Authors Take Sides on the Spanish War*, and Marcus counters the accepted, and erroneous, account by Stephen Spender and T. S. Eliot, which either rejected political messages that didn't fit or omitted key figures from the public record of anti-fascist activism during the Spanish Civil War. Cunard's contact with Langston Hughes, Pablo Neruda, and Samuel Beckett, but also with more minor but important figures in the cause, such as Nicolás Guillén, Jacques Romain, Regino Pedroso, and George Padmore, fills out Marcus's reading of the history of this activism, as she asks "What does it mean now, especially for Black British readers, working-class readers of all races, and women, to reconstruct the response to the Spanish war and the rise of fascism as white, male, and upper-class, while denying the presence of African, West Indian, and Asian postcolonial intellectuals in anti-fascism?" The chapters in this section record Cunard's involvement, organization, and activism on behalf of racial justice in Spain, which, for Cunard, "was always tied to fascism's primary endorsement of racial and colonial oppression." Her subjects are controversial and her reportage impassioned as she documents "the sellout of Ethiopia, the price of non-intervention in Spain, the concentration camps in France holding Spanish refugees, fascism's driving force as racial fanaticism, modern European war as a battle between colonized Blacks," topics, Marcus points out, "not objective enough to survive in the textbooks."

Perfect Stranger seeks to reshape canons and avoid "narrow national narratives" in its bid to rethink the radical, the modern, gender, race, and class within the context of Cunard's involvement in the politics and culture of her contemporary times. Anna Girling's recent essay, "More than a Muse,"[11] and her recovery of a never-before published short story by Cunard, "A Lost Night," point to the need to reassess Cunard's reputation, which *Perfect Stranger* speaks to, as well as to renewed interest in Cunard's literary and political contributions. As Marcus argues, bringing the work of Cunard and her circle into focus, "out of the murk of the minor, gives their movements for social change the same kind of resonance the dominant class has with its own movements and the art that was produced in them." *Perfect Stranger* not only recovers Cunard's example for today's readers, but also interrogates the machinations and systems that led to her erasure and dismissal in the first place, urging us to rethink, dismantle, and revise such systems in a bid for a more just and equitable world.

Introduction to the Original Text

Nancy Cunard (1896–1965) was not an ordinary woman. And this is not an ordinary biography. It is the story of a woman artist and political activist, poet, and passionate journalist, a white woman who devoted her life to the cause of the recognition of the civilizations of Africa in the West and freedom struggles everywhere in the early part of this century.

In exile in France she found a culture more receptive to the exciting mix of races and classes in which she began to find a role, a cosmopolitan culture personally and intellectually more open to her international vision of the importance of the cultures of the Black Atlantic, as it was more open to women and homosexuals. The principles of Surrealism as they interacted with French Marxism and communism in the late twenties and thirties shaped her politics and her activist work for the rest of her life.

To write the story of Nancy Cunard as a major European public intellectual in the twentieth century has meant reworking the myths and legends about her extraordinary career, to try to see her, as she struggled but failed to see herself, as a producer of knowledge about Black cultures that the West, white and black alike, has so far failed to incorporate into their histories and political genealogies. So this is not the story of Nancy Cunard as an English heiress of the Anglo-American shipping line family. This is not a family romance about the ungrateful daughter of Maud (Burke) Cunard, silver mine heiress from San Francisco, who married Sir Bache Cunard, and grew up at Nevill Holt, a magnificent Leicestershire estate and grand country house for the parties of the Edwardian elite. This is not about Nancy's failed marriage or Lady Cunard's discreet but public affair with Sir Thomas Beecham, among others. Or even about the poor little rich girl who finds meaning in life. It is about the making of a female public intellectual out of some very odd clay. It would have been easy to understand Nancy Cunard as an upper-class rebel, like her father figure, the Irish writer George Moore. But adventuresses like her mother end up under the protection of marriage or their money. For a while it looked as if Cunard would end up dead from drink and drugs and syphilis. With immense courage and steely nerves, she remade her life as a fighter for good causes and it is the triumphs and tribulations of that life from 1928 until 1965 that I would like to emphasize here.

In restoring her to the political context of the principles for which she fought, I hope to reframe her life in terms of her work. To my mind, her family name, her English birth, and her notorious sex life have muddied the waters, obscuring, even for Cunard herself, the importance of her great achievements for the Black cause and the struggle against fascism. The researching, organizing, and editing of the 800-page *Negro* anthology was, by itself, a major achievement in the cause of racial justice. This is not to claim that Cunard was free from the prejudices of her time, or even some of the prejudices of her class and country. None of us is. Certainly it is true that her desire to promote the cause of Black freedom was inspired by her love of a particular Black man. But surely one cannot despise that very human method of learning respect for the Other. Strange bedfellows have made some very interesting politics, to reverse the old maxim.

It is also true that her interest in African arts coincided with *le tumulte noir*, Europe's Orientalist love affair with all things African. Does the fact that many French intellectuals, as well as ordinary people, were caught up in passion for the cult of Africa, in art, music, and anthropology, cast doubt on either her sincerity or her taste?

It is my intention to take Cunard seriously in these pages, even when the subject is her face as an icon of the wild and decadent twenties in Paris, London, Cannes, and Venice, or her diva-like cultivation of her own image. Visually, in the famous photographs and paintings, she remains the white woman adorned with and enslaved by African objects, the things of the Other; her bound body a sign of empire's despoiling of the culture of a continent, carrying away its despised and feared religious and ritual objects to recover their "value" as art in the West.

Such forms of primitivism still exist. I am writing this in Delhi after two months in India. What I have chosen, not without a pang of conscience, to take back to New York is a patchwork of tribal handwoven cloth, made by the so-called "Indians" of India. Cunard would have loved it, as she traveled the world with her African and South American Indian woven cloths to spread in dreary hotel rooms as she typed her reports for the wire services and the Associated Negro Press from the battlefields of the Spanish Civil War, the refugee camps in France, and the recruitment points, barracks, and prisons of Black troops in France and North Africa. For her gypsy life, the ivory bracelets and carvings and the prehistoric stones wrapped in "native" African or Amerindian boldly patterned handwoven cloth were her home altar, set up wherever she went to worship the *lares et penates* of a determined and exhausting rootlessness.

As a poet Cunard made some interesting choices. She wrote and published in *Wheels* with the Sitwells before and during World War I, and her early volumes bear the marks of her high modernist mentors and sometime lovers. We detect in them echoes of T. S. Eliot's bleak hymns to alienation, Wyndham Lewis's Vorticist social destructiveness, and Ezra Pound's erudite, irreverent Imagism. But she rejected the kind of poetic practice Pound demanded from women disciples and declared that she would not sacrifice her political interests to be his next H.D. This was a momentous decision, for she was already established as a modernist voice, known as a poet, and a publisher of poets at the Hours Press.

Her circle also included John Rodker, Laura Riding, Samuel Beckett (one of her first young poet "discoveries"), Richard Aldington, Robert Graves, Walter Lowenfels, William Carlos Williams, Louis Aragon, Eugene McCown, Harold Acton, Roy Campbell, Robert McAlmon, and Brian Howard. W. H. Auden's "Spain" was first published in an anti-fascist collection edited and published by Cunard. It is worth considering why she withdrew from the world of high modernism and its little magazines, where she had established herself as a poet, publisher, and editor, for the more exciting world of political activism, polemical poetry, pan-African struggles and Black freedom struggles everywhere, and Surrealism.

As she moved away from the dominant aesthetics of the age, she found a way to write political poetry and to enlist poets in her campaigns against fascism in Spain in *Writers Take Sides on the Spanish War* and, later, *Poems for France*. As a left artist, she did not despise the work of her early apolitical, right-wing, or conservative avant-gardist comrades in London. But she found a voice for her anger in an engaged poetry of the thirties, which, along with that of Valentine Ackland and Sylvia Townsend Warner, has yet to find an appreciative audience. For Cunard not only became involved in the politics of Harlem and the American South, with the Scottsboro Case and Marcus Garvey, with Claude McKay and his family and friends in "Banana Bottom" in Jamaica, but she took Black poets like her lifelong friend Langston Hughes as her models in poetry as well as comrades in struggle.

This, I think, was the most shocking thing of all to her European compatriots. She was rejecting, not only her mother, her mother-country, and her family's money, but Western culture, as it is (still) canonized in the poetry of Eliot and Pound. Imagism, Futurism, and Vorticism were the correct European modes of artistic rebellion for alienated artists. To actually try to write a blues lyric or a poem in the voice of a white southern redneck sheriff about a lynching was going too far. (I am not saying she did it well. But the point is that she did it at all.) All the male modernists were influenced by Black culture, African or African-American speech rhythms, and jazz and the blues, as well. They quoted Black styles from minstrel to gospel, but they did not acknowledge that what they were assimilating was in any way an art or culture comparable to their own. (The same issue is acted out in Picasso and the European modernist painters' wholesale "primitivist" annexation of the shapes and forms of African sculpture.) Nancy Cunard did not become a good Black poet, but she became an apprentice Black poet the way some whites took up jazz, in precisely the way that she told Pound that she would not apprentice as a new H.D. She tried to bury or disguise everything in her voice that was white, privileged, female, or European. She was unable to do it, but in the process she developed a left poetics, which served her political purposes, and she also gained the courage to take up reportage as a serious writing career.

Cunard's engagement with Black culture, like many Black artists' interactions with European culture, scrambled her identity into a bizarre form of the cultural splitting W. E. B. Du Bois named "double consciousness" in Afro-Americans. Acting as a self-made Black public intellectual and political radical, a white agent of Black Power for the three decades of her prime, she was unable ever again to inhabit her white skin with impunity. Sunburnt and starving herself, Cunard in old age wore her once white skin and its class privileges like a thin, brown, leather cover for the skeleton that signified its membership in the same species as Africans. Cunard's political achievements, staged as many of them were by hiding her white skin behind a black mask, are important to the history of the struggle for freedom in the modern world. She was truly an international figure on the left, and figuratively an interracial icon in the struggle for the recognition of Black culture.

She found her voice as a Surrealist polemicist (in *Black Man and White Ladyship*, 1931); as a (sometimes unbearably high-pitched) communist editor in the major example of thirties collective ideology, the pan-Africanist *Negro* anthology (1934); and as a champion of the refugees of the Spanish Civil War in her role as a reporter for the *Manchester Guardian* and Sylvia Pankhurst's pro-Ethiopian *New Times*. Leaving Madrid for North Africa in 1936, she began to report on "the way the Moors were impressed (mainly) into a war that was no concern of theirs." Her pro-Black pieces earned her a place as a correspondent from this war through the next, all over Europe, North Africa, the West Indies, and South America, for the Associated Negro Press International, a wire service based in Chicago, servicing Black papers all over the world. That byline, Nancy Cunard, reporting race issues from Spain through World War II and on into the fifties, appeared in many newspapers in Ghana and Nigeria, in hundreds of Black papers in the United States and the Caribbean, and was read by Black readers. Like the monumental *Negro* anthology, which was banned in many of the English-speaking African countries and colonies and ex-colonies in the West Indies, and her anti-colonial pamphlet with George Padmore, *The White Man's Duty* (1943), these articles on issues of interest to Black readers and left readers alike kept her name alive in radical Black circles in Africa, the United States, the Caribbean, and Latin America. Her name was recognized internationally, particularly in Africa and among the future leaders of emerging African countries in the West African Students Union in London and among the Senegalese intellectuals in Paris. She was an important intellectual influence on C. L. R. James, and he is reported to have carried a copy of the *Negro* anthology with him wherever he went to teach and lecture.

The more she lived in a Black-identified world, concerned with pan-African issues and the cultures of the African diaspora, the more she became alienated from the privileged English world of her youth. What wasn't closed to her as a champion of Blacks was closed to her as a leftist. But she wasn't really a great success as a Communist Party fellow traveler either. The Party was certainly not going to claim an independent anarchist with a mind of her own as one of their own. She was as ideologically slippery as her fellow travelers (at different periods of time), Langston Hughes and Claude McKay. And the Soviets never published a Russian version of the *Negro* anthology as they had promised when she visited in the thirties. Neither did they produce her film script on the history of slavery, which reads like an early version of *Roots*, following individual characters from Africa into slavery and beyond.

The film script on Black cultural history languishes in various drafts and pieces of typescript with her papers in the Harry Ransom Humanities Research Center at the University of Texas, Austin. It was a thirties project whose time came later in the sixties. The remains of other monumentally grand projects lie there with it—a precise scholarly art-historical book on African ivories and a collection of notes, photographs, and museum postcards and reproductions from all over the world on the representation of Blacks in Western art. Nancy Cunard was a woman who lived and struggled well before her time.

Some of her works survive. As a public intellectual, she lived the life of a committed radical to the hilt. She was among the ranks of those brave souls who invented modern life for women. As a girl she demanded to be educated. As a young woman she escaped her mother by marrying. Bored by marriage, she chose her lovers and friends on her own terms; divorced, she worked hard at anti-war poetry, drank and danced and committed herself fiercely to the cause of social justice. Her personal life was a disaster.

Cunard began the thirties with a chip on her shoulder and she got angrier and angrier. The anger, the isolation from movements and people that had sustained her, the drinking, dissipations, and solitary work alone in a house in the Dordogne, the refusal to eat finally did her in—she did not go gentle into that good night. She went raving and cursing, writing her last great poem and then burning it, drunk in Paris in 1965. She died fighting, fighting at last with her friends Janet Flanner, Raymond Michelet, Georges Sadoul, her long-time allies. It was not a good death and her friends recorded it with horror. But it was somehow an appropriate death for the fierce freedom fighter that Cunard was, a death that suits a life of struggle as an artist, as a woman, and as an activist.

Nancy Cunard was not a lady. She was a fighter, and it is as a fighter I want to remember her. I take courage from the impassioned speech in her defense given by a young man from South Africa at the panel on the *Negro* anthology at the Modern Language Association meeting in 1996. After many negative things had been said about the book and its design, its eclectic contents, and its high-toned Party-line pronouncements about American Blacks like W. E. B. Du Bois, her "racism" and her politically incorrect "primitivism," he rose to speak eloquently on her behalf, reminding the mainly white Western audience that Nancy Cunard's name and the name of the *Negro* anthology mean a great deal to African freedom fighters. He said that it was a matter of great importance to Black South Africans that she had sought out one of the founders of the A.N.C. to write for *Negro*. He spoke of her respect for, and friendship with, African intellectuals. It is that Nancy Cunard I salute in these pages.

Cunard's life is an interesting problem in the study of the history of left internationalism, especially for feminists. Her white racial identity was more important to her than her gender identity, though it was her androgynous sexuality that catapulted her image into the public eye as the epitome of modernism. So she is a very different figure from the women artists of modernism who have occupied the attention of feminist critics. But precisely because of her racial consciousness, Cunard's story leads one to want to rethink Gertrude Stein as a nice Jewish girl, as Linda Wagner-Martin does brilliantly, and then to think of her as an American version of Isaac Deutscher's non-Jewish Jew, to look seriously at her relationship to French nationalism and fascism. Djuna Barnes invites the same inquiry regarding race and so, of course, does Virginia Woolf.

World War I is the other crucial issue for Cunard's identity aside from race. Primitivism emerged in her early anti-war poetry and not only engaged her intellectually and emotionally in the idea of Africa, but also in a life-long attraction to peasants, working-class men, and tramps. Cunard's class primitivism was equally important and even more difficult to discuss, but it was a serious component in her radical and communist fellow-traveling activities, as it was for Sylvia Townsend Warner and Valentine Ackland, for example. In this book I want to place these particular primitivisms in relation to others in the period, in literary culture, the arts, ethnography, photography, travel writing, reportage, and political propaganda in England, France, and Spain, in Moscow and in the United States. We spend time in T. S. Eliot's wastebasket, where Ezra Pound deposited the waste products of *The Waste Land*, his portrait of Nancy Cunard as Fresca, upper-class poet and whore. And John Banting, the English Surrealist painter and photographer who went to Harlem with Cunard, and later to help cover the

Spanish Civil War, not even a minor figure in the canon, appears here as an example of the international and interracial gay left. Both his work and his life are important politically.

Perfect Stranger is concerned with the visual in modernist primitivism and Cunard's image is at the center of that discourse. *Perfect Stranger* looks closely at some of the images of Cunard that signify modernism: photographs by Man Ray and Cecil Beaton, for example. But other photographs by John Banting, Barbara Ker-Seymer, and Curtis Moffat are examined for different reasons. The photographs of Black workers in the *Negro* anthology, as well as Michelet's drawings of African museum collections, are described in another section.

The fictional icons in Michael Arlen's *The Green Hat* and Aldous Huxley's novels are also addressed. How Cunard did not continue writing a column for *Vogue* and so did not become another Janet Flanner is another story included here. The critical use of her *Authors Take Sides on the Spanish War* to tell various canonical versions of thirties culture without acknowledging Cunard's formative role in the landmark survey is considered in some detail. The Scottsboro Case and the refugees from the Spanish Civil War were the subject of much organizing and writing by the left activist, and we see her as well in Paris, with her lover, Louis Aragon; in Venice with the Black pianist Henry Crowder; in Spain with Pablo Neruda; in London putting together a magazine called *Wheels* with Edith Sitwell; and then again in wartime, working for the Free French, translating her old friend Ezra Pound's fascist broadcasts. She discovers and publishes a young Irish writer called Samuel Beckett. She brings three Black poets together: Langston Hughes, Nicolás Guillén, and Jacques Roumain.

Cunard's concern with whiteness is traced to the influence of the Irish writer George Moore. Consequently, the text moves back to Moore's own "white writing," his self-styled "white nympholepsy" or obsession with white girls in white dresses in the paintings of Édouard Manet, whose reputation he helped to establish. The Impressionist turn to white nostalgia, I argue, is the result of colonialism and the encounter with the racial Other. Manet's *Le Linge* moves the scene of cleanliness and order, the woman and the washtub, from the urban and sexualized sweatshops of Paris to the backyards of the suburbs. The painting feeds the imagination of the French soldier or sailor abroad, the settler or the explorer in the colonial hinterlands (and dirt) of Africa and Asia, with a vision of home. In a parallel discussion, *Perfect Stranger* traces the supposed sketch for this painting by Manet to its ownership by Moore, who gave it to Lady Cunard, who left it to her estranged daughter, Nancy. Writing about the drawing in her biographical sketch of Moore, *Grand Man*, Cunard effects a rapprochement with her dead mother.

Cunard's refusal to write an autobiography and her creation of a self between the lines of the memoirs of her two *grands hommes*, George Moore and Norman Douglas, is the subject of a chapter on Cunard's identity as a sexual outlaw and minor figure in modern life. In "Intellectual Nomads," her dream of the desert is related to her heroine, the Russian traveler Isabelle Eberhardt. Texts by Moore and Douglas contributed to the texture of exile and primitivism that she wove around her, and so they are re-read in this text, for context.

But other texts take up space as well. And it is not so easy to see the connections. There is an extended reading of Mulk Raj Anand's radical 1936 Indo-Anglian novel, *Coolie*, whose heroine reads Michael Arlen's *The Green Hat*, the most popular fictionalization of Nancy Cunard. *Coolie* is concerned with the parallel lives of an Indian peasant boy and a white memsahib on the order of Virginia Woolf's *Mrs. Dalloway*. Anand connects the rise of the white woman with the fall of the colonized peasant in terms of sex and power in an absolutely brilliant fiction. The issues of race and sex and power and nationality are played out here in a way that sheds light on Cunard's relations with Black men like Henry Crowder, while avoiding the heavily charged atmosphere in following the libidinal currents, to use Joseph Boone's telling phrase, between white women and Black men. It is with the same intent that we look closely at Claude McKay's Marseilles stories and their participation in a primitivism of the Arab Other that they shared.[1]

Nancy Cunard's many lives—as poet and publisher at the Hours Press; as working journalist reporting race issues for three decades for the Black wire service, Associated Negro Press International; as co-author with George Padmore of *The White Man's Duty*; as author of the pamphlet accusing her mother of racism, *Black Man and White Ladyship*, a spoof ethnography of the elite to be read by the marginal—were lived in a burning intellectual intensity, a proud demand for pleasure, and as an effective political organizer. Her days and nights were full of rage and red wine. Anger gave her energy but it also destroyed her. Nancy Cunard's life was an experiment in modern living for the woman public intellectual. No blood ties restrained her and no blood ties sustained her. Her legacy of work for racial consciousness and a way of living outside family and class is a formidable example of how to live by your principles.

East Hampton
August 1998

PART I

Outlaws: The Making of the Woman Poet as Perfect Stranger

Figure 1.1. Nancy Cunard in a coat and hat designed by Sonia Delaunay, 1925.
Photograph by Curtis Moffat © Curtis Moffat / Victoria and Albert Museum, London

CHAPTER ONE

The Cunard Line
A Poet's Progress, 1925

Nancy Cunard was a poet. A woman poet. An anti-war poet. An English poet. A modernist. But she wrote sonnets and villanelles. She was also a propaganda poet of some substance. She was a jazz poet and a would-be Black folk poet. She was a gifted and very active linguist and translator (in both directions) of contemporary French and Spanish poetry, her own and many others, famous and unknown. From her own center as a poet she wove a strong web connecting poets to each other around the world. She supported and published unknown poets at her Hours Press and besieged other publishers with the manuscripts of new writers. Samuel Beckett was one of her discoveries. She published his first work, *Whoroscope*, and introduced him to the worlds of Black jazz and the Surrealist left in Paris. He then translated their poems, essays, and manifestos for her *Negro* anthology. In her sad old age Beckett sent her signed copies of *Whoroscope* to sell to support herself. Cunard ended her uncomfortable sojourn in the world like a Beckett heroine, buried alive with only her voice left, cursing.

Old-fashioned in form, her early poems, often sonnets, were avant-garde in content. Her short, brilliant career as an English poet began with *Outlaws* (1921), *Sublunary* (1923), and *Poems (Two)* (1925, 1930), collected after her first public successes with the forgotten provocative wartime anthologies with the Sitwells, called *Wheels* after Cunard's signature poem. Yeats's gyres and visionary cycles of history are the poetic figures that survive from the period, but one may argue that Cunard's "great revolving of the spheres / Under the trampling of their chariot wheels" where "Our words are turned to spokes that thoughts may roll / And form a jangling chain around the world" is as challenging a figure for modernist angst in the aftermath of World War I.

War Dance

Wheels (1916–21), a yearly anthology of new verse begun and edited by Cunard with Edith Sitwell, and later edited by Sitwell alone, was a brave and exciting cultural venture. The slim volumes with jackets and endpapers by Severini, or the startling red masked figure of a warrior by William Roberts, or Lawrence Atkinson's "The Sky Pilot," give a rich sense of the mixed and motley modernisms that were a vital part of the English poetry scene before canonization of Eliot's *The Waste Land* eclipsed its variant voices. *Wheels* is European, Futurist, Vorticist, and carnivalesque. Nancy Cunard's apprenticeship as an anthologist began with the establishment of *Wheels*'s anti-war group attitude, not pious and pacifist but defiantly calling up the devil for a dance of death.

In the whirl of wartime angst and excess the odd group of poets made few attempts to tell the dancer from the dance. The dance itself was all. For me, the simultaneously heartbreaking and hysterical sound of the pipe and drum as it survives from mediaeval Lenten carnival pageants in Basel, for example, gives the mood of dancing skeletons that these volumes still possess. *Wheels* revolves in the somber and hilarious mood of Vernon Lee's *Ballet of the Nations* in *Satan the Waster*, another neglected masterpiece of World War I.[1]

The bloody orgiastic dancing of Stravinsky's *Rite of Spring* is answered by the clowning of circus acrobats. Léger's brilliant puppet costumes worn by actors on stilts animate Darius Milhaud's ballet for Blaise Cendrars's version of a *faux*-ethnographic African creation myth, *La Création du monde*, performed by the Ballets suédois in Paris at the height of *le tumulte noir*.[2] It was the production of *La Création du monde* that captured Cunard's imagination and stimulated her interest in African cultures, an interest that became a cause and then a life's work. The making of new and freer dance forms that began in these productions is one of the most telling examples of modernist primitivism at work. Europe wanted the ecstasy of African dance and ritual, the energy of Russian folk dance, and the rhythm of Afro-American jazz dance for its own new rituals.

Cunard and her cohorts, like Sitwell, had begun to explore their own experience of such manic gestures of the body, the frenzied dancing with officers on leave from the Front, as part of women's "work" in the war. The women were haunted by memories of fleeting pleasure, lost lovers, and the grisly grind of syncopated sex and death. Sitwell's "The Dancers" captures the mood:

> (During a Great Battle, 1916)
> The floors are slippery with blood:
> The world gyrates too. God is good
> That while his wind blows out the light
> For those who hourly die for us—
> We can still dance, each night.
>
> The music has grown numb with death—
> But we will suck their dying breath,
> The whispered name they breathed to chance,
> To swell our music, make it loud
> That we may dance, —may dance.
>
> We are the dull blind carrion-fly
> That dance and batten. Though God die,
> Mad from the horror of the light—
> The light is mad, too, flecked with blood, —
> We dance, we dance, each night.[3]

Bad Reviews

Despite the serious reception of the modernist experimentation in tone, if not form, of the early volumes and the *Wheels* anthologies, Nancy Cunard's major work, the long poem *Parallax* (Hogarth Press, 1925), following T. S. Eliot's *The Waste Land* in the prestigious series edited by Virginia and Leonard Woolf, was dismissed in two important literary journals as derivative of Eliot's poem. Since the history of Cunard's career as a poet consists simply of the repetition of this accusation, it seems worth examining the original charge.

"Miss Nancy Cunard's poem is modelled so closely on Mr. T. S. Eliot's *The Waste Land* that it is impossible for anyone who is familiar with the latter to keep it out of his mind while reading the present volume," it was argued in an unsigned review in the *New Statesman*.⁴

> *Parallax* is indeed *The Waste Land* "seen at some distance from its true and proper being"—if I may borrow the text its own author has chosen for it. In form, thought, rhythms and phraseology Miss Cunard follows in the wake of her model. It is her misfortune that in planting her feet in her master's larger footprints the original sharpness of the trail is somewhat blurred.

He then quotes Eliot's "I have heard the key / Turn in the door once and turn once only" with Cunard's "Closed doors, where are your keys? / Closed hearts, does your embitteredness endure forever?" But I cannot see what Cunard's question has to do with Eliot's pronouncement. Nor can I see what he calls "stealing" in the move he cites from Eliot's "the loitering heirs of city directors" and Cunard's wonderful "Or how many thousand prodigal francs / From serious patriarchal banks."

There are parallels, of course:

> Lil and her friend in the pub become "Two old women drinking on a cellar floor / Huddled with a beerish look at the scavenging rat," ... while Mr. Eliot takes us through Highbury, Richmond, Kew and Moorgate to Margate, Miss Cunard's itinerary will be the Embankment, Gravesend, Kew, Oxford Street and Fitzroy Square; though Mr. Eliot's crowd "flowed up the hill and down King William Street" Miss Cunard's is to be met with "On the rim of the tide along Commercial Street."

The reviewer notes the shadowy third in each poem and ends by praising the sincerity "of her borrowing": "*Parallax* is echo-stricken in a bad sense, as *The Waste Land* is echo-stricken in a good sense ... *Parallax* is a 'Waste Land' with none of the deadly precision of Mr. Eliot in literary expression." What the critic doesn't allow for is what *Parallax* is about—precisely the difference in the skewed and distorted angle of vision that displaces the object when the observer is not in Eliot's position but in Cunard's, and seeing postwar London otherwise, as the marvelously tilted vision of the jacket by Eugene McCown makes clear.

The reviewer in the *TLS* also went so far as to suggest plagiarism, and there is no doubt that this review did irreparable damage to Cunard's reputation as well:

> Miss Cunard has a very considerable expressive power. Her language is alive, colloquial, free from the poetaster's timeworn turns of speech. The debt, which *Parallax* owes to Mr. Eliot's *The Waste Land*, cannot, however, be overlooked. The conclusion is unavoidable that Miss Cunard's poem would never have been conceived in its present shape without the example of Mr. Eliot; and the parallelism even extends to verbal reminiscences in certain passages.[5]

The reviewer notices the poet's "dissociation of elements," and is willing to follow when "This poet-foot must halt in every tavern / Observing the crusty wrecks of aftermath." "She describes the emotions of aftermath with remarkable subtlety," the same critic concedes, allowing that there are other ways than Eliot's for expressing the despair of the period, and he praises her "resilient mind." *Parallax*, he writes, "has a complexity and grasp of reality which is so frequently lacking in women's poetry." It's not really original but it may be "the prelude" to an original poem. She lacks, he thinks, a "climax of emotion." Is he writing about sex or about the major modernist long poem whose reputation he has just destroyed? *Parallax* was chosen for publication by Leonard and Virginia Woolf at the Hogarth Press as the successor to *The Waste Land* in the same avant-garde series. The review was an attack on their taste as well as a stunning blow to the young woman poet's self-confidence.

A volume of Edith Sitwell's poems, under review in the same piece, gets similar treatment. Both women are scolded and told to practice "self-criticism." Sitwell's new manner is almost as dangerous as the "verbal harlequinade" of her earlier work, the reviewer sneers. The writer's struggle with himself and the English language over expressing the value of poetry in the opening paragraph makes clear that, to him, both books are worth little. By his own gold standard they are small change, and he chides the women poets "to see that the abortions and experiments of the mint are not passed over the counter." His job as reviewer is to protect the public from counterfeit culture.

This remarkable mixed metaphor is expressive of the author's and, obviously, the literary world's fear of what the woman artist and her sexuality will do to the "market" for highbrow verse, the fear that is the subtext of the review.

"Abortions" is rather a strong word here in the culture bank he sets up. One keeps trying to imagine the poem as a child-coin aborted in the mint of the imagination (to coin a phrase), the woman's poem as a twisted piece of scrap metal, shrapnel left from the war perhaps, when she was a social necessity. Of baser metal, the woman's poem may infect the golden coin of the realm that is English poetry. Is that what he means?

Women's poetry like Cunard's and Sitwell's is in tune with the aftermath of the war. The culture of the aftermath itself is not much remarked, as historians leave the dreary period of fallout from the war to look at the rise of fascism, the class struggle, and the economic collapse leading to the next war. They call the period Between the Wars. But the aftermath, that frightening period of slow recovery from self-destruction, a world without men as they once were, as the wounded and maimed tried to re-enter the world they had left to fight, was of special significance to women. Ousted from jobs and professions, the still mourning (but now well-trained) women workers were sent back to the home as unemployed and homeless men thronged London's streets in desperation. It was a desperation for which the women poets could offer no consolation. Nancy Cunard was, in fact, the great poet of the aftermath, after T. S. Eliot, of course. Her land was really wasted, her vision much bleaker than his, for she had faith in neither the Church of England nor canonical English culture to revive the dead lands. They *were*, in her view, the warmongers. "Contemporaries," she cried, "what have you done?" In one reading of the passage, we may hear her cry as a strong rebuke to her fellow men for making the bloodthirsty war that was fought in the name of civilization. The point, to Cunard and other left intellectuals, was to dismantle the institutions of Church and state, for they were the source of war.

The reader of the *Times Literary Supplement* in 1925 would, of course, have connected the word "abortion" in this anonymous review with Cunard's public presence as a sexually dangerous New Woman, known to have had affairs with many writers and artists in London and Paris. She was a divorced woman without children. Cunard's gynecological operations and subsequent hysterectomy had become a topic of public interest the year before (1924), due to a scene in Michael Arlen's popular romance *The Green Hat*. The novel, the play, and the film, with Cunard as the acknowledged model for the dashing heroine, Iris March, established the twenties type of the racy, boyish, promiscuous "woman of honor." She was independent and anti-maternal. The childlessness of Sitwell and Cunard would have been seen as a refusal to do their patriotic duty in the aftermath of war by replenishing the pool of soldiers as cannon fodder for the next one. By writing at all they were competing with the few men left to revive the culture. Did the critic think he was being patriotic by clearing off the women from the literary battlefield? Certainly, it is obvious that both anonymous reviewers were soldiers in the war, doing their duty by killing off female poets who had survived it.

The pages of *Vogue* in the middle twenties, where Cunard's picture had appeared as a society girl, were now running her photograph in a series with great philosophers and scientists *as a poet*. *Vogue* was inventing celebrity culture as we know it today by mixing stories and photographs of society women with puffs for artists, and portraits of performers and intellectuals. But Cunard was cut down to size in the literary papers. There she and Edith Sitwell are only small change. To the *TLS* reviewer only Eliot's poems are stamped with the right logo to mark modernism, a "personal image" that "draws the credit of the buyers" of modern poetry. Eliot was indeed a sober and respectable banker. But he had rhythm, and his poetry had personality, and a remarkable, marketable manner, and he was a good investment like a Burberry trench coat, *pour le sport*, another icon from this period of the aftermath, rejuvenating dapper English dress with elegant war surplus. It took some time before his now classic poem was regarded as abstract and impersonal. The trench coat has had a similar cultural life. Only recently have critics begun to read *The Waste Land* again as the very personal poem Eliot always claimed it was.

Whatever the cause of the split between Edith Sitwell and Nancy Cunard, having their poetry jangled on the counter from the critic's small change pocket did their friendship and their collaboration as editors of *Wheels* no good. The praise of Cunard's voice and her "individuality" is lost in the review's devastating accusation of counterfeiting the master's coin. The money metaphor used to undercut the reputations of two upper-class poets was very effective. Both poets had extravagant flamboyant mothers often in the public eye. Cunard never lived it down. Nor did Sitwell. The hysterical logic of the *TLS* review did its work. In a bankrupt world only male voices can produce golden notes. Now is the time for women to be silent. Women with money can't write. Women with money shouldn't write because they queer the market for male writers who must write.

"In this market he who can stamp his own metal with his own image naturally draws the credit of the buyers," writes the anonymous reviewer in

1925, though it sounds quite like 2000. He is arguing that Sitwell and Cunard just don't have enough personality, when the problem for him is obviously that their voices are too distinctive. The "dissociation of elements" that the reader is asked to follow rather than "assisting at their synthesis," a process that he identifies in Cunard's work, will from now on be defined as the key element of Eliot's style. Anyone else who does it is derivative. Even if they did it before he did it. Even if they did it simultaneously. Especially if they did it after him. That technique, produced by the anxiety of the age, and evident in the earlier *Wheels* poets Osbert Sitwell and Aldous Huxley, for example, is now authentic only when used by Eliot. It is as if *The Waste Land* now had the only strong cultural currency to get the nation through the endless crashes and devaluations of the aftermath. *The Waste Land* became the Bank of England. To some extent it still is the Bank of England. Or a Burberry trench coat.

Edgell Rickword: Lovers on the Left

It is now possible to identify anonymous reviewers in the *TLS*. What a shock it was to discover that the reviewer was Nancy Cunard's lover and comrade, Edgell Rickword. The war poet and critic (1898–1982), a decade later, as a fellow leftist and editor at Wishart, worked day and night for over a year setting up and proofreading the *Negro* anthology with Cunard. It was a mighty effort in a great cause. But how did he reconcile the one thing with the other?

Why dwell on the devastating anonymous review of Cunard's brilliant poem *Parallax* and the reviewer himself so early and anti-chronologically in the story of Cunard's career as a poet? First, to show the climate of hostility to women writers even among their friends, that is, anonymity served patriarchy. Second, to show how little there was to choose from among prospective mates for a woman artist or intellectual at the time. Edgell Rickword is only one of the men Cunard chose as combination lover, comrade, and collaborator throughout her working life, and a not very important one at that. But the fundamental disloyalty of his relationship to her, the fact that Rickword had had it in his power to wreck her career as a poet, and did, and then acted as editor and lover to the same woman, points up the fact that other disloyalties and power inequities like this one recurred throughout Cunard's life. She sought companions and partners for an intensely lived life of work and love and struggle without giving up her own freedom. Few men could keep pace with her. Radical men proved in the end just as patriarchal in sexual politics and domestic expectations as men who didn't share her politics. Louis Aragon attempted suicide when she left him. Richard Aldington wrote to say he wanted her to meet his wife and child, forgetting, perhaps, his vicious portraits of her in fiction and drama. After her death the gigolos and academics to whom she gave all her "things" had a field day—Charles Burkhart in the snobby sensationalism of *Herman and Nancy and Ivy*, Hugh Ford by breaking his promise and publishing a bowdlerized version of her masterpiece, the *Negro* anthology, defacing her all-Black book with photographs of her as a celebrity and fashion icon. Henry Crowder's *As Wonderful as All That?* is in the same genre, and warns Black men to stay away from white women, but it is hardly trustworthy since the story was supposedly told to a reporter in the thirties and only surfaced after all of them were dead. Something about Nancy Cunard aroused men's desire to ruin and deface her.

Rickword's biographer points out that they lived together, worked together, and drank together until the *Negro* anthology was done. Then Cunard went out to meet the Hunger Marchers, bringing one of them home to displace Rickword in the role of lover. (They parted amicably but with the usual violent drunken scene.) They were comrades; he joined the Communist Party in 1934 after his experience working with the radical woman poet, though he did say he was sure the British comrades would not have accepted her in their ranks. Again, when she couldn't find a publisher for *Authors Take Sides on the Spanish War*, he offered the pages of the *Left Review*, of which he was then editor.[6]

Twice, then, Rickword was the midwife to collective projects of Cunard, projects on the Black international struggle for freedom, and the struggle against fascism, both rejected by scores of other publishers. So history owes him a debt of gratitude. Did Rickword have a change of heart or a change of conscience? Did he ever tell Cunard that he had written that review? Or did he always lead a double life? Surprised by his biographer's mention of a "favorable" review of Cunard's poetry, I turned to *Essays & Opinions: 1921–31* (1974), and looked in vain for it.[7] Rickword helped edit this volume himself and obviously chose to leave it out. What is there instead is a review from the *New Statesman* in 1921 of poetry by Robert Graves, Maurice Baring, Nancy Cunard, and Charlotte Mew. Here he reviews her earlier volume, *Outlaws*.[8]

Again two women poets are paired but now they "display a very definite personality in their poetry, which is nevertheless not entirely satisfactory."[9]

You can't win. He dislikes the wonderful switches of diction in Mew's splendid ballad "The Farmer's Bride" and finds Cunard's "Wheels" too abstract:

> She treats her emotions intellectually and discusses with vigour where Miss Mew rambles … in spite of her frequent lack of success, one can feel the pulse of an original mind beating through a rather uncongenial medium. The language, though often striking, lacks that essential rhythm, that dominant note which absorbs and unifies the diverse elements of a poem…[10]

It seems doubtful that either woman would have called this review favorable. Sitwell's, Mew's, and Cunard's places in the canon of modernist poetry were lost because of reviews like this. Can we hold Rickword accountable? When he prepared his essays for publication, was Rickword perhaps attempting to spare posterity or his own reputation by suppressing the brutal capitalist sexism of the TLS review? The language was surely an embarrassment. He had become a figure on the left and possibly did not want his early praise of Eliot known; in 1920 he thought Eliot England's finest critic. Clearly, at the time, he couldn't bear feeling the pulse of an original mind at work in poetry when that mind lodged itself in a woman's body. And he was at a loss to deal with the long poem by a woman.

In fact, during the twenties Rickword supported himself by reviewing for all the literary journals and undermined the careers of many poets with his negative tone. Nancy Cunard, wounded by the TLS's dismissal, recovered from the rebuff by starting the Hours Press in Paris to publish, support, and encourage poets like Samuel Beckett.

Rickword's doubleness, his secret attack on and later public support of Cunard, may simply reflect his fear that women were taking over the masculine territory of poetry. In one of his reviews Rickword deplored the claim to exclusivity made by Michael Arlen's subtitle for The Green Hat, A Romance for a Few People. Did he resent the place of Cunard (and Sitwell), already among the exclusive because of their class and social position, and then again because of the publicity of figures based on them in literary caricatures? Rickword could bar them from the exclusive clubs of poets, and he did.

But one wonders who it was that supplied British Intelligence with the page proofs of the Negro anthology before it went to press, and shared with American Intelligence the evidence of Cunard's subversive political activities.

Cunard later told Hugh Ford that Tom Wintringham had also helped with the preparation of the volume. (He worked with Rickword on the *Left Review* and was later expelled from the Party.) The question of the ethics of sleeping with someone whose work you have reviewed negatively is also an interesting one. Perhaps in some circles it is permitted after ten years? The situation would make a fascinating literary novel. Or a Tom Stoppard play. Then again, the cloak of anonymity is often paired with the dagger of the undercover agent. And I am only speculating on the man's motives, with no evidence whatsoever. Both of them were heavy drinkers. Maybe they left the proofs in one of the pubs they drank in after a day's work on the *Negro* anthology.

Rickword and Cunard met in 1932 in London between her two trips to Harlem for research for the anthology, when he agreed as an editor at Wishart to include race-related books in their list. She was with Henry Crowder, and Rickword also knew of her affair with Wyndham Lewis in Venice. Returning in the spring of 1933 from Cuba, Jamaica, and Paris, where she and her assistant and lover Raymond Michelet had finished editing the immense volume, she turned to Rickword and Wishart, after being turned down by Jonathan Cape and Victor Gollancz. He had begun working for the press in 1927 and it published several of his books. Wishart, the communist publisher, became Lawrence & Wishart, and published George Padmore, Karl Radek, Subhas Chandra Bose's *The Indian Struggle*, and the proletarian novels of working-class writers. The *Negro* anthology was part of a very progressive international list.

Edgell Rickword was shaped by the war in the trenches, Oxford, and a tragic early marriage to an Irish "girl" named Peggy (*girl* was the poet's favorite word) who shared his love for French poetry and helped with his book on Rimbaud. They had two daughters. Peggy was institutionalized after violent outbursts relating to sexuality, contraception, and confession. (She sewed his shirt to his trousers.) The poet visited her once, gave his daughters to relatives to raise, and never saw her again. He was attracted to women and had several lovers in the course of his life.

When Cunard took him up on his promise of publication of the *Negro* anthology by Wishart (at her expense), Rickword was of two minds about her anti-racist pamphlet *Black Man and White Ladyship*, as he imagined himself to be of two minds about her poetry: "he thought it both scurrilous and hysterical, yet he had to admit that it had opened his eyes to injustices of which previously he had only been partly conscious."[11] Provoked by injustice or cruelty, Nancy Cunard could become violently angry. Working from an unpublished memoir, Rickword's biographer writes: "She would have felt at home with Clodia and Sempronia, those patrician ladies of the late Republic who dabbled in revolutionary politics, and might have inspired Catullus to write greater poetry than poor Nichols' sonnets" (Robert Nichols, another World War I poet, had assaulted Cunard with bad sonnets).[12] Rickword's double standard is an interesting one in that it will allow political action in a woman of the upper class. In poetry, however, she merely serves as muse.

> She rented an attic flat in Percy Street, in the heart of Fitzrovia, deco-rated it with [Henry] Crowder's assistance, and furnished it with paintings presented to her by her many artistic friends, and with African sculptures, some of them disconcertingly phallic. At first all went well; Crowder had found himself a black girl friend, and Rick-word and Nancy were wholeheartedly engaged in getting *Negro* into its final shape.[13]

Hobday calls *Negro* "a ragbag" and points out that while Crowder may have inspired it, he had "taken little interest in it," nor was he prepared "to play the political role as champion of Black rights for which she had cast him."[14] Rick-word's "Slavery Papers," extracts from evidence on the treatment of slaves laid before the House of Commons in 1790–91, are praised as "scholarly." Hobday, wrongly asserting that *Negro* was not well received in Britain, takes the view of the Fabian colonialist Lord Olivier in the *New Statesman* that Cunard's essay on Jamaica (which attacked non-radical Blacks) was "grotesquely inaccurate": "when Miss Cunard writes the manifest nonsense and displays the one-sided-ness which cannot but appall any instructed sympathisers she prejudices the whole case of her clients."[15] After the *Negro* anthology went to press, Cunard set off to join the Hunger Marchers (the Scottish contingent and the Tyne-side contingent were on the road to London). "She wore a man's overcoat, an airman's helmet and several scarves, (partly for warmth, she explained, and partly for disguise), and carried a small film camera."[16] Dressing the part, Nancy Cunard, the poet, was now Nancy Cunard, the radical journalist.

Judging from *Collected Poems* (1947)[17] Edgell Rickword was a poet much like Nancy Cunard. His forms were traditional, his subjects (like the *Wheels* poets) war, sex, shame and fetishism, masquerade and carnival, the Spanish Civil War, censorship. His quotes from Eliot, and his "hyacinthine" imitations of Eliot's manner, style, and tone, unlike Cunard's, are quite shameless. Neither Cunard nor Rickword are poets of the caliber of the much-maligned Edith Sitwell or the forgotten Charlotte Mew. Rickword shrewdly saw that Cunard's failing as a poet was a lack of rhythm. He shares the failing.

Rickword also shared with Cunard a love of the French poets, Baudelaire, Rimbaud, Verlaine. The early war poems are striking: "The Soldier Addresses His Body" ("I shall be mad if you get smashed about; we've had good times together, you and I"), "Trench Poets" ("I knew a man, he was my chum, / but he grew blacker every day, / … He stank so badly, though we were great chums / I had to leave him; then rats ate his thumbs"[18]). In the satire *Twittingpan* Rickword's characteristic doubleness manages to mock the homosexual aesthete ("Don't you think Wyndham Lewis too divine? / That brute male strength he shows in every line!") while attacking the "fire and brimstone" directed at gays by James Douglas ("vice-hound and highbrow-baiter") of the *Sunday Express*.[19] (Rickword's imitation of Pope may be compared with Eliot's Fresca section of *The Waste Land*, deleted by Pound, though its personal spite and rage clearly gave energy to the work. See the next chapter.) As a critic, Rickword called for the return of negative emotions in poetry on the grounds of mental health, to allow for "explosions of spleen or long-rumoured fulmi-nations" to bring "relief and cleansing of the mind."[20]

Rickword's most powerful poem, inspired, it appears, like Eliot's, by hatred for women, was addressed "To the Wife of a Non-Interventionist Statesman" (March 1938), "whose suave compliance sealed the fate / of thousands left to Franco's hate— / (those very Basques whose fathers drowned / to keep our food-ships safe and sound."[21] The force of the poem's anger is not addressed to the errant English statesman but to his wife, as the speaker "invades" her bedroom and "intervenes" in her "co-habitation with a beast." The statesmen, Neville Chamberlain in particular, responsible for the "Gentlemen's Agreement" of appeasement with Italy and Germany, and Anthony Eden, Sir Samuel Hoare, and Lord Chatfield, who were the chief non-interventionists, are just doing what their class always does. The real culprit, the poem contends, is the wife who didn't stop him from acting out his own beastliness. "A thinking wife" would have condemned her husband's evil deeds. Are men in power natural killers who have to be constrained by women to be civilized?

Cunard's friend Hugh Ford and Rickword's biographer, Charles Hobday, quarrel about the effectiveness of the poem addressed to the statesman's wife. Ford, whose book was written with the help of Cunard's files on Spain, finds the poem's invective vents rage on a false hate symbol.[22] Because Rickword had written in favor of returning the negative force to poetry, Hobday reads Ford's distaste for the poem as part of the modern resistance to harsh satire. He argues that the poem's confrontation with the wife of the statesman in her boudoir expects her to go on a sex strike, as the Greek women who want to end war do in *Lysistrata*. I'm afraid his argument is not at all convincing. The poem's anger is directed at the statesman's wife in another typical burst of misogyny. It blames her for the horrors of the war. It condemns all mothers whose sons make war, all wives whose husbands make war. Men, military or diplomatic, do not enter the bedchamber where these accusations are made. Nancy Cunard and her anti-fascist friends wrote many powerful poems for Spain. This is not one of them. What it reveals is that the poet's rage against upper-class women was still far stronger than his hatred of the men who allowed Franco to win in Spain. If Cunard was experimenting in making a modern life for a woman, one of the difficulties she had to overcome was the fear and hatred of women still motivating the men she worked with, in politics and the arts. A man might be anti-racist and anti-fascist but still feel that woman was his worst enemy. Her mother, Lady Cunard, was always complaining about Nancy's friendships with gay men. But it was always among the sexual outlaws that she found the comradeship lacking on the left.[23]

In the next chapter Cunard's relationship with Eliot will be discussed in more detail. Here I want to suggest what a blow this then anonymous dismissal was to an already established poet, and to encourage a re-reading of *Parallax* on its own terms as Cunard's personal vision of a dead culture, an example of the suspicious "white look" from that characteristic sidelong glance of hers captured by Cecil Beaton's photographs, looking askance at the wreckage of her world, the aftermath of World War I, and demanding that her generation do something about it—not an attitude one associates with *The Waste Land*. Edgell Rickword may have been a communist in politics but in the arts he functioned as a conservative guardian of culture. Could it be that his editor and biographer do not mention the *TLS* review because it reveals his failings as a critic and as a man? After Cunard died Rickword gave a copy of her poems to David Holbrook, inscribed "In Memoriam N.C. / A fiery Soule, that working out its Waye, / Fretted the Pigmie Bodie to Decay. Christmas. Human Rights Year."[24]

The Hours Press and Other Anthologies: Cross-racial, Internationalist Documentaries of the Thirties

After establishing the Hours Press in Paris and Normandy in the late twenties, Cunard discovered and published writers established and new: George Moore, Norman Douglas, Louis Aragon, Ezra Pound's *XXX Cantos*, and several other avant-garde volumes in a mixed list she describes vividly in *These Were the Hours*. Among her authors was the American Bob Brown, who first conceived of books on tape. The tape was ticker tape of the kind used by Wall Street stock traders and the text was to be read with a magnifying glass. He called the tapes *The Readies* (Roving Eye Press, 1930) and Cunard joined Gertrude Stein, Kay Boyle, Robert McAlmon, Paul Bowles, William Carlos Williams, and Ezra Pound as producers of text for the Readies (Roving Eye Press, 1931). This experimental new technology of reading had little success, but it shows, perhaps even more clearly than Stein's writing, how radically inventive the modernists were. Brown's reading machines and their tapes were the prototypes for today's innovative technologies of communication. Poets like Cunard wanted to be immersed in the production of writing at the level of setting type by hand and running the printing press, choosing paper and type, and producing the book as a work of art that was a product of the hand and the machine, relishing technology as handmaiden to creativity, not its enemy. Just as McAlmon worked in film and Man Ray, Léger, Antheil, and the experimental composers brought strange sounds, images, instruments, costumes, and sets to theatre, opera, dance, and the concert hall, Cunard was part of a movement that was fascinated with things that moved, with machines and their "wheels." Audiotapes and videotapes and websites developed and are developing in the same spirit.

Cunard ended her stint with the Hours Press with another kind of anthology, a tribute to the influence of jazz on modernist poetry. *Henry-Music* (1930) published Henry Crowder's music with songs written for him to play and sing by the modernist poets Richard Aldington, Samuel Beckett, Walter Lowenfels, Harold Acton, and herself. Man Ray's black-and-white collages for the cover echo Cunard's experimental attempt at mixing Black jazz and white poetry. A photograph of Crowder, with Cunard's African-braceleted arms on his shoulders as she stands behind her man, is dominated by a phallic tribal figurine; masks and ivory bracelets appear on the back with the date in large figures. Nothing could be more evocative of Paris primitivism in 1930 or Cunard's commitment to collaboration and cross-racial exchange. It is not clear from the other poets' lyrics whether they were meant for Crowder or Cunard. There was a recording by Sonabel, but it never achieved the effect of capturing what Afro-American jazz meant to European intellectuals, let alone what white modernist poetry meant to Black musicians. But *Henry-Music* is a landmark record of the postwar meeting of the white expatriate poets and the Black expatriate musicians in the *boites* of Paris, like Le Boeuf sur le Toit, and the blues they made out of trying to talk to each other across the class and race and cultural conditions that divided them at home. The "American-ness" of the experiment in music and words, not unlike a set of numbers played by a jazz musician or band, is marked by the thirties internationalism of the players, the Irish-French Beckett, radical American leftist Walter Lowenfels, who, with his wife, remained close to Cunard through the bad times to come, and the British poets—the faithless Richard Aldington, who worked closely for a time with Cunard in Paris at the press, and Harold Acton, a Bright Young Thing from London's gay literary scene. I see it staged like the Stein–Thompson *Four Saints in Three Acts*, the Sitwell–Walton *Facade*, or the plays of Langston Hughes and Zora Neale Hurston.

Cunard's "Equatorial Way" and "Memory Blues" from *Henry-Music* come closest to the interracial spirit of the moment, a moment we may call "Paris in the thirties," and they mark her move to Black syntax and diction as the white poet tries to capture Black idiomatic speech. "Equatorial Way" was written while Cunard was eagerly trying to find a way to go to Africa with Henry Crowder to research the African sections of the *Negro* anthology. She found no way the pair could travel together by ship because of the color bar. The poem speaks in Crowder's voice as an African-American going back to Africa, cursing the South and its Jim Crow trains from the land of his ances-tors with a conflagration of heat from the equator to douse the lynchers' fires, imagining taking musical revenge against the racists: "Goin to beat up Fear on the octaves, / Tear the crackers limb from limb— / Goin to take on each-every vengeance / Drum one blood-blasting hymn—."[25] Cunard's use of "cracker" betrays her English origins: "southerners with violent prejudice apt to explode," her own (amusing) definition as a reference to firecrackers. By the time she had been to Harlem twice she revised the definition for her useful and comic visitors' guide "Some Negro Slang" in the *Negro* anthology as "a pestilential white, lousy with race prejudice, generally a Southerner who can't keep it to himself, but makes trouble."[26]

The highlight of Cunard's career as an anthologist was the *Negro* anthology (1934), a collective documentary of over 800 pages on African arts and culture in Africa, Europe, the Caribbean islands and Latin America, and Harlem, with histories of slavery and anthropological studies mixed with photographs of the stars of sports and film, and diatribes on the role of the Communist Party in the freedom struggle. The works by white modernist poets in this volume, written in solidarity with the Black cause, as well as her own problematic poems on the Scottsboro Boys (problematic from class and feminist perspectives),[27] may be seen to overstep the bounds of taste in artistic encounters between the races—as in William Carlos Williams's nostalgic race fantasy "Colored Girls of Passaic," for example. But I find it does no harm to bring a blush to white cheeks in the classroom, particularly when dealing with sentimental racism of this sort, and I don't think poems like this by "well-meaning" whites should be suppressed to preserve the reputation of the poet. On the other hand, neither should they be used as sticks to beat the benighted writers to death.

The raw communist sloganeering of *Negro* as well as the sometimes patronizing white gestures toward Blacks have to me a certain thirties charm that ought to be preserved and studied, if one may use such a word in this obviously politically incorrect way. The charm, or perhaps one should say, unmediated personal responses to the making of a race documentary, like the signing of a public petition for a cause one believes in, takes the artist into a collective political act to support Black freedom struggles. And that is not an action to be sneezed at. Knowing as we do now Cunard's genius for circulating her calls for contributions and her extensive networks among European poets, the list is as important for poets not represented as it is for those who responded to the plea for solidarity.

The works of whites are meant to play a supportive role to the Black poets in the volume, like Langston Hughes, whose work is the centerpiece of the American section, along with poems by Arna Bontemps, Jonathan Brooks, Sterling Brown, Carrie W. Clifford, Countee Cullen, Thomas F. Fletcher, Walter E. Hawkins, and Donald J. Hayes. West Indian poets Nicolás Guillén, Regino Pedroso, Jacques Roumain, and Georgia D. Johnson appear in a separate section in which Cunard edits the Caribbean islands into a federation, at least culturally, along a left-wing ideal, and to some a lost cause, though the Trotskyist intellectual C. L. R. James supported the idea. It is interesting now to see these particular names called "West Indian." Cunard's editorial note says that these poets, whose work is translated from the French and

Spanish by Langston Hughes, unlike their forebears, do not imitate European models: "Regino Pedroso has put into verse his background as a factory
worker in Havana, and as a child of Chinese and Negro blood." Pedroso's
"The Conquerors" is a rather sophisticated attack on American imperialism
for a Cuban factory worker. "Poetry by White Poets on Negro Themes" is
a carefully controlled category containing Cunard's "Southern Sheriff," Jean
de Journette's "Cedric" and "Hittin' de Grit," Alfred Kreymborg's "Miss Sal's
Monologue," Norman McLeod's "Night out of Harlem," William Plomer's "The
Scorpion," Carl Rakoski's "The Black Crow," Florence Ungar's "Elevator Men,"
"The Song of the Washboard" by Ildefonso P. Valdes, and "Poem" by Louis
Zukofsky. In *Paris Was Our Mistress* the American Rabelais scholar-translator
and editor of the *New Review*, Samuel Putnam, calls Norman McLeod "one
of the best young poets of the time," quoting his "The philosophy of our time
was written by bootleggers" from *Thanksgiving Before November*.[28] McLeod's
Harlem speakeasy poem addressed to Henry Crowder ("Your large shoulders
are bunched with easy power") captures a white mood "tense with expec-
tancy": "It is a dark country in which we live / Or there would be less need
of electrification / Certifying the hour; it is black in our heart / And we are
desperate with defense mechanism... / Can I ask you all that is in your travel
/ (Your courage there and distinction?) / You sing like a chorus of warriors /
With black blood in your jaws."[29] The poet is referring to the memoir by Henry
Crowder in *Negro* called "Hitting Back," in which he recalls several instances
in Atlanta and Washington, D.C., of resistance to white violence, a relief from
the mass of horror stories of lynching and terrorization in the anthology; in
the tradition of verbal boasting called "the dozens," he always wins.[30]

Cunard's modernist poetic, beginning with the *Wheels* volumes, was
always an affront to the audience and often brought the critical response, "in
bad taste." It was a label she seemed to court deliberately and it united her work
with the Surrealists in Paris. Although the Surrealists published a manifesto
in the *Negro* anthology, the fact of their early anti-racism is often obscured in
labeling them all as communists. The translation is by Samuel Beckett, who
also translated so many other articles and poems from the French avant-garde
in the text that his reputation as a translator and as a man will be altered
when scholars examine his work and his involvement with Cunard and her
Black and revolutionary milieu.[31] A new European Beckett in black and red
now appears on our intellectual maps. Nothing less than a full-scale revision
of definitions of modernism, most of which are in flux already at the end of

the century, is called for, when these neglected books are used for a revaluation of the problematic primitivisms we are discussing here, as well as the meaning(s) of race in shaping the work and politics of the artists and the age. What strange sites those rare books, *Henry-Music* and the *Negro* anthology, appear to be when we push them out of the margins and into the center of our cultural maps of a cross-racial and international mix in a new geography for understanding modernism.

Black outsiders are centered in these texts. Who their supporters are among white writers is a revelation and a historical challenge to the narratives as we know them, of modernism and cross-racial exchange. If the *Negro* anthology is restored to its place in the history of modernism, a new story will emerge. It will include alliances between white women and Black men. It will include stories of support and withdrawals of support by the Communist Party in the United States and the Soviet Union. It will include different sets of literary misalliances, mistakes, and betrayals as well as different sets of sexual relations—interracial, heterosexual, homosexual, and lesbian. *Henry-Music* marks a brief moment in Paris in 1930 when avant-garde white poets collaborated with an expatriate Afro-American jazz musician. This experiment in a modernist mixed-race art form belongs with Gertrude Stein and Virgil Thompson's opera for Black voices, *Four Saints in Three Acts*, as Steven Watson's brilliant revisionary *Prepare For Saints* makes very clear, in a revaluation of the international interracial modernism in which Nancy Cunard was also a significant figure.

Authors Take Sides on the Spanish War, a survey of intellectuals that Cunard published as a special issue of *Left Review* in 1936, because publishers were not interested, was Cunard's next anthology. *Authors Take Sides* has served as a major source of documentation for studies of the effect of the Spanish Civil War on art, poetry, and politics in Britain and Europe. Too often authors of studies of the thirties or of left-wing culture, many of whom quote extensively from this work, have removed Cunard's name as its compiler from the record. More significantly, they have failed to mention that *Authors Take Sides* included the views of Black intellectuals, like Marcus Garvey. This document, whose hallmark phrase "taking sides" has named the decade and the art produced in it for its open political engagement, appears in the history of the thirties as if it were the brilliant product of the collective ethos of the age. Cunard, one assumes, would not have minded that, since some form of Bahktinian *heteroglossia* or sampling of the voices of the time was what she was after. But that standard version of the story must be challenged because it invalidates the work of two groups, women and the Blacks with whom women allied in the Spanish Civil War and on the left.

Cunard oiled the old press again to publish a series of six poems for Spain, *Les Poètes du monde defendent le peuple espagnol*, including her own "F.A.S.C.I.S.M.E." and "To the Mothers of the Dead Militia" by Pablo Neruda in her translation. She translated Neruda's "Almeria" for the *Left Review* in 1937 and Jacques Roumain's "Madrid" in 1938; her Spanish poems were published in 1938 in *Life and Letters Today*, the *New Statesman and Nation*, and *Voice of Spain*. Perhaps her most important work on race in this period, she wrote "Three Negro Poets" for the *Left Review* in 1937, introducing left readers in Britain to an international circle of Black writers who shared their politics. Translation, as she practiced it, was a political art. Her political acts were driven by a poetic energy.

"Man-Ship-Tank-Gun-Plane" appeared in 1944 along with *Poems for France*, another anthology (La France Libre, 1944), which was also published in France (Pierre Seghers, 1947). "Sonnets on Spain" was never published, nor was "Visions Experienced by the Bards of the Middle Ages," from her last years, a return to her Provencal troubadour poetry of 1925. Cunard left a manuscript edition of her collected poems with Sylvia Townsend Warner and Valentine Ackland before she died. Her papers contain many drafts and translations of her own poetry and that of the young poets whose work she championed. (An important piece of modernist history lies waiting for study in the thousands of pages of Spanish poems and plays in her papers in Texas. One of these is her 1939 translation of *The Refugee*, a one-act play by Miguel Hernandez from *Teatro en Guerra*, Nuestro Pueblo, Madrid-Barcelona, 1937.) She wrote on ships and trains all over the world. She left manuscripts in many South American cities in the early forties and left suitcases in train stations in France and Spain during a lifetime of exile. Many of her manuscripts and letters were destroyed by the Nazi occupiers of her Norman farmhouse and press during World War II.

A Poet First

Nancy Cunard never stopped writing poetry, however much her late career was focused on race journalism as a reporter for the Associated Negro Press wire service from the thirties through the early sixties. The identity of a poet was her most basic identity. She abandoned her daughterhood and was never a wife or a mother. She was a poet first, and then a lover and a friend to many outsiders like herself, especially lesbians and gay men. She was a foreigner and a translator, at home in languages, adept at bringing intellectuals together across borders. She was a radical poet and a political activist for the international left, a champion of Black culture, a friend of Black poets. The career of Cunard's poetry from London high modernism to the contradictions of formal sonnets composed as anti-war poems, from French Surrealism to the blues and Black protest poetry, is an arc of exile from high to low as the white poet searches for a Black voice, and the woman poet who came into voice in mourning for the dead of the Great War spoke her mind about the next wars and the culture of war.

Cunard created herself as a poet out of the consciousness of her racial identity as white. While other white women modernists created their writing selves in passionate affirmation of gender identity, Cunard performed whiteness, not womanhood, as a way into writing. Race, her own race, was of deep interest to Cunard. What did her mother's (repressed) Irish-American roots mean to her identity? Or the shipbuilding Cunards' artisan origins in America? I want to argue that she believed that "making," working with her hands, was primary to her heritage and identity, seeing her father's ironwork as not just a craft but a creative endeavor like her own mastery of printing and the mysteries of ink, paper, and typesetting, a combination of strenuous physical effort and art. Like a certain school of craftwork, Cunard's poetry bears the marks of its making, proudly announcing its production as a response to a political event. Sometimes the hammer-marks are too prominent and we wince at the crudity of "Southern Sheriff," for example, or the poem about Lincoln. But making poems was not in her life an ascent to an ivory tower or a retreat from the everyday world. Tranquility seems to have escaped her altogether, so that the notion of a poem produced out of recollection in tranquility is foreign to her habits. She wanted the poem to trap the heat and the intensity of her anger, her ardor. For many years her favorite poet was Sterling Brown, and one may see his influence on her work. Rapping away in righteousness, Cunard would have been at home with the most ferocious Black rap music of today.

Cunard's early influences and alliances (aside from the seminal ones of her Victorian mentors George Moore and Norman Douglas) were with a certain rural romantic England; high modernism; T. S. Eliot, Ezra Pound, and the canonical male modernists; the Hogarth Press; Edith Sitwell; and the poets of the six *Wheels* anthologies (1915–21), including Helen Rootham, Victor Tait-Perowne, Harold James, Iris Tree, E. Wyndham Tennant, Osbert and Sacheverell Sitwell, Aldous Huxley, and Wilfred Owen. But the most important event in the poet's self-creation was her move to Surrealist Paris and her rejection of experimental modernist poetry with traditional values. She made a permanent aesthetic commitment to Black arts, and with it a difficult and not always successful shift from Western classical models for writing to African, Afro-Caribbean, and Afro-American styles. Her liberating primitivism and identification with the fierce Black folk alternative voices of the Harlem Renaissance brought her to champion the work of Sterling Brown, Langston Hughes, and Zora Neale Hurston. Her cross-cultural literary apprenticeship placed her with Blacks and white radicals as they created an American low modernism in the thirties. This Afro-American low modernism might usefully be looked at with the Surrealist low modernism of Aragon and the British low modernism of the *Wheels* poets.

Public acting out of literary battles was an essential part of all three movements as they thrived on publicity and protest. There is a low modernist link between a Surrealist *manifestation* at the ballet, Zora Neale Hurston's notorious act of self-promotion at a Harlem Renaissance prize-giving ceremony, and Edith Sitwell's performance with a megaphone of *Facade*. All three women, Cunard, Sitwell, and Hurston, could be said to share Hurston's streetwise boast: "I Love Myself When I Am Laughing And Then Again When I Am Looking Mean and Impressive." It is not too much to say that both Sitwell's and Cunard's success at looking mean and impressive was derived in part from images of African women circulating in metropolitan culture where the commanding gesture, the natural hauteur, and shameless gaze had not been tamed. Hurston found such pride closer to home in an African-American tradition of self-respect and female power not quite crushed by slavery and oppression. Sitwell and Cunard adopted primitivist profiles of power, oversized bracelets and rings and richly woven fabrics to conjure up royalty and reserve in bold personal styles unusual for white women in this age. They carried themselves as regally as African women did. The effect was often electric.

But then again people often found that Cunard looked "out of place" wherever she was. A certain form of camp was not far away from some of Cunard's voguing attitudes, like the double-crossing of the exaggerated whiteface she wore in Black company, or the shiny marcelled hair and bold ethnic jewelry she wore in sedate white bourgeois company. Sitwell invented a royal queen bee self as a kind of extravagant oriental nun, while maintaining a discreet lifelong relationship with her musician-poet governess and public relationships with gay male artists. My point is, however, that a significant source of their style was derived from copying the postures of figures of African art and photographs of African women circulating in art and anthropological exhibitions. Both women emphasized their racial whiteness rather than their gender, a style we may now see as a response to the newly revealed beauty of Blackness. For Cunard, in particular, racial identity was crucial to her character. This proud flaunting of the raced female body was surely what provoked hostile responses to Zora Neale Hurston's claim to be an American public intellectual as well as the agent of her own sexuality. For Hurston, Sitwell, and Cunard, the proud carriage of primitive women was the basis of a modernist self-making that broke bourgeois taboos on femininity by deliberately taking up space in the public world with a noticeably bold walk and a loud, clear, distinctive voice that rang with authority and self-respect. When white women strutted, they stopped being white. Even if the diva style was an act, it was a hard act for heterosexual men to take, black or white, while gays, lesbians, and bisexuals were in their element. For Hurston, Sitwell, and Cunard, admittedly an odd trio, gender was theater. The most outrageous and successful of their acts of writing were also in the theatrical mode, performances of folk tales in dialect, shouting poetry though a megaphone to music, or using Surrealism's shock techniques for political demonstrations.

Nancy Cunard invented her own character. The expatriate English poet's life journey as a stranger in her own culture, moving backward along the old slave trade routes, from England and France to Africa and then to Harlem, the Caribbean, Latin America, and back to France, is the story of a white woman traveling back and forth across the Black Atlantic and trying to make sense of, and come to terms with, the history of white people, their commerce, and their urge to empire. Bearing the name of the Cunard Line, the glamorous transatlantic shipping company, the young artist became an obsessive traveler, a wild and tragic figure of modernist *angst*. She appears obsessed, like Wagner's Flying Dutchman or a one-woman cargo cult. The Cunard ships had not been part of the slave trade and her family no longer had an interest in the company. She satisfied her conscience on that point before embarking on her crusade for Black culture. Her white skin, haughty carriage, expertise, and confidence in her own creative powers and research and organizing skills confused enemies and friends alike. Speculation on the venality of her motives continues to this day. Carrying the historical guilt of her race and her nation for the evils of slavery, and not always conscious of carrying this baggage with her or sure of what her role was in exposing it, Cunard became a wandering prophetess, preaching her cause in righteous anger, alienating white people and Black people alike with her public espousals of free love and racial mixing. Now that we have some distance from that historical moment, one may read her life (however ethically questionable such a choice may be) as an act of atonement for the crimes of her race against Africa as the mother of culture. She knew perfectly well not only that no such atonement was possible, but that she herself had no right to take on such a burden.

But it is not really as simple as that narrative implies. And, of course, she did not see herself in this role at all. Her own particular romance of the idea of Black racial purity, for example, as well as her notion of what constitutes the beautiful in a work of art, participate very much in the outdated primitivism of the anthropological discourses of the day. Cunard's life as a wanderer and an artist takes some remarkable turns as she moves from the oppressive mentoring or the aesthetic corrections and rejections of Ezra Pound working to harness her to his gait and the territorial maneuvers of T. S. Eliot, to take Sterling Brown, Langston Hughes, and the Black vernaculars as a model for writing. Literary history has many models of the outsider's mastery of the tropes of the dominant culture. The rejection of that culture from one who is inside it, insofar as any woman could be inside high modernism in England as we know it, to embrace French Surrealism is far more easily understood than the aesthetic choice of Black low modernism's folk rhythms à la Hurston and Hughes.

Other white modernists assimilated the primitive Other into their own discourses. Nancy Cunard—and this is one of the reasons she is a difficult subject for many people to discuss rationally—came to think she was Black or an incarnation of the white negress. Early on she made the unpardon-able blunder for a radical (a blunder with which many radicals are familiar) of attempting to speak *for* the other in the other's voice, a ventriloquism so unnerving to read that it often threatens to wipe out her impressive record of enabling so many African intellectuals and writers and radicals of color in the African diaspora. So politically incorrect and psychologically and socially embarrassing has this position become that her passionate lifelong commit-ment to Black culture has made her into the invisible woman of modernism. Angering some critics by her presumption, her practices as a public intel-lectual may now appear appropriative of the African cultures she sought to legitimize. It is, after all, much harder for a white person to be a Black fellow traveler than a communist fellow traveler. She brought her primitivist poetic to the newly emergent practice of committed race journalism while writing poetry but publishing less of it. For Cunard and other left writers of the thirties, poetry and reportage were the genres of truth telling. Fiction, always already a lie, they often feared. Herself the slandered subject of so many of the fictions of the twenties, Cunard shied away from the form.

For three decades then, as a left-wing, anti-racist poet, Nancy Cunard played an important cultural role as an international public intellectual, reporting events from the Spanish Civil War through the American Civil Rights movement to Black readers all over the world and to white and Black readers on the left. Hers were the readers of Black newspapers from Chicago to Ghana, Liverpool to the West Indies, and even now her name is recognized more often by older Blacks than by the Anglo-Saxon literary establishment. The admiration of Marcus Garvey and the friendship of Langston Hughes and the comradeship of George Padmore did not polish her reputation as a poet in the white literary world.

Nancy Cunard's public life was shaped by two Black men, an artist and a revolutionary, the Afro-American jazz pianist Henry Crowder and the Jamaican communist organizer George Padmore. Crowder set her studying the history of slavery. She was so shocked when she learned what had been done to Blacks by white people that she became obsessed with understanding why, and she researched the history of slavery as an autodidact with excellent skills and access to important libraries and collections. The young West Indian communist Padmore advised her by letter as she put together the huge anthology *Negro*, strongly influencing its radical tone. Padmore's praise of Ethiopia in that volume supposedly led to his expulsion from the Communist Party. As a loyal fellow traveler like her friend Langston Hughes, Cunard lost faith over Padmore's treatment by Moscow. *Negro* is a testament to a brief moment when the Party and its Black and white political workers, Padmore and an international array of prominent intellectuals, put the race issue first in a show of solidarity toward Africa and the cultural diaspora. Padmore and Cunard collaborated again later in London and in her house in Normandy, when they wrote and she typed the hard-hitting pamphlet *The White Man's Duty*. Nancy Cunard spent most of her adult life doing what she thought was the white woman's duty toward Blacks.

Figure 2.1. Nancy Cunard, 1935, posing for Man Ray wearing her iconic wood, gold, and ivory bracelets. In addition to working with Man Ray, she also collaborated with John Banting, Barbara Ker-Seymer, Curtis Moffat, Brian Howard, and Humphrey Spender. Curtis Moffat introduced Cunard to African art. © Man Ray 2015 Trust / ADAGP – ARS – 2019; image: Telimage, Paris

CHAPTER TWO

The Artist as Antichrist

Thamar the Demon Lover[1]

One passionate poem of Nancy Cunard's, "Answer to a Reproof," now speaks directly to the woman reader and writer as fellow "perfect strangers," defiant in their "glorious discontent." The contradiction between "perfect" and "strangers" implies a certain performance of exile from the culture of those who were already Other in gender and race. It was necessary to master the master's form and to teach it to say what hadn't been said, before abandoning it for freer experimental forms. Cunard's prophetic early poem may surely be read as the declaration of independence of female modernism as it has been studied by two generations of feminist critics, beginning with Shari Benstock's *Women of the Left Bank*.[2]

Cunard's poem sets a tone of talking back to authority that became her literary and political signature. This was not always a sensible move for a woman. Combined with her bad girl posture in highly publicized photographs by Man Ray and Curtis Moffat and her public appearances with boxers and jazz musicians, Cunard's writing and publishing as an outlaw from her family, class, and culture suggested the dangerous possibilities for public activities by once private women. When the woman poet also declared that the finest poets of her age were not going to "grammarize" or "prison" her imagination, she made the leap from humble apprentice to the masters of modern culture to claim the status of "master-mind itself" for woman, marking her mentors as enemies, herself their match—even as an enemy. Of course they and their biographers have outmatched her as enemies, as she certainly knew well before she died, vilifying or leaving her out of the literary and cultural "modern" she helped to make so vital. The communists have seen no reason to claim her as their own and her steadfast Black friends have not had the cultural power to assert her claims to influence. The artist who had chosen the figure of the outlaw as her first poetic mask, much as Virginia Woolf defined herself as an "outsider" as a woman and a pacifist in *Three Guineas*—joining the despised and rejected and their left-wing defenders—and became an outlaw herself.

Much of the modernism that has become legendary is about exile and expatriatism: Pound and Eliot in London, then Italy; Stein and Hemingway in Paris, the Sapphic modernists making a new Mytilene in Natalie Barney's French salon; homosexuals chasing the south wind from Berlin to the isle of Capri or North Africa; African, Caribbean, Latin American, Asian, and Indian intellectuals in London and Paris, in the cafés and at the European universities; White Russians and Red ones in the European capitals; Romanian painters and Spanish ones in Montparnasse; Afro-American jazz musicians in Venice and Paris; the International Brigades fighting against fascism in the Spanish Civil War, giving Madrid a particular situated meaning in modernist discourse; European communists visiting Harlem; refugees everywhere, from Spain, from Belgium, from the horror of World War I; and to the new apolitical and unassimilating communities of rich English and American expatriates settling in the South of France from Nice to Cannes after the war. Nancy Cunard's journeys touched all of these ports and others, engaged many forms of exile and displacement, though some were more alienating than others.

Cunard's first step as a poet was to reject Western culture and define herself in relation to it as an outlaw. *Outlaws* (1921) predicts the course of her career outward from the inner circles of alienated high modernism to find the sources of a life-affirming philosophy in primitive works of art. The voice of the volume is Cunard's alter ego Thamar. It is a voice primed for talking back to authority. War is the subject, love lyrics and despair among the zeppelins; there are French poems, odes to opium, allusions to Pierrot and Tristan, masks and dances. Her writing and that of the community of poets writing for *Wheels* was an important early instance of a counter-culture in England. Euro-centered and liberated from class boundaries, they also made their modernist experiments in many different ways, one "lower" than the next in tone and diction while dancing to ancient formal rhythms. What they brought to poetry was an urge to say the unspeakable and a deep suspicion of classical and traditional ideas and values, along with a powerful masochistic drive to master them, digest them, and write their disgust and fury in classical forms. In *Outlaws* Cunard called up a demonic world of sex and death, corruption and despair. Her "Psalm" and "Prayer" were curses: "Oh God, make me incapable of prayer, / Too brave for supplications, too secure / To feel the taunt of danger! / [...] / Make me symbolic'ly iconoclast, / The ideal Antichrist, the Paradox."[3]

That a young privileged Englishwoman should be brought to such despair by the ravages of World War I is understandable. But to choose for herself the role of Antichrist, imagining herself the precursor hastening the Second Coming and the end of the horror and bloodshed, is to demand a position of critical agency as self-proclaimed "iconoclast" that Nancy Cunard was to occupy for the rest of her life. She had a very strong presence and used her reputation as an icon for the artists and photographers of the twenties to call attention to the social necessity of political iconoclasm in the thirties. She reveled in the role of Antichrist and believed that she could (and should, for her sins) carry the suffering of the world on her shoulders. Delusional as her vision might have been, it was one with the ethical imperative of thousands of pacifists in this war, and along with the socialists and revolutionaries in the Spanish Civil War and World War II. As female Antichrist she saw herself as mistress of sexual excess, embodying female agency in the extreme, like the Georgian Queen Thamar around whom the Bible and literature had created many myths that stirred her imagination. Cunard's complicated poetic identity defines itself as Outlaw, Antichrist, Iconoclast once and for all in this first volume of poems—all-powerful active figures who break the law, reverse the rules, like the female Byronic hero Thamar was to the poets. Cunard identified with the role of romantic demon lover Thamar had come to represent. For a woman poet it was an interesting choice, given the revival from this period of the much more problematic (in terms of gender) mythologizing of H.D.

The figure of Queen Thamar stands for the Georgian Renaissance. She ruled from 1184 to 1213, conquering the Armenians, Turks, Persians, and many local tribes. For Georgian epic poetry Thamar is both a beauty and a learned woman, a protector of the arts and religion, the opposite of the cruelly amorous Thamar of Lermontov's romantic verse and Nancy Cunard's poem.[4] In "The Demon" the Russian romantic poet Lermontov casts Thamar as the cause of the devil's fall; she is an ice-maiden, her castle and church on a peak in the lonely Caucasus are haunted by her ghost. For Cunard the legends around

Thamar weave elements of her self-image as a lonely princess in a castle and her identity as an intellectual, already formulated in adolescence. She worked and studied to impress her mother and never lost the habit. The Georgian folk tale and the Old Testament stories served Cunard's desire for a primitive and Orientalist identity, escape from her proper English girlhood in an "improper" setting where her mother acted as mistress to the (also married) conductor Thomas Beecham, and the classical music, painting, and literature of Lady Cunard's salon. Her mother's departure to London, depriving the odd girl of the romance of her childhood home, with its remains of a castle's glory, she always regarded as a punishment.

The legend's medieval setting cast Thamar and her lovers as a Lady and her troubadours in a northern version of the Provencal legends and poems she had found for Ezra Pound in the Dordogne during her poetic apprenticeship. Woman's sexuality in these legends, either her icy chastity or her mad desire, kills men. This element of the stories touched the deepest chord in Cunard's self-consciousness. She was a woman who had made love to many men in her youth and they had all died in the trenches. She came to believe at some primal level that she had killed them. Sex with her had marked them for doom. I am sure that many women were obsessed by the same feelings of guilt that tormented Cunard after the war. Because of the war, they had been allowed to express desire, as women never were in peacetime. It was natural to feel the connection between desire and death, sex and the loss of all the young lovers on the battlefields of France. Cunard's assumption of the Thamar myth as her own may be seen as a way of dealing with the pain and loss the women of her generation suffered in a senseless war. The Thamar myth allowed Cunard to see herself both as the war widow besieged by ghosts of dead lovers and the scholar-poet who would write that story.

Why does Cunard choose the figure of Thamar as her muse? Is her alter ego the Thamar of 2 Samuel, daughter of David, raped and cast out by her half-brother Amnon, revenged by Absalom? These are the Old Testament Thamars behind the Georgian queen's legends. Or is she Thamar, the daughter of Shem, ancestress of David, the Canaanite, wandering on the border of Judah in the wilderness? That Thamar lost her first husband; his brother Onan refused to make her pregnant and was struck dead. Judah refused to give the widow his third son so she dressed as a prostitute and seduced him, keeping his ring, his bracelets, and his staff as evidence, to save her life when her pregnancy was revealed. The Thamar figure was supposedly related to Ishtar, the mistress of the Babylonian fertility god Tammuz, associated with blood sacrifice in primitive rites of spring and adopted by the Hebrew war texts of the Bible as a sexual outlaw.[5] Was this Thamar the figure called up as Samuel Beckett's "Shining Whore" in the text he wrote for Cunard's Black lover Henry Crowder's music?

Cunard's choice of the ancient figure of Thamar as her muse is important. Thamar demands that her desire be fulfilled. She is a woman feared and outlawed because of her sexuality. The uncanny early identification with Thamar suggests that Cunard sensed that she would be cast out of the upper-class world of her youth and the canons of high modernism. Did she foresee that she would be demonized for her unruly interracial and tabooed sexual activity, for acting out her desire, that she would become a legend, a witch whose powers are exorcized in the perverted portraits of her in the poems, plays, and novels of colleagues, friends, and former lovers? Thamar appropriates the ring and bracelets and staff of the king, the symbols of his power. Always attired in such royal amulets, her arms and hands adorned with oversized tribal jewelry, Nancy Cunard not only imagined a nomad muse for herself as a woman poet in exile, but she dressed like Thamar (in the multicolored garments of a desert king's daughter) all her life, calling attention to her sexuality and her power. Thamar is clearly a figure for her of the outlaw white negress she wanted to be and the dark desert queen, a figure first of freedom, sexual and political freedom, but also a vision of the value of human life as it was preserved and revered in her imagined holy land, the Africa of origins that sustained the wandering artist trying to recover from the death culture of the European war and its aftermath. Cunard had a recurrent dream of a desert storm from the time she was a six year old. The young Nancy imagines herself in a tribal scene in the desert in ancient times. It is a scene that enacts the reconciliation of the tribes and the races by the acceptance of the foreign woman into the circle of the ritual dance as she recalls:

> extraordinary dreams about black Africa—"The Dark Continent"—
> with Africans dancing and drumming around me, and I one of them,
> though still white, knowing, mysteriously enough, how to dance
> in their own manner. Everything was full of movement in these
> dreams; it was that which enabled me to escape in the end, going
> further, even further! And all of it was a mixture of apprehension
> that sometimes turned into joy, and even rapture ... And now for

years ... I saw the desert in a sort of mental vision, almost photo-
graphically. But which desert? It seemed that I should recognize it
the day I found myself there.[6]

The young Nancy's recurring dream of dancing in the desert will be discussed
in detail later in this study. It is the primal scene for the European modernist
artist as primitivist, dramatizing escape from the Victorian patriarchs who
made the empire, and, more significantly for women, from the bourgeois
family at home where women were trained to consume the products of that
empire. In its drama of belonging and not belonging, its primal fantasy of
racial unity or her own role as female messiah, the scene casts Cunard as the
outlaw and outcast Thamar. It is the dream of exogamy; the daughter is sent
to a strange tribe. In her dream the other tribe understands and accepts her.
She knows their language and the steps to their dance. Her exile is full of fear
and joy—but someday, the narrative implies, she will "escape." The sandstorm
in the Sahara, the whirlwind in the heart of Africa is the landscape she longs
for—escaping back to the beginning of everything, to the scene of human
origins as Virginia Woolf imagines so powerfully in her primal scene of the
dog fox and the vixen facing each other in fear and desire at the end of *Between
the Acts*. The biblical Thamar saves her people and her race by producing twin
sons from her seduction of her father-in-law. Her story is often interpreted by
Jews and Christians as about the survival of the House of David and so also
of the line that produces Christ. As the Antichrist of Cunard's poem "Prayer"
hastens the end of the world and the Resurrection, Thamar's bad behavior
brings good results for her people.

Cunard's reputation for outlaw sexuality and the breaking of taboos
was constructed on the basis of her interracial love affairs. But her adoption
of Thamar as alter ego was early enough to predict a career of even more
sexual excess than the young woman had already experienced, an extension
of that excess into similarly shocking Surrealist political acts, and a period of
wandering in the wilderness. Like Thamar, she experienced the patriarchy's
wars with a series of unsatisfactory lovers. Cast out, she chose promiscuity
over chastity in the name of life. What did not happen in Nancy Cunard's
story was a version of Thamar's reconciliation with her tribe and Judah's
ultimate recognition of her righteousness. She had no children. She did not
continue the Cunard line. Her chosen childlessness was political. No family
were there to ease her agonized end. As an instance of primitivism, Cunard's

self-creation as Thamar, in the same way that Christian genealogy creates the Old Testament race savior as ancestress of David and so of Christ, is the ultimate white European fantasy of being one with human origins of all the tribes in Africa, the "heart of darkness" that colonialism has destroyed, being accepted as one of them by the Other. In assuming the persona of Thamar as her outlaw identity, Cunard fearlessly faced herself as a woman of insatiable sexual desire and predicted the life of exile, activism, and adventure that lay before her.

Cunard's own story was a tragedy. And if Europe was the place of escape in her dream, Cunard the poet never loses her vision of European culture as devastated by war. The European tribes have not accepted each other into their rituals, their languages, their dances. The poet predicts the ash-white end of the world in the closing of the drama of World War I:

> The curtains of the sky are tightly drawn;
> As in a horrid sunken maze the sun
> Is veiled with wickedness, and all the streets
> Shine horribly and wanly at noontide.[7]

This is a vision of the end of white Western civilization. That vision never fades. It is a visualization of the familiar message heard by an age in the lines "not with a bang, but a whimper." The ghastly whiteness appears again in her Spanish Civil War poems, her poems of World War II, and the late long poem raging against war. She set fire to the manuscript of her anti-war epic, staggering up the stairs of a Paris hotel, like a mad Brunnhilde throwing her torch at Valhalla, as if she were going to bring down the old gods once and for all, destroying instead herself and her oppositional texts. Ashes, ashes, we all fall down, as the children's rhyme has it. In the end she was Thamar again, outcast, wandering in the wilderness, but a modern Thamar as well as a modernist Thamar, out of tune with the rhythms of the dominant culture into which she was born, in step with all the arts of African origin.

The Thamar legend that Cunard identifies with in her poem is the story of the Georgian princess whose lovers died after being with her, a story obviously based on the biblical Thamar whose husbands died, embodying the ancient fear of a sexually free woman. Cunard and her women friends, as Diana Cooper points out in her autobiography, had spent the war years making love to officers and men on leave, and most of them had returned to the Front and been killed. Their experience of their own sexuality in the course of the war might well have led to an association of desire with death:

> Thamar in distant Georgia watched the sun
> Sit in voluptuous solitude; the hills
> Brought to her lovers, and she bound their wills
> Under her own firm spell, and everyone
> Of pleasure tasted, marvelled and was dead:
> Cast into night after a little hour
> Of paradise incarnate, for her power
> None might escape, by fate thereunto led
> But in the silent hall where love had lain,
> Captive of all her beauty, wisdom, pride,
> Rose clamouring ghosts that made her turn aside
> Her longing eyes, as yet she waved again
> (Herself now prisoner of the loves that died,)
> Signal continuous o'er the endless plain.[8]

The Georgian Thamar is figured as a flying virgin, her desire never satisfied, a killer of men. Cunard's poem sets her as a star in the night sky over the desert/plain/battlefield (Beckett's "Shining Whore" again), not guiding men, but signaling their deaths in great numbers, one by one. She waves and signals, a goddess of misguidance, luring men to pleasure and danger. Is Cunard's Thamar the figure of woman as war, monstrous, evil, and lustful that war literature always encourages? The poem expresses the collective guilt of her generation of young women, accepting the myth that the source of war is their own unbridled sexuality, blaming themselves for the loss of their lovers.

The figure of the woman waving or signaling in Cunard's poem creates love as a battlefield where the dead hold her prisoner. We assume she is cast in this role forever as the dead are dead forever. The poem asks what is the relation of love to war. The answer is: as cause and effect. Many survivors of World War I experienced guilt in the same way that Cunard's poem works. It certainly speaks for that lost generation of women and their self-lacerating griefs, suggesting obsessive repetition of its S.O.S. of pleasure and pain. Sex and death, as in the Tristan and Isolde story Cunard also loved, were always intertwined.

The American poet Robinson Jeffers created a demonic Thamar in 1921 and self-published as *Tamar and Other Poems* (1924) and *Roan Stallion, Tamar and Other Poems* (Boni and Liveright, 1925). It is not clear whether he read Nancy Cunard's *Outlaws* before writing his violent poem about incest, rape, holocaust, but he, too, was responding to the horrors of World War I. The poem is set on the California coast at Point Lobos where Jeffers lived, and, while he appears to use the story from 2 Samuel, Jeffers's Tamar is also a postwar Ishtar, sister of Tammuz, the fertility god, whose modern self is assaulted by tribal gods on the beach so that she loses the child. When she seduces her father, she brings the world down in flames. The poem is dramatic in form with interludes and chorus-like Greek drama, a powerful primitive reworking of the myths of death and regeneration that characterize the literature of this war. Tamar's ritual lovers are mutilated and she laments the dead like the speaker in Cunard's poem—she insists she must talk to the dead and later feels she has been assaulted and eaten by the dead. Tamar's dance, in Jeffers's poem, as in Stravinsky's *Rite of Spring*, is an orgy of rape by savage gods or ritual prostitution, that dance that haunts the imagination of World War I writing and seems to be at the heart of Cunard's identity as a poet. Jeffers writes of Tamar's new strength:

> She was white stone,
> Passion and despair and grief had stripped away
> Whatever is rounded and approachable
> In the body of woman, hers looked hard, long lines
> Narrowing down from the shoulder-bones, no appeal,
> A weapon and no sheath, fire without fuel...[9]

Tamar calls down fire and Armageddon on her house/race as dark horsemen ride out from the war. The wheel of fortune "dips toward" Asia as Western civilization burns itself out; Tamar imagines herself "standing back of the evening crimson on a mountain in Asia" or on the evening star as the world comes to an end.

The Georgian legend of Thamar the ice princess had haunted the Russian poet Mikhail Lermontov (1814–41) in his famous poems "Thamar" and "The Demon," where we meet the queen of the black castle: "Her beautiful face was angelic, / Her spirit demonic and mean." In his poem the dead are "impetuous women and men / Who gathered for feasting and orgies, / Who reveled again and again." The river crushes the bodies as "A wave to a wave would be rushing/ A wave would be driving a wave ... / A face or a handkerchief whitened, / And somebody whispered 'adieu.'"[10] The confluence of waving and drowning in Lermontov's poem is very moving, and if Cunard read it, as she certainly seems to have, her remaking the wave into a signal of both love and war is a tribute to the masterful Russian lyric. Cunard's identification with the Georgian siren, however, is closer to the historical Queen Thamar than Lermontov's *femme fatale*.

Women of Affairs: Lempicka, Garbo, and Cunard

But the *femme fatale* is not a figure to be dismissed in the history of Nancy Cunard's adventure in self-making. There was a real-life Tamara in postwar Paris, a beautiful White Russian refugee from the revolution, married to a Polish aristocrat. Tamara de Lempicka (189?–1980), a publicly bisexual and passionately promiscuous woman, was both a celebrity socialite and a brilliant painter.[11] Did Cunard take the stunning Slavic beauty herself, as well as the Slavic legend, as her example? This Tamara, too, danced all night in the jazz clubs, mixing cocaine and drink, flamboyantly flirting with girls and boys, "adoring" Josephine Baker. But she also drove herself all day as Cunard did in an amazingly prolific production of paintings that only now are beginning to be taken seriously as art.

Working against the grain of all the definitions of modernism in painting, Lempicka's pictures were as classical in style and elegant in form as Nancy Cunard's and Edith Sitwell's poetry. It was the content that was radical for all the women artists. The poets worked as far from Eliot's free verse as Lempicka did from the Cubism of Cézanne and the Post-Impressionism of Matisse. Sitwell and Cunard and their fellow poets in *Wheels* wrote of death and desire, war and the end of civilization. Class prejudice certainly took its toll on the reputations of women artists born into privilege. Yet it is only logical that they would be the ones to break the barriers for their sex. Cunard voluntarily gave up her position as Lady Cunard's daughter, and Lady Cunard herself denied the poet an allowance from her heritage, disinheriting her for all intents and purposes, after refusing to end her affair with Henry Crowder. She embraced the 1917 revolution from which Lempicka fled and made her life as an outlaw among the artists of the left, pan-African intellectuals, and Surrealists in Paris; Lempicka flirted with the right, with Marinetti, D'Annunzio, and the titled rich in Italy, and in Paris with the lesbians of Natalie Barney's salon, Jean Cocteau, and an international crowd of socialites. Marxists and fascists, both serious and *dilletantes*, made up the Parisian intellectual scene. Cocteau was a particular hate of Cunard's and her politics turned her toward a nightlife among Black jazz musicians, sailors, and artists of a different stripe, though she and Lempicka doubtless frequented the same lesbian and homosexual underworld and the bars where drugs were to be had. But Lempicka had a husband and child to come home to, a mother and a community of White Russian exiles to provide a secure base from which to experiment with life.

Where Cunard and Lempicka's paths crossed in the twenties is in the intersection of fashion with the art world, one's picture appearing in *Vogue* and the other's in *Vanity Fair*, Nancy then writing a column for *Vogue* and Tamara doing a series of astonishing covers for *Die Dame*. Cunard didn't last long as London *Vogue*'s Paris arts correspondent. She apparently commented harshly on Cocteau, and Clive Bell, who was neither as intellectual or as critical, took her place. Cocteau was a lifelong friend of Lempicka's and they shared the same attitude about socializing with the rich and famous and publicizing their work. As society women of style and artists in their own right, Nancy Cunard and Tamara de Lempicka were in the extreme position of acting as visual icons of the age. Images of their faces and bodies caught the fashion camera's eye and aspiring artists who wanted their work taken seriously photographed and painted and sculpted them as well. Cunard's grace and beauty lives forever in the Brancusi sculptures, the Man Ray photographs, and the paintings of Wyndham Lewis and Eugene McCown. The fashion magazines went through a phase in which they did profiles of Einstein and Bertrand Russell, and the celebrity culture they created placed Cunard and Lempicka with the most important intellectuals of the day before their achievements matched their looks. It was part of the New Woman's mystique that she worked and drove a sports car, wrote nihilistic poems, and painted daring lesbian nudes.

Lempicka painted women's bodies with a woman's eye for deep curves and shadows in firm flesh as buffed and polished as the racing cars that symbolized their Jazz Age glamour. At odds with mainstream modernism, her pictures reward attention to modernist hyperreality with a vision of the age that contradicts the standard narratives of art history and literature. The strict musical rhythms and classical forms of Cunard's poems gave off a certain *frisson* under the weight of their cargo of despair. What has been called the decadent Mannerism of Lempicka's painting gives the world and the flesh a hard edge and shine that appealed to audiences at the millennium as they did to those recovering from the insane and destructive debacle of World War I and the leveling displacements of the Russian Revolution.

Lempicka cared about finish and form in an age of impressionist smudge and surrealist games. Her work was hyperreal, a combination of classical Italian Caravaggio in grand nude bodies and modernist Futurist color work with glossy and slightly menacing machines and phallic skyscrapers. Her erotic female figures were as sleek as machines but they had an excessive mass and volume like both Picasso's classical figures and Léger's tubular shapes, along with a Mannerist gloss and the hard edge of Renaissance painting.

Lempicka's *Autoportrait in a Green Bugatti* has had at least two lives in publicity, first as a cover design of the New Woman of the twenties for a German fashion magazine, widely circulated as the icon of an age of Deco and decadence, and more recently as an icon of the celebrity singer Madonna's outrageousness. Because Madonna and other American movie stars and celebrities have bought and collected Lempicka's work, as they have the work of Frieda Kahlo, her status as an artist has not risen while her extraordinary images are proliferating in calendars and posters in the age of mechanical reproduction. Lempicka also has a cult following as a publicly active lesbian and painter of gorgeous lesbian bodies.

Tamara de Lempicka and Nancy Cunard were taboo-shattering divas in Paris in the twenties, present and photographed at all the parties and balls. Traffic stopped and people stared at the living glowing tragedy of beautiful women courting death, dancing, drinking, taking drugs and lovers in mad pursuit of pleasure. Whether or not they met in person, they are likely to have seen each other at the 1925 Art Deco exhibition in Paris where Cunard modeled Sonia Delaunay's multicolored coat and Lempicka showed her portraits. A famous photograph of Cunard in this coat graces many of the books about Delaunay, another Russian émigré artist whose work is at the crossroads of fashion and art. She did brilliant textiles, stage sets, carpets, clothing, and book design as well as painting. But her work in the decorative arts somehow diminishes her reputation as a painter, while her husband's status is secure because he only painted. Lempicka exhibited *Irene and Her Sister,* and began working with well-known Paris couturiers and designers to provide dresses for her models or for the many portraits she painted of society women. A more sanguine view is taken of such relationships between male artists, photographers, decorators, and art dealers. But in judging women's work the very confluence of fabrics and dresses, jewelry and hats, and high art, the suggestion that creativity acts itself out in different media, puts her name in pink lights around a dressing table skirted with masses of pink gauze and tulle, not fiercely facing an easel. The rather ferocious femininity of both artists, each of whom had as great a sense of self as they had a unique personal style, only added to the confusion of body and sexuality with work. Lempicka painted frantically to restore her family to their lost elite social position. Along the way she created a past that excluded her Russian Jewish businessman father. Cunard publicly disavowed her mother, Lady Cunard, as she dedicated her writing to wider social causes. But as we have seen, her name forever invoked her class; she was fused in people's minds with the glamorous figures in elegant clothes in the Cunard Line's famous advertising posters; reviewers thought her poetry derivative of Eliot's and tainted by her class origins in money and her reputation for (unreproductive) sexuality. The secret upper-class past was always bursting through in her new life as a radical, just as Lempicka's fear of revolution made her paint as if the wolf were at the door. It was there in her walk. It was there in her speech, her command of languages, her knowledge and experience of travel and cultural history. Even drunken promiscuity couldn't make her into a girl of the streets.

As divas Tamara de Lempicka and Nancy Cunard have a reluctant and belated aura about them. They seem to resist as critics and biographers attempt to bring their stories and their works out of mothballs for new readers and viewers. Nowhere is this mood more pronounced than in the peculiar film *A Woman of Affairs* (1928), based on Michael Arlen's *roman à clef The Green Hat*, called by one critic an advertisement for Hispano-Suiza motorcars, with Greta Garbo playing the Nancy Cunard figure. Lempicka's punning *Autoportrait* is a hard-edged version of the soft-focus film, more like the brittle sophisticated writing of the novel than the stilted languorousness of Clarence Brown's MGM movie, a belated silent film in the age of Talkies, censored so stupidly that it could never match the popularity of the theatrical performances. The film makes no sense now because the novel and the play are not in circulation to fill in the blanks for the audience.

Lempicka later played tennis with Garbo in Hollywood, hoping to paint her heroine. In fact her painting, the "auto-portrait" and her life, as well as Cunard's looks and life, are far more suited to Arlen's "gallant" heroine than the fading, passive Garbo, who doesn't look very competent behind the wheel of a fast car. Garbo does kiss the foolish hero, John Gilbert, with an open mouth, and the way she slouches around in her Burberry trench coat and pouts under her cloche hat are classic acts, though they don't suit this partic- ular heroine. Garbo is entranced into acting a bit by a bouquet of roses that she romances with all her might. But the film is a failure because Garbo lacks backbone, the bisexual independence and stiff-upper-lip "honor" projected by the brazen boyishness of tough characters like Cunard or Lempicka or the heroine of *The Green Hat*.

The Iris March character based on Cunard from Arlen's novel (and playscript) connected brilliantly with the careers of stage actresses Tallulah Bankhead and Katharine Cornell, both of whom participated in the celebrity cult of the gentlemanly "woman of honor":

> Iris March was absolutely a post-War institution, of course. She couldn't be taken seriously today. But then people were fascinated and charmed by that "gallantry of a hungry heart" point of view; by that fair small Iris with tiger tawny hair and eyes the color of the sea at Capri. Her green hat *pour le sport*, her "thousand carnal Calvaries," her yellow Hispano-Suiza, her spectacular suicide, seemed exciting and glamorous stuff.[12]

But they had Arlen's lines to speak and Arlen's plot to act. The film censors cut the risqué dialogue as well as the husband's syphilis, so the scenes make very little sense.

What seems interesting in *A Woman of Affairs* for audiences now is that the film as it exists, hanging on to the fabled green hat by only a thread, is a story about men's love for each other. The memorable performance is the homosexual hysteria of Douglas Fairbanks, Jr. over his "best friend's" marriage to his sister, the Garbo character, who is most in character when she flirts with her brother. The marriage is never consummated; David commits suicide on his wedding night and Fairbanks then drinks himself to death while refusing to see his sister ever again. The real love-death drama is between men, as the traditional wedding-night scenario is reversed, and the bored, impatient (read "experienced") bride drums her fingers on the bedstead as the "virgin" male delays and then jumps out the window. Was it a fate worse than death to sleep with a woman like her? The film censor changed David's sin to embezzlement so Garbo can claim he died for decency. But in the novel he dies for "purity" because he has syphilis. The censored syphilis in the film we would now see as the sign of homoeroticism, the heroine's "theft" of the boy from his boyfriend. While the plot relates all this to Garbo, her diffidence as an actress and Fairbanks's manic eye-rolling and tense body language tell another story of another triangle than the one supposedly shaping the plot, the incestuous competition between a brother and sister for a lover. With the woman of affairs, the manly woman of honor that the sad and listless Garbo does not begin to impersonate, and the gay men dead, English country life, we presume, is saved for heterosexual marriage and the family.

Images of the woman writer and the woman painter have become inextricably mixed with images of Garbo and perhaps tainted by Garbo's failure as an actress to fulfill the role of the character as a "woman of honor." Garbo is too weak and traditionally feminine to be believable as either a wicked woman of affairs or the honorable English girl who kills herself because her lover has to tell his father she was innocent all along. The self-creating Garbo named herself in Swedish as "wood nymph," just what she is in the film. Kenneth Tynan wrote that the Spanish word was applied to a high-spirited, controlled, animal grace in bullfighters. That *garbo* Garbo doesn't have in *A Woman of Affairs*. But Tamara de Lempicka and her painting have it. And so does Nancy Cunard.

Betsy Erkkila sees Garbo as not in the least passive, but an active presence in her films, combining mannishness with sensuality.[13] But none of that New Woman mannishness comes out in this film. She also sees the substitution of male for female sleeping beauty under Garbo's passionate sexuality, her desire and yearning lingering after she is dead. Certainly she exudes desire and all the characters are seen looking at her longingly; she does kiss her lover's wife's photograph and brilliantly captures her desire as well. I would argue that this scene and the scene in which Garbo vamps the armful of roses are all part of a hysterical discourse of queer looking that is most visible in Fairbanks's acting. His excited spectatorship with binoculars in the stands as David wins the Oxford/Cambridge boat race is definitely homoerotic. The other men in the stands are there for the same thing but have been socialized to repress it and they disapprove. Fairbanks's rolling eyes at first seem to be a throwback to earlier silent films, the broad gestures of minstrelsy. But then the protruding eye, the goggling eye, aghast at his sister, or furious with her, indicates that it is a gender-dysfunctional minstrelsy, not the male gaze that feminist critics have analyzed that is dramatized by Fairbanks as a queer white Al Jolson figure. Garbo does not seem distressed about his death as she stands in the frame of the window out of which David has jumped. She appears to be wondering, eyes cast down, what there is about her that causes men to commit suicide. She appears to acquiesce to her brother's accusing gaze at the woman he thinks murdered his beloved.

Can one suggest that Garbo colludes in making *A Woman of Affairs* a gay film? She doesn't star in this film the way she stars in other films. Garbo was of course taking on a role that was still being played by a real woman from Michael Arlen's enormously popular novel, *The Green Hat*. But the role was also played on stage in London and New York by Talullah Bankhead and Katherine Cornell in her first starring role. These two formidable actresses and the presence on the international scene of Nancy Cunard as a celebrity herself were perhaps a warning to Garbo that she would be marked as more openly mannish than she wanted to be if she played the role of autonomous tragic woman of honor as it was being played by the heavy competition on the stage.

Despite the fact that she called the play that "Armenian mishmash" in her memoirs,[14] Tallulah Bankhead claimed it brought her the attentions of Lloyd George, Ramsay MacDonald, then prime minister, and various Churchills. It also made her a star who drew a nightly "gallery" of hundreds of London working girls, who enjoyed the scandal of an actress appearing in a play about what was reported to be her own outrageous social set. She played up the heroine's death wish and wore the green hat offstage as well as on, creating her own celebrity out of the role.[15] James Agate declared the production obscene, not to mention "oversexed" and "overdressed": "It is the attempt to gild sensuality with the trumperies of sham generosity which is objectionable. Also I take it that Mr. Arlen's metamorphosis is wrong in fact. Lady into fox may be thinkable; vixen into goose is absurd." But he, like the girls in the gallery, admired Bankhead's "husky charm" in the role of "a young woman careening in canary-colored motor-cars between Deauville and Nice." "All praise ... to Miss Bankhead, impersonating to the life a joyless creature whose spiritual home was the gutter."[16] The green hat was reborn as a verb when Agate wrote of Bankhead's next stage appearance that she "greenhatted it to perfection."

Years later, when Kieran Tunney gave her the script of his play *Aurora*, based on Nancy Cunard and her mother, Lady Cunard, Bankhead mentioned that she had always thought *The Green Hat* was the story of Nancy's best friend, Iris Tree. Curtis Moffat, Tree's husband and Cunard's close friend as well, had been Bankhead's ("very expensive") decorator: "He was brilliant.

An artist, photographer—they say it was he who taught Cecil Beaton how to make everyone look gorgeous."[17] It was Moffat of course who had transformed Cunard from soft English girlishness to hard-edged, African-braceleted icon of the twenties. His photographs and Cecil Beaton's had established and publicized a brazen "look" she kept all her life. Tallulah Bankhead was styled by Moffat and Beaton as well, but in her case, the look was also lodged in the voice. A photograph of a scene from the play in Brendan Gill's *Tallulah* shows the actress in a low-slung twenties dress that could have been Cunard's, "not only braless but waistless."

"Tallulah had less to play against than I had," Katharine Cornell said of her own more successful run in the New York hit version of the play. "Tallulah's life in those days was a series of extreme melodramas, and mine was not. I had to work my way into Iris; Tallulah was already there."[18] Cornell attributes her success (the play ran for two years in the United States) to downplaying the role, and to the fact that Guthrie, the director, cut the lines he didn't like, replacing them with the best lines from Arlen's other novels.[19] And Leslie Howard played Napier Harpender, who has loved her since childhood. Reading the reviews now one is startled to find that all the reviewers remark on Arlen being an Armenian. George Jean Nathan's review went after Arlen as "an alien" and "a swell dresser," calling his play "a backstairs piece of literature brought into the drawing-room, seeking to hide its nervous embarrassment behind a screen of ultra-tony and elegant writing."[20] Robert Benchley asked for a performance an eighth of an inch broader for a delightful burlesque; a Chicago reviewer called it a "civilized melodrama … sophisticated, polished till its rouge and rhinestones blush and sparkle like real."[21]

The racy language of the play was still in the public memory and the novel still in print when Garbo's film version muddled it up without green-hatting a bit. Erkkila quotes the French critic Edgar Morin on the ways the film characters infect the star and the star infects the characters. Something like this seems to have happened with Cunard, the model for the character in Arlen's *The Green Hat*, and even de Lempicka's painting and persona of the vamp in the sports car. Censorship seems to have diluted (or diverted to the homoerotic) the romantic energy of the film. A woman of affairs in the French sense, that is, a competent woman, is a role Cunard and Garbo both played well in real life, embodying the freedom of the woman who wants to be alone.

Nancy Cunard made a new way of living for a woman artist. And that was no small social accomplishment, although it may have been a personal tragedy. She chose to live and work alone. In a productive and effective life as a political activist, a public intellectual and a poet, she lived the new paradigm of the independent woman. It was not easy. There were few comforts—no home, hearth, children, garden. Sexual partners and political allies came and went. Without ties to parent or child, nation or language, Cunard was one of those larger-than-life figures who created modern life. She cherished her friendships and supported her lovers in their work. Work was indeed the center of her life, as if to make up for the work not done by her mother and the women of the luxuried class she left behind. Free in her love habits and strict in her work habits, she was the very model of the new woman of the world. She sought lovers who would also be partners in work. When she first met Louis Aragon she wrote to one of her girlfriends that she had at last found an ideal lover—he was capable of intense work sessions at all hours, a match for her own energies. Some of her most significant contributions to modernist experimentation were not in poetic forms, a free or freer verse, but in making a life as a radical woman.

Cunard's work embodies the crisis of white identity at the heart of modernism. Her political work, her poetry, her art collecting, her editing and journalism, and her free-loving life are acknowledgments of the vitality of primitivism as a force in European culture and her own psyche. Not only did she not deny that Africa and its arts inspired her; she wanted to *be* African, to suffer oppression and to fight for freedom, to expiate in some real way the sins of colonialism against a continent. It is a choice one comes to respect in reconsidering the import of her life and work for our time.

Race matters were of vital importance to her development as a public intellectual. But the impact of World War I, its waste and loss, shaped her literary imagination. Cunard's life may also be seen as part of the collective pacifist epic made by the lives and works of women driven by a powerful anti-war ethic in the twentieth century, from Virginia Woolf to Grace Paley, from Olive Schreiner to H.D. The figure of Thamar, making love, not war, demanding sex and seducing her father-in-law, was a powerful enough evocation of sexual freedom and cross-cultural connection among the warring tribes, as rebellious in-law and performing outlaw, to call Nancy Cunard out of her name, her class, her nation, and into the life of an artist and rebel.

Outlaw: "*Not* H.D."

"I love the gesture of your open hands / Expounding things," the title poem of Nancy Cunard's *Outlaws* begins seductively, in the traditional posture of the student sitting at her master's feet, pretending to listen while absorbing the master's technique to get up the courage to speak, herself. The forms she uses are often the old Provencal ones used by the troubadours in the wars of the heretic Cathars and the Albigensians. In "The Knave of Spades," a lover is called, "A fiendish rebel with no heart, and yet [the poet says] / "You are my love, the witchcraft of my faith."[22] It is a nice reversal of the courtly love tradition. Cunard admired Pound and Eliot and Wyndham Lewis and Aldington and Huxley and John Rodker because they were opinionated and engaged intellectuals, because they were full of theories and arguments.[23] Her faith was art. They were its priests, adepts at its arcane practices. The men seem to have taken it in turn, the task of mentoring the aspiring poet. They had great difficulties treating her as an intellectual equal. One fiendish rebel after another proved to have no heart. The trouble was that they could not bear an answer or an argument or even the slightest move toward expounding anything from the women writers they patronized and were determined to change from aspiring poets into patronesses of the expounders.[24] They kept the secrets of their (witch)craft to a specifically male circle, for the most part. For what their rites were like the reader is directed to the letters of Eliot and Pound. The young Nancy Cunard met many of the modernist men as they came to beg patronage from her mother. The daughter's claims to be taken seriously excited them sexually. How many other lovers wanted to hear their ideas? Her open mind and willing body met no equals in their circle. The problem was that she often disagreed, talked back, and appropriated the expounder's tone herself.

The Provencal form of verse disputation, a child of the courtly love traditions that Pound studied and mastered for his *Cantos*, eventually became Cunard's form as a poet. It was called a *tenson* and was derived from the *canso*. The *sirventes*, a verse diatribe, was a form both Pound and Cunard learned to use very well for differing political ends.[25] As she came into her own in the thirties, Cunard jokingly called her Spanish Civil War poems "Nanción's Cancións," playing across languages and traditions and recalling her apprenticeship in Provencal languages, texts, and history with Pound and Rodker, an apprenticeship that shaped her idea of herself as a poet, scholar, and researcher, and then as an expounder like Pound himself of a set of serious but very different social values. She was indispensable to Pound it seems as a determined researcher in the libraries of Languedoc. Cunard returned to the Dordogne, the scene of their sojourns together in the twenties, many times later in her life, and then settled after World War II near Lot in an old stone castle, like the heretic politically active queens who were the heroines of the troubadours. Cunard's *Poems (Two)* (1925) records her Provencal adventure: "At les Baux," "To Vaucluse Came Petrarch and Laura," "At St. Rémy," "Saintes Maries de la Mer," "By the Dordogne," "A Night in Avignon." In *Sublunary* (1923) she writes of her rebel governess from Toulon and a prostitute in Bandol, poetic versions perhaps of Picasso's *Les Demoiselles d'Avignon* and her identification with Thamar's sexuality; "The Siege" calls her heart a castle in troubadour tradition.

Pound, for his part, in the tradition of William IX of Aquitaine remembering his good companions before going into exile, memorializes the similar chivalric pleasures of Cunard's companionship as a scholar and an intrepid walker on the rocky mountain paths of southern France in Canto 80: "Nancy, where art thou?"[26] Remembering their days in the Dordogne, deep in Provencal poetry, courtly love, and their own relationship, and the Paris days with Orage, Ford Madox Ford, and the Surrealist René Crevel, whose "Negress in the Brothel" was refused by the censor for the *Negro* anthology and secretly printed and tipped into all the volumes by Cunard herself, Pound both mocks her poetic language and memorializes their friendship.

Cunard reverses the sentiment of both William and Ezra in "From Afar":

> I sit thinking of you
> Friends, partners of other times …
> Gay, lusty, destitute and unsobered …
> Do you not see I am estranged from you?[27]

Estranged she certainly was, and not entirely because of the poets' misogyny. Unrecognized as a poet in Pound's circles as part of the Provencal revival and rejected as an expounder of modernist angst by Eliot's conservative *Criterion* crowd and *The Dial* alike, Cunard grew intellectually over the next decade into an expounder of radical socialism, pan-Africanism, and anti-fascism. The peculiar primitivism they shared in the search for ancient cultural traditions in old books, local language, and customs, an eclectic scholarship of the self-educated to remake history that they also deeply shared, actually led to one ideological convergence, admiration for the work of the controversial scholar Frobenius on Africa. Pound wrote a piece for Cunard's *Negro* anthology; primitivisms of the left and right seemed not to cancel each other out at this point. As male modernism moved to the right, Cunard moved to the left and to the Europe that she and her fellow poets on *Wheels* had embraced (in French) in their six wartime anthologies of poetry published from 1916 to 1921. For Cunard the ancient cave drawings and rock formations of the Dordogne, the scene of the ruins of splendid civilizations, was a spiritual center for her modernist primitivism, a place where she could follow the urge to find the origins of art and the meaning of life after the war. Her primitivism, like that of many Europeans devastated by the waste of war, was an affirmation of the life instinct over the death drive. It was a religion in which art and anthropology were enjoined to argue the essential brotherhood of man in common racial origins. The arts of Africa were read as the vital signs for the survival of humanity. Despairing of the West, its worn-out ideals of Christianity, commerce, and empire, Cunard embraced Black culture out of hope for the future.

This is the story of Nancy Cunard the poet and how she came eventually to expound her own ideas, to break with her mentors, to insist to Pound that she was "*not* H.D."[28] One cannot imagine her as "N.C., Imagiste." But she did in fact learn a great deal from Pound's immense powers as an editor. Cunard's own powers as a poet are very different from H.D.'s and both women are neglected in modernist canons, but H.D.'s best work is a protest against the wars that shattered their lives. In a sense one could say that H.D. and Cunard are linked as women anti-war poets whose styles have nothing in common, across the dead body of Ezra Pound's controlling canonical modernism.

George Moore, Cunard's first and faithful mentor, was perhaps right in his review of *Outlaws* in acclaiming her genius as a poet and her utter lack of talent, by which he meant tact or judgment. What Moore valued was her passion, which he compared to Heloise, Saint Teresa, and Emily Brontë, and he urged her to cultivate restraint.[29] Oddly enough, it was Cunard's lack of passion that was commonly cited, even by Moore himself, captivated by the same coldness in her mother, as explanation for both her charm and her ability to survive on the cultural edge. In *The Radical Twenties* John Lucas writes: "Nancy Cunard wasn't really a poet, but it is understandable that she would have wanted to be one."[30] Of *Outlaws* her future comrade and fellow poet Edgell Rickword, who later helped to edit the *Negro* anthology, in a critique Lucas finds "both just and generous," notes "her frequent lack of success," but says that "one can feel the pulse of an original mind beating through a rather uncongenial medium. The language, though often striking, lacks that essential rhythm, that dominant note which absorbs and unifies the diverse elements of a poem, drawing them to an awkward conclusion."[31]

It is ironic, given Cunard's strong identification with Black culture and jazz, her passion for dance and her dream of joining an African dance because she knew the steps by instinct, that her verse should lack rhythm, but Rickword is correct. Cunard was the Black-identified white poet who was sure she had rhythm and didn't, dancing furiously all through the twenties to find the source of that rhythm. Surely, she was not the only white person, whether intellectual or political, radical or not, who ever dreamed that dream. Her failure to capture the rhythm of Black speech despite an awesome intellectual and linguistic command of Afro-American and Caribbean slang, Creole, and Patois is actually more tragic than it is anything else.

The name Cunard was already powerful. She wanted to make it stand for more than ships and speed and glamour and money. And she did. Her father, Sir Bache, had lost or sold the family interest in the shipping line. He spent his time fox hunting or working with his hands at his craft of ironwork. Her mother's name as Lady Cunard, first Maud, then Emerald, came to stand for the blossoming of the arts in England, as she funded the opera, ballet, music, and painting in the brilliant and lavish salon she kept to promote the career of her lover, Thomas Beecham.[32] Lady Cunard was already cultivating a new generation of artists, the men who were to make classical modernism as we now know it. When her daughter emerged from the debutante stage into the character of poet, and the women, her daughter's contemporaries and friends, who were meant to succeed Maud Cunard as London's patroness of the arts and society hostess, Nancy rejected the emerald tiara for a printing press.

In 1921 Pound, ever the teacher, sent Cunard a serious critique of her writing that she kept in her poetry scrapbook. Pound criticizes Cunard's diction and encourages her to avoid the cadences of Alfred Lord Tennyson while praising how she evokes faithful images without artifice or exaggeration. Her style is decidedly not Georgian, in his view, and he offers the same counsel that he offers in the margin to a draft of Eliot's *The Waste Land*: "Ils detachent des sentiments pour les accomoder a leur vocabulaire." In fact, Pound must have had Eliot on his mind while dispensing advice on how Cunard might fine-tune her recent submission to the *Dial*, as he names Eliot in the same letter as the only one in England who "knows anything" about poetry.[33]

It is likely that it is his criticism to which the speaker is replying as well as Eliot's (though it could be Rodker or Aldington or another one of her poet friends) in Cunard's brilliant "Answer to a Reproof":

> Let my impatience guide you now, I feel
> You have not known that glorious discontent
> That leads me on: the wandering after dreams
> And the long chasing in the labyrinth
> Of fancy, and the reckless flight of moods—
> You *shall* not prison, shall not grammarise
> My swift imagination, nor tie down
> My laughing words, my serious words, old thoughts
> I may have led you on with, baffling you
> Into a pompous state of great confusion.
> You have not seen the changing active birds
> Nor heard the mocking voices of my thoughts;
> Pedant-philosopher, I challenge you
> Sometimes with jests, more often with real things,
> And you have failed me, you have suffered too
> And struggled, wondering. The difference lies
> In the old bulk of centuries, the way
> You have been fashioned this or that; and I
> Belong to neither, I the perfect stranger,
> Outcast and outlaw from the rules of life,
> True to one law alone, a personal logic
> That will not blend with anything, nor bow
> Down to the general rules; inflexible,
> And knowing it from old experience;
> So much for argument—*My* trouble is,
> It seems, that I have loved a star and tried
> To touch it in its progress; tear it down
> And own it, claimed a "master's privilege"

Over some matter that was element
And not an object that would fit the palm
Of a possessor, master-mind itself
And active-ardent of its liberty.

We work apart, alone; conflicting tides
Brim-filled with angers, violences, strife,
Each championing his own idealism,
Romanticism and sceptic bitterness ...
The last I leave you, for this present mood
(The name of which you have expounded so)
Has turned against you, bared insulting teeth
And snarled away its rage into the smile
Of old remembrance: "You were ever so,"
Exacting and difficult; in fact the star
That will not, cannot change for all the price
Of love or understanding—mark you *now*
I have concluded we are justified
Each in his scheming; is this not a world
Proportioned large enough for enemies
Of our caliber? Shall we always meet
In endless conflict? I have realised
That I shall burn in my own hell alone
And solitarily escape from death;
That you will wander guideless too, and dream
(Sometimes) of what I *Mean*, the things unsaid,
Vacant discussions that have troubled you
And left me desperate as a day of rain.

Then we shall meet at crossroads in wild hours
Agreeing over fundamental fates,
Calamities of a more general kind
Than our own geniuses have kindled up.
But at the fabulous Judgment-day, the End,
We shall be separate still, and you will find
That destiny has posted you once more
Back in the sky—and I shall be on earth.[34]

In 1921 when *Outlaws* was published Nancy Cunard saw herself as "the perfect stranger," "outcast and outlaw from the rules of life," a rebel in conflict with her intellectual companion, the "philosopher-pedant" who finds her "inflexible" and intent on mastery. The contradiction between "perfect" and "stranger" suggests the driven perfectionist she became as well as her continual need to pack up and leave wherever she was for the nomad's life of exile that was her calling. The struggle she describes is mental and emotional. How can two masterminds maintain a relationship with each other and keep their own integrity and liberty? This is a question many artists and intellectual couples have asked themselves. For Cunard it was particularly important to assert her identity as a poet. Her defiance of the "rules" of the grammars of art and life was unusual for a woman and her self-defense is heartening. She celebrates her wanderlust, her "glorious discontent" in words that express the feelings of many other women whose creative work is constantly being corrected by male mentors. "Let my impatience guide you now," the poet commands her reprover, challenging him to further conflict, not giving in, asserting her "genius" the equal of his. Defending the authority and authenticity of her own "personal logic" against his demands for order and rationality, the speaker of the poem insists on her dignity as "the perfect stranger." The word "perfect" is a challenge to his idea of order, a contradiction of "stranger" in its assertion of the nth degree of alienation. There is nothing civilized about me, she is saying. "We work apart, alone." She chooses to remain at odds with him in a world big enough for "enemies of our caliber." They'll be perfectly matched enemies says this bold rejoinder to a catalogue of her faults, refusing defeat. She has no intention of submitting to his criticisms, nor will she be handmaiden to his genius. "Answer to a Reproof" is the woman artist's declaration of independence.[35]

Of course, Pound's criticisms of her work were very much appreciated. She had met Ezra Pound first at Lady Cunard's tea table in 1915 where he begged successfully for a grant from "the King's Bounty" for Joyce and for Wyndham Lewis's appointment as a "War Artist." His mannerisms and appearance were "astonishing," Cunard wrote: "He looked singularly like Rodolfo in *La Bohème* … He was dressed … in black and white check trousers, black velvet jacket, with a large-brimmed black felt hat. He wore a sweeping black cape and carried yellow chamois leather gloves and a cane." She was fascinated by the "green, lynx-like eyes, a head of thick, waving red hair and a pointed red beard" belonging to the "alarming," "vibrating," "dynamic," and "ecstatic" character who recited Greek poetry in restaurants. Perhaps Cunard's invention of herself as an eccentric poet, using her body, her bound head, and severe *maquillage* against her white skin, was acquired in imitation of Pound's self-dramatization. The bohemians of her age, from Augustus John to Edith Sitwell, also cultivated a distinctive personal presence, using the body and the voice to call attention to their art. Pound should also be credited with teaching modernism how to do its own publicity.

But it was Pound's "learning," not his red hair, which seduced her and, however much she later denounced his fascist delusions, she always declared that the *Cantos*, thirty of which she published at the Hours Press, were great poetry. She shared his interest in music, admiring the opera on Villon and his essay, *Antheil and the Treatise on Harmony* about their common friend, the American avant-garde composer George Antheil. Immersed in opera during her mother's London years as patroness of Thomas Beecham, she knew the classical repertoire well before developing a taste for modern music, jazz, and African tribal music. Cunard was very well educated for a girl of her class. Like Virginia Woolf she was basically an autodidact, teaching herself what she needed to know by reading and research, though she had formal schooling in London, Paris, and Germany to strengthen her command of languages and her interest in art, music, and history.

Pound was an excellent critic and she very much admired the way he pushed his friends and their careers. His "great appetite intellectually," his "flamboyance," and his "driving energy" were traits they had in common. To Cunard, Dudley Fitts's defense of Pound's learned citations of obscure historical periods and personages as *masks* was correct. The primitive for Pound was in Provencal culture, or various Japanese, Chinese, Italian, and troubadour cultures—an analogy to her own interest in Africa. Her final "home," in a primitive ruin near Lot in the Dordogne, was the site of a last poetic effort at reclaiming the primitive for her anti-war epic in the language of the troubadours and the legends she had explored with Ezra Pound walking in Provence after the Great War.

CHAPTER THREE

Between Men
Eliot, Pound, and Fresca

Eliot's Bogey

When the news of T. S. Eliot's death was broadcast on the radio on January 7, 1965, the 68-year-old Nancy Cunard, still in exile in France, breathless with emphysema and emaciated from illness and pain, struggled to her typewriter at Jean Guerin's Villa Pomone in Saint-Jean-Cap-Ferrat. Eliot's companion John Hayward had told her that Eliot suffered from emphysema as she did, and she recalled that his taste for gin was almost the match of her own. Writing a letter of condolence aroused intimations of her own mortality. But it also brought back her own past as a promising young English poet during the darkling years of World War I.[1]

"He will know what to do with Death," Cunard wrote to Hayward, remembering Eliot as a "solitary eagle," herself "seized" by his looks, his way, his eyes, at one of Lady Cunard's grand balls in 1922. Meeting death herself three months later, she decidedly did not know what to do—or how to do it.

Punning that she was already "somewhat versed" in him by then, her poem-letter of consolation explains that E. W. Tennant, the young officer-poet whose death in Flanders she mourned all her life, had given her a copy of "Prufrock" in 1917. Lines from "Prufrock" had got into her "fibre" as a private dirge for the dead soldier-lover, her fellow poet, and remained there for life. Eliot's death shocked her into recalling the American poet and his writing,

and her own work with the avant-garde editorial collective of the provocative annual poetry anthology *Wheels,* and the subsequent sinking of her
circle and their cycles, as the star of Eliot and his journal *The Criterion* rose.
Cunard remained as "versed" in Eliot's poetry all her life as he chose to remain
unversed in hers, or any other woman's. Being versed in his poetry meant that
his lines rang in her head when she started to write. His paralyzing literary
presence, like the frightening figure of Milton's bogey in Virginia Woolf's *A
Room of One's Own,* blocks out the sun as it blocks the woman writer's power
to write. It is in her poetry that the struggle against his shadow takes place,
the battle, we might say, against "Eliot's bogey." Unlike women writers who
struggled with "the angel in the house," the internal censor who speaks in the
voice of the mother urging convention and ladylike behavior, Cunard had no
such inhibiting angel. Her actual mother was no angel herself and was either
absent or controlling with her daughter. Her struggle was with the authority
of Eliot as he assumed the mantle of English poetry.

It is not clear how consoling Hayward found the other poem she sent to
him when Eliot died, written at night in a pub in London in 1942. War had
called her into poetry in the first place and war and the politics of war were
always her subjects. War had again fueled her poet's rage. And she makes clear
that her early experience with Eliot had put her back up against the wall, a
wall he had erected as her horizon, as he claimed London as his cultural territory, rejecting her as disciple and in effect banishing her to France. But she
takes her writing hand, the hand that drank with Eliot in the cold cruel month
of April, and characteristically follows Ibsen's Peer Gynt: "If you cannot go
forward, go round," she reasons with the "Scandinavians" Eliot found so
pernicious an influence on Fresca, his caricature of the upper-class English
poet in *The Waste Land,* escaping from Eliot's need to control the London
literary scene: "this is no longer London, this is the world," says the poem.

Out of her exile and homelessness Cunard made a life of political engagement in Paris, Madrid, Barcelona, Toulouse, in the West Indies, Harlem, and
the Dordogne. She bids Eliot's ghost be gone with its "fit of the quotes" that
robs her of her own voice in "the gin we drink from weariness, / Gin we drink
through dreariness," as she tries to write about the new generation of soldiers
who will die in Russian snows. "Metal-mouth gin" (gin/gun? or the drink as a
killer of words?) fills her head with lines from Eliot, whose imitator the critics
had called her, crippling her creativity. She was well versed in him, indeed.
Or, "And How," as she wrote to Solita Solano in the American slang she found

so appealing. "Here comes an angry little moon" is a line from the poem of her London return and World War II that catches her mood, a self-portrait, perhaps, of the displaced poet returning to the territory she had been driven from.[2] It is instructive of her critique of her work as repressed to think of the poet welcoming "an angry little moon" to the scene of writing (again)— London in wartime.

In *Parallax* (April 25, 1925), published by Leonard and Virginia Woolf at the Hogarth Press in the same series as *The Waste Land* (263 copies were sold by August 30, 1926; Virginia Woolf set the type by hand with the help of Dadie Rylands after delays because she had a cold),[3] Cunard gave a different spatial perspective on the struggle of the male artists with the female over the naming of London as the waste land. She chronicles her loss of lovers in the war and her loss of a self, a history or identity in family, gender, class, or nation. This parallax vision in modernist poetry that Cunard opposes to Eliot's search for order and tradition may be compared to Tamara de Lempicka's close-up perspectives and odd angles of vision in painting. The speaker asks: "Or how many thousand prodigal francs / From serious patriarchal banks / Must build the card-house for this / Grand Amour?" Her London is almost too real, summoning youthful heartbreak, the "war's dirges," "London, the hideous wall, the jail of what I am, / With fear nudging and pinching / Down one street and another, lost—." London is a wall obstructing her progress, a figure that recurs in the later poem about Eliot. "What wings beat in my ears / The old tattoo of journeys?" the poem continues. "The foot's impatient ... (where?) / the eye is not convinced." "(Out, out, clear words!)" she castigates herself, a theme that appears again as she struggles with Eliot's presence and hears in her head lines from his poems as obstacles to her own creativity, the powerful beat of the eagle's wings. What a question she asks, "Are the living ghosts to the dead?," a desperate question for the generation that lost so many sons and lovers, brothers and fathers. "Or do / the dead disclaim / This clutch of hands, the tears cast out to them?"[4] This passage, and its haunting question "Are the living ghosts to the dead?," is the embodiment of Cunard's parallax vision, seeing things from the other side. It is strange, skewed, out of joint, and as utterly modern in content as Eliot is in form.

Interestingly, Laura Riding and Robert Graves read *Parallax* as a conscious reply to Eliot, mocking his "utterly hopeless and unpurposed pessimism."[5] They saw that her growing political consciousness rejected his fear of the idea of revolution she was soon to embrace. But it was hard to escape from

Eliot. The *Manchester Guardian* found *Parallax* obscure and the *Daily News* heard "a rather delirious echo" of *The Waste Land*, while the *New Statesman's* reviewer detailed the links between them.

Beckett always admired *Parallax*; his respect and friendship were based on regard for it. To Raymond Mortimer it was unbearably poignant, "one of the most moving poems of our time," its point of view that of "one who perseveres through a life whose point he continually seeks in vain, too intelligent either to be content with one or to accept the facile explanations that soothe others."[6] In *Outlook* for July 1925 Louise Morgan (later Theis, and eventually to become a good friend) pointed out that "The peculiar characteristic of *Parallax* is an almost sensational repression; one feels in the reading as if one were treading a clear swept, trimly bordered garden path around the crater of a volcano." That sensational repression was what Cunard later remembered talking about to Eliot as the salient characteristic of *The Waste Land*. But it is a perfect description of her method.

The career of Cunard as a modern poet is what concerns me here. The story is a melodramatic one, though I doubt that she would have seen it that way. Biographers have argued that Cunard was the model for the fearful Fresca of Eliot's infamous 70 couplets, written in disgust à la Pope, venomously reducing an upper-class woman writer to her physical appetites and bodily functions in "The Fire Sermon" section of *The Waste Land*, lines cut by Pound and restored by Valerie Eliot in the facsimile edition of 1971.[7] Cunard's claim to the title of poet seems to have so enraged Eliot that it inspired one of the great works of art of the age. One could say that he was moved to write out of rivalry with Cunard and her companion poets of *Wheels*, perceived by him to be privileged by class and nationality to express modernist angst. In the Fresca fragment Eliot un-versed Cunard's career as a modernist poet, as he and Pound and their circle cleared the cultural ground of all the women writers, editors, and artists who were in the way of their own hegemonic dominance.[8] In her 1942 poem Cunard recalls being up against the "cold curve" of Eliot's wall, cutting her off from poetic progress that April in London, but also providing a new international perspective that was to be her future career. In *Parallax* she had first renounced personal and class "heredities," maternal protection and cultural identity "in the folded curve of Origin." As a poet she left Eliot at the wall of English traditions and individual talents and made a beeline for Europe, political education, and engagement, and a new series of collective artworks.

Eliot saw himself as a victim, an unrecognized (American outsider) genius, without the class and social connections that he imagined ensured the smooth progress of the poets of *Wheels*. The traces of that rivalry were removed from the poem's life and legend until its primacy was firmly established. When, in 1971, the facsimile edition of the drafts of the 1922 poem was published by Valerie Eliot, it clarified, among other things, Pound's important role as editor and exposed the detritus of the great poem's creation, including the nasty portrait of Fresca. By then it was too late to re-evaluate the poem or the poet. Cunard and the *Wheels* poets had been wiped off the street by the Biggest Wheel of all. *The Waste Land* is so entrenched as the canonical work of modernism that the biographies and histories of its makers do not matter.

How oddly things had turned out. Eliot, the conservative American who captured the rhythms of modernism in working-class and Afro-American speech, had become the quintessential English poet, speaking for tradition and individualism. Pound, brilliant poet and maker of poets, wearing the mask of Afro-American speech, ended up broadcasting hate from Mussolini's Italy. Leaving the United States, Eliot and Pound had revitalized English high culture with the beat of Afro-American speech in a patriarchal classicism of obscure and learned references to world religions, anthropology, and Eastern mysticism. Cunard, the English poet whose classical voice rose from the depths of social despair and futility over the waste of human life in World War I, the writer of hopelessness in sonnets and elite formal verses, had become a rough realist, a white blues artist, a radical champion of Black, Caribbean, and Latin American, and working-class writers. Now she was totally forgotten and Eliot was being called the greatest poet of the century. Eliot's voice had rhythm, to say it clearly, though his message was anti-modern. It was syncopation that made his poetry live. The complaint about the sterility of modern life had already been made by the poets of *Wheels* during the war. Cunard and her cohorts were still squeezing their violent revulsion for the culture of war into decorous and musical forms. Cunard dreamed of a pulsating circle of African dancers and her own miraculous entrance into the circle because she knew the steps.[9] But her feet got there before her voice. The jazz rhythms she danced to changed her writing voice by the end of the twenties. She tried singing the blues—but she never did capture a voice as suited to the age as Eliot's St. Louis sound.

Things had started out very differently. As the very visible and highly praised author of *Outlaws* (1921), *Sublunary* (1923), *Parallax* (1925), and *Poems (Two) 1925* (1930), and coeditor of the anthology *Wheels* with Edith

Sitwell, Cunard was a rising star of the avant-garde when Eliot was struggling for a place in the London literary scene. Like James Joyce, he denied her claim to be a poet, preferring that she reproduce her mother's role of patroness of the arts and male artists. Cunard's passionate wish to be an artist, rather than the promoter of artists, was both disconcerting and threatening. Later when she espoused the cause of racial freedom, certain Black men could only see her as a patron, not a comrade in the struggle, and some critics to this day insist on casting her in the hated role of her mother, Lady Cunard. Eliot and Pound manipulated many intelligent women into providing for the men of modernism in every possible way, as angels and editors and publishers and getters and givers of grants.

Eliot saw Cunard as much more of a threat to his hegemony than she ever was. He resented her success as a poet and an editor and one might argue that he founded *The Criterion* as a (much more respectable) rival journal to *Wheels*, where he had control of who would write and what was written and published. By ignoring *Wheels*, he dismissed its importance. He was killing off his mother culture in its latest avant-garde appearance, to the joy of the conservative guardians of high culture, destroying a vital counter-culture and clearing a way for a complete family reconciliation with the English traditional canon. As poor but proud English aristocrats, like Bache Cunard in fact, married Americans with money who longed for "culture," like Maud Cunard, Eliot and Pound brought "hot" American subcultural voices to England, bathed in a multicultural glow of foreign languages and esoteric references to the literatures of India and Japan. Like a couple of white professors acting out blackface minstrelsy, they acted out modernism's new sounds and dances while calming the fears of the natives.

Cunard started the Hours Press in Paris in 1928, in some ways to extend the work of the Woolfs at the Hogarth Press, who had published her work and that of other modernists, but also to provide a place for new "outlaws." She published Pound and discovered Beckett and produced volumes of the work of John Rodker, Brian Howard, Louis Aragon, George Moore, Norman Douglas, Laura Riding, and other avant-garde writers. The press was not the plaything of a dilettante, nor was it her attempt at patronage. She always worked with groups and intellectual communities, seldom making critical decisions herself. The actual physical work of typesetting and printing was a challenge she took up and mastered, despite the Woolfs' warning that her fingers would never be free of ink stains.

But she did not stop writing poetry. She pushed Eliot's demotic method to the extreme and worked at the border between poetry and journalism until, for her, news and poetry were practically the same thing. She became a radical race writer, a left-wing crusader against fascism in the Spanish Civil War, a champion of the Africans and African-Americans Eliot primitivizes in the Hoo Hoo Hoo of *Sweeney Agonistes*.[10]

How Cunard came to embody Eliot's fear of the woman writer can only be imagined if in fact her writing itself or the cultural power of her writing was threatening as well as her sexuality. His vicious portrait of Fresca was excised by Pound from the published *Waste Land*. Only many years later, after Eliot's dominant position in modernism was secure, did the original typescript appear, showing how important Pound's cuts were in the shaping of the poem. ("If you must needs enquire / Know diligent Reader / That on each Occasion / Ezra performed the caesarian Operation."[11]) Lyndall Gordon, in a chapter on the writing of *The Waste Land* called "Eliot's Ordeals," argues that he "seems to have regarded a seductive woman not as a human being but as a man's ordeal, a figure of sin with whom the man had heroically to consort."[12] The immersion of the poets in the culture of courtly love is assumed: "Eliot allowed Pound to groom him as a sophisticated poet in some ways as Gurnemanz groomed Parzival as a knight. Parzival obediently polished his manners, Eliot his diction and versification."[13] Now the poem is read as a very powerful case of artistic collaboration, and it is no longer new to notice how threatened Eliot was by women writers in general and by Cunard in particular. Fresca was in some sense Eliot's response to Joyce's Molly Bloom. The real Cunard spoke her yeses into the ears of many modernist poets. But she also wrote her noes into the cultural record. What was he afraid of? Male chastity still seems to be the issue, here, as Parsifal's purity was threatened by a witch-like Kundry.

In the passages Pound cut from the Fresca section, Eliot's rage at Cunard, her birth, social connections, and success as a poet, is almost pathologically chilling. His obsession with Cunard, writer and woman, creates her as a kind of *grand guignol* slut muse for his great poem. She is his enemy, his female reader-writer, his *soeur-lectrice*, the literary woman and competitor who figures as the cause of the downfall of Western civilization. The suppressed Fresca/Nancy now appears to be the secret source of the power of his poem.

But Nancy Cunard did not know what kind of fury she inspired in Eliot's imagination and never saw herself or her radical life of sexual freedom and poetic license as either a threat to his genius and eventual cultural hegemony or as the embodiment of disorder. He was an eagle; she was seized by the power of his genius. But Eliot's Fresca is just another vampire icon like Huxley's Lucy Tantamount and Myra Viveash and Michael Arlen's Iris March, though the Fresca figure is more honest in open acknowledgment of its author's resentment of and rivalry with the woman artist.

Cunard was literally on her last legs when she wrote to share her memories with Hayward in 1965, and, in fact, she broke one of them a few weeks later and then recovered enough to begin her last odyssey in rage and pain to Paris by train, a journey toward a wretched death, cursing the fascists and burning the manuscript of her epic poem against war, like an ecstatic bacchante or a drug-driven Brunnhilde setting a torch to the worn-out gods of modernism and primitivism. These were the gods she had worshiped and these were the gods that failed her. Cunard was always intoxicated—possessed by poetry, inflamed by revolution, enraptured by African art, tortured by the suffering of the refugees from the Spanish Civil War. Wild-eyed bacchantes of a certain age are probably not the nicest companions on a train trip.

But from 1916 through 1923, when she moved to Paris permanently, Cunard was both a real poet for Pound and Eliot to reckon with and a woman who made a messy triangle of their relationship with each other. Wayne Koestenbaum has written eloquently on the erotics of the collaborative relationship of Eliot and Pound in the creation of the text of *The Waste Land*.[14] The triangulation of the relationship of the two men complicates matters even further with the knowledge that Cunard was the source for Fresca, the scatological character of the woman poet as filthy whore in Eliot's draft, edited out by Pound, who had a serious relationship with Cunard as lover and critic. Cunard was situated "between men," in Eve Sedgwick's construction. Her character was created and then killed off, deleted from the poem by the better "man," *il miglior fabbro*, the better maker of poetry as well as love.

Koestenbaum is interested in Eliot's passive submission to a mesmerizing man, to use his language, as a scene of analysis of hysteria in the process of collaboration on *The Waste Land*. He sees the author(s) producing a text as an act of intercourse involving the exchange of women/texts. Nancy Cunard was in reality a "shared woman"; Fresca an obsessively anal text. Cunard had some sort of sex with both men, and some sort of experience as a poet of being edited, or "submitting" her writing to be criticized by both of them. Like Anna O., the patient who taught Freud the technique of the talking cure, Cunard rejected the role of patient (etherized on a table or not) and refused to be edited or "grammarised" by the modernist men. I want to claim that her brilliant poem "Outlaw" speaks for all the women artists badly mentored by men, the partners in pairs or collaborators who got the short end of the stick, the ones who refused to be the next H.D.s.

The lack of anger in Cunard's memory of Eliot is instructive, since anger was her *modus vivendi*. She talked to him about poetry, about aesthetics, unaware that inwardly he was seething with anger at her gender, her sexuality, her social position, and her claim to be a fellow poet. She never envied his success. She never saw him as a rival. His crisis in masculinity was clearly exacerbated by their (failed?) tryst at the Eiffel Tower restaurant. He even tried belatedly to enlist in the navy—with Cunard's help.[15] Perhaps Roberts's striking war pictures on the walls of the Eiffel Tower restaurant and Cunard's vitality as a woman and a poet contributed to his distress.

Eliot had been one of the most powerful of those strange gods of her youth. His broken rhythms and images of the fragmentation and decay of Western culture shocked her generation of English writers and specifically shaped her own poetry in its later learned but rough and bitter voice. He and Pound between them convinced her and her generation of English poets, already experts in creating the moods and themes of *The Waste Land*, to abandon the old forms, the sonnets and rhyming verses that limited their power. Her confidence as a poet was practically destroyed by reviews of *Parallax* that mocked her as an imitator of Eliot when she and the *Wheels* poets had been writing of a world of alienation and emptiness, uneasiness, fear and guilt for many years. But the success of *The Waste Land* in expressing the miseries of the age was due to its language and its rhythm, its abstruse bits of learning layered in collage with fragments of rhythmic voices, I often think overheard while dancing in wartime. As a poet Cunard was never able to do what it does. But she held no brief for the poet as priest, dispensing absolution and spiritual control.

Echoes of Eliot in form and style may be heard in her later left lyricism of the thirties and her realist attempts to write the "voices" of her time. She was indeed influenced by Eliot, but the poems she produced in that modernist vein were as politically committed to revolution as his were to conserving the past. Cunard's late poems have been dismissed as propaganda, as her earlier efforts were ignored as precursors of Eliot's poems. If Eliot and his characters could "do the police in many voices," she could "do" the "cracker" or white southern sheriff, the old peasant French washerwoman or the English soldier from the Midlands. What she learned from him, and used for far different political ends, was to listen to the voices of ordinary people around her, to try to bring them, without Eliot's irony and contempt, into speech on the page. Some of early Eliot's rage and hatred remained in her style; she attacked racists and fascists with the same ferocity with which he attacked rich women, Jews, and radicals. She rejected Pound's editorial attentions to her poems without knowing that such service to the typescript of *The Waste Land* had deleted her own part in its creation, as Fresca, the woman writer, a figure who aroused Eliot's fury, envy, and sexual panic.

But Eliot's death reminded her of what his brilliant and disturbing poetry had meant to her life. In writing and editing *Wheels* she had freed herself from the salon culture of her mother ("The hostess, that small termagant, in all her glitterings," her Eliot poem says about Lady Cunard) and began to create herself as an intellectual. Eliot wiped out the old forms. That he would not and probably did not approve of the ideas and politics she produced from his example hardly matters. His radical voicing of the words of cockneys and the Irish, secretaries and timid old men, his use of jazz, slang, and Afro-American idioms set writers like Cunard free to produce a writing now sometimes referred to as low modernism. Eliot's subsequent position as a conservative Anglo-Catholic, his ascent to the realms of high culture and defense of tradition and the individual talent did not prevent others from profiting from his radical style.

Eliot was the poet-prince in an elegant "smoking" who talked to Nancy about poetry at one of Lady Cunard's balls in 1922, she wrote to his friend, John Hayward. She left off dancing with the Prince of Wales in her gold and red gown from Poiret, panniered "with cascading white tulle on the hips," gathered up the shy American, and took him off to eat supper alone. She convinced him over the lobster and champagne to meet for a tryst at the Eiffel Tower restaurant the next evening, where they drank gin and talked philosophy and did not to go to the Hutchinsons, where both were expected for dinner. What more there was to their brief encounter we do not know. She was "entranced." He was "pale, restrained, impassive," and she "admired his gradual unthawing": "And then?," she questions herself and finds her memory blank. She seems a little taken aback by the fact that she cannot remember the great poet as a lover. And puzzled as well. "Not every life-moment's recalled, though all of that night certainly is ... / Not every moment goes into one's histories, / Be they written, or even spoken." Is this for the sake of her reputation, or his? Eliot, one imagines, was first impotent, then anxious, then angry. In Cunard's poem about Eliot she casts herself as abject lover and reader, too "obtuse" to perceive the poem's "full import, its span, its entirety." She loves *The Waste Land* even though she doesn't understand it. "It put its rightful frenzy into me," but its soul remained a mystery. The poem changed her life she says, unaware that her ghost walks behind its pages, unaware that that night whose privacy she does not or will not unseal out of respect was an occasion of such disgust on his part that Eliot wrote the Fresca scene and showed it to Pound and to his wife, Vivien. Her "obtuseness" about *The Waste Land* is perhaps a blessing. Eliot spent that night with Fresca, a creature he regards with utter contempt. Cunard recalls talking about "repression and passion" with "a great poet."

Eliot was writing modernism's great poem of renunciation of the world and women as the life force. Cunard's answer in *Outlaws* was an embrace of the world and the flesh. And it looks as if Cunard excited the poet's disgust, his anger, his fear of female power, and his desire to assert his masculine hegemony in the province of poetry. If indeed Cunard was the source of the unflattering portrait of Fresca, prudently removed by Pound from "The Fire Sermon" section of *The Waste Land*, she did not know how little the poet(s) who meant so much to her own intellectual development thought of her and her work.[16]

Eliot's (fortunately) excised imitation of Pope's *Rape of the Lock* in which "The white-armed Fresca blinks and yawns and gapes, / Aroused from dreams of love and pleasant rapes," takes the heroine from defecation to masturbation to writing letters about the latest in French literature and the horrors of parties at Lady Kleinwurm's (Lady Katzegg in another draft). The white arms were Nancy Cunard's signature, and they make their phallic appearance in other modernist literary and visual texts, with their armor of ivory bracelets announcing the birth of the New (white) Woman as artist and intellectual as surely as Josephine Baker's Black bottom announced the arrival of the liberated (Black) body.

Between Men

To return to Eliot's Fresca fragment, "Not quite an adult, and still less a child, / By fate misbred, by flattering friends beguiled," Fresca is called a "can-can salonnière."[17] Cunard certainly did admire the aesthetes as well as the Russians and the Scandinavians, especially Ibsen, but the critics still said she was a follower of Eliot. She danced in French nightclubs and she wrote about

Josephine Baker and the Paris nightclub scene for *Vogue*. Eliot met her, let us not forget, at one of her mother's salons, though she says she first met him in 1919. The word "misbred" refers to the rumor that Nancy was the daughter of George Moore, the Irish writer and long-time admirer of her mother who was one of the flattering friends who reviewed her poetry. Pound also reviewed her poems with flattery and criticism. Cunard seems to have spent part of the summer of 1919 on a walking tour of the Dordogne with Pound. According to his letters, Eliot also spent August of 1919 on a walking tour of the Dordogne with Pound.[18] Did they meet? She had known Eliot beginning in 1919. To Hayward she confided in 1965 that she was glad that they had decided against showing anyone at all the poem on Eliot. Hayward must have been relieved. Cunard told him that Solita Solano got too excited about her connections with other poets and might have concluded more than was intended and spread gossip as gospel.

The difference between Cunard's conscious memories of Eliot and what her poems reveal is remarkable. Her (aborted) love scene with Eliot appears to have taken place in London in April 1922, remembered by both as the cruelest month. She sent Eliot's friend a poem written in the winter of 1942 in Fleet Street during the crisis over Libya and Penang, that recalled drinking London gin with Eliot at that cold moment in April that seems outside of time's reach. The poet-speaker banishes the quotes from other poets and other wars that fill her gin-besotted mind as she thinks about soldiers fighting in Russian snows. She wants to feel outside of the oppressive weight of his influence, commanding him to be gone so that she can get her furrow straight. The poem's concern with the straight furrow and the roundabout passage to the end of the wall may be read in sexual terms, as well as about the way quotes from Eliot's work block her progress as a writer. The startling figure of the glove as a poetic straitjacket suggests that her mentor puts a condom on creativity, that his influence is a form of mental birth control. Cunard speaks here, I think, for many women artists in partnerships with creative and successful men.

The word "misbred" in the Fresca fragment indicates Eliot's fear of hybridity, racial mixing, and all the threats to his adopted culture that a flamboyant figure like Cunard represented. Not only did she write. She wrote like him. He was tainted by association with her. Women poets were, to Eliot and Pound, altogether a misbreed. Bent on taking over the little magazines and the big reputations as the two American men were, women poets represented stressful competition for mastery of the cultural world. The letters of the men, plotting the takeover of the journals to exclude the women writers, are both paranoid and misogynist. Like Blacks, women could supply the scripts, the tunes, the jokes, the language used by "real" poets, but they could not be poets themselves. Nancy Cunard and her ilk had a role to play as mistress of the poet: "the lazy laughing jenny of the bard," not himself, of course, or the "strolling slattern," her body "A doorstep dunged by every dog in town."[19] The goddess Fresca in Eliot's draft is recognized "by her smooth celestial pace," a reference to Cunard's inimitable walk, and the parody ironically declares "Thus art ennobles even wealth and birth, / And breeding raises prostrate art from earth."[20]

A milder version of the Fresca episode appeared in print under the initials of Vivien Eliot's pseudonym, Fanny Marlow, in the journal that Eliot edited, *The Criterion*.[21] *The Waste Land* without the Fresca section had appeared in the first issue of his journal. Valerie Eliot, in her edition of the drafts of *The Waste Land*, does not suggest that her predecessor either wrote or rewrote the lines attributed to her. Pound's unerring poetic judgment told him that the couplets were neither as good as Pope, nor successful as parody. So Eliot's publication of the rejected lines under his wife's name constructs a situation in which a bad woman poet publishes in an important literary journal a bad poem about another bad woman poet. There were then four people involved in the Fresca story, the waste product of *The Waste Land*, the draft cut by a brilliant editor, saving his friend from making a fool of himself and making some dangerous enemies, for Nancy had not yet broken with her mother, the real-life *salonnière* hostess whose largesse supported many modernist writers. Pound's editorial decision was wise aesthetically and socially. Eliot could get the attack in print without having to be responsible for its undignified expressions and unsuitable anger. In attributing it to his wife, he contributed to the cultural assumption that women hate women and to the notion for the contemporary audience and posterity that Vivian Eliot (as Fanny Marlowe) was mentally disturbed in her portrayal of Fresca's toilet, her "hearty female stench," her role as "bitch," "trull," and "strolling slattern in a tawdry gown, / A doorstep dunged by every dog in town." The dog whose habits Eliot most cared about, of course, was Pound, his publicist and editor; it appears that Pound and Cunard had been lovers, or at least very close companions.

Pound not only saved Eliot from a libel suit, but he remained on good terms with Cunard, as well, until her ultimate denunciation of his fascism;

when she began the Hours Press in Paris, he was glad to give her *XXX Cantos* to publish. Pound later told Charles Olsen, perhaps in the spirit of the Afro-American voices and masks that he used to *épater* the Europeans, that he and Henry Crowder who worked with her at the Hours Press, a pianist he named "Nancy's coon," were "the only civilized creatures,"[22] aligning himself with an imagined natural primitive masculinity that he projected onto the American musician, a man whose memoir paints a self-portrait as a temperate and gentle Christian. Pound's verbal blackface minstrelsy was, like his self-drama-tizing, part of what attracted Cunard. When later, in *Negro*, she published a glossary of Black English, it was done in the same spirit of sharing a new language that she and Pound had done with Provencal. Pound's relationship with Cunard was based on his admiration for her considerable linguistic skills in French, German, Spanish, Latin, and her skill in researching problems in Old Provencal. Obviously, the pleasures of the language of the French trou-badours and the *patois* of Harlem and the American South were part of their shared passion for expressions of the primitive.

For Eliot, female creativity, the body and its sexuality, and the female mind and instinct to make art were the primitive. Unlike Pound, he feared it. Fresca was the excess of the poet's rage against disorder, evidence of its origin in personal paranoia, hatred and fear of women, and Eliot's erotic textual connection with Pound on the doorstep of Nancy Cunard's body. Valerie Eliot introduces the edition of the typescript of *The Waste Land* with Eliot's words: "To me it was only the relief of a personal and wholly insignificant grouse against life; it is just a piece of rhythmical grumbling."[23] Purists will always argue that the published poem has a life of its own, unassailable by the facts of its genesis, place in history, or its author's problems. But critics of culture continue to learn from drafts and diaries and letters more than the writer wants us to know. Always demystify the priesthood is a good *modus operandi* in such cases.

Educated to take on the class and gender burdens of high culture as a patroness of the arts in the wake of her mother's extravagant support for the traditional high arts, the opera, the ballet and the nurturing of the musicians, painters, and poets of the age, Cunard struggled to find her own voice as a writer in a low modernism she helped to create by infusing radical ideas into the ancient poetic forms and trying to write in a Black voice. These practices link her in England with the poetics of the much misunderstood Sitwells, Sylvia Townsend Warner, Anna Wickham, and Charlotte Mew—poets whose

Figure 3.1. Henry Crowder by Man Ray, 1930, silver gelatin print.
Image courtesy Harry Ransom Center, The University of Texas at Austin

primitivism took other forms. The love of song, popular and classical, and serious training in music is one of the things the poets have in common, and links them to the surrealist followers of Rimbaud in France and the Black and left poets in America, like Walter Lowenfels or Claude McKay. It is instructive to place Cunard with Lowenfels, a writer from the *other* group of American expatriate poets in Paris in the twenties and thirties, who brought a radical voice to the sonnet. Cunard's transatlantic connection with Lowenfels marks an engagement with a certain white radical American modernism that shared her interest in traditional form, left politics, and public action against racism.

William Carlos Williams's awkward contributions to *Negro* mark an odd moment in literary fellow traveling down the intersecting roads of "progressive" politics and the struggle against racism.

While Williams and Lowenfels were part of her circle, Cunard's work (and life) may also be seen in relation to another expatriate radical poet of this period, an Australian working in the United States, a writer for *Broom* and an activist, Lola Ridge.[24] I raise these names now in the interest of seeing Cunard as a modernist public intellectual, one among others in a wide-ranging Black Atlantic culture that created modern life and marked out ways of being in the world that combined political activism with making art among those who staged the public performance of independent female sexuality outside the bonds of family and motherhood as a necessary freedom. I am not claiming that Cunard was another Emma Goldmann, Rosa Luxemburg, La Pasionaria, or Zora Neale Hurston. But these are the other modern "strangers" who come to mind as outlaws in life and work, other makers of modern life. The outlaw lives of some of Cunard's dearest friends, Solita Solano and Janet Flanner, Langston Hughes or Louis Aragon, already belong to public culture as part of other narratives of race, expatriatism, or the Communist Party. I am shaking up the kaleidoscope of modernism here, making other patterns with the same pieces, so that different stories may emerge.

In the wake of inadequate histories of British radical writing, Bonnie Kime Scott, Andy Croft, John Lucas, Mary Joannou, Angela Ingram, Claire Tylee, David Bradshaw, Janet Montefiore, Julia Briggs, Arnold Rattenbury, Phyllis Lassner, Mary Hamer, Gay Wachman, Robin Hackett, and others have been recuperating writers from Sylvia Townsend Warner and Valentine Ackland to Mary Butts, Edgell Rickword, Vernon Lee, and Naomi Mitchison, for example, along with pacifists, suffragettes, sex radicals like Edward Carpenter and Havelock Ellis, banned lesbians like Radclyffe Hall, the many others who went to Spain and fought fascism aside from Auden and Spender, and wrote about it. This book is part of the effort to rethink the radical, the modern, and race in the context of primitivism. I would like to see such work continue to reshuffle canons and avoid narrow national narratives, as well as expanding to include the work of colonial and postcolonial writers like Mulk Raj Anand and C. L. R. James, writers of color as well as figures like the homosexual Surrealist painter and photographer John Banting, and others who would have marched with Cunard at the rallies she organized in Trafalgar Square for the Scottsboro Boys. They are there, in the photographs, with their homemade banners and their fedora hats, the Bantings and their working-class comrades, the Black intellectuals and Indian writers of the time. Bringing them back into the picture, out of the murk of the minor, gives their movements for social change the same kind of resonance the dominant class has with its own movements and the art that was produced in them.

In the next chapters we follow the poet up to her break with class, country, and high culture, and subsequent emergence in the role of editor and activist in the low modernist discourses of international revolutionary Surrealism in Paris in the twenties. Cunard's relations with the Bright Young Women, Iris Tree and Lady Diana Cooper, are examined, along with her place among the bohemians in Stulik's Eiffel Tower restaurant in London.

Henry-Music: Henry Crowder

The very telling disjunctures of such a black and white left modernism may, perhaps, best be heard in the relation between the modernist poems of Cunard's extraordinary Hours Press volume *Henry-Music* and the music Henry Crowder composed and wrote down.[25] It is a critical commonplace that jazz was a major influence on modernism, but little evidence that this is taken seriously. The book itself is very rare and has not been discussed in any study of modernism. And yet here are all the elements of cultural meeting and exchange in one place: poems by famous modernist writers, songs by a popular jazz musician playing nightly in the Paris clubs, a collage design in black and white by Man Ray of African art objects and ivory bracelets. It should be a prime example of the cultural moment. But the music isn't played and the poems are forgotten. There was a recording but it was not a success. Music that was meant to be improvised in the moment seems frozen on the page, though it is lively enough when used in a "classical" piece by Stravinsky. The allusions in many of the poems expect a learned audience, not necessarily a dancing crowd.

One of the few passages in Henry Crowder's memoir that ring true is his warning to other Black men that Nancy Cunard refused to pay for sex and insisted, despite their enormous race and class differences, on being friends and equals. Crowder speaks as if the white woman as sexual predator who pays for her pleasures is a well-known figure to the men for whom he is writing. But beware, he is saying, of being seduced and abandoned by a woman who acts like a sister artist.

Cunard claimed to have no color prejudice, so she assumed that the conditions necessary for her own creativity were the same as those necessary for his, as she assumed that their sex life was based on mutual attraction. She had a piano moved up to a remote mountain village in the Dordogne and set him down to compose and write down his music. But he was not an English poet brought up in a tradition of artists as individual geniuses. He was a jazz pianist and he improvised nightly with his band, Eddie South and his Alabamians, or the group that showed up at Le Boeuf sur le Toit. Their instruments spoke with and against each other in a collective conversation, responding to each other and to the audience, sometimes alone, sometimes with another instrument or several, sometimes all together. It was a different cultural form. They made music together and were pleased. The joy was in the making, the pleasure in the moment, the performance.

In Cunard's tradition music had to be written down, printed, recorded, attributed to individual artists. She got her friends to write words for his songs, and Samuel Beckett, Walter Lowenfels, Harold Acton, and Richard Aldington provided texts, and she printed *Henry-Music* at the Hours Press, with a collage of her African art collection by Man Ray as the jacket cover (enclosing his music in her arms as another collector's item?), as her ivory-braceleted arms form a phallic protection for the photograph of his face. She stands behind her man, faceless, but with the upper hand. He is known as "Henry," as the mistresses and boyfriends of her friends are known by their first names. *Henry-Music*, that rare oversized book, a prize for modernist collectors, is a monument to cultural misunderstanding, or a basic document of modernist hybridity, if you will (imagine *Nancy-Poems* circulating in Harlem or Kingston).

The poems and music are at odds with each other; even Cunard admitted that the recording on Sanibel, the short-lived record company she financed for Crowder, was not successful. Her own "Blues," however, and Samuel Beckett's "From the Only Poet to a Shining Whore" actually work quite well, perhaps because they spent so many hours together drinking, dancing, and listening to jazz and other forms of Black American music in the Paris clubs. Beckett sometimes wondered what he was doing there, but Nancy obviously felt right at home, noting in *These Were the Hours* that she had read a great deal of African-American literature and admired all forms of jazz; these sources inspired her own blues effort in *Henry-Music*.

There is a note of regret, an Edith Piaf note, in Nancy's Paris blues. It is hard to think of Henry Crowder as being upset by what he sees in the mirror, as the speaker is. Cunard, not "Time," often paid the expenses of Crowder as her own personal "piper," court musician to her informal semi-surrealist salon. She, far more than her former lover and assistant at the Hours Press, wanders from capital to capital, losing herself in drink, music, and memories, obviously worried over decisions—which lover, which city, which life, which work to choose. She doesn't choose; she goes. She leaves and then comes back, looking for lost joy and mystery among the leftover remnants of her old life. She's a miserable traveling woman. Somehow, the figure of the miserable traveling woman seems even more bereft than the classic figure of the "miserable travelling man." *Henry-Music* succeeds less well than the music of Darius Milhaud or George Antheil or George Gershwin in crossing racial and cultural boundaries. The music survives, despite being written down. It is harder to move the words from the page to the voice. It's not that something is lost in translation. The modernist poem has abandoned rhythm and has no physical relation to the music.

Low Modernism

Cunard's last anthology, *Poems for France* (1944), was not widely acclaimed, nor was her anti-war effort "Man-Ship-Gun-Tank-Plane" from the same period. Her last efforts as a poet were to collect and revise her work for a volume that was never published but copied and sent to her dear friends, the English left-wing poets Sylvia Townsend Warner and Valentine Ackland, and kept with their papers in Dorset. They had all been radicals, Warner in the Party and Cunard as a fellow traveler (Ackland converted to Catholicism in the end), and the lesbian couple were loyal to Cunard during her worst spells of alcoholic mental illness and hospitalization.

Perhaps it is in that last distillation of a life's work for other women poets who shared her class politics and left idealism that her lasting legacy as a poet lies. But the context of low modernism in which this book attempts to understand Cunard's work, gender does not take the foreground. We may place her with a group of artists from Sylvia Townsend Warner to James Hanley, texts from Vernon Lee's *Satan the Waster* to Hope Mirrlees's *Paris*, Claude McKay's Marseilles novels to Zora Neale Hurston's raunchy folk tales, the popular novels of Nancy Mitford and Elinor Glyn's strange romance *Three Weeks*, Louis Aragon's pornographic fiction or Mulk Raj Anand's harrowing Indian novel *Coolie*, and that mixed company of low modernism with other lost upper-class and working-class writers like Osbert Sitwell and Sherard Vines who wrote for *Wheels* during World War I. We may track her progress along that cultural low road that rejected the urge of Eliot to assimilate with a classical English culture of the cathedral close. The two roads were separated by antagonistic responses to the chaos of war, Eliot driven backwards to find an ideal of order, Cunard and her cohorts trying to make their experience of disorder implode in a sonnet. The effect was one of "sensational repression," as one critic wrote of Cunard's *Parallax*: "one feels in the reading as if one were treading a clear swept, trimly bordered garden path around the crater of a volcano."[26] The effect of *The Waste Land* was immense release from the burden of history, absolution and a washing away of the sins of the age. Cunard's work was unforgiving, and it asked its readers to take responsibility for the war, for the history of slavery and the excesses of empire. Perhaps it is fitting that we revive her for contemporary audiences and succeeding generations.

Despite the class credentials of the writers involved, the low modernists may now be seen as rejecting religion, nationalism, class, and capitalism, rejecting even that experimentalism that projected their peers into the spotlight in the stubborn use of old forms. If they were important poets of the Auden generation, their names do not appear in that particular canon. They are a collective of perfect strangers, to each other now and to the canon, outlaws to the end.

Cunard's protest poem may also be read in an international context of the colonized performing the forms of the mother countries before claiming or reclaiming the local traditions devalued by the metropolitan modern—as the work of cultural studies has demonstrated. The timing of Claude McKay's brilliant early Jamaican dialect poems is a case in point. But the Europeanness of his Marseilles novels still seems problematic to critics who expect the Jamaican-born writer to write only of his roots, when much of his life was spent in the Mediterranean. Like other expatriates he was also trying to write the great American novel. Mulk Raj Anand's mastery of "the English novel" is another lost example. *Coolie* never received the critical acclaim it deserves as an English novel, while Chinua Achebe has become part of the canon. V. S. Naipaul's "English" fiction and travel writing functions exactly as *The Waste Land* did for the English national psyche. It gives consolation to the victors and brings inside knowledge of the sins of the others to the center. He has become a figure on the postcolonial stage who is strongly identified with traditional English culture and values, much as Eliot's religious conservatism served British cultural needs in the post-World War I era to divert attention from the war to the sinister activities of internationalists, Jews, and women, and the Bolshevik revolution.

Eliot, Picasso, and Stravinsky have been forgiven their raids upon the speech rhythms and jazz tunes of Afro-America and the brilliant three-dimensional visions of African masks and ritual carvings incorporated into their work. That work is seen and read and heard as major masterpieces of Western modernism. Anthropologists like Michel Leiris enjoy the status of heroes in French culture because the loot they stole from African villages with the help of government troops in violence and bloodshed was mounted in the Musee de l'Homme, classified and studied by Western "experts" before its significance was lost by natives entering the modern world. It is now a commonplace to attribute the characteristic African and Afro-American images and rhythms to the genius of the European artists. In Nancy Cunard's case the movement is easier to follow precisely because she was not a genius and did not attempt to assimilate Africa into her work, but because she did not have the state or an institution to send men and guns and bearers to remote villages to carry out their cultural wealth for her private collection. Content with mimesis, she often fails or falls flat. But we can see clearly what is now part of the deep structure of an Eliot or Picasso work in unassimilated form on the surface of Cunard's work. The artists and the critics have buried the roots of modernism in African arts in building the reputations of the major poets and painters of our time. The free-ranging egos of Eliot and Picasso and Stravinsky devoured what they needed from alien cultures and forged ahead. Crippled by anger, masochism, and cultural guilt, Cunard, one might say, attempted to negotiate a truce in the culture wars over modernism and primitivism. Neither side, it must be said, accepted her credentials as a legitimate representative. She remained an outlaw in Europe when other modernists and their work were naturalized into classics, and historians of Black culture have ignored or forgotten her contributions to their struggle.

In the case of Cunard her own whiteness became a problem. The history of white people enslaving Black people became her problem. Empire and the rape of African colonies became her problem. Lynching and racism in the United States became her problem. The color bar in Europe became her problem. She did not always make very good art out of her problems but she did make good politics. Her story is the other side of the story of how primitivism revived a moribund Europe and revitalized Western culture. It is also, in her adoption of a Black voice, the other side of the ventriloquism that Alain Locke urged on Black writers of the Harlem Renaissance, the adoption of the voice of white Europeans to express Black consciousness, to prove their worthiness.

In Cunard's version of the white Rites of Spring, the color of the dark sacrifice is acknowledged. The false notes in both diction and ethics that we find now in her Scottsboro poems, for example, are interesting and instructive. In their failure we read the history of the Communist Party and its white fellow travelers as they took up the cause of lynching in the United States, releasing the hornets' nest of sexual, race, class, and labor issues central to U.S. politics in the thirties. In "Haywood Patterson in Jail" (1934) Cunard's imprisoned hero speaks in dialect for class solidarity across racial barriers ("I lie on de stone and gits to thinkin' / White boss-justice rotten all thru'"). The figure talks Black folk wisdom and left rebellion. Would Haywood Patterson have spoken or written this way? Does it matter?

Walter Lowenfels: American Radicalism

Walter Lowenfels (1897–1976), an American radical poet and modernist expatriate who was a member of Cunard's Surrealist circle and published in *transition* as well as the *Criterion*, left Paris in 1935, according to Louis Aragon, to take on the editorship of the Pennsylvania edition of the *The Daily Worker* (1940–55). He was arrested, tried, and convicted under the Smith Act in 1953 for communist activity. Like Beckett, Lowenfels was published by Cunard at the Hours Press (*Apollinaire*), joined in the jazz scene with Cunard and Henry Crowder, and contributed a poem to *Henry-Music*. A loyal friend during one of Cunard's worst periods in an asylum in England, Lowenfels issued an international call for her release from what he and Aragon saw as a case of political reprisal like his own imprisonment for his political beliefs.[27]

It was Lowenfels who was accused of imitating *The Waste Land* in a *TLS* review of volumes by Robert Graves, Laura Riding, and Cunard's *Poems (Two)* in 1931. Why Cunard's book was included so long after publication is unclear, except that it allows the reviewer to pair her with Lowenfels, as Graves and Riding are paired under the rubric "Modern Riddles." They are all obscure and gnomic, but Lowenfels's obscurity in the elegy for Apollinaire is not as "richly suggestive" as Eliot's. So it seems one set of obscure references is better than another. But Lowenfels's obscurity is "licensed" compared to Cunard's.

Her "disconnected images" force the reader to puzzle out cryptograms in a series of fragments. "And the drawback to this," the reviewer writes, "is that fragments have to be so good. It would be a rash poet who would cheerfully accept for his works the fate of Sappho's poems."[28] They survived from 1925 to 1931 when he reviewed them, but his reference to Sappho and his naming Cunard a rash poet consign the poet and the poetry to Sappho's fate, while suggesting perverse female sexuality. Even the universal masculinity of the poet in his sentence has a sinister ring. She was always rash, but cheerful seems odd in the circumstances, except for the reviewer's glee in pitching the poet over the cliff.

I raise the name of Walter Lowenfels here because he seems to have disappeared even more completely than Cunard, and his defense of the Marxist sonnet lets us see another side of the international discourse about radicalism and form. Party cultural debates often endorsed certain socialist realisms while claiming some classics for the left, though they differed from place to place and journal to journal. The rejection of difficult experimental work as elitist in England did not convince Cunard to reject Pound and Eliot. She worked in both modes and tried to breach the gaps. In Lowenfels' defense of the use of the old forms for modernist poetry, we may see how differently the issues translated to the American scene in the fifties from Paris and London of the twenties and thirties, and why, perhaps, Afro-American modernism gives us some of the most interesting examples of these formal problems.

Like Cunard, Lowenfels was another one of those "perfect strangers" at odds politically with their cultures while keeping up a reputation with the formal literary avant-garde. Their commitment to Black culture always united them and Lowenfels continued the work of Cunard's 1934 *Negro* anthology with his own *Poets of Today: A New American Anthology* (1964) by including twenty Black poets among the eighty-five neglected poets he chose to reprint. The introduction notes that he had reviewed what he called "The Oxford Book of (White) American Verse" fifteen years before, and that the situation hadn't changed. Lowenfels and the American radical poets of the thirties of all races may usefully be read with their English and French counterparts, Spanish and other European radicals, Latin Americans and Caribbeans for a cross-cultural view of the period that makes intellectual sense.

The Only Poet: Samuel Beckett

None of the young poets Cunard read and admired whose advice and company she sought—Pound or Eliot or Rodker, Robert Nichols (the war poet who smothered her with love lyrics), or Richard Aldington—passed the test or entered her canon of "great men," writers whose style was matched by the straightforwardness of their ideas. Louis Aragon and Samuel Beckett were the great writers in her life who weren't afraid of her as an intellectual or as a woman. Beckett's *Whoroscope* appealed to her and she gave it a prize of £10 and published it at her Hours Press in 1930 precisely because of its erudition, its allusiveness to an enormous cultural past. The poem's difficulty was a quality she valued. The long and important friendship she and Beckett shared was based on her faith in his genius, giving him a start in the world of letters where she was already known as a poet and publisher. Beckett never forgot her generosity. She didn't pay the contributors to the *Negro* anthology but there seems to be a possibility, mentioned in Henry Crowder's memoir, that she paid Beckett for the many excellent translations from the French he did for *Negro*.[29] It was a characteristic act, and Beckett's complaints in a letter to the collector Quinn about the work should not be taken to mean that he did not use his talent well. Cunard, after all, spoke and wrote French like a native. There was no need to give Beckett this work unless she was acting as Comrade Patroness to a poor fellow artist, a role he could accept while men like Joyce could not. If taken seriously, Beckett's translations for *Negro* place him ethically and politically among the internationalists of modernist primitivism, taking sides against racism and fascism.

Among the pieces Beckett translated was the Surrealist manifesto "Murderous Humanitarianism," signed by André Breton, Roger Callois, René Char, René Crevel, Paul Éluard, J. M. Monnerot, Benjamin Peret, Yves Tanguy, André Thirion, Pierre Unik, and Pierre Yoyotte; two essays by Robert Goffin on the origins of jazz; a poem called "Louis Armstrong" by Ernest Moerman; and Georges Sadoul's "Sambo Without Tears." The bond between Beckett and Cunard as artists, friends, and translators indicates that he shared her left political agenda to some extent, and that on the issue of race he was her ally. If, as Alan Friedman argues, we rethink Beckett's contribution to *Negro* as a serious part of his intellectual work, he emerges as less of an Irish exile and more of an international figure with a strong base in French culture and language, as Cunard herself was, allied with Surrealism and familiar with the Black jazz scene—a modernist minimalist more like Gertrude Stein than James Joyce.

Certain images have been used over and over to evoke the life of expatriate artists in Paris, including images of Cunard in her ivory bracelets or Hemingway and friends at the Coupole. One might conjure up instead the scene of Cunard and Samuel Beckett drinking and dancing with the mixed crowd at one of the Paris jazz *boites*. Henry Crowder comes to the table between sets. He sings and plays a blues song with Nancy's lyrics and then performs Beckett's "From the Only Poet to a Shining Whore," a song published in *Henry-Music* (1930) and written for the musician to set to music along with texts by other modernist poets.

The ironies are delicious. Beckett the recluse in a Black bar in Paris. Jazz fans dancing to a Beckett song. Crowder, Afro-American piano player, negotiating at least two worlds simultaneously among Black fellow performers and a multiracial, not all heterosexual crowd. His flamboyant white lover dances out her pleasure at bringing them all together, playing the shining whore for all she's worth.

PART II

Poetry, War, and Primitivism: Making Modern Life

CHAPTER FOUR

The Rites of Spring

T. S. Eliot was dead. Nancy Cunard remembered the dress she wore to dance in his arms in 1922. Her friend Eliot had rhythm. He loved to dance. In his early letters home he expresses delight in finally finding modern English girls who could dance; he frequented dance halls and the ballet and was as madly smitten by Massine, Diaghilev, and the cult of muscular primitivism of "The Rites of Spring" as he had been by Afro-American jazz rhythms. The Russian dancers captured for audiences in the European capitals the spirit of primitivism that promised renewal for European culture's dry roots in the frenzied dancing of primeval rituals of sacrificial death and creation myths.

For Nancy Cunard the primal scenes that shaped her consciousness as an artist were not the death dances of Diaghilev and Nijinsky but the earth-shaking and, for her and many other European intellectuals, Western-paradigm-smashing performances of African creation myths in Paris by the Ballets suédois in October, 1923 in Blaise Cendrars's ballet *La Création du monde* with music by Darius Milhaud and curtain, set, and costumes by Fernand Léger.[1] Cendrars' (early, amateur, and ultimately inaccurate) collection of African folk tales *L'anthologie negre* had contributed to the cultural excitement of the *vogue noir* in the French capital, and in an important sense the book and ballet based on it may be seen as inspiring a second generation of European primitivism as well as providing a model for Cunard's *Negro* anthology. I think it is very important to see the embrace of African art and ideas after the war as an alliance with life-affirming cultures, celebrating birth and desire rather than sacrifice and death.

Eliot blames the woman poet's "unreal emotions and real appetite" on the influence of the aesthetes, Arthur Symons, Walter Pater, and Vernon Lee—and the baleful effects of reading the Scandinavians and Russians. Her writing is a "chaotic misch-masch potpourri," a reference, perhaps, to her many languages as well as the political internationalism Eliot abhorred, but, interestingly, the words are equally applicable to that other "chaotic misch-masch," *The Waste Land* itself. Pound had written that Eliot was "too weary and too polite" to give her a critique of her work. The Fresca scene shows him as quite energetically obscene in his criticism of the woman poet.

Rites of Spring: Vernon Lee, *Satan the Waster*

It was true that Nancy Cunard admired the aesthetic writers for their philosophies of form and their opposition to Victorian preaching and morality in art, but to her they were an enabling set of precursors. All three were also "outlaws" like herself, sexual radicals and exiles from English propriety. To Eliot and Pound, the aesthetes were weak and effeminate, despised for their lack of virile diction and strong rhythms. But to Cunard, as to Virginia Woolf, they were a breath of fresh air. They challenged law and social convention in their lives and wrote, shall we say, against the grain of gender, assuming a feminine tone of voice that Pound and Eliot found threatening and dangerous. Cunard entertained Symons in Paris with another one of her outlaw uncle figures, George Moore, and published him at her Hours Press.

The English philosopher of aesthetics, Vernon Lee (Violet Paget) (1856–1935), might also be seen among the sex radicals in exile, like Norman Douglas, whom Cunard regarded as exemplars and fellow experimenters in free living and free loving. She would have been, and probably was, very much at home among the uncles who were Cunard's personal *grands hommes*. Like her good friend, the swaggering and brilliant lesbian composer Dame Ethel Smyth, Vernon Lee was very much a *grand homme* herself. A lesbian who lived and worked in Florence, Lee had a long career as a serious writer and thinker, known for developing the psychology of empathy, for her novels and music criticism, as well as for her feminist critique of patriarchal institutions. Lee's international presence as a public intellectual was surely an important example for Cunard.

Satan the Waster (1920), incorporating the excruciatingly grotesque *Ballet of the Nations* (1915), is surely Vernon Lee's masterpiece. It is also a *grand guignol* anti-war opera of major importance to a revaluation of the relation between international modernist primitivism and World War I. It is a major critique of the Stravinsky–Diaghilev ballet *The Rite of Spring* (1913) and the belief in much of Europe in its theme of social renewal through sacrifice, the bloodbath of war as a purification rite. Modris Eckstein's reinterpretation of this myth and its widespread embracing by European intellectuals as crucial to inciting war to begin with, as well as inspiring the fascism that led to World War II, are challenging and, I think, ultimately convincing arguments.[2]

Vernon Lee's *Satan the Waster* may be read as a pacifist feminist reply to the blood sacrifice cult of *The Rite of Spring* in European modernism. The discourse of primitivism that *Satan the Waster* participates in is very similar to that of Cunard and the poets of *Wheels*, a dance of death on a stage filled with clowns and harlequins, obscene masques and skeletons acting out passion plays in the name of grand abstractions like Patriotism, Science, Fear, Comradeship. Gillian Beer's important essay recuperating *Satan the Waster* places the ballet-historical pantomime with *Faust, Back to Methuselah*, and Hardy's *The Dynasts*.[3] It seems to me to respond so wholeheartedly to the primitivism of *The Rite of Spring* that I want to read it in that context as well as in the language of *grotesquerie* of the English Rimbauds describing their own hells in the poetry of *Wheels*. That is, Lee's cohorts are more likely Osbert and Edith Sitwell and Cunard, and her form is the form of the provocative primitive ballet. Satan the warmonger is a waster: he destroys. There is no ritual death as renewal. It is death and destruction for its own sake. Lee's text seems to perform an answer to *The Rite of Spring*. There was a powerful and grotesque anti-war discourse in English culture before and aside from *The Waste Land*, but it has been eclipsed by a canon that allows this kind of macabre satire when it comes straight from the trenches, but not from women philosophers or aristocratic poets. Beer finds Lee too caught up in the language of the war frenzy she is attacking. But one might see her anger as removing the sexual glamor both from the belief that blood sacrifice can cleanse the nation and from violent death in war, in a form that was very popular and wildly exciting in the Stravinsky–Diaghilev *Rite of Spring*. *Satan the Waster* did not, of course, join *The Waste Land* or *The Rite of Spring* as classical texts of modernism. The poems of *Wheels* did not survive the age either. But after the fact they appear to have a profound resonance compared to Eliot's cynicism about his voices and his strong belief in Christianity and its ideas of order, and the religious emotionalism of *The Rite of Spring*, both of which may now assume the uncomfortable status of (using Eksteins's imagery) pandering to and glorifying a "celebration of life through sacrificial death."[4]

Eliot's hysterical response to Cunard is indicative of the profound misogyny he shared with other modernist writers. It is very different from the misogyny of the Surrealist intellectuals whom she joined in Paris later on. Upper-class rebels, dead war heroes, society girls, disaffected intellectuals parading as poets and communists who wrote in religious metaphors enraged the critics and Eliot alike. His anger at their success in thumbing their aristocratic noses at the bourgeoisie fueled the writing of *The Waste Land*.

On *Wheels*

Taken out of their original context of publication by Edith Sitwell and her co-editors on *Wheels* (1915–21), the poems of Wilfred Owen have gone on to become a canon of their own, as a body of work by an individual poet and as part of two discourses, anti-war poetry and the Great War discourse of homosocial brotherhood. As a text to Benjamin Britten's *War Requiem* his words are used in unwitting testimony, as is the music, to make beautiful the senseless deaths of young men. Owen has also emerged as an icon of a lost generation of Englishmen, a quintessential example of a nationalism he despised. In the same way Vera Brittain's *Diary*, however flawed and false to her original feelings, has become a classic text, representing a certain discourse, mourning their lost men, as *the* discourse of women during wartime. *Wheels* has its share of soldier poets, anti-heroic or simply observant of life at the Front, and elegies to their dead contributors like Owen and F. W. Tennant, are sung by women poets who were their comrades on the English wartime counter-culture front. But *Wheels* is interesting because these bits of canonical verse are interspersed with the decadent and the Dada, the Surrealist and the sensualist, translations of Rimbaud and new poems in French by English poets, working-class poets and radicals. Social critique is deliberately carried out in the pages of the anthology by poets of all classes. The experiment is unusual, especially as gestures are made toward an international readership of avant-garde work that is seriously anti-elitist while giving certain "elites" plenty of room to express themselves.

Osbert Sitwell's "London," in the Second Cycle of *Wheels*, suggests Eliot's "Unreal City," a forlorn deserted Babylon with "beggars watching motor cars roll by," "And whelks piled high upon a wheel-barrow / That almost smells of salt and tar and sea," "an antheap overturned," crowds of "beggars and deported aliens / Who listen to a crazy clergyman, / Unbalanced politician, or to those / Who sing the patent virtues of a pill, / Or hear the views of some pale Hindu / Explaining theories to a scoffing crowd / Or mock the Bacchic singing of some sect / Who hymn the Almighty in a ragtime strain ..."[5] There is a great deal of merit in Sitwell's poetry. Reading it, one comes to see that Eliot's gift for diction was a shared one.

A forgotten poet of the class struggle, Sherard Vines (1890–1974) calls on "Christ Communist" to canonize the socialist martyrs Karl Liebknecht and Rosa "now grown *mystica*" Luxemburg as "New Saints":

> Let labourers build a church to shew
> The history of their clean emprise
> Whom, at your dictates, we will now
> Beatify, then canonise.[6]

Vines's poem on strikes in wartime, "Last night we nearly killed a scab," appears next to Edith Sitwell's Rimbaud-inspired "Singerie" celebrating "a summer afternoon in Hell."[7] Vines also invents Sir Bonian Boggs, the soap magnate, and Osbert Sitwell creates characters like Lady Carabas and Mrs. Kinfoot:

> The British bourgeoisie
> Is not born,
> And does not die,
> But, if it is ill,
> It has a frightened look in its eyes.
>
> The War was splendid, wasn't it?
> Oh yes, splendid, splendid.
> Mrs. Kinfoot is a dear,
> And so artistic.[8]

His "Mrs. Freudenthal Consults the Witch of Endor" begins,

> A nose, however aquiline,
> Escapes detention in a throng.[9]

But Eliot's debt to Osbert Sitwell, as well as his skill as a poet is also evident in his poem "De Luxe":

> But Mrs. Freudenthal, in furs,
> From brioche dreams to mild surprise
> Awakes
> …
> Mrs. Freudenthal day-dreams
> —Ice-spoon half-way to her nose—
> Til the girl in ochre screams,
> Hits out at the girl in rose.[10]

These poems may have inspired, influenced, and enraged Eliot, who refused to publish with the *Wheels* poets, but most of the traces of those local London literary battles were removed from the story of the poet and *The Waste Land*'s evolution by Eliot's brilliant early career handler and editor, Ezra Pound, who worked out a more dignified and classical set of predecessors for the poet.[11] Meanwhile Huxley was writing "Nero in the Circus" for *Wheels*:

> [I too
> Have heard in the hanging beer-gardens, I too,
> In the violet nights of June, have heard
> Minna von Barnhelm, welt berumte
> Kornetapiston virtuosin play
> Puppchen and The Blue Danube. What a
> Soul!]][12]

What the *Wheels* poets have in common with Eliot is primitivism, from Edith Sitwell's "The negress Night devours that gourd the sun— / Grown over-ripe, and lets the gold juice run / Staining her body" to Osbert Sitwell's "Rag-Time" dirge for the war dead in the trenches where "live men tread on dead men in the dark," the dance tune a "gay—yet terrible" reminder of their youth.[13] These volumes of verse are like a wild carnival dance of the dead out of their trench graves. Osbert Sitwell's "This Generation" ends "For, entering life, they found it was their tomb …"[14] Also in the 1918 anthology in "Beauty V" Huxley speaks for a modernist generation of soldiers: "Troy is the birthplace of my homesickness. Troy is more than a patriotism …"[15] Then he shifts ground to the instabilities of the home front, adding Dada to the poets' tactics in "Evening Party":

> 'Sans Espoir, sans Espoir,
> … sang the lady while the piano opened its
> box of old sardines in treacle. One detected ptomaine
> in the syrup.[16]

These poems undermined the English cultural landscape before *The Waste Land*. And they crossed the Channel to France for more cultural contact than the deaths of many of their number in the trenches allowed. There was a powerful connection to French modernism, Surrealism and Dada in the avant-garde volumes. The poets are forgotten. Literary critics do not take seriously claims that there is a certain radical social content in the poems of the Sitwells, and Aldous Huxley recycled his second thoughts in fiction. His first ones, like "Siesta Thoughts," published in an early round of *Wheels*, run to what is now called the Eliotic:

> Oh, these distressing heavy lunches …!
> They tend to ecstasy—ecstasy reversed
> When from soul the body stands
> Triumphally apart.
> Oh, Afternoons, Afternoons …
> Snug rectories where no foot crunches
> The sleek gravel except the pad-paws of baboons,
> Black and hairy curates dressed
> In ecclesiastic frock coats
> And dog-collars.
> Oh Afternoons, Afternoons …!
> I must take to eating bread and jam again.[17]

Edith Sitwell's "Mothers" and "The Drunkard" do not fit the critical response to the anthology as a clever cynical Edwardian nursery game with

Bakst designs and Beardsley drawings either.[18] Huxley wasn't sure at first about associating with "Society" and "the Shufflebottoms," the "Wheelites" who take their "horrible production" so seriously, but he became a major presence.

Women on *Wheels*

Seven of Nancy Cunard's early poems appeared in the anthology *Wheels*, which she and Edith Sitwell and Iris Tree put together in 1915. There is some difference of opinion about who edited the collection, but the painter Nina Hamnett, in her memoir *Laughing Torso*, says it was Cunard.[19] The collective project of young poets was named after Cunard's signature poem in the first number, "Wheels":

> I sometimes think all our thoughts are wheels
> Rolling forever through the painted world,
> Moved by the cunning of a thousand clowns
> Dressed paper-wise, with blatant rounded masks,
> That take their multi-coloured caravans
> From place to place, and act and leap and sing,
> Catching the spinning hoops when cymbals clash.
> And one is dressed as Fate, and one as Death,
> The rest that represent Love, Joy and Sin,
> Join hands in stage-learnt ecstasy,
> While Folly beats a drum with golden pegs,
> And mocks that shrouded jester called Despair.
> The dwarves and other curious satellites,
> Voluptuous-mouthed, with slyly-pointed steps,
> Strut in the circus while the people stare.
> And some have sober faces white with chalk,
> Of sleeping hearts, with ponderance and noise
> Like weary armies on a solemn march.
> Now in the scented gardens of the night,
> Where we are scattered like a pack of cards,
> Our words are turned to spokes that thoughts may roll
> And form a jangling chain around the world,
> (Itself a fabulous wheel controlled by Time
> Over the slow incline of centuries.)

So dreams and prayers and feelings born of sleep
As well as the sun-gilt pageantry
Made out of summer breezes and hot noons,
Are, in the great revolving of the spheres
Under the trampling of their chariot wheels.[20]

Don Alvaro de Guevara, who designed the endpapers for the 1918 volume, painted portraits of both Edith Sitwell and Nancy Cunard.[21] Sitwell's biographer attributes her break with Cunard and Cunard's exit from *Wheels* to Sitwell's jealousy.[22] But intellectual and political differences as well as issues of editorial control were surely the problem. Cunard did not care much for the attentions of "Chile," as the painter was called, or his picture. But when he returned from three years in South America, he redeemed himself with the perfect gift for her primitive art collection, some enormous ancient stone Easter Island heads.

Among the reviews included in the second edition of *Wheels* was Ezra Pound's review in *Poetry*, praising Cunard's sonnet "Uneasiness," but lecturing her (and Sacheverell and Edith Sitwell) on their failure to suit the modern unpoetic content of their poems to the old-fashioned form:

Miss Cunard shows at times surprising closeness of thought, and a talent for epithets with her dwarfs "with slyly pointed steps" and her aged abstractions, Love, Joy, Sin, "in solemn stage-learnt ecstasy." She uses the sonnet, like most poets at the beginning of their course, without recognizing that the sonnet is a peculiar costume. Like duck trousers or a scarlet hunting coat, it is suitable on some occasions and not quite fitting on others. Few forms, save the classic quantitative measures, are a better drill ground for one's early effort, but a sense of form is not shown by trying to fit matter which is not a sonnet into essentially a sonnet-shell.[23]

The failure of the poets to respect the proprieties of writing as a form of maneuvring on a drill ground, as a war game with elaborate rules, deliberately exploiting the clash between subject matter and formal structure, roused the admonitory editor in Pound. Sonnet-shells were to be filled with sonnet stuff or they wouldn't explode. Real poetry, when the content suits the form, kills. (I'm assuming Pound's figure refers to the dangerous filling of shells for the heavy guns done by women workers in the ammunition factories, the shells painted so powerfully by his friend Wyndham Lewis in *A Canadian Gun Pit*.) What was sonnet stuff? Was it sonnet stuff that he cut out of *The Waste Land*? Love was more appropriate than war, one presumes, as the narrator of *A Room of One's Own* says regarding why poetry was different before the war. The love lyrics of Tennyson and Christina Rossetti had a different *sound* from modern poetry. "[T]hey were accompanied by a sort of humming noise, not articulate, but musical, exciting, which changed the value of the words themselves," wrote Virginia Woolf.[24] Pound had gotten rid of that humming noise. It was too feminine, too Victorian. No more innumerable bees in scented gardens, no more hearts like singing birds. Why were the *Wheels* poets still pushing their prams down the old garden paths? If they were going to write Victorian verse, they should stick to the subject of love. Rhythm, the rhythm of a strong drumbeat, drove out rhyme. But the poets of *Wheels* did not take Pound's advice. They kept on writing about war in the forms that were usually used for love and about love as an epic adventure.

Pound's American origins are perhaps evident in calling the hunting coat scarlet instead of pink; he knew that young Nancy Cunard had had a passion for hunting. But the hunting coat and the duck trousers are costumes that men wear when they are engaged in upper-class sport, fox hunting or sailing. He goes after the "promising" Sitwells for their "inexcusable carelessness as to meaning and fitness of expression," when they get the forms down so correctly. This lack of fitness of expression is what makes the Sitwells interesting as poets. *Dulce et decorum est*. The poets of *Wheels* give us another side of modernist poetry, the opposite of conservative thoughts in radical speech rhythms in their intentional courting of bad taste by trying out radical ideas in elegant and neatly contrived forms.

In Celeste Schenck's important revisionary essay "Exiled by Genre: Modernism, Canonicity and the Politics of Exclusion," the definition of the only modernist poetic as "experimental" is seriously challenged in re-readings of Edith Sitwell, Charlotte Mew, Anna Wickham, and Djuna Barnes, among others, and in a close contextual and historical examination of the supposed female affinity for fixed forms. She begins by exposing a chilling attack on rhymed verse from *The Little Review* in 1914. The poet writes:

> Suppose I were a Bluebeard who had enticed a young girl into my
> dim chamber of poetic thought. Suppose I took the little knife of

rhyme and coolly sliced off one of her ears, two or three of her fingers, and finished by clawing out a generous handful of her shimmering myriad-tinted hair with the hands of meter.[25]

Schenck's argument against such murderous gender-bound distinctions is that modernist women poets are caught in a double bind in a socially prescribed "exile *from* and *to* poetic form."[26] "If gentility in poetry carries the disparaging connotation of soft and female, or worse, not male enough, it can also bear the opposite meaning of conservative and rigid, rhymed, and therefore masculine and hard." Sitwell tries to avoid the pitfalls of gender by writing "in as hard and glittering a manner as possible" with "strange" images; forging a technique for oneself, she says "there is no help to be got,"[27] a sentiment Woolf shared in *A Room of One's Own* on the problem of male models for women writers.

Pound liked the satiric yellow cover of *Wheels*, "displaying a scraggy nursemaid and a makeshift perambulator. It is the perfect sort of inkpot to hurl itself in the face of senile pomposity." But Cunard as editor, quoting his review among others in the second cycle of *Wheels*, has the last word. She quotes "We are in especial bored by male stupidity," from Pound's "The Condolence." Having the last word was an editorial habit that cost her dearly later in the editing of the *Negro* anthology, when she could not resist correcting W. E. B. Du Bois and alienated an important ally as well as many mystified readers.

In their day, the poets of *Wheels* were called morbid, macabre—nightmare followers of Rimbaud and Baudelaire, sinister dwellers on war, death, hopelessness, and fear. They were condemned for their collective "bad taste" as a "conspiracy" of "young and cultured amateurs" in pointing out the emptiness and futility of life, or, as in Osbert Sitwell's preface to the 1917 volume, commenting on the likeness between the grand old men who send each other's sons out to war and the critics who massacre young poets and call for the abolition of free speech. The anthologies were sneeringly labeled after ladies' "vanity bags"; the poets seen as so wedded to the inappropriate that their "harpies [were] like nightingales and nightingales like harpies" (*The Nation*) for their collective failure to please.[28] They created the cultural landscape of European alienation and despair that named *The Waste Land*. But they continued to produce that musical buzz that so enraptured Virginia Woolf. They no longer hummed "My heart is like a singing bird." Cunard's sonnet "Remorse" complains "I have been wasteful, wanton, foolish, bold, / And loved with grasping hands and lustful eyes … but now am old / And ill and bad—content with discontent."[29] They wore their duck trousers to the opera and their hunting coats in the city.

Wheels presented itself as Babel with disparate voices crying doom for the "20th century harlequinade"; "the pantomime of life is near its close," they prophesied, calling up grotesque Pierrots, Black Masses, primeval terror, malignant dwarfs. Their angst is reflected in Cunard's "Uneasiness," a nightmare like Charlotte Perkins Gilman's classic story of the woman artist deprived of her work, "The Yellow Wallpaper":

> To-night I hear a thousand evil things
> Between the panels and the mouldering floor;—
> Small bitter things with hearts and, maybe, wings,
> That curse their bondage yet entreat for more
> Free wicked time to hurt our lives,
>
> …
>
> Armies of corpses hid behind the wall
> That creep and grind and tear each other's souls.[30]

It looks as if Nancy Cunard edited the first two volumes of *Wheels*; Edith Sitwell signed the rest. But it is not my intent to restore her lost signature to the texts. Cunard's mark is on the volumes of *Wheels* in two important ways. The first is the (socialist) collective publication of very different writers in different styles protesting for a cause, here, of course, the horror of war, and this was a cultural gesture she continued to make throughout her career, as in *Authors Take Sides on the Spanish War*, *Poems for France*, and the immense labor of the *Negro* anthology. Once in an author's note she described herself as an anthologist. This is meant as a claim to collectivity and a concern for the cause before the individual. Cunard's definition places herself in opposition to Laura Riding and Robert Graves's New Critical aesthetic in *Against Anthologies*.

The second is the anarchist's "direct action" bold attack on authority, as in her scathing pamphlet *Black Man and White Ladyship* (1931). She thumbed her nose at the critics by publishing their reviews in the next edition, putting an extra anti-establishment spin on *Wheels*. These tactics earned her the admiration and comradeship of the French Surrealists and the respect and love of Louis Aragon. One may see in these volumes a cross-class gesture of English avant-garde culture to Dada and Surrealism in Paris. Printing the bad reviews was a brilliant move for the project of undoing cultural hegemony and this rude tactic was used throughout the life of *Wheels*. In Eliot the rudeness of the characters emphasizes the authority of the controlling imagination. Cunard was always engaged in a conspiracy to mock entrenched institutions. Eliot mocked the low; she and her fellow poets in *Wheels* mocked the high.

But the eerily prophetic lines of Edith Sitwell, "With children our primeval curse / We overrun the universe," are typical of the dark, anti-war vision of the *Wheels* poets. The rickety baby pram on the jacket of the first volume marked it as a site of pacifist, rebellious "un-reproduction," to use Angela Ingram's term, during World War I, a blow against the wartime glorification of motherhood.[31] Sex in these bleak poems does not lead to family happiness. This thought was practically treason in wartime when women were being urged to reproduce for the state. Edith Sitwell's class origins and those of her brothers, like Nancy Cunard's and, until quite recently, Virginia Woolf's, have kept critics from taking their social critiques quite seriously.

Wheels at War: The Eiffel Tower, William Roberts, and Wyndham Lewis—Visual Terror, Race, and Masculinities

The dying Nancy Cunard remembered without rancor how T. S. Eliot resisted her seductions at first (Ackroyd quotes Haigh-Wood, his wife Vivien's brother, on her attempts),[32] and then she recalled the figure of Joe, the Austrian waiter at the Eiffel Tower restaurant, who came upstairs to her flat to see that she was all right, smiling and bringing more double gins to the couple sitting on the floor "as close as could be."[33] On the walls were paintings by William Roberts, a Futurist painter whose work captured the anti-war mood of the *Wheels* poets in jackets and illustrations for the 1919 and 1921 collections (not exactly an inspiration for lovemaking).

Roberts's *Gun Drill* appeared on the 1919 jacket of the number that included war poems by Wilfred Owen. On the inside front and back covers his startling red, black, and yellow constructivist paintings show workers and soldiers playing darts. Roberts's red masked head of a warrior on the 1921 jacket of *Wheels* combines the Vorticist with the hieratic Japanese. It is like the address to their critics that prefaced the second edition of the first cycle of *Wheels*, "In Bad Taste":

> On a triumphal car, and with cavalcades,
> Rides Moloch, God of Blood,
> And in his hand a fingered treatise on Simplicity.[34]

A critic in *Commonwealth* wrote that "the very cover of the volume is calculated to establish a reign of terror on any respectable bookshelf."[35] Roberts's extraordinary paintings were silent witnesses to the battle for modernist turf fought between Eliot and Cunard, a war within a war over culture.[36] Roberts's abstract Vorticist robots lead to a more realist grotesque in the later work. In *The Gas Chamber* (1918) the gassed soldiers are stumbling in clumsy disorientation, struggling with their gas masks, the stylized postmodernism of their uniforms and boots, like Roman gladiators and Star Wars droids, at odds with their heavy, groping bodies. The point of view is tilted so we may experience the nausea and dizziness of the gas.

Roberts's massive *The First German Gas Attack at Ypres 1918* and Wyndham Lewis's *A Canadian Gun Pit* done in the same year, both commissioned by the Canadian government, move toward Expressionist realism and away from the abstract Cubism of their earlier work. Pound had sought Lady Cunard's help in securing these wartime posts for modernist artists. The same tensions about form animate the poetry in *Wheels*, and the same loathing of war. Everything is either experimental and fluid, moving machines and men like the wheels in the poets' signature, industrial, deadly, and beautiful in speed and precision, and unbearably destructive, or stopped dead, an immobile mobile, a stasis in crisis. Both pictures are about the destruction of white Anglo-Saxon masculinity and feature the problematic presence of primitive others as allies.

In Roberts's picture the French frontline Algerian troops with their dark skin and mustaches, their red and blue uniforms like ethnic remains from an earlier war, stumble into the khaki-clad Canadian field battery as the white men whose skin is highlighted by the painter are loading the big guns. The sacrifice of the Zouaves in their folk costumes is violently portrayed, like a terrible ancient ritual from a primeval celebration of the "rites of spring." We see these blinded and poisoned French soldiers from above, retching and running from the German gas, among them a one-eyed bleeding Canadian who has seen the deadly attack. The contorted muscular bodies of the blonde and red-headed Canadian gunners in their acid green, yellow, and pink shirts, looking like powerful stevedores, their arms extensions of the shells and the gun barrels, will try to avenge the losses of the foreign and feminine-looking Zouaves in their Turkish trousers and embroidered jackets.

Wyndham Lewis's *A Canadian Gun Pit* is a static nightmare of desolation, catching the "stupid, sullen and phallic" stubborn-looking objects, as Lewis called the shells in a letter to Pound, before they are deployed in further destruction of a burnt-out landscape. The white men's faces are stylized masks from Lewis's Vorticist past. They are feeding the heavy shells into the maw of a giant monster aimed at a target far away from the gun pit. In the right foreground is the figure of an enormous romanticized Black worker, like a Paul Bunyan folk hero, carefully and skillfully lifting the shells. The romantic realism of this figure in a shocking pink muscle shirt is created in stark contrast to the alienated and dehumanized white soldiers, all of whom are frozen in action, as if for a photograph. The raw masculinity of the Black man includes a calm and dignified confidence. In *Blasting and Bombardiering* Lewis remembered "we had attached to us a lot of West Indian negroes, principally for the purposes of shell-humping."[37]

In both pictures dark men carry a different form of masculinity than the white men; they are both feminized as objects of beauty by their colorful dress and endowed with mythical power as saviors of their white brothers. The workers/enlisted men are separated from the uniformed officers in these paintings. They are naked from the waist up or shown in bold colors emphasizing their physiques. Class and race and caste are important in making wartime masculinities come alive on the canvas, in a primitivism shared with the writers of the age. Cunard shared this wartime fetishizing of powerful muscular bodies of workers and Blacks instigated by the fear of the destruction of European culture. She and Wyndham Lewis and William Roberts welcomed that destruction on one level, but I think they shared to some degree the contemporary Social Darwinian fantasy that European culture would be saved by the workers and the "darker races," who had not "lost" their masculine strength.

This is no single explanatory argument for Cunard's personal cult of muscular dark men. But the primitivism of the war paintings and the war poems makes clear that she was participating in a shared cultural fantasy. The historical line between the cult of hard masculinity, fetishizing muscles, uniforms, and boots has easily been drawn to the culture of fascism. Such Vorticist visual pleasure existed on the left as well. Ferdinand Léger's workers and soldiers are similarly eroticized. Roberts and Lewis were training the eyes of their viewers in a sense to *see* the French foreign troops in the front lines who were taking the brunt of the German attacks with enormous casualties as men—supermen, perhaps, and mysteriously masculine-feminine. Lewis humanizes rather than demonizes his Black shell-lifter's noble face in contrast to the stylized gunners' Roman warrior profiles. The color that the dark men's uniforms and shirts and mustaches carry and the color of the working-class soldiers' bright, unmilitary bodies, shirts, and hair signifies class, sexuality, and power; their labor makes the khaki-clad soldiers seem invincible. These radical bright paintings making the battlefield look like a bed of tulips and the poems of the *Wheels* poets about Blacks in Nassau and Trinidad, Tahiti, Rimbaud's French hell, Babel, negresses and jungle animals, carnivals and primeval terrors are part of a powerful cultural discourse of World War I around "the Rites of Spring," imagining bloody scenes of sacrifice and death in an orgy of primitivism leading to rebirth. Nature might be destroyed in Europe but the African continent was full of life: "and vigilant on the terrace / One palm tree, deputy from Africa" negotiates a meeting with the poet of *Sublunary* (1922). In "New Coasts" Cunard imagines the pleasure of dealing "with Africa / Giant unknown across the azure storms."[38] The work of Cunard and the *Wheels* poets, as well as of the avant-garde painters of the war with their troubling references to race and gender, speak the discourse of the war as part of the purifying of a decadent world in bloody but renewing rites of spring.

Both large paintings dramatize the battlefield as a theater of war. We the viewers of Roberts's massive portrait of struggle and turmoil feel as sensually assaulted as the men whose eyes are blinded, bandaged, or smarting from gas, whose mouths are vomiting the poison, hands tearing at their damaged throats or covering mouths with their handkerchiefs to keep the gas from getting at them. We are treated to a low-flying pilot's view of a scene of amazing confusion, contortion, and cross-thrusting movement. *The First German Gas Attack at Ypres* could be looked at as a painter's version of Stravinsky's *Rite of Spring*. The French soldiers writhing in pain in their ethnic costumes look like the pagan Russian maidens he imagined being sacrificed in a great primitive ritual, dancing themselves to death. The gorgeously colored gunners are the dancers Diaghilev imagined and Nijinsky performed, with the khaki-uniformed officers as the old men for whom the Dionysian rites are performed. *The Rite of Spring* enacted a sensational eroticizing of death, unleashing a lust for war shared by Europeans who sought authenticity and their own rebirth in ancient and primitive objects. The huge shining golden shells in Roberts's and Lewis's pictures glow like golden idols for ancient altars. Are the men priests of the cult of the golden phallus? Is the gunpit a shrine to Moloch?

Cunard's lamentations and dirges at the senseless slaughter predicted a scene at the end of the world:

> I saw the people climbing up the street
> Maddened with war and strength and thought to kill
> And after followed Death, who held with skill
> His torn rags, royally, and stamped his foot.[39]

Figure 5.1. "Iris Tree was a poet, a Bohemian and later a celebrity with a distinctive style and a nomadic life"; Marcus reads her work along with Cunard's in *Wheels* "as a sapphic analogue to the homoerotic male poetry and painting seen as constitutive of the World War I imagination." Married to Curtis Moffat, Tree studied alongside Cunard at the Slade School of Fine Art and was "her inseparable girlfriend." Photograph by Curtis Moffat (or Man Ray), 1923 © Man Ray Trust / ADAGP, Paris and DACS, London 2018

CHAPTER FIVE

Girlfriends, Boyfriends, and Bright Young Things

Girlfriends

The poets of *Wheels* were a motley crew and the volumes are notably unparochial as well as unpatriotic in their translation and publication of poetry in French, a radical cultural move during the war. There was Edith Sitwell and her ex-governess, Helen Rootham, as well as Nancy Cunard and her inseparable girlfriend, Iris Tree (and E. W. Tennant, the promising poet-lover whose death in the war has been understood as the cause of Cunard's future reckless abandon as well as Tree's). Rootham was Sitwell's music teacher and poetic mentor as well as her long-time companion after helping her escape from a miserable and soul-destroying home. She was an accomplished poet and a brilliant translator of Rimbaud; *Wheels* contains poems the women dedicated to each other. The slightly Sapphic coexists in these volumes with the anti-heroic homoerotic of Wilfred Owen and the war poets. The history of modernism does not attribute to Helen Rootham the popularizing of Rimbaud in Britain.

At first glance it is hard to connect the women behind *Wheels*, Sitwell, Cunard, Rootham, and Tree, with each other. A critic in the *Saturday Review* said that "Miss Tree is venomously alive," despite her cry in "III," "Mouth of the dust I kiss, corruption absolute," decadent poems from the 1916 first cycle, or "Black Velvet" from the second cycle in 1917:

121

Candelight
Snuffed in the flooding darkness, and the train
Of queens that go to scaffold for a sin—
Or splash of blackness manifest of pain,
Hamlet among his court, a Harlequin
Of tragedies … Mysterious … And again
Venetian masks against a milky skin.[1]

Or "Revision":

We see your wounds and weep,
You meet our pity with a traitor's kiss—
No,
You are schooled in suffering and schooled
In teaching pain to others—
And all that mob of furious accusation
To which you turn the cheek, or curse so well,
Are but the ghosts of bodies you have murdered,
That drive you on in vengeance to fresh crime.[2]

If we see the poets as two couples, mermaids murmuring each to each, and
not to Mr. Eliot or Mr. Pound at all, pupil and teacher in the case of Rootham
and Sitwell, and devoted girlfriends in the case of Cunard and Tree, in classic
lesbian configurations, their work in *Wheels* may be read as a Sapphic analog
to the homoerotic male poetry and painting seen as constitutive of the World
War I imagination. Together they perform a stately dance of death with strange
animals, a carnival of unreproductive love, mourning their friends, the mad
soldiers. Tree and Cunard set up a secret studio where they could write, dress up,
and see their friends and each other. They were agents of each other's struggle
for freedom from family and the social pressure to conform, as Rootham as
Sitwell's music teacher played a similar role, encouraging her pupil's confidence
in her genius. They were caught and their keys confiscated and then they set up
together again in Fitzroy Street, and Cunard also rented rooms above the Eiffel
Tower restaurant. Together they moved to Paris, sharing a famous flat and their
bohemian friends, writers and painters, sculptors and photographers.

Iris Tree was a poet, a bohemian, and later a celebrity with a distinctive
style and a nomadic life. The daughter of the actor Herbert Beerbohm Tree, Iris

was a beauty who always wore her blonde angel hair in a bob with a fringe, like her friend and fellow art student at the Slade, Dora Carrington, who painted her (on colored tinsel under glass) riding a white horse as Joan of Arc. She was painted by Vanessa Bell, Duncan Grant, Roger Fry, Don Alvaro de Guevara, and Augustus John; Epstein's bust captures her look of a young page or knight.[3]

Tree's cultivation of a particular look and the rush of artists to capture her avant-garde image links her to both Cunard and Sitwell, whose bodies also served as icons of the age and their own *difference*. The costumes and make-up they affected were extraordinarily *feminine*, though often from another age, and ranged from the royal to the religious to the primitive peasant. Dressing up, they learned to assume authority, distinctive identity, and stage presence. From a family of actors Tree learned and taught her intimates a sense of style that included walking the walk and talking the talk, training the voice for establishing dignity and distance or the opposite. The visual playing of the *femme* role also highlighted their "masculine" independence and distance from other women and their confined domestic lives. They stare back at the viewer of their portraits with utter confidence and control. Cunard and Tree played at dressing up in their studio, and one of their favorite props was Sir Bache Cunard's top hat, later topped with a mask in a famous photo of Janet Flanner, the Genet of the *New Yorker*, by Man Ray. Flanner's lover and Cunard's dear friend, the poet and journalist Solita Solano, had been a favorite of Tree's actor father when he was performing in Boston. All of these remarkable women loved both men and women; Tree's adventures included marriage and children with two men, one of whom, the photographer Curtis Moffat, introduced Cunard to African art.

In the 1918 cycle of *Wheels*, Iris Tree perhaps captures the mood of her rebellious and difficult relationship with Nancy Cunard and their New Women's studio flat in "Return":

> The curtains are drawn as though it still were night,
> A slip of dawn between them is a dangling silver ribbon
> And all about the room is quietness—Each patient chair
> Erect, alert, in place. A letter on the table and a book
> Lie as you left them, now bereft of purpose—
> Garish a little in the room's sedateness, you
> Returning dressed so frivolously in all your colored clothes!
> How grey and sober, full of placid with

> The furniture, the pictures on the wall
> How steely swift the light, stabbing you to the heart
> As you stand at the window, bright as rushing blood.
> Garish your hair, your shoes, your startling chalky face,
> And white, white gloves …
> What time is it? … Still ticks the tireless clock,
> with face grimacing … nearly six it is …
> Yet hurries not nor lingers, like our hearts,
> For in its dial eternity is housed,—
> A cock should crow … there are no cocks in town?
> But a water cart with surly noise below
> Grates unconcerned along the disconsolate street,
> How cold and how familiar all these things,
> To you so lonely in the enormous dawn
> Slowly unfastening that vermillion dress …[4]

At one stage Tree wore eccentric natural linen and wool dresses from the Omega Workshop, lived in Augustus John's ménage, and was painted as a Belgian war refugee looking, in John's words, "voluptuously virginal, passionately pure."[5]

Another of Cunard's girlfriends, Sybil Hart-Davies, first a very close friend of Iris Tree, annexed by Cunard when Tree went to America with her famous actor father, was thought to be a bad influence on her.[6] Hart-Davies gave Cunard a copy of Norman Douglas's *South Wind* (1917), a brilliant farce about the gay and lesbian exiles on Capri. Douglas later became a dear friend and hero, one of Cunard's *grands hommes*, along with George Moore (see Chapters 6–8), outlaw artists whose sex lives were far from respectable. Cunard promptly broke off her brief marriage to the Australian officer, Sydney Fairbairn, and afterwards dubbed Hart-Davies "my liberator." When their husbands had returned to the Front, the older woman, with her children, set up housekeeping with Cunard, reading Meredith, Swinburne, and Havelock Ellis's *The Psychology of Sex*, and she fell in love with one of her husband's brother officers, Broughton Adderly, and had an affair of five days that ended with his death at the Front. Robert Nichols, one of the young war poets, became obsessed with Cunard and poured out his feelings in execrable verse and was dismissed.

John Lucas associates women's independence with lesbian sexuality and cites Cunard's strong ties with Janet Flanner and Solita Solano, begun in

Figure 5.2. Lady Diana Cooper. One of Cunard's childhood friends, who was "deeply attached" to Cunard's mother and "thought of as a surrogate daughter" after Cunard's break with Lady Cunard. According to Marcus, Cooper "had the gift of keeping up appearances" and her "social life among the aristocracy protected her from the scandals that Nancy Cunard seemed to court."
Photograph by Curtis Moffat © Curtis Moffat / Victoria and Albert Museum, London

Paris in the early twenties, as evidence: "To treat Nancy Cunard as an archetypal flapper is to dishonor a brave and good person."[7] But her passionate relationships with women friends and the invention of herself in the early twenties as a permanent third to the lesbian couple Flanner and Solano, and later to the communist poets Sylvia Townsend Warner and Valentine Ackland, suggest one of the ways in which the exile constructed "home" for herself, in the domestic sphere of women who did not dominate and control their surroundings as Lady Cunard had done, women who allowed each other as much sexual and personal space as was needed, while remaining loyal friends.

Diana Cooper was Cunard's friend from childhood, a woman far more suited to the role of Evelyn Waugh's decadent society girls, a great beauty, deeply attached to Lady Cunard for her entire life, thought of as a surrogate daughter after Nancy's break with her mother, and sharing with Nancy a young man who was Lady Cunard's escort in her last years the estate and its Impressionist paintings. She also had the gift of keeping up appearances, and her marriage to Duff Cooper and her social life among the aristocracy protected her from the scandals that Cunard seemed to court.

The Roaring Queen[8]

Wyndham Lewis, who painted her stylish portrait in Venice in 1920, recalled first meeting Nancy Cunard as a lively debutante, "very American and attractive after the manner of the new World, rather than the Old."[9] As a modernist poet who published her work in the circles of T. S. Eliot and Edith Sitwell, as well as a member of the "Bright Young Things" crowd, Cunard had a well-shod foot in both camps, walking and talking with the serious intellectuals all day and dancing all night with "degenerate" artists and aristocrats. Like Virginia Woolf, Cunard was essentially an autodidact, extremely learned and knowledgeable about European literature, art, music, and languages, but insecure with university-educated men. Unlike Woolf, she experimented with sex as well as maintaining an intellectual interest in its extreme and "perverse" forms. Later, at her Hours Press in Paris, she published as its last volume Havelock Ellis's *The Revaluation of Obscenity* (1931). Arthur Symons brought "the great savant" to dinner at her apartment on the Île Saint-Louis in 1926. She told the sexologist excitedly how she and her friends had marveled over his rare and "magnificent" seven-volume *Studies in the Psychology of Sex* toward the end of World War I:

> There, so interestingly described, were all these case histories, quirks, peculiarities and habits sometimes conditioned by a way of life imposed by circumstances and not by choice; (at random I remember some remarkable passages about homosexuality among tramps in the U.S.A.). [...] Interest in *all and any* of the facts and doings of human beings cannot be dismissed as a lewd thing; it is one part of anthropology [...] the study of stone and insect, of star and psyche is all interlinked [...] By the time Malinowksi's *Sexual Life of Savages* came out [...] there was less prudery and fuss over writings on various aspects of human behavior.[10]

It is interesting to note the themes that recur at the end of her life—a fascination with tramps and their (forbidden) sexuality, a view of sexual practices as formed by "circumstances," and a defense of "erotic fetishes." Her claim to find sexual case studies of anthropological interest does not extend to leaving posterity a record of her own sexual practices, subject as they were to so much gossip, and the fiction, poems, and dream lives of rejected lovers. Reading Malinowski in her youth, she began to think of her work as a branch of anthropology, the collecting and disseminating of African objects and ideas. As intellectual missionary to her peers, she sought to familiarize the West with Africa's kinship in the human family, while as anthropologist *manquée* she was plainly fascinated by exotic difference. Is it cultural difference or gender authority that allows the French anthropologist Michel Leiris to write of his own sexual desires and dreams instead of the practices of the African peoples he has come to study on the Djibouti Expedition?[11]

Havelock Ellis's "serene lucidity" impressed Cunard, as well as his early defense of homosexuality.[12] His essay asserts that the excremental obscene arouses only a social taboo, while the sexual obscene incites moral and religious attacks. Ellis redefines the obscene as "what is *off the scene* and not openly shown on the stage of life," and what is off the scene has nothing to do with pornography, he says, "the literature and art that is a substitute for the brothel."[13] Ellis argues that the legal definition of obscenity based on "what excites sexual desires" makes the sexes themselves obscene, as well as (in Cunard's words) "the things that act as erotic fetishes (to conscious and subconscious minds alike)."[14] For Cunard and many other metropolitan intellectuals, including anthropologists like Malinowski and Leiris, and painters, sculptors, choreographers and dancers, critics, composers and photographers, poets and political activists, primitivism was a powerful force in personal life, in sexuality, fantasy, and dreams, as well as their work.

Nancy Cunard and the Bright Young Things (they were white young things as well, though they often took Black or brown lovers) were involved in sexual experimentation in a more flamboyant and risky way than their friends in the Bloomsbury Group. They had more money and more friends with houses in the south of France than the Bloomsbury Group, but there were a lot of crossover figures—Carrington, for example, and Julia Strachey. The painter John Banting, who took many photographs at Lytton Strachey's Ham Spray, writes that membership in the set demanded that one be very attractive to both sexes as well as talented, and bisexuality was practically *de rigueur*.[15]

Judging from the photographs taken by Barbara Ker-Seymer in the south of France, they were indeed bright and thin and muscular and beautiful, and Blacks, gays, and lesbians were visibly present among the (tanned) white glamorous expatriates and artists.[16] Tanning was another part of the "'20s Primitive" a cult of deliberate identification with "the darker races" that horrified the white colonials as much as the boyish bobs and bold body language of postwar girls threatened the sentimental idea of home and family values. Hemingway's fiction connects the cult of tanning among the exiles in Europe with bisexuality, role switching in couples where the men are passive and the women very "manly." Feeling connected in their sunburnt skins with bronzed working men, dark French and Spanish peasants, and Italian farm-workers, Hemingway's exiled Americans and Brian Howard's Bright Young Things, alike, crossed boundaries and reversed roles in race, class, and gender.[17]

They could afford to conduct their experiments in Havelock Ellis's neutral zone of "off the scene," in Cannes or North Africa; as photographs kept by Howard, Cunard, and Banting testify, they even skied in Austria with Henry Crowder, the Afro-American jazz pianist, enjoying the shock they caused in the village. They were part of a "scene" that still exists. Crowder was a race object as well as a sex object as the Bright Young Things played in the snow. His reaction can perhaps be found in the title of his memoir *As Wonderful as All That?*[18]

Lucy Tantamout: Huxley's Perfumed Monkey

In *Point Counter Point* (1928), Aldous Huxley's white writer, Philip Quarles, demonizes female desire and collusion with colonized men of color in his dream of the Indian feeding meat to the monstrous green and white crocodile he sees when Lucy Tantamount (the Cunard figure) opens her mouth. White women aren't supposed to open their mouths. Black and brown men aren't supposed to feed their appetites. Huxley's novelist invents his own version of the comic-romantic green hat as a deadly vagina dentata, as he fetishizes the vampire-woman. His (fetish) is made of genuine imported crocodile. Indian men feed the "sacred" animals in a foreign culture that the narrator and "author" suspect may, unlike their own civilized and repressed culture, acknowledge female power and desire.[19]

Lucy's provocative scrawls from Quai Voltaire in Paris, inviting the writer to orgies in brothels or "twenty thousand simultaneous sadistic *frissons* at the bullfights in Spain," or telling of the break-up of their friends Tim and Eileen because she can't continue lying naked "while he sets fire to newspapers over her and lets the hot ashes fall on her body," convince him that "the repressed functions don't die; they deteriorate, they fester, they revert to primitiveness."[20] Lucy's "pencilled scribbles," which do, alas, sound very much like Nancy Cunard's letters to her English literary lovers, challenge his jealous rages, insisting that she won't be "cursed or whined at," "reproached or condemned."[21]

She tells him of her adventure picking up an Italian "brown savage" in the street for a "sordid" bit of "fun" in a cheap hotel:

> He came at me as though he were going to kill me, with clenched teeth. I shut my eyes, like a Christian martyr in front of a lion. Martyrdom's exciting. Letting oneself be hurt, humiliated, used like a doormat—queer. I like it. Besides, the doormat uses the user. It's complicated … Beautifully savage he looked, a Red Indian. And as savage as his looks. The marks are still there where he bit me on the neck. I shall have to wear a scarf for days. Where did I see that statue of Marsyas being skinned? His face was like that. I dug my nails into his arm so that the blood came…[22]

To Huxley's hero's friend the scientist, Lucy is "a refined and perfumed imitation of a savage," a "putrefaction"; she and other society girls like her are acting like monkeys, "white negresses."[23] The voices of Huxley's novel speak the scientific discourses of racial and sexual degeneracy, Social Darwinism and eugenics, and Lucy's "perversions," her sadistic slapping of her lovers, her need to reduce them to abjection, are a "throwback" to atavism; she is the product of an over-intellectual civilization. Primitivism and decadence are two sides of the same coin, like Huxley's plot which sets idealist communists murdering gentlemen fascists in a musical "point counterpoint" social suicide.

The style of Arlen's Iris March and Huxley's Lucy Tantamount is a style of *femme fatale*, boldly taking the initiative in sex: "The strong gardenia perfume was in his nostrils; he was breathing what was for him the very essence of her being, the symbol of her power, of his own insane desires. He looked at her with a kind of terror."[24] She is like Richard Dyer's description of the women in *film noir*: "The femme fatale (like the nymphomaniac) is an image of frustration, alive with sexual desire that cannot be satisfied."[25] Nancy Cunard's fictional, visual, and real-life acting out of the role of nymphomaniac, and Hollywood film conventions regarding white women, along with the artificial constructions of *film noir*, are participating, I want to argue, in a major crisis of white identity. Cunard's *look*, and the look of heroines created to caricature her reputation, project what Dyer calls in discussing the images of women in *film noir* a "startlingly unreal sensuality."[26] This comes close to the mode of artificiality that one senses in Cunard's careful cultivation of her image, even when she was old, sick, and in pain. Dyer examines the particular case of Veronica Lake:

> It is above all in the faces that this quality is produced. Make-up and coiffure are used in a way that draws attention to their own artifice while at the same time they create surfaces of considerable tactile impact and draw attention to aspects of the head such as the mouth and hair which are particularly associated with eroticism in our time ... The hair is groomed and lit lustrously, it flows in "natural curves" that have yet somehow obviously been coiffed; the foundation make-up makes the face very pale while the lips are heavy and dark. To this combination of artifice and sensuality is frequently added the use of luxurious clothes made of highly tactile yet man-made fibres, and, of course, furs are often used to identify women with savage nature.[27]

Huxley lingers over descriptions of Lucy Tantamount's "short black hair, oiled to complete blackness and brushed back from her forehead. Naturally pale, she wore no rouge. Only her thin lips were painted and there was a little blue round the eyes. A black dress emphasized the whiteness of her arms and shoulders..."[28] He writes as if for a film script:

> Lucy Tantamount had just emerged from the dining room and was standing under the arcades, glancing in indecision this way and that. Against the mourning of her dress the skin was luminously white. A bunch of gardenias was pinned to her bodice. She raised a hand to touch her smooth black hair, and the emerald of her ring shot a green signal to him across the room.[29]

Or, again cinematically:

> They were passing a street lamp. Through the window of the moving
> cab the light of it fell on her face. It stood out for a moment palely
> against the darkness, then dropped back into invisibility—a pale
> mask that had seen everything before and whose expression was one
> of amused detachment and a hard, rather weary languor.[30]

Performing whiteness, Nancy Cunard crossed the borders of morality
and politics. How could she represent both the purity of English national
honor with what people always call her "cold sensuality" (a description George
Moore also applied to her mother) and at the same time embody the adventuress? Dyer discusses the making of "stars" and photographic conventions
which were adopted, as lighting codes were developed by the film industry
specifically in relation to the white face: "codes of glamour lighting in Hollywood were developed in relation to white women, to endow them with a glow
and radiance that has correspondences with the transcendental rhetoric of
popular Christianity."[31]

Huxley's Indian Primitive

Aldous Huxley was above all a survivor. He took his principled pacifist self to
California before the war. *Point Counter Point* might have survived if he had
continued to write in the tone of the opening, in his best *House and Garden* or
Vanity Fair voice: "'You won't be late?' There was anxiety in Marjorie Carling's
voice, there was something like entreaty ...'"[32] This voice haunts Huxley's work
and the "literature" of romantic fiction. . It would not be out of place in Michael
Arlen's *The Green Hat*, while Mulk Raj Anand's *Coolie* might quote it as an
example of degeneracy. Wyndham Lewis used this passage from the opening
page of Huxley's highly regarded and best-selling *Point Counter Point* in his
mocking "The Taxi-Cab Driver Test for Fiction" in *Men Without Art* (1934). To
Lewis, Huxley's style was an example of the "tone of vulgar complicity with the
dreariest of suburban library readers" in the "cozy ... accent of the newspaper
serial," telling the reader that the novel he quotes cannot possibly be thought
of as "a serious work of art," but that nevertheless it is regarded as "one of the
landmarks of English literature in the last decade."[33]

But Huxley's racism in the Bombay chapter runs deeper than what Lewis shows as his "lady-novelist's" tricks or even Arlen's casual barbs about French food. It would be instructive to read this chapter with Salman Rushdie's *Midnight's Children*. Philip Quarles and his wife are being entertained by Sita Ram, an Indian legislator. They are swamped by lower forms of life; a "squashy" toad, mildly tolerated by their host, hops across the veranda, to Elinor's disgust. They find the fish "toad-like," the rissoles "dubious," and the sweets "much fingered," rolled in something "at once slimy and gritty, and tasting hauntingly through their sweetness of mutton fat."[34]

Sita Ram's speech is given in a dialect used for American negroes: "'Dere is one law for de English,' he said, 'and anoder for de Indians, one for de oppressors and anoder for de oppressed ...'" which robs it of serious political meaning. Sweat pours down his face, Huxley writes, so that "he seemed to be weeping for Mother India. One drop had been hanging, an iridescent jewel in the lamplight, at the end of his nose. It flashed and trembled as he spoke, as if responsive to patriotic sentiments ..."[35] Ridiculing Ram's demand for "fair play," the Quarles couple make the usual speech about birth control.

Crossing "the sordid suburbs of Bombay," with the air smelling of tropical flowers, sewage, curry, or burning cow dung, they congratulate themselves on their "civilized" marriage, in which she introduces him to possible mistresses for the sake of his fiction, negotiating the social world for the intellectual who is only "an intelligent tourist in the realm of feeling."[36] A dog breaks its back chasing a bitch in heat in front of their car, and Quarles thinks that "primitive societies are apt to be more seasonal than cultivated ones ... a bad reputation in a woman allures like the signs of heat in a bitch. Ill-fame announces accessibility ..."[37]

Huxley renders the Indian primitive in the debasement of the English language, the only thing his hero really cares about. (Could these passages once have been read as comic?) Quarles's immoral, loveless marriage and affairs are described as the actions of what the D. H. Lawrence figure calls "Intelligent primitives. Big game with a soul." "Atavismuses with all modern conveniences."[38] India is the inconvenient animal primitive. London intellectuals have science—birth control and "operations" to allow for the sexual experiments of authors attracted to women of bad reputation, and wives glad to spend the money earned by the pornographic scenes in their husbands' books.

The first page of *Point Counter Point* assured Lewis's taxi driver that it was a romance novel. But to what genre does the broken English, not even a good rendition of "Indian English," belong? Yellow journalism, like *Mother India* perhaps, written to make clear that Indians were too "primitive" to govern themselves? The pages of scientific argument earned *Point Counter Point* its "landmark" status, but they have dated as much as the racist discourse. But the description of the sadistic heroine in action would leave no doubt in the taxi driver's mind. Huxley's best-seller formula combined romance with political murder, suicide, maudlin scenes of the death of a child, ignorant dark people in exotic foreign lands imitating "civilized" life; and the intellectual discussions about evolution and the future of the race are conducted between passages of semi-pornographic prose. This is called melodrama.

Huxley's fetish was cars, despite his novel's claim that he was, by heredity, "under-acquisitive," and the fact that he couldn't see to drive. His wife drove, and a special seat was built to measure for his outstretched legs in the scarlet Bugatti racing car with dove-gray leather upholstery that they bought with the proceeds from *Point Counter Point*.[39]

Vogue versus *Vanity Fair*

Huxley's working-class scientist works himself into a righteous rage that condones murder by reading *Vogue*, a journal in which daring photographs of Cunard sometimes appeared, and, for a brief time, her column, "As I See It: Paris Today." He rants about fur coats and advertisements for fat-reducers, cursing the "strumpets and gluttons" whose latest perfume is *Songe Negre*. His (and his author's?) class hatred is fueled by sex hatred and jealousy. Huxley's bread and butter was earned as the founding editor of Condé Nast's publication *House and Garden*. In *Vanity Fair* (also owned by Condé Nast) in June 1925, Huxley had ranted about "The Horrors of Society: The Unutterable Boredom Involved in the 'Diversions of the Leisured Classes,'"[40] a slap at his one-time lover Cunard's indulgence in a Black dream, a "nightmare" of primitive sexuality, *Songe Negre* as *singe negre*. His novel explicitly connects the right-wing "outlaws," the British Freemen (Mosley's British League of Fascists) with self-proclaimed outlaws from upper-class society, like Cunard, who embrace Africa, its music, art, and dance, and other outrageous art forms out of boredom and the stress of finding cultural ways to fill the vacuum of their (non-working) lives. *Outlaws* was the title of a volume of Cunard's poetry, as Huxley's readers were sure to have known.

In *Vanity Fair*, Huxley bemoaned the international influence of primitivism on modernist art: "many artists cultivate a deliberate nativism, when the technical practice of the primitives is freely imitated and art is simplified and conventionalized to the utmost. There is obviously nothing remarkably modern in imitating the primitives."[41] In both fiction and essay Huxley was expressing his fear of the resurgence of the barbaric and atavistic in a degenerate art akin to the decadent and primitive sexuality of the Lucy Tantamounts who liked it, inspired, it, and bought it. He praised Schoenberg's serious intellectual music and denounced the primitive in Stravinsky's "backward" appeal to "the primary emotions and the nerves." This places Huxley at odds with the writers of *Wheels*, once his comrades in an English wartime "rite of spring." In particular, he argues against the common claim that primitive art is abstract and that it shares this formal quality with modernist art. Primitive art is non-realistic, he says, but it was full of meaning in its cultural setting, while modern imitations of primitive form do not express modern ideas or values. The appropriation of the formal aspects of primitive art without creating a new European historical context for them is a dangerous backward move for twentieth-century culture, according to Huxley's evolutionary philosophy. The modern must be new; it must not have a past.

Cunard's Paris letter to *Vogue*, which it is tempting to compare with Janet Flanner's longer-lived letter to *The New Yorker* as "Genet," lives up to Huxley's expectations of decadent primitivism, offering the rich and leisured a taste of Paris diversions while making fun of "*le snobisme*," describing the excitement of the bicycle races, touring the Surrealist galleries and the *mondain* "Au Sacre de Printemps" (a "gallery-cum-tea-parlor," she says not quite approvingly), with stocks of pictures and new music, dedicated to Stravinsky and run by Princess Lucien Murat.[42] She announces the Paris "classical" concert season of her mother's lover Thomas Beecham, as well as the plans for new ballets by Cocteau and the Ballets Russes dancing works by Constant Lambert with curtains by Ernst and Miro; reviews the new books and literary magazines; reports on the troubles of the "legion of Russian taxi-drivers"; and signals that "gaiety" is welcome among the artists and celebrities dancing at her favorite nightclub, the Boeuf sur le Toit.[43] The "'orientalism' [...] and interminable series of naked women contraptioned into fans [...] might very easily be called rotten" in the new Folies Bergère show—except for the "astounding"

Josephine Baker, contorting her "surprising" form "in her necklets, bracelets, and flouncing feathered loincloths (ending with) a scant one of golden palm leaves. The fuzz has been taken from her hair, which shines like a dark blue crystal as she yodels (the nearest one can get to expressing it)," as the Afro-American dance sensation performs better on her own than with the *Negro Revue*.

Songs Negre / Singe Negre: Josephine Baker

In her column in *Vogue*, Cunard critiques the vulgar Orientalism of the acts at the Folies Bergère with their "sparkling headdresses and trick-jazz couples." She defines Josephine Baker as an original "native" artist whose work has been appropriated by the Folies dancers, as African and Oceanic arts, which she had been discussing in the previous paragraphs, have been appropriated by modern artists—she names in particular "Léger's Negro ballet *La Créa-tion du monde*"[44] and Man Ray's paintings in the Gallerie Surréaliste in the rue Jacques Callot as derivative of "magnificently executed" and "beautiful" pieces from Africa and New Ireland which are exhibited with them.[45] As a collector of African art, selling pieces in the front of her Hours Press shop on the rue Guenegaud as well as buying pieces for the Gallerie Surréaliste, she had as much of a stake in valuing the primitive as primitive as dealers like Kahnweiller or his son-in-law, Michel Leiris. "No one thinks any longer of disputing the influence of African and Oceanic work on contemporaneous painting," Cunard wrote in 1926, not anticipating the tremendous controversy over this issue that would develop, the denials of the artists themselves that they had seen or were influenced by African and Oceanic art, and the writing of critics and curators in defense of the originality of the Europeans or the better execution or higher value of their painting and sculpture in comparison to the "primitive" works.[46] For her the issue was that "the work of 'savages' is no more incomprehensible than would be thought nowadays an abstract painting."[47] She did not, like Huxley, attack abstraction as an evil in itself.

She was as concerned as he was about the "authenticity" of the primitive in relation to dead bourgeois values, and quite sure that she knew authenticity when she saw it. Almost a decade later in the *Negro* anthology, Cunard lamented the fact that a "dreary gang of French critics" had usurped Josephine Baker's authentic energy, and she quotes examples of their assimilating and "civilizing" the cannibal beauty with her fetish face—She is anyway too exquisite for a Negress—she seems to whiten as we gaze at her ... What a difference between the little savage of the early days and her delirious, grotesque dances and the toned-down refined *artiste* transformed by Paris ... Her limbs have retained those thin, disproportionate lengths which ensure her the indispensable aspect of the monkey ... [Not the evolutionary discourse again.] No longer do we see mere exhibitionism—She shows us now that she has a choreographic sense bordering on pure art ... what an exquisite way of prostrating herself at the white man's feet.[48]

Baker is now appearing at the Casino de Paris in a sketch called "Josephine est blanche..." The French are making her into a "Gallicized actress" fit for the Comédie Française.

Disgusted with European culture herself, Cunard cannot accept or imagine the African-American dancer's desire to become French, in the same way that Virginia Woolf couldn't imagine a Black Englishwoman. When Cunard immersed herself in French "culture" at the same moment as Josephine Baker, she was part of the "French" audience for everything African, and it was necessary to repress all her English lady's expertise in high European culture. French was the medium through which she approached the African. She was shedding all traces of "refinement" as Baker was acquiring them as fast as she could in a bid for survival. Granting that the French are far less racially prejudiced than the Anglo-Saxons, she admits that their colonial policy approves racial intermixing and that they want to bring superior French culture to the Africans. Regretfully, Cunard mourns the loss of her Black role model's "whirlwind," "wildfire," "fierce," "beautiful brown electric body" to be "whitened" by French taste, kitsch diamonds and feathers replacing the "magnificent tornado's" more tasteful (read: more primitive) "spare gold banana fronds." Baker's gleaming, plastered-down hair with its curls stuck to the face, and her huge beads and bracelets, were translated across race to Cunard's ash-blonde bob and emaciated body with phallic arms and shoulders doing the fetishizing work of Baker's famous buttocks. Her arms in their heavy bracelets were often perceived as weapons and Henry Crowder tells of being assaulted by them; others remember her using them to chastise her lovers in public, and in Huxley's novels, the adventuresses are fond of flexing their bare white arms.

As Baker performed the jungle to win a place in French culture, and then left the jungle behind her for the glamor of the metropolis, Cunard performed the white negress in British polite society and earned exile, a permanent exclusion from Anglo-Saxon mainstream social and literary life. One may question her right, of course, to judge Josephine Baker's choice. The French needed her to be "African" and chose her as Queen of the Colonial Exhibition in 1931—until it was pointed out that Baker was not African at all, but Afro-American. Cunard's need for savagery and violence in her life was derived from a childhood of beatings and abandonment in upper-crust England. It had nothing to do with her political commitment to Black culture and freedom, to the art of the African diaspora. But these contradictions run all the way through the *Negro* anthology, and much of Cunard's political work for the Black cause is fraught with embarrassing appeals to "pure" African essences, uptight scolding of those who do not toe the party line, lectures in Communist Party jargon about political correctness to the likes of W. E. B. Du Bois. She is disappointed that Baker has lost her "African" virginity to act out the jeweled and feathered fantasies of the French bourgeoisie instead of the cruder ones of Cunard and the intellectuals, artists, and working people who were her early audience.

Josephine Baker created herself, just as Nancy Cunard did. But her desire to assimilate into French culture was a more socially acceptable desire than Cunard's to be an "outlaw." Baker could fetishize herself and her body without losing her identity. The poverty and insecurity of her past were a motivating force. Having it all and giving it up is different from never having had a thing. Cunard became the renegade figure she had acted in the twenties, and then found that she could not go home again. It looked like only a few gay men and lesbians and some French leftists mourned the loss of the person under the mask. Other "authentic" members of her generation, like her friends René Crevel and Brian Howard, truer to form, committed suicide.[49]

Cunard's critique of Baker raises interesting questions. By "civilizing" the savage Black dancer, France gives itself a cultural alibi for its own imperialist adventures. Baker willingly trades the jungle act she had created for less outrageous forms of seductive dance. She stops "shaking that thang." All of it was a performance, including playing the Black Frenchwoman, and one suspects she was always in control. The Russian-Jewish artist Sonia Delaunay, it seems to me, became a Frenchwoman in a similar way to Josephine Baker. Her outrageous foreign "primitive" Slav-Jewish-folk-gypsy artist persona appealed to the French. She erased this past to assimilate French culture as the wife of Robert Delaunay and to end her days as a representative French-woman designer of fabrics.

Baker became French to the French in sentimental ways that Cunard's political writing, publishing, and translating could never accomplish. She married, adopted many children, and played the role of woman "correctly." But, for a time, Josephine Baker's bouncing bottom, her prancing legs, and banana-belted body brought the African statue of European modernism to life, animated the wooden fetish figures, and unloosened the libidos of a generation of men and women.

Vogue-ing and Writing

It was for the readers of *Vogue* that Nancy Cunard posed in 1926 for her portrait as the savage modernist poet, her back to the camera, "wearing a fantastic headdress of feathers" and staring threateningly into a mirror, dark mouth turned down, eyes deeply shaded with kohl. The woman poet as part vampire, part harpy, identified as the author of *Parallax* and two earlier volumes of poetry, looks like a bird of prey. She was acting the female Rimbaud. For English modernists and French Surrealists, Cunard played the devouring woman, the *femme fatale* in the same kind of knowing perfor-mance as Josephine Baker's jungle act. The photograph was taken by Olivia Wyndham and Curtis Moffat, an American designer who married Cunard's old friend, Iris Tree. It was Moffat who first introduced Cunard (in 1921) to African art, and she includes a photograph of one of his pieces in the African Art section of *Negro*. The society photographer Olivia Wyndham later fell in love with a Black American actress, Edna Lloyd Thomas, who was performing in London. She followed her to Harlem, where, among other roles, Thomas played Lady Macbeth at the Lafayette Theatre in and out of costume, and there she remained. Wyndham's assistant, Barbara Ker-Seymer (1905–93), took over the studio, taught herself technique from German photography magazines, and photographed her friends—the Bright Young Things—Brian Howard, Frederick Ashton, Eddie Sackville-West, David Garnett, John Banting, Julia Strachey (who helped out in the studio), and took, with John Banting staging the scenes, the brilliant and disturbing fetishistic photographs of Nancy Cunard that constitute a major modernist *oeuvre*.

Figure 5.3. Barbara Ker-Seymer was a radical, innovative photographer of the British avant-garde. She opened her London studio in 1931, painted all the walls black, set up a radiogram (a combo radio/record player), and hung paintings on the wall by friends such as John Banting. She took a number of photographs of Cunard, the most famous a portrait of her veiled head against a tigerskin rug. This portrait of Ker-Seymer is by Humphrey Spender, 1930s, vintage bromide print
Photograph © National Portrait Gallery, London

In her attempt at producing a *Vogue* column, Cunard's writing was much too opinionated to survive the editor's pencil. They preferred looking at her anorectic face and body in murderous and self-destructive photographs, photographs much like the fashion photography of the late 1990s, glorifying the drugged and abused female form, than arguing with her over literary style. Josephine Baker made Paris's beloved Tiller Girls look insipid, she wrote, and French cycling is the sport that replaces the old Roman games for the masses; Miro's colored balloons will appear revolutionary in England, and she hopes that the French translation of Ford Madox Ford's *No More Parades* will retain some of the vigor of the original. The writing is as vivid and rapid as her letters, nothing like the shaped and controlled prose of Janet Flanner's amusing Paris Letters. She is present in the text in a personal way, telling us with relief that you can drink at the bicycle races, and that she is too tired to tell "whether it is illusion or fact that the street lamps shine here through the young chestnut leaves as in no other town." The food is good at the Boeuf sur le Toit, you can dance there before midnight, and you don't *have* to drink champagne. "Paris Today" is very much as Nancy Cunard sees it, and, much as one would like to have had her comments on the scene for the next four decades, the anti-fascist work she did for the Spanish Civil War and her subsequent causes were more important. I doubt that she read *The New Yorker* columns of her dear friend Janet Flanner, or even discussed politics, for they were very far apart on most issues. Re-reading Flanner's essays today, one is shocked at her conservative and often right-wing opinions. Toning down her writing would have been as immoral to Cunard as Josephine Baker's metamorphosis into a French chorus girl. *Vogue* had a brief moment of *avant-garde* literary style (Man Ray's photograph of Cunard appeared in *Vogue* on February 5, 1927), but it would hardly have been the place for her communist articles about racism and the history of slavery. But *House and Garden* and *Vanity Fair* seem to have suited Aldous Huxley very well. It is difficult now to understand the basis for Huxley's reputation as a serious public intellectual and Cunard's as a white cannibal "fetish face."

Cunard wrote to Flanner from Paris on July 14, 1926, that she had just arrived to "find *Vogue*, my second letter all emasculated and bereft of its rather-more-lively-than-the-rest attack on Cocteau" (written to please Aragon; later, she was friendly with Cocteau). She complains to Flanner of "loneliness" despite the fact that "A [Aragon?] is delicious—in perfect training *always* to write at will, any place, of anything. And he is a very sweet person— were I not myself so irreductably [sic] myself, I would be very happy—I am, as far as can be." "At lunch just now read a fine piece of muck by Clive Bell," she told Flanner,

> and don't know which it stinks of most, idiocy or nastiness—he is the fool of England—and what is his article [in *Vogue*] on? "Round About Surealise"! (Were you still here when Todd was frantically clamoring to know which side up she was to reproduce a painting of a horse's head?)

Dorothy Todd was for a short time the editor of *Vogue* and the cause of its brief interest in the arts and writing by artists. This letter was really a cry to a fellow writer about the lack of professional respect shown her as a woman, as well as the difficulties of explaining one cultural scene to another, problems Flanner knew well. Cunard may have been an expert on Surrealism, but Clive Bell was a member of the Bloomsbury Group, and encouraged by his friends in the belief that he was an art critic.

While she was in England, Cunard told Flanner, she went to Southampton "to look for African and Oceanic things ... now a very large interest in my life," and found herself in a suburb "in the middle of the largest collection of these things ... in England." It is likely that Aragon was with her and that they brought back objects both for her Hours Press shop and for the Gallerie Surréaliste around the corner. She writes of the "drunkenness and inner violence" of her nights, and that her reputation for being "The Green Hat" was causing many disagreeable moments with Guardsmen at parties, while Arlen, "the Baron," was enjoying a great success. "As for the Hat, it is indescribable."[50]

Aragon's Prick, or the Revolution in the Service of Surrealism

The title of this section is not gratuitous. It is meant to suggest the simultaneous sex-obsession and misogyny of the band of elite intellectuals who called themselves Surrealists and communists in Paris in the twenties and thirties in their discourses on politics and art. Because the Surrealists agreed that "automatic" writing of one's sexual fantasies was a radical political act, the French writer and dandy Louis Aragon (1897–1982) enhanced his masculinity by becoming Nancy Cunard's lover. He earned his avant-garde credentials by publishing an exhibitionist essay in erotica that was supposed to have cured him of his despair and checked the suicidal impulses that beset him when she left him. In 1928 Aragon published anonymously a piece of pornography called *Le Con d'Irene*, though *tout le monde* knew that, the *Le con*, or cunt in question belonged to Cunard, the English poet who had been his much-paraded public lover for several years. Why this adolescent fantasy added so much to Aragon's reputation as an intellectual and became a much-cited underground classic is a problem I cannot begin to solve, though it has always had literary admirers. "All this will end up in a story for the cream, the elite, the upper crust, the ultra-chic of stupid cunts. Arranging everything into a story is a bourgeois mania ...," Aragon writes at the end of his tale, getting his class credentials in order for the literary left.[51]

The French know how to take care of the reputations of their public intellectuals. Aragon is a major figure in the history of French politics and culture in the twentieth century. One smiles at his poses, his perversions, his polemics. They are part of the privilege of his status as a *grand homme*. His muse may have departed the scene soon after Cunard left him, but Aragon and Elsa Triolet retain an aura as the left's signature modern couple, second only to Simone de Beauvoir and Jean Paul Sartre. De Beauvoir is perhaps the only woman on whom a comparable status is conferred. But the public surely prefers Colette because most of her work concerns the private, not the public life.

It is true that Cunard has far more of a following among the French, for, after all, she lived there for much of her life, and died there publicly and horribly. Still, despite mad scenes, alcoholic rages, and wretched health, she was beloved by many old comrades, faithful French artists and intellectuals, as well as the expatriate community, particularly Janet Flanner and Solita Solano, Samuel Beckett and Georges Sadoul. In Britain the patriarchal left and the academic experts in the field are divided about her, some remembering all she did in the Spanish Civil War and for the cause of Blacks in anti-colonial struggle, others, like Valentine Cunningham, despite Anne Chisholm's evidence of a history of commitment and service to social justice, even blotting out her name from that crucial document *Authors Take Sides*. A circle of left feminists reviving interest in British women writers of the thirties, including Maroula Joannou, are now engaged in recuperating Cunard's work for the history of politics in her own country. Even as this is happening, however, we can see that the revival of Virginia Woolf, largely accomplished by American feminists interested in her socialist and pacifist writing as well as her fiction, has entered the backlash stage. The Woolf who is celebrated now is no longer the public intellectual, but the aesthete of Bloomsbury. As Sylvia Townsend Warner pointed out, women are here regarded as bombs, and only one can go off at a time. Under these conditions, the necessary work of situating Cunard internationally, which was, after all, the way she situated herself and her political writing and organizing, is all the more imperative.[52]

The attack on women and narrative strikes the Surrealist note perfectly. The credit for converting Cunard to communism is certainly Aragon's in part, but that particular part of her body had become part of the collective well before it met Aragon's still exclusively Surrealist member. The damage Aragon's "dirty" book did to Cunard's reputation was, some would say, almost irreparable, but time will perhaps allow us some leeway in rethinking this little history as a way of understanding where the Party line primitivism of Cunard's *Negro* anthology came from, to see its roots in French political debates at the Café Cyrano and Surrealist battles about revolutionary art at André Breton's studio in the rue Fontaine. Cunard was there when Breton, Paul Éluard, René Crevel, Jacques Prévert, as well as André Thirion, Georges Sadoul, and Aragon argued about Marxist-Leninism and the role of the artist in the revolution. Here she found the ideology and the intellectual rigor she had been looking for, the mental stimulation, creativity, and committed activism which was to shape her life on the left.

In *Revolutionaries Without Revolution* (1972), while crediting himself with the conversion of Aragon from Surrealism into a "tool" of the Communist Party in France, André Thirion nevertheless venomously attacks Aragon's double standard (since he was a pornographer himself) when he abandoned the Surrealists over the "Dulita Incident," Salvador Dalí's publication of "Reverie" in *Surrealism in the Service of the Revolution*, a masturbatory scene based on watching a little girl look at an album of pornography.[53] The break was over Aragon's compliance with *L'Humanité*'s editors' demand for condemnation of the "daydreaming writing," which was so important to Surrealism's practice. "Total submission to the Party brought Aragon (like so many other weak minds) a cozy spiritual comfort," wrote his comrade. "This was the shipwreck of one of the most celebrated dandies of the Western world."[54] Thirion's text drops its pretext at objective history as he resorts to the Surrealist practices of his youth and brings Dalí's Dulita to life. Forty years later, in 1967, at Georges Sadoul's funeral, where Thirion hears him speak, "Dulita" makes a date with Aragon for 1968.[55]

Thirion's portrait of Aragon is based on his initial experience of sharing a flat with Aragon, who was recovering from a suicide attempt in 1928 after Nancy Cunard had left him. He was unable to make up his mind between two women and, as Thirion tells it, Elsa Triolet, being the boldest and most decisive of the three, despite the fact that they all suspected her of being a Soviet spy, entered and took over his life. To him Aragon's character is the essence of weakness and vacillation. The son of an accomplished musician and composer in Baccarat, then in Nancy, André Thirion joined the Party as a high school student, and he also arranged for the second Surrealist show in Nancy of all places, as part of a cultural exchange called Paris-Nancy that the provincial intellectual prodigy organized with Georges Sadoul, famous later as a film critic, but then a comrade in both camps, Surrealism and the Party. Like Aragon, Sadoul, and other members of the group, Thirion came from a well-to-do family and was a gentleman revolutionary who enjoyed the sacrileges of Surrealism and the violence of a Party life of "action." As a teenager, he wrote a novel called *Black Mass* for serialization in the local Party organ in Nancy, but gave up writing for action after failing his exams and not attending classes at the Sorbonne. He and Sadoul desecrated churches in eastern France while on their way to and from family visits, pissing in holy water fonts and carrying away sacred objects and altarpieces to decorate their super-cinematic surrealist flat, as he relates with some relish. His book proudly pictures the crucifixes they used as toilet handles and chain pulls. He broke with Sadoul, whom he regarded as a Trotskyite when he became a "professional revolutionary" devoted to the cause of the workers.

Marcel Duhamel had repaired and restored an abandoned pavilion at 54 rue du Chateau in 1924, and it was decorated like a film set by Yves Tanguy, with a fantasy covered courtyard furnished as if it were an outdoor garden, with ambiguous confusing entrances as in dreams and a trapeziform mirror inspired by *The Cabinet of Doctor Caligari*. Thirion describes the decor in great detail, just as he describes the furniture and design in his father's various residences. One has the impression of a young man who spent his Paris days organizing the workers in factories, checking in with the Surrealists at the Cyrano on his way to a Party meeting, then heading back to Katia, his Bulgarian girlfriend in the rue du Chateau. But the same intense and starving provincial intellectual also went home for serious consultations with his father about the design of his new furniture in Nancy. One of the photos in the book is of the pink parlour in the family house in Baccarat, burnt down by the Germans in 1914. The Art Deco furniture, he says, is by Tony Selmersheim. He devotes loving attention to describing the family silver and the contents of the wine cellar looted by the invading troops. (He was seven years old at the time.) Deeply concerned with things, Thirion's bourgeois autobiography remembers Surrealism by the things it produced, the style it affected, and the manner in which its adherents dressed. He recalls the thrill of playing modernist music in Nancy, and then Darius Milhaud performing *La Création du monde* for him personally in Paris when he didn't have the money for the concert. He judges people by the paintings they own and lists what is hanging on whose walls. He must have been impossible in meetings. No wonder his workers' cell in the Party expelled him.

This aggressive young dropout from Lorraine, with his materialist taste for modernist culture and his penchant for looting churches, found that Aragon had moved into his room in the rue du Chateau after one of his refurnishing jaunts in Nancy. Man Ray's photograph of Nancy Cunard, her arms sheathed in ivory bracelets, was blown up to life size on the wall of the big ground-floor room, and Aragon in agony, "literally a broken man," shared "the sorrows of young Werther" with the other occupants of the flat—Thirion, whose Katia had gone back to her husband in Bulgaria, and Sadoul, in love with "Suzanne," who had no use for him.[56] Maurice Blech, an old friend of Thirion and Sadoul, was there to share in the dancing to jazz and blues records he had brought. Blech was respected because he had been Josephine Baker's first lover in Paris. The stylized primitivism of the flat included an alcove with four black leather mattresses, and low walls covered in movie posters for visiting women. There was "a leather-lined ancestral figure from Gabon" in one of the bedrooms and under the loggia was

> a kind of tabernacle wrapped in striped fur and dotted with a vertical line of glass eyes. On top of it there was a human-sized head in fur, with glass eyes, a leather nose, and real teeth; perhaps it was a mummy's head wrapped in fur. On either side of the tabernacle hung an arm of light in gilded bronze, à la Louis XV.[57]

Michel Leiris, Raymond Queneau, Jacques Prévert, Benjamin Peret, Georges Malkine, and André Masson were often to be found there. Nancy Cunard had been a regular visitor in its earlier phase, when Duhamel, Prévert, and Tanguy occupied it, and Aragon had stayed there.

PART III

Grands Hommes:
Fabricating a Father

Figure 6.1. Montague Eliot, "Nancy Takes G.M. for a pleasant walk."
In two memoirs by Cunard on George Moore and Norman Douglas,
paying homage to both as father figures, Marcus writes she
"legitimates their masculinity" at the same time as she creates
herself as "the daughter of two queer men."
Image courtesy Harry Ransom Center, The University of Texas at Austin

CHAPTER SIX

Closet Autobiography

Bones and Stones

This chapter and the following one, "White Nympholepsy," are based on two odd books written by Nancy Cunard in the fifties, *GM: Memories of George Moore* and *Grand Man: Memories of Norman Douglas*. The fragments of autobiography which form the frail skeletons of her tender and delicate portraits of Moore and Douglas are a tribute to the "difference" between her life and theirs as political or sexual outlaws, and the difference of all three from standard patterns of English life. Both Anne Chisholm's *Nancy Cunard* and Hugh Ford's anthology *Nancy Cunard: Brave Poet, Indomitable Rebel,* and, certainly, this book, are deeply indebted to these volumes about obscure Victorian men of letters for the facts of her life, the only autobiographical writing we have. We are indebted as well to the structural power of Cunard's writerly reading of her own letters to the men she created as her own personal *grands hommes,* to bring herself to life as someone other than the "Cunard Line heiress," or the daughter of a London society hostess. In these memoirs of men of letters of her own class, but outlaws like herself from English social conventions, Cunard left us her own story. We find it, hidden between the lines of the lives of two distinctly odd gentlemen, a skeleton in their closets.[1]

In the 1950s, when she was writing these books, Cunard actually looked like a skeleton, her body a reliquary of old fragile bones, always breaking, her spirits kept up by rage and red wine. Perhaps the most moving image of this much-photographed woman, her face and body the subject of so many

149

startling paintings and sculptures by Dadaists, Surrealists, Vorticists, and other modernists, is the X-ray of her broken leg, filed, practically, among her papers. (She was eccentric, but eminently practical with the remains of her photograph collection, along with the disturbing experimental *rayographs* and *solarizations* by Barbara Ker-Seymer and Man Ray that reversed black and white to further polarize her looks.) The broken bone is an apt object to call up the memory of Nancy Cunard, a modern woman with a prehistoric look about her, like an extinct bird surviving the disappearance of her species, a mythical creature from a painting by Leonora Carrington or Max Ernst.

The personal voice she uses in these books is dialogic. They are staged conversations, one-woman shows with one-way speeches. She asks her dear, dead men to tell her about herself, shouting her questions across an abyss, like Billie Whitelaw playing one of Beckett's ravaged women. Her interlocutors come alive, as it were, as straw men, silent witnesses to a life of bold action and intense self-loathing. The rhetoric is yet another instance of most active women public figures' inability to write their autobiographies except in some ingenious form, which foregrounds the other.[2] Cunard only exists in relation to others, to her causes, her friendships. To be herself she needs someone to talk to. But who will listen? She even amuses the reader by introducing her village wine seller to the dead writer's portrait, in a distinctly postmodern pause in her writing at LaMothe, in tiny Fenelon, her old stone house in the Dordogne. Toasting George Moore with a French peasant stirs her memory of their conversations with Leicestershire farmers and shepherds as they walked up Drayton Hill. In the gorse on the hilltop she showed him where she "had been 'blooded' out hunting, at the age of six or so, and given the fox's brush." They marked the mineral stone palette of color and veinings at the old quarry at Ironstone, singling out some "with an angry, reddish suffusion" near the gypsy camp, which was one of her favorite haunts.

The kiln of Adam, the old blind potter, was also on her pilgrimage with her father-figure to Ironstone, that "fierce, wild place that had something ominous about it and something holy in a pagan way." Always a devoted mentor to her education and to her writing, even from the grave Moore draws from the reluctant Cunard this vivid writing about the English landscape, seduces her into admitting her love for the Midlands, sharing her romantic passion for the rocks and stones and trees of home, and confessing the earliest stirrings of her love for gypsies and tramps.

Old stones, old bones. Fossils and shells. Cunard escaped the carefully ordered world of the social consumption of art and music at Nevill Holt to be alone on a mountain. Do artists need to do this in order to create, returning to the scene of origins as Nancy Cunard did, imagining the violence of the primeval struggle with nature, the savagery and power of the cave drawings, the Easter Island stone heads or the African masks as the cultural expression of her own alienation from the prospect of an upper-class Englishwoman's life? Old Adam, making his clay pots in a hut, "turning shapes out of great gobs of wet clay," was her hero, man the maker as he had been from time immemorial. All her life and all over the world she stopped to talk to peasants working the soil and craftsmen making useful objects, out of respect perhaps for her (rejected) father's ironworking, silently acknowledging her roots in the English Midlands and her descent from a family of artisans—woodworkers and shipbuilders.

The virulence with which she hated England was matched by her mentor's hatred of Ireland and Catholicism ("The two dominant notes in my character—an original hatred of my native country, and a brutal loathing of the religion I was brought up in").[3] Cunard's hatred was for her class and for England in its posture as Mother Country. They became cosmopolitan. They reinvented themselves as French. Moore had to "shake himself free from race and language and to recreate himself as it were in the womb of a new nationality, assuming its ideals, its morals and its modes of thought …,"[4] an interesting precursor to Joyce's Stephen Daedalus, wanting to forge in the smithy of his soul the uncreated conscience of his race. Gertrude Stein needed to live in France unassimilated to create, as she said, the American language. Nancy Cunard gave herself totally to France two generations after George Moore, and her identification with the avant-garde in French intellectual life, her participation in movements like Surrealism and communism, her establishment of a small press and a shop selling African objects along with the books of new poetry were a way of setting down the cosmopolitan exile's roots—she was going to assimilate into French culture as fervently as the other expatriates in Paris in the period were not. The Nouvelle Athènes, where the young Irishman met Manet and Degas, Mendez, Pissarro, and Cabaner, was replaced by Cunard with a series of cafés with different crowds for serious daytime work and discussion of the relations between Surrealist politics and art; for her evenings were spent listening to Black jazz and blues at the Boeuf sur le Toit—as his were spent at the *bal musettes* in belle époque Belleville. Moore forced himself to leave France when he could no longer write and think in English. Cunard always moved easily from French to Spanish to German to Italian, and sometimes her English poetry reads like the translations, which were her contribution to the struggle against war. Her final disillusionment with France was like that of someone betrayed by the nation-mother she had adopted in place of her real mother. And her public anger with her beloved France was as violent as her earlier repudiation of Lady Cunard and all she stood for.

Bones and stones were Nancy Cunard's element—her furniture and her signature. Her rooms and her body bore them in abundance as amulets and armaments against her fear of the domestic and the comfortable. She wore her ivories and her amber, enormous turquoise and onyx rings, massive carved Indian bracelets, bright beads of semi-precious stones to ward off the spell of the blue-eyed devil, the evil eye of white European respectability with its buildings separating the body from the earth and her mother's real emeralds only a ghost of the power of ritual objects in the primitive cultures she admired.

Closet Autobiography

Books were the closet in which Cunard buried herself. Following her, rattling the bones in the two "grand man" books, we wonder what they had in common, Nancy Cunard, Norman Douglas, and George Moore. What is the reader meant to find? Secrets? Hints and suggestions of bizarre sexualities? Moore's obsession with women's clothes and Douglas's male pedophilia—are these related to Cunard's "nymphomania," her lifetime of lovers, her reputed sado-masochism? She writes so affectionately to her dear dead mentors, the memoirs recall the semi-private world they shared—the love-letters, as Moore said, of a little girl to her "first friend," letters to be read by others in their circle, letters carrying messages they don't know they are carrying, for the communication is really intended for the other, her mother, whom they both love—or they reach out to "Uncle Norman" in Capri as the person who named and valued the rootless anti-authoritarian lives they both lived as "intellectual nomadism." The form vacillates between covering up the sexual secrets of Moore and Douglas—narrating them out of the tawdry stories of their contemporaries and biographers into a girl's story of grand men/mentors, making them into proper fatherly and grandfatherly heterosexuals—and discreet disclosure of some details in her own life.

Because Cunard's closet autobiography is written between the lines of patrimonial tributes to dead writers, it legitimates their masculinity at the same time as it creates Cunard as the daughter of two queer men. They are her (ironic?) pantheon of "great forebears," replacing her family and erasing the Cunard line from her personal history. The act of placing herself in a lineage descended from such unlikely fathers is another audacious act of self-creation. The act of writing these apparently dutiful daughter's sketches of eccentric unrelated misfits is not innocent. It insults her name and class once again and links *Grand Man* and *GM* to her 1931 pamphlet *Black Man and White Ladyship* as a deliberate provocation. It removes her from the world of the artists and writers who were her contemporaries, as well as from the Black revolutionaries, Surrealists and communists who were her comrades. Nancy Cunard's closet autobiographies unsettle us, as I am sure they were meant to do. She places herself "between men," a strategy that Eve Sedgwick's classic study *The Epistemology of the Closet* examines.[5] The grandfatherly men of letters are cast as maternal replacements for Lady Cunard, and she fathers herself as Nancy Cunard the poet, mentored by eccentrics whose literary judgment could never be dismissed on the grounds of their having been her lovers.

What is she doing hiding out from history among the mothballs in old men's closets? Publishers had besieged her to write of her affairs with the men of her generation. Her failure to do so has left her out of the lives of Eliot and Pound, for example, to whom she was very important, as well as Aragon and other French intellectuals. The looting of her house in Normandy has deprived posterity of their letters to her. What a story she could have told, from experience, of the famous men of her day, and the not-so-famous for that matter. But she didn't.

There were two strategies for dealing with her in the biographies and autobiographies of prominent men with whom she had had affairs and/or passionate intellectual relationships. Feed the image of Nancy Cunard as vamp or vampire, or erase her traces, as the wives of Aragon, Pound, and Huxley did. The effect of distorting the sexual part of her relationships was to diminish the power of her intellectual relationships with the men of her generation. They literally "wrote her off." If she appears in the history of modernism (other than in Shari Benstock's *Women of the Left Bank*), it is not as a poet, a political activist, a publisher, a Spanish Civil War journalist, or a champion of African culture. She is summoned up as a narcissistic face in the mirror of modernism, or its Nighttown Vampire. Why did she ally herself with men of a previous generation? In their "closets," and from their point of view as elder literary uncles, she was still a brave writer and a courageous political activist—she was safe from scurrilous footnotes and accusations of nymphomania.

It seems to me that her mother had interfered with her relations with her peers in an extraordinary way. Lady Cunard had annexed Nancy's women friends like Diana Cooper, who remained her friend for life, and she had entertained Ezra Pound and Wyndham Lewis, whose letters remind us that she managed to get a subsidy for James Joyce as well as an appointment for Lewis as an official war painter when Pound pointed out the senselessness of Gaudier-Brzeska's death in the war. In *These Were the Hours* Cunard tells of Joyce's refusal to see her in any other role than that of a patroness of the arts like her mother, and his rude insistence that she help with a subsidy for a singer who was his protégé.[6]

The assumption that Cunard had money to subsidize the arts troubled her relations with artists and often prevented her from forming relations with other modernists as a peer rather than a provider of money and sex like her mother. Her mother's name recurs as a patroness in the index of many a modernist biography in which Nancy Cunard, writer and woman, is only a ghostly echo. It is clear that the fictions about her by her peers, as well as the visual icons in circulation, were too compelling to be answered by an autobiography of her sex life, and she had wanted to be remembered for her work. Her own version of a life that had already become public property could not compete with portraits painted in revenge, misogyny, or disappointment. Lady Cunard's Grosvenor Square salon introduced many young artists to patrons; she not only promoted the career of her lover, Thomas Beecham, but supported composers, funded the London opera season and the ballet, and provided connections to the rich and powerful. In comparison, publication at her daughter's Hours Press did not make the careers of Beckett or Crowder, nor any of the other poets and artists she published.

"Personal Literature"

Her name brought shame and misunderstanding to her relationships and she had constantly to struggle to define herself against the ring of "Cunard" like sterling coins in people's ears, inciting a knowing smile. By writing the lives of Moore and Douglas, Cunard was creating an artistic lineage for herself among exiled writers. She was choosing her niche in history next to the minor writers with whom she compared herself. The Moore of the *Confessions* and the Douglas of *South Wind* were radical anti-authoritarian rebels, sexual "dandies," eccentric and, this is crucial, deeply *learned* writers, the alienated intellectuals of an earlier age. As the writing "daughter" of Douglas and Moore, Cunard could perhaps salvage a more honorable place in literary history (with the minor eccentric exiles) than as the dangerously perverse ex-lover of the major writers of her time, or as the "shipping heiress" who fancied "blackamoors" of the popular press.

"Personal literature is the only literature," wrote Moore, "for the age it is written and the age that follows."[7] What a tremendous cultural and historical gap has opened up between what he meant by personal at the end of his life in the 1920s, and what we mean by personal now. Presumably the author of at least one famous autobiography, *Hail and Farewell* (and many other memoirs and "personal" essays), was predicting that the kind of "public-personal" tone of the European Man of Letters in which he writes, the (to us) pontificating tone of a man who has never doubted that not only is he responsible for culture, but imagines (as do other people) that he may actually *be* the very embodiment of culture, would be dated. The memoir has a short and intense shelf-life. At two generations' distance, faded subjectivities, like old photographs, lose their power to enchant.

The mutual "knowingness" that this cultural intimacy between a literary figure and (his) audience presupposes does not survive into the next generation. In Moore's case this is a pity, for, if his sometimes stilted pronouncements as a critic of culture strike us now as absurd, he is credited with making the reputation of his friend Édouard Manet in *Manet and the Impressionists* and *Modern Painters*, as well as with building up the cult of Wagner in England. The visual pleasure provided by Manet's pictures has survived and increased in popular appeal, while the words of his champion in *fin-de-siècle* personal criticism, it seems, no longer bring a *frisson* of pleasure to the reader. It might be interesting to look at the studied casualness of Moore's mode of writing as an early instance of the anti-authoritarianism we think of as modern. It is a "personal" more familiar from the prose of Walter Pater as it comes to us through Virginia Woolf, a "personal" which opposes itself to the high moral Victorian "we" of the pronouncements of the patriarchs like Leslie Stephen. The "confession" in his *Confessions of a Young Man* was that he hated his father as much as he loved him and was greatly relieved ("glad" is the word which shocks him when he feels it) when he died:

> My father's death freed me, and I sprang like a loosened bough up to the light. His death gave me the power to create myself—that is to say, to create a complete and absolute self out of the partial self which was all that the restraint of home had permitted; this future self, this ideal George Moore, beckoned me, lured like a ghost ... the voice that said "I am glad" was not my voice, but that of the will to live which we inherit from elemental dust through countless generations. Terrible and imperative is the voice of the will to live: let him who is innocent cast the first stone ... Terrible is the day when each sees his soul naked, stripped of all veil; that dear soul which he cannot change or discard, and which is so irreparably his.[8]

This contrived and distanced autobiographical mode served the interests of a bachelor like Moore, who could not anticipate descendants reading his private thoughts in diaries and keeping them in the family. The semi-private voice of the "personal literature" in which he produced a version of himself for his readers is avuncular and often charmingly pompous. It is a voice which is confidential, not confessional, a formal voice which presumes the reader's respectful attention. Such a semi-private tone seems to be echoed in the work of Roland Barthes, for example, and Nancy Cunard sportingly attempts it in the two memoirs, but misses the mark, unable to make that leap of the imagination which assures the writer that the reader is listening. Cunard was even more "secretive" than Moore was, and always claimed to have no confidantes.

Moore made his reputation with *Confessions of a Young Man*. He had managed to find a way to express in a mild, inoffensive voice, as if in a private conversation with the reader, the accumulated fear and loathing his generation felt for their Victorian fathers and their patriarchal ways. Cunard's tirade, *Black Man and White Ladyship*, attacked her mother in the voice of a political agitator. The tone was harsh and angry. I am sure it never occurred to her to call upon *the will to live* as her defense. And if she had, it would have made her tirade seem all the more matricidal.

Moore's "personal" voice has no interest in laying bare his soul or discussing his childhood or analyzing his sexuality with the common reader.

Like Augustine, he confesses his sins, making clear to the "exquisitely hypo-critical reader" that his character was formed by youthful excess. He describes the church vestments and the incense of his decadent apartments shared with a dandy friend, a python fed on guinea pigs, and a large white cat. "I think that I might equally have been a Pharoah, an ostler, a pimp, an archbishop, and that in the fulfilment of the duties of each a certain measure of success would have been mine," he boasts.[9]

But the choice of the subjective style in criticism was itself subversive, Moore warned Cunard, as indeed it must have seemed in comparison with the muscular, masculine prose expected of a Victorian male. When he slyly insisted that the mature Cunard abandon the polemical mode of the commu-nist propagandist, her no-holds-barred calls to rebellion or her Harlem street *patois*, surely even less a forum for the personal, for a portrait of her privileged childhood in the tones of genteel Edwardian English nostalgia he assumed were still in her range, he did not consider how hard it had been for her to suppress that personal voice.

Not for her the nostalgia of Moore's writing of what I am calling, using his own language, "white nympholepsy." Like the narrator of Michael Arlen's *The Green Hat*, he rhapsodizes over the flesh of women and the fabrics which adorn them in endless descriptive titillation without climax, imagining for his readers Arlen's "things you had never done with women you had never met." They display their charms and he looks. Cunard's sexuality was about things she had done too often with everyone she ever met. There were too many affairs in her life to make an interesting autobiography. It would read like Leporello's list.

Again, she was no Nancy Mitford, and the avuncular voice of the Irish essayist in his popular "autobiographies and conversations" is not compatible with the harrowing pain, the inside-outing I sometimes call it, of contempo-rary personal criticism. One of the Mitford sisters could move between these two incompatible modes of socialist realism and society entertainment, but Cunard could not write again in the voice of her class. "Darlings," she would begin, and then outrage poured forth in a polyglot tongue of left modernist politics. Moore's manner was not a suitable model for Cunard's committed prose. He was not cut out for the role of muse to her muckraking, except insofar as the terrifying "facts" of his Zola-esque novels, *Esther Waters* and *A Mummer's Wife*, gave her a taste of a sensational realism she could use to great advantage in her own reportage. Moore's "French" fiction was as important

to English feminism as Thomas Hardy's problem novels. From him, Cunard
learned to write bravely of the wages of poverty, injustice, disease, and drink.
She carried the techniques of Balzac, Zola, and Moore into her writing about
the ravages of racism, war, and the dispossession of refugees. But autobiography was not journalism.

The gap between Moore the novelist and Moore the essayist is as great
as the gap Cunard perceived between the scruffy "Golden Boy" portraits by
Manet, and the later "Great Man" pose in the Sarah Harrison portrait she
reproduces in her book. If Moore's personal essay was not a form she could fit
to her needs—Cunard was always uncomfortable in any mode except poetry
and journalism—she did learn from him the art of the *exposé*. The "femininity"
of the personal essay's voice, as in Moore, Douglas, and Walter Pater, although
quite suitable for their rebellion against Victorian patriarchy, was too close to
what was expected of women of her generation for her to find a comfortable
register in which to speak. Diana Cooper, Margot Asquith, and Nancy Mitford
lightly dished up their diaries in its frothy champagne. Virginia Woolf adapted
it from effeminate male reaction to Victorian thunder and preaching to fit the
timbre of a woman's voice. It was from Pater that Woolf learned to "write like
a woman." Rebecca West responded in eighteenth-century periods, rolling,
rational, and masculine. Nancy Cunard reacted against the style of Moore's
personal writing, while taking his iconoclastic self-making as a model. Her
journalism brings the life of the other, the suffering refugee, the conscripted
soldier, the Black prisoner of war, into the homes of readers who could not
imagine the other as human like themselves. In demystifying the alien, especially in her reporting the speech and concerns of Black soldiers, she was a
pioneer against racism in the daily press.

George Moore developed the English essay as the Impressionists developed painting. Its only object was pleasure. It was not political. It made no
moral claims. Neither does it style itself as a version of the small personal
voice of the individual against the masses. It was not a voice suited to Cunard's
purposes as a polemicist. Here she had to reach back into the Irish branches of
the family tree to fashion patriot Robert Emmett into her role model.[10]

Moore does not cast his lot with that modern mighty cast of victims
and martyrs waiting to claim our sympathy. He demands blood and circuses
and curses the education of the masses. His is a confident vocalization in
full rounded tones of what we might call the "Big Personal Voice." He speaks
as a gentleman to an audience constructed as gentlemen (ladies admitted if

they accept the rules) about questions of artistic taste. For his semi-private taste was meant to be shared with a semi-private coterie like the members of Lady Cunard's salon, where his discreet voice whispering in her ear as her own semi-private Sotheby's ensured the buying and selling of pictures. When Nancy exposed the capitalist underbelly of her mother's musical and artistic soirées with her lover Thomas Beecham, in the shockingly Surrealist pamphlet *Black Man and White Ladyship* (1931), sneering at the salon as a cover for business deals made in the art world, she did not mention George Moore as one of the players of this rich man's game. He wanted to influence public taste, and he kept faith with Wagner's genius, for example by recording his experiences on visits to Bayreuth, and fostered Manet's reputation by writing essays recalling details about the artist's methods. His role as a man of letters was to bring Wagner and Manet to the drawing rooms of English country houses, to bring French culture to the vulgar rich. In this role he was as invaluable to Lady Cunard's reputation as Hindu pundits were to the courts of the Mughal emperors.

But to her daughter, alienated from the luxury and materialism of Nevill Holt and her mother's frenzied modernization, restoring the ancient parts of the house, pitching out the dark Victorian furniture of her predecessors, expensively redecorating and electric-lighting the enormous old stone castle, George Moore was less an arbiter of taste, consulted for his artistic eye and his musical wisdom, than her only friend and walking companion among the hordes of consuming grown-ups who depleted the hostess's extravagant entertainments, eating and drinking and smoking and devouring chocolates and all the latest novels in rooms full of exotic flowers and fruit. Cunard's asceticism and her later hatred of eating (her own strong words) took root here in the house of abundance and waste that her mother built for a life of flirtation and cultural influence, where there was no love to spare for Nancy, clever but not very pretty, watching the pageant from the sidelines.

Because he was an artist, a writer, Moore was allowed to say all the wicked things Nancy wanted to say, and that lesson was not lost on her. It is Moore she remembers encouraging her reading and writing as a small child, as well as writing seriously to her as she grew up, offering detailed criticism when she began to write and publish her poems. Amused by her mind, he set her intellectual tasks, like learning the names of all the wild flowers and their times of blooming. But in her dearest memory he is associated with her introduction to sex, defending her right to read a risqué novel. Writing about sex was another thing altogether. It was over sex that the prepubescent girl and the closeted bachelor poet sealed their friendship, and sex was its subtext, forbidden sex, for thirty years.

While Lady Cunard and her guests conducted their love affairs in plain view, pig-tailed Nancy escaped from the schoolroom, and walked miles with her friend in the countryside, showing him all her secrets, the world of tramps and itinerants and farmers she had made her own, to ground herself as a person in face of the flighty moods of her mother and the hothouse atmosphere of Nevill Holt. She was as physically strong and as high-strung as the horses from her father's splendid stable that she rode in her adolescence, and grew up to become one of those unmistakable Englishwomen one sees in foreign places walking the hills and mountains with natural aplomb. She belonged outdoors and was happiest there.

Later Cunard worked outdoors when weather permitted, at home at Le Puits Carré or in cafés in Paris, in the south of France, in Spain. She did without what most people consider the ordinary comforts of home. With Norman Douglas she shared the feeling that England was *too green*—being there was like being in a salad. He mocked the remains of her love for "my darling River Nene ... The Midlands! God help me! Beets and swedes and turnips and mangle-wurzels—all that *ridiculous* agriculture—and not a feature, *not one*, in the whole landscape."[11]

Biography as Séance

It is conceivable that for Moore, the subject of the artist's sexuality might enter the semi-private writing chamber, but not that of the author—or, shall we say, in honor of the man who was satirized by his contemporaries (and the generation after) as a man who told without ever having kissed, sexual adventures of the purely fictional kind were consistent with the genre. Such was the epistemology of Moore's closet that the elaborate mask of the retired *roué* fooled no one, and he could denounce "pederasty" to Nancy Cunard while spending much of his time with homosexuals. He could giggle with her over "What do lesbians do?" when at his insistence many of the women Cunard brought to meet him in her Paris flat in the twenties were lesbians. The semi-private voice loved scandal but spoke of an intolerance or ignorance of "vice."

When Cunard pushed him on the color question, telling the reader of her shock that he has never met so much as an Indian, Moore said he could imagine going so far as meeting a yellow person, but never a Black. (As an art critic Moore wrote in an elegant vocabulary of color gradations. It was he who first raved over the white light in Manet's paintings.) As memoirist, Cunard is clearly trying to come to terms with racism and homophobia in someone she dearly loved, as well as trying to bring him out of the closet of the semi-private after his death. She talks to Moore and argues with his ghost on the pages of her memoir, semi-biography and semi-autobiography that it is, clearly wondering how she had kept up their intimacy over such a deep political divide. Her posthumous pique at his utter political incorrectness has the delightful effect of bringing him to life on the page. Arguing politics with our beloved (and stubbornly wrongheaded) dead, as a way of remembering them, is something human beings do all the time. But Nancy Cunard's two memoirs record a way of turning this talking to ourselves into a literary form.

Cunard's wonderfully honest technique as a biographer mimics not only this common practice, but it openly acts out what we seldom ever acknowledge—that the life of the other is a fiction perceived through our own lives. The reader is aware of the writer's wish to understand Moore's racism, of course, but wants even more to know the Nancy Cunard who forgave or ignored for so many years what she now finds so shocking. Her questioning mode is passed on to the reader. We start to interrogate her subject position and our own with a certain discomfort. The contemporary reader notes that Cunard's voice, the private voice of the poet and then the increasingly public voice of the protester, the editor, the journalist, speaks to men, to white men and men of color to be sure, to the comrades and the intellectuals. Missing from the range of Cunard's famous, hoarse, radical voice is a specifically female register or either an open address to women or a private register for women friends. She seldom speaks to her peers in print, though her friendships with women were deep and lasting. Perhaps all that make-up and extravagantly flamboyant jewelry was an elaborate act of "femininity as masquerade." Perhaps the voice of Nancy Cunard as a public intellectual was of necessity the authoritative voice of a man. Perhaps the voice of any woman who aspires to be a public intellectual has to be male-identified to be heard. And who could be a better teacher than a masquerading male? The writer of "white nympholepsy," a lover of women's flesh and dresses in the Impressionist mode of Manet, acts as mentor for the writer accused of "negrophilia." Growing up indulging Moore's fetish for white women's clothes of the belle époque, she imagines he will understand her fetish for images of African men.

The voice of the memoirist, calling George Moore and Norman Douglas out of their graves, insists on a man-to-man conversation with each of her evasive ghosts. They shuffle along like characters in *Waiting for Godot* as we see them shamefacedly try to answer her charges. She indicts their politics, can't understand why they didn't march for the Scottsboro Boys or fight in Spain against fascism. She forgives them, of course, all their myriad sexual sins, as they undoubtedly had to forgive hers. Transgression she understood, and in their transgressions they were all outlaws together. (She called her first volume of poems *Outlaws* before politics came to rival sex in her rebellious identity.) They do not, however, rise from the dead to comfort her.

A Midlands *Rosenkavalier*

To be heard above the brilliant remarks of the artists and wits of her mother's salon, Cunard had spent her childhood learning everything she could about history and culture, and acted as a learned foil to her mother's femininity. As she had learned about sex from the fashionable trash her mother's friends read, and she had learned about wild flowers to lure George Moore out of the house as a playmate, she built the foundation of research skills which were to last a lifetime, mastering many languages, a talent that surfaced when she began to do serious translations, and a great range of history, literature, and the history of art and music. Edward Marsh asked a friend if he knew the eleven-year-old girl: "I went to *Figaro* the other day and between the acts Nancy said in her high little squeaky toneless voice, 'The Count is exactly like George the Second. The Countess I should put a little later—about 1790.' What are children coming to?"[12] Nancy was very bright, well-educated in languages and the arts, though she deplored the weaknesses in her background. (Her feared, intellectually demanding French governess was also Vita Sackville-West's governess.) She claimed no place but the amateur's in art history, anthropology, or the history of slavery, and yet she did more research in primary documents and acquired more theory in all of these fields than most people who have earned doctorates in them. She was not witty, but she was thorough and hardworking in her raids on libraries and institutions. Here her upper-class manners and background were a big help in getting the rare books and documents she wanted. It was her mind that she used to win her mother's love and the friendship of her mother's lovers.

The voice Nancy Cunard reluctantly coaxed out of herself to write the memoir of Moore had been formed as a girl who joined her mother's lovers in the circle of courtship. Did she recognize this as she wrote herself back into that long-suppressed voice, the voice of the girl at the door of her mother's room as she prepares for one of her lovers? The bonds between the young girl and the old admirer had strengthened as others moved into the inner circle of Maud's attentions. They played their parts well in the grand opera Lady Cunard created in her life as an English Lady. The opera that the Cunards' family life, if it can be called that, suggests most strongly is *Rosenkavalier*. Nancy passionately courted her mother in the "pants role" of Octavian, while George Moore was in and out of the lady's boudoir and her intrigues like Baron Ochs. But there came a time when Nancy could no longer play her part in her mother's charades. There were too many suitors. She relinquished the role of pageboy to Lady Cunard to her dear friend, Diana Manners. And, in the manner of all good divas, she never sang the role again. But "Her Ladyship" lacked the wisdom of the Marchellin, and stayed too long with the younger generation, demanding court from Nancy's friends and cohorts, the Sitwells and the painter Alvaro Guevara as well as Diana Manners, and even Ezra Pound and Wyndham Lewis. Janet Flanner and Solita Solano recall Cunard's fear that they would meet and be taken up by her mother; she brought them to George Moore instead. Her attitude toward Yeats and Joyce was cool—they were, after all, her mother's protégés.

As the rift between mother and daughter grew wider, more public, and more melodramatic, Lady Diana shifted her role from pageboy to the princess to act the devoted daughter to her Ladyship, and so she remained until the *grande dame*'s death, and so she was treated in the will. An English opera, we'll call it, though Strauss does capture the cynicism of story, and Moore's Irish tenor adds a necessary grace-note and a little clowning as a distraction. Like the Baron, he was often a figure of fun at Nevill Holt, and Cunard recalls the laughter as a great deal of "Moore-baiting" went on at Maud's house parties. (He managed to remain on good terms with both Maud and Nancy after the breach, though he was quite upset when he learned that Maud had changed her name to Emerald.) Thomas Beecham conducts himself badly and the orchestra superbly for the most part in the Cunard family *Rosenkavalier*, but eventually he too deserted the ageing Marchellin.

Whoever heard of mother and daughter divas? Impossible. Lady Cunard wanted Octavian and Sophie too, along with all her other courtiers. She competed with her daughter and she won. One of them had to find another stage and another voice. And that was Nancy. The story has been told by all concerned as the story of Nancy's rebellion against a charming mother and an enviable life of dinners and theater and opera, trips to Paris and New York. But her mother was not only a patron of the arts—she was a fancy whore, albeit a wealthy one, a lady of fashion, as her mother had probably been before her. Lady Cunard, it seems to me more likely, pushed her daughter out of the feathered nest by annexing all her artist friends and their avant-garde movements.

With a powerful and ambitious courtesan as a role model of feminine behavior, Cunard had no refuge from English society's expectations of further discreetly scandalous liaisons in the next generation, more money, more marriages, certainly not a brilliant career, unless it was in the beds of the rich and famous. She tried studying. She tried marriage (briefly). She tried modern poetry (and with it, modern poets, including T. S. Eliot, Ezra Pound, Wyndham Lewis, Aldous Huxley, John Rodker, to name a few). She tried what one of her mother's society friends called "drink, drugs and Negroes." She had an abortion, or a miscarriage; no one knows for sure. She took up Surrealism and Surrealists. She gave up England and her Edwardian mother's false extravagant world of consumption and display. She became a Surrealist herself, although she did not count her work as a writer, publisher, and editor as of the same value as a poem by Aragon or a piece of sculpture by Brancusi. Her reputation as an "heiress," or a "patroness" of Black artists denies that she produced work of her own, and has reduced her to the role of consumer of culture she hated in her mother.

Semi-Private Parts

Cunard was attempting a belated response to Moore's earlier request that she write autobiography when she wrote GM: Memories of George Moore. The "personal" in the anti-modernist mode he meant had been abandoned along with the high modernist poetic of her years under the influence of Eliot and Pound, and the "Tragic Imagism" they encouraged in women poets. One of her greatest accomplishments as a writer was to develop the personal voice in committed journalism. (We hear this voice now from another generation of women public intellectuals in Lillian Robinson or Blanche Cook or Eunice Lipton writing in The Nation or The Women's Review of Books. Nancy Cunard has yet to be claimed as the radical reporter she was.)

Performing for her mother's attention, the young Nancy learned to attract her through her lovers. Like Salome dancing for her mother's lover, Nancy once stripped naked for Moore and then cherished his description of her back as "like a weasel"; not exactly the kind of compliment a nice English girl might expect. But then Nancy Cunard was never anyone's version of a nice English girl. Writing the memoir of Moore chastens her a bit and softens the righteous rage she has nursed so long that it twists her body in pain. She finds a route to her mother in writing with a passion she has not lost after all her years as a radical reporter, of the fashionable love of the feel of fabrics, describing for the delight of her dead mentor the dresses in her memory of her mother's boudoir. The old habits of pleasing him came back. And with them an echo of the lisping voice of the daughter of the English upper classes.

Almost all of what we now know about Nancy Cunard's life is written as the voice of the Interlocutor in the minstrel-show manuscript of her memoir as she sifts through her letters to him in the performative rather than the common nostalgic mode of memoir, trying to make sense of the dialectic between her life as a political activist and his as an ageing Irish *flâneur*. As she recounts her political adventures to the dead Irish writer out of her own letters, Nancy Cunard, the realist, the militant anti-mystical mind, makes her memoir into a *séance* to speak to George Moore's loving and maternal spirit, summoning his Irish ashes from across the water.

One might say that the writing of the text of *GM*, the memoir (I think of it as *White Man, Black Sheep*), is a companion piece to her famous 1931 *Black Man and White Ladyship*. The text's construction of Moore's character as the incarnation of whiteness, Cunard's uncanny repetition of the word *white* in relation to a certain set of feminine curves, and her deliberate retro-recall of Manet's palette for a black-and-white portrait of Moore as the ultimate *flâneur*—her child self-dressed à la Manet in little white socks and black patent shoes—allows Cunard to substitute Moore's maternal body for both her mother and her mother-country, and to forgive them both. (There is no evidence to suggest that she learned to forgive herself.)

She relives her *Rosenkavalier* days in this book, reluctantly and without much self-knowledge, and grudgingly gives the dead Moore the gift of her description of home and mother, the grounding ties of almost every woman's life, ties which she had cut forever. I see her weak autobiographical self-representations here as a last-ditch effort at racial (and national) bonding with—I will boldly enter her consciousness here—the transvestite figure of her mythical George Moore in the breast-plated costume of a Celtic Britannia, armed and maternal to be sure, but also domesticated as her own dear phallic mother. Still, I imagine, he was more approachable than her mother.

Not only rejected as a heroine or a political leader, but also simply erased from Black history by white communist (and anti-communist) historians and by the Blacks whose cause she had so eloquently espoused; remembered, if at all, by African, Latin American, Caribbean, Spanish, and Afro-American intellectuals to whom she had been comrade, friend, lover, mentor, ghost writer, editor, publicist as some kind of sex maniac, the very role in which the white capitalist press had cast her to discredit her politics, Cunard allied herself with the closeted gay expatriate male artists who were all the "England" she could stomach. Perhaps fetishizing that "whiteness" helped her come to some kind of terms with her own racial identity, the daughter in herself she was always denying.

However much Moore's semi-private mode of personal writing may be claimed as non-generative, it inspired Nancy Cunard to the only autobiographical efforts she ever made and they are notably more impersonal than her mentor's. Neither the raving emotional nor the thundering denunciative mode make their appearance here. Her prose is as demure as one might expect from a lady of quality. The current vogue for autobiography may revive interest in the very strange form of "personal literature" in which Cunard recorded her own life between the lines of unofficial biographical sketches of minor men of letters, whom she had invented as a "family," years after a bitter public denunciation of her own English upper-class connections. Feminists might read this self-closeting (mistakenly, I would think) as an extreme form of female self-sacrifice, when it might also suggest a natural move for a woman who lived in the public eye and was always traveling, as a way of keeping her personal feelings safe in a secret hiding place, the ditch of last resort where her class and national identities lay buried. Letters to Norman Douglas and George Moore were the expatriate's letters home; they the fixed points on her compass, she the traveler.

The Semi-Public Voice

If George Moore, in whose well-bred tones the modern reader hears the ring of the outmoded snobberies of another age, for nothing dates like self-congratulation, is master of the discourse of semi-privacy, the inventor of the Big Personal Voice, then Nancy Cunard acts out in that unusual register for a woman, the semi-public. She lived and worked out of suitcases in hotel rooms and bars all over the world, conducting the daily business of what one calls "private life"—eating, sex, fighting, drinking, cursing—very much in public view. Like Hemingway, she was an expert at local color in a story about war or the plight of refugees.

Where other women need only write in the "personal" voice of their semi-private letters and diaries, Cunard had stifled that voice (she was famous in life and fiction for hastily scribbled pencil notes), except when sitting safely in Ebury Street with George Moore, or on Capri with Norman Douglas and the expatriate community of upper-class sexual outlaws who were her only permanent community. (One may recapture the mood of gay Capri in the twenties in Douglas's *South Wind* or Compton Mackenzie's *Extraordinary Women*.) In such a genealogy of artists she could act "the mummer's daughter," to play on the title of one of Moore's most famous books. She could tell and "keep mum" at the same time, though she does pay tribute as an alcoholic to his brilliant portrait of a woman done in by drink. Moore might not fit her myth of him as her "real" father, but she could acknowledge his paternity by writing as his literary daughter.

It is here in her role as literary daughter to George Moore, incidentally, that I see Cunard's feminism emerge, despite her seeming diffidence about women's issues. For women of her generation, the feminist literary men of the 1880s were important mentors: Ibsen, Wilde, Shaw, and Meredith for Virginia Woolf; for Nancy Cunard the other George Moore, the George Moore who wrote as the English Zola in *Esther Waters* and *The Mummer's Wife*, the feminist in spite of himself. Here in his fiction was the politics of class (as well as gender) in which he pretended no interest. Posterity does not take him seriously, but both novels had a powerful influence on the formation of feminist consciousness in *fin-de-siècle* culture.

Expatriate internationalist that she was, Cunard could construct the slippery Irishman as a palatable version of England or "home" in a shared Celtic racial identity. Nancy Cunard, according to most accounts, kissed more than she could possibly tell, though her chasteness of demeanor in these volumes may be intended to mend the class breach opened by her life of public crusades. Writing her own story between the cracks of slender sketches recording "the lesser side" of the lives of already forgotten minor "men of genius," as Moore wrote of Whistler, where did Nancy Cunard see herself in history? In *Grand Man: Memories of Norman Douglas* and *GM: Memories of George Moore* she created a pair of male mothers as muses. Both are created as monumental figures in her own history as *les grands hommes*. At a moment in history when her own brilliance as poet, publisher, cultural critic, and radical journalist was in eclipse, she found security in an alliance with closeted asexual, homosexual, or bisexual expatriate artists who had always befriended her. They had not abandoned her in her personal tragedy of public drunkenness and awful tragic loneliness when her comrades in racial and revolutionary struggles no longer had patience for a woman who made public scenes.

The only "public" category for a woman has traditionally been as a whore or an actress. Nancy Cunard walked the streets of the cities of the world as a cosmopolitan political woman, and she sat and argued in cafés in public squares and Party congresses, organized and marched in demonstrations with those who shared her vision of racial justice. In Geneva she reported the struggle over Ethiopia. From Madrid she described the feeling of being bombed from above. Women were not only supposed to confine their energies to the inside of their homes but to stay put inside their nations. The flaunting of female radical homelessness, as in Virginia Woolf's *Three Guineas* (1938), produces a profound feeling of *uncanniness* in Freud's sense of the word, a loss of cultural bearings in those who need woman to represent a stable home/womb for the individual or the state. Some of the nervousness caused by Cunard's presence is, I suspect, at her public lack of the signs of permanent personal or national ties. She refused motherhood and her mother, denied England for France. Her bold, bony, flamboyantly dressed body announced that it was not about to be a home for anybody but herself and it was clear that even she was uncomfortable in it. Eventually she was outlawed from the cafés she had frequented in all the capitals of the world, the cafés she sang in her "Memory Blues" for Henry Crowder.

Cunard's place in the history of Black historiography and the struggle for racial freedom is lost, partly because she cannot be placed, as it were, in an established category for heroism, and Spanish Civil War history has already so diminished her role that simple restoration of her reputation is now a serious threat to an established cultural narrative in which participants and historians have invested. In the light of the left history provided by men like Stephen Spender, and more recently Valentine Cunningham, white Englishmen exclude their compatriot, her gender clearly an embarrassment, and, as her achievement goes from dim to fully faded, the historians of other nations take their cue from her compatriots.

Norman Douglas and George Moore did not share her politics. They were quite conservative in political and social matters. But in personal and sexual matters they were kind and liberal. They were eccentric in their sexuality, scandalous and disapproved of, living in exile. They accepted Cunard's rages, her "inappropriate" lovers, her need for pain, her drinking. It was in this non-judgmental world of genteel tolerance that we now recognize as a form of gay culture that the outrageous, globe-trotting, pro-Black journalist found whatever "home" she had for a large part of her life. It seems strange then to read of her activities in favor of racial justice and the Spanish Civil War in the pages of "lives" of men who had steered clear of the public commitments she made so wholeheartedly. In the privacy of the personal memoir the most public of women leaves her "personal" story in a kind of literary closet. The flamboyant self-defined Outsider inscribes her life inside the Inside, in the secret place of her racial identity as a white expatriate Briton. It is no wonder, then, that the semi-public Nancy Cunard, having lived as the ultimate *fin-de-siècle déracinée*, would write her "life" in the semi-private pages of the semi-private lives of her semi-private friends.

Mauve Declining …

Cunard's record of Moore's amusement at lesbians is undermined by naming Solita Solano, Dolly Wilde, and Janet Flanner. Was she making the memoir into a closet? If so, for whose sake? She quotes Moore's loving letter to her from 1926 insisting that she "write (her) own story," beginning with "a retrospect" and enclosing a model short story:

> When you came here you were very winning, tender and inclined to confidences, moods that are dear to me, who know that love is not stinted to three primary forms, like the colours, red, blue, and yellow… A few understand love in secondary aspects, to continue the colour comparison, purple, green and orange. Some know love in still finer stages, delicate shades of mauve, mauve fading into grey, mauve rising out of grey into rose, mauve declining from rose into blue …[13]

It is hard to refrain from reading Cunard's "wistfulness," her "color purple" of the twenties as regret for a lesbian love affair in the phrase, "mauve declining...," as Moore so delicately puts it. "Confidences!" she exclaims. "I remember about whom and why," she hints without telling.[14]

If her own love story then, well after the death of her beloved in the war and just before her famous public transracial affairs, was not to be found among the three primary forms of a "stinted" notion of what love was, where was it to be found? Of course the text does not tell. Cunard then constructs an elaborate tale of a walk in Paris with Moore in which he pointed at closed shutters to show her the scenes of his "prowesses" with women, wherein he claims to have been "a great dab at making love." She laughs at his use of the word "dab"—to me it suggests his role as a scene painter, and this scene that they create together is an unsubtle heterosexual mask (a dab/daub) in far too primary colors. But the dictionary gives *dab* as French slang for boss, and in English a sign of the expert or dab hand. Recalling this walk through the Ile St. Louis back to her flat, Cunard undoes the restoration of Moore's heterosexuality, which she at other points seems to undertake. Unable to tell her own life except in the context of someone else's, Cunard claims a special kind of "manhood" for her mentors. They become women.

Moore's figure of "mauve declining..." was also, we may assume, a figure of Maud, Lady Cunard, declining his advances, such as they were, forever recalled in his memory of her pink and gray shot-silk dress, defining his role in her circle as "finer" than that of an actual lover in his letters to her. The story of Maud and Moore seems to be a fine romance, as in the romantic Edwardian portrait by John Lavery of the pair at Nevill Holt. Spun by both parties, with hints of his fathering Nancy, Maud contributed to the legend by keeping Moore's letters from his biographer, and then destroying all but 276 of them. What she kept does nothing to deny the possibility of an affair. One cannot help feeling that this lifelong friendship provided cover for other more intense (or perhaps, forbidden) affairs for both of them. They were very close. He remarked on her "cold sensuality," the same description many ex-lovers were to give to her daughter. She was the "dear lady of [his] thoughts ... an evening fountain under embosoming trees." He signed himself "The Discoverer of Maud and Manet."[15]

Cunard learned from Moore that femininity was a masquerade, and masculinity too. Her own obsessive desire for the masculine was a mirror of his passion for the feminine. Certainly Norman Douglas's masculinity was a tragicomic masquerade for public appearance, and George Moore's masculinity was a masquerade from a belle époque operetta. Obsessed as the

Confessions is with women's looks and women's things, the message emerges that he has essentially escaped their clutches while enjoying their favors:

> For years it seemed to me impossible that women could love men. Women seemed to me beautiful and desirable—men so ugly, almost revolting. Could they touch us without revulsion of feeling, could they really desire us? I was absorbed in the life of woman—the mystery of petticoats, so different from the staidness of trousers! the rolls of hair entwined with so much art, and so much colour and perfume, so different from the bare crop; the unnaturalness of the waist in stays! plenitude of slenderness and silk, so different from the stupidity of a black tail-coat; rose feet passing under the triple ruches of rose, so different from the broad foot of the male. My love for the life of women was a life within my life; and oh, how strangely secluded and veiled! ... I loved women too much to give myself wholly to one.[16]

The private closet of the personal memoir was also the place where Nancy Cunard, who loved men so much that she could not give herself wholly to one, might atone for her denunciation of her mother as a racist in her very public *Black Man and White Ladyship*, by sharing her *faux* father's position as the eternal gentleman suitor in Lady Cunard's salon. Moore's round white body leads the estranged daughter back to her mother. By fetishizing his whiteness as the substitute mother's breast/phallus, she can recapture her childhood in a shared fantasy about her mother's dresses and, in particular, their bustles, which she disguises as indulgence in *his* outmoded tastes. She kept for many decades a pair of 1830s poke bonnets, "a prosaic one in yellow straw with red tartan ribbons, and the airiest flimsiest dream in peach-coloured cambric and gauze" that Moore had sent "to Maud and Nancy," setting the stage for Lady Cunard's appearance as a vision (to both admirer and daughter) from Boucher or Watteau, tumbling out from under her charming hat "the shining surprise of her golden hair."[17] And the memoir lingers over descriptions of

> beautiful and exciting ladies ... in sables or long fox stoles, a bunch of Parma violets pinned into the fur on the shoulder. Summer-long, in shot silk and striped taffeta they stroll laughing and chatting across the lawns. All those toilettes with their ruchings and flounces, the

veils with big, smart spots on them, the feather boas … It was a much corseted period of busts and shirt-waists, but in the early evening some of the ladies went floating through the warm atmosphere in trailing tea gowns of beige lace, of lilac, wisteria and cream-colored chiffon.[18]

In this sensuous world of feminine fabrics, recalled by the older Cunard, ill and forgotten in an old stone house in the Dordogne, it is as if we are privy to her first lessons in femininity as masquerade. The belle époque descriptions do double duty here. They recall the lost prewar golden days at Nevill Holt, and they suggest Manet's women, the subject of Moore's most gorgeous writing, while imitating unashamedly his practice of writing "white nympho-lepsy." As she writes to and for the dead Irish writer, Cunard recreates the triangular romance of her youth spent watching with the voyeur Moore her mother trying on dresses in the intimate semi-private flurry of her boudoir.

"Of course," Moore wrote, instructing Nancy on how to write in the "personal" mode, "a preface of the kind I suggest would cause that cheerless soul, T. S. Eliot, to frown."[19] And after his pronouncement about the short shelf-life of autobiography quoted at the beginning of this chapter (personal literature is the only literature), he admonishes her: "It isn't easy, and it has to be cultivated." I am not suggesting that it was easy for Nancy Cunard to speak in a personal voice. She had lived her life and written her books and articles in the public mode and at the top of her lungs. In these biographical sketches of exiled "gentlemen" she creates texts in which her own life is a subtext. Moore and Douglas serve as hosts for certain parasitical autobiographical acts.

Is Cunard performing for the only audience she felt cared? Moore had compared the "impulsive music" of her poems to the "personal passion" of Heloise, St. Teresa, and Emily Brontë, while her contemporaries found her passionless. She and Norman Douglas had spent the years of World War II in bed-sitting rooms in bomb-shelled London, working for the Free French, the odd-couple expatriates suddenly subject to a patriotism neither knew what to do with. Between men, between the lines of their expatriate intellectual lives, the English exile leaves a legacy, claims a past with no Cunard lines in it, no aristocratic blood or land. She gives herself an identity as an outlaw again, at the end of her life as she had at the beginning, so that, looking for a place to put her, we would find a radical woman intellectual, a permanently displaced person.

CHAPTER SEVEN

White Nympholepsy

George Moore, Manet, and the Modern

Artists and Models

"Once my youth moved through thy whiteness, O City," George Moore addressed the Paris of his youth in the 1870s among the Impressionist painters in 1906, "and its dreams lay down to dream in the freedom of thy fields! Years come and years go, but every year I see the city [...] in the happy exaltation of spring [...] it has come to me to think that Paris and May are one. I drive to breakfast through the white torridities of the Rue Blanche."[1] Moore conjures up the paintings of Manet and Monet, which he did so much to make famous, a French pastoral myth of green gardens and white girls, white flowers and green trees, white dresses and flowered hats, the pleasures of the country in the city, a veil of virginal and bridal white, hiding the harsh realities of European industrial life.

Like Manet and Degas, Moore moved back and forth between a respectable life and life among the artists' models and prostitutes, his "white writing," as in the above, contrasting with the dark dramas, the Zola-like novels of female degradation—*A Drama in Muslin*, *A Mummer's Wife*, and *Esther Waters* of English naturalism. There was a certain thrill to be found in comparing the dreadful lives of the models to their exquisite images made eternal and universal by the painters. The model was an actress embodying the painter's vision; the sordid scenes of her own life, off the canvas so to speak, enlivened the opera, the stage, and the naturalist novel.

George Moore called his obsession with the painters' models of the belle époque "nympholepsy." The fetish fixed on white flesh—white women nude or in white dresses, especially as they were painted by Édouard Manet. The sight of the white world of the Parisian models, dancers, actresses, and opera performers was enjoyed by men in each other's company. The rooms of their dressmakers and the restaurants they frequented were places where artists and dandies and men about town gathered. Manet and Moore were among them, feeding their own and the period's taste for the melodrama and passion of the brief lives of the *demimondaines*. Manet's violent and crude naturalism turned from painting the threatening desire of the white woman *Olympia* to "impressions" of the sunlit outdoor world which would not disturb the viewer, like *Le Linge*.

But Manet's white palette, grey at one end, yellow at the other, at the height of his powers, captures European culture at the high point of its concern with racial origins and evolution, with scientific definitions of racial purity and national identity, in a blazing celebration of whiteness that was hailed by poets and critics from Mallarmé to Baudelaire to Zola to Moore. "His paintings are light-coloured and luminous," wrote Zola, "with a concrete and tangible pallor. The light in them is white and widespread," from the "soft and blonde" street singer to his gray color harmonies expressive of "Dandy and bourgeois tones." "This 'blond' grey of Manet's will take its place beside the luminous grey of Titian, the severe Spanish grey of Ribera, the aristocratic grey of Velasquez," wrote Baudelaire, declaring that Manet had taken painting out of the shadows by refusing to paint shadows.[2] "Manet's white is the rarest," raves Moore; "he alone can endow the breast blossom that shames a peony," but, Moore makes clear, "Manet's white is mundane..."[3] His own white writing, in tune with these extremes in modernist Impressionist painting, is both mundane and excessive: "Marie Pellegrin is enshrined in my memory like a miniature in a case. I press a spring, and I see the beautifully shaped little head, the pale olive face, the dark eyes and the blue-black hair. Marie Pellegrin is really part of my own story."[4]

Moore's fictional tragi-comic opera of the Parisian world of models and artists tells a story we know well—joy and pleasure in excess, suffering and dying young, beauty corrupted, illness and impoverishment, from rags to riches and back again. "Marie Pellegrin" was the subject of a portrait by

"Octave Barrès," which Moore tells us he saw in the studio when sitting for his own portrait:[5] "The portrait was crude and violent, but so was Octave Barrès; he had painted this portrait when he was a pupil of Manet's, and he had painted it well [...]"[6] Moore is intrigued by "the thin, olive-complexioned girl with fine, delicate features and blue-black hair lying close about her head like feathers—she wore her hair as a blackbird wears his wings ... black silk dress covered with black lace, the grey pearls in her ears, and those upon her neck."[7] And he describes the painter in an "impressionist" visual vocabulary, which survived in art criticism well beyond its usefulness. Moore's painter is always bathed in a glow of blond masculinity, a knight in shining armor who rescues women from the ravages of daily life on the street into the eternal life of art: "He wore his jersey as if it were a coat of mail."[8]

He learns from Barrès in the course of sitting for his portrait that "she was the daughter of a concierge on the Boulevard Extérieur and had run away from home at fifteen to dance at the Élysée Monmartre ... But one day a Russian prince caught sight of her and built her a palace in the Champs Élysées."[9] (He had met her at Alphonsine's.) Moore describes Alphonsine's, the restaurant where gentlemen, artists, models, and prostitutes met:

> The green door in the crumbling wall opened, and I saw an under-sized woman with two cats purring about her legs; and her portrait, a life-size caricature by Octave including her cats, faced me from the whitewashed wall of the hencoop. Underneath it he had written, "*Ils viennent après le mou.*"[10]

He found the woman whose image he had been staring at in the studio:

> it was she, Marie Pellegrin, and so like her portrait that she seemed to have walked out of it, as the saying is, in black silk and white lace, her hair worn swathed about her shapely little head as in the portrait. She was her portrait, and something more, for Octave had omitted her smile, a wayward, sad little smile in keeping with her grave face...[11]

> Marie asked me if I played cards, but I excused myself, saying that I would prefer to sit and look at her; and just then a thin woman with red hair, who had arrived at the same time as Marie, and who sat next

to her at dinner, was introduced to me, and I was told that she was Marie's intimate friend, and that the two lived together whenever Marie returned to Montmartre. She was known as "La Glue"; her real name was Victorine, and she had sat for Manet's picture of Olympe, but that was years ago. The face was thinner, but I recognized the red hair and the brown eyes, small eyes set closely, reminding one of "des petits verres de cognac." Her sketchbook was being passed round, and as it came into my hands I noticed that she did not wear stays and was dressed in old grey woolen. She lit cigarette after cigarette, and leaned over Marie with her arm about her shoulder, advising her what cards to play. The game was "ecarte," and in a little while I saw that Marie was losing a great deal of money, and a little later I saw "La Glue" trying to persuade her away from the card table...[12]

They went to the "bal" at the Élysée Montmartre where she was to spend her last night before going off with a Russian prince. Moore's description is exactly like the scene in Gustave Charpentier's light "Bohemian" opera Louise.[13] Marie is presented with flowers by the dancers and crowned "la reine d'Élysée."[14] (Manon Lescaut, the queen of all the French prostitute-heroines, is destroyed by her desire to be "la reine.") The lesbian lovers dispense absinthe, cigarettes, and brandy; fireworks are arranged in her honor and two women dance a quadrille in which they kick off men's hats. Marie leaves for Russia and he hears nothing for a long while and then she is back in Paris and very ill. He goes to see her and she is in bed dying, playing cards with "a good deal of jewelry and money among the bedclothes."[15]

Marie remembers he doesn't play cards and tells him to look at Victorine's new drawings. "She has done some better ones." Victorine, "with her red hair and untidy dress," shows him her pictures, while another Marie, "une grue" (literally a crane, a slang term for a prostitute), plays cards with five women. Clementine accuses Marie of unfair dealing. Victorine Meurent, whose nickname "La Glue" means bird-lime or glue, a reference to her relationship with Marie Pellegrin,

told Clementine that she was not wanted—"qu'elle ferait bien de débarrasser les planches," a vulgar phrase which her coarse voice made seem still more vulgar [...] The women caught each other by the hair, tore at each other's faces; Marie raised herself up in bed and fell back crying.[16]

Moore listens to her laments and offers to go to her dressmaker to see that her dress for the evening's dance is delivered. She doesn't appear at the ball, but her friends are there, drinking and celebrating on her money. The next day as he is sitting next to Barres, some women come to look at Marie's portrait. They tell him that Marie was found dead on her balcony in her new dress. Why the balcony? She was watching the fireworks.[17]

In Moore's memoir of his "dead life," it is the women's dresses that come alive, and his interest in them that fascinates the reader. His role in the story of "The End of Marie Pellegrin" is to see to it that the model-prostitute, the beloved of Victorine, has her new dress delivered in time for the ball—in time actually to die a sentimental operetta heroine's death, "Louise's" death, gallantly watching the fireworks, sign of the brief and sparkling brilliance of Paris bohemian life. Cinderella doesn't get to go to the ball, but her Fairy Godmother/Godfather knows it was really the dress she wanted, to die in the masquerade of femininity that the culture and Moore's story demands.

The real life of "Marie Pellegrin," George Moore hints, is in her relationship with the ex-model and painter, the now poor and worn-out Victorine Meurent, once Manet's shocking white Olympia. Though he appears to have made up the name of Barrès the painter, readers in his own generation and the next, according to his pronouncements about "personal literature," might be expected to know who was who, and what was fictional here and what was not.[18] The modern reader is lost in a twilight of half-knowledge and suspicion. The story cannot be enjoyed as pure fiction. Neither can it be read as "real." The reader might wonder, Moore tells us, about the relationship between a story by "Paul" called "The End of Lucie Pellegrin" and

the story that I have just finished writing. How is this? the reader asks, and I answer that I undertook to write one of Paul's stories, the best he ever wrote, because when I spoke to him of Marie Pellegrin, he was surprised to hear her name was Marie; he thought it was Lucie, and then I learnt that he had never been to Alphonsine's, and had told her story as he had picked it up from the women who turned into the Rat Mort at midnight for *soupe a la oignon*.[19]

This postmodern slide from Marie to Lucie, from one author to another, in search of some dubious authenticity, some fit between life and fiction, asks us to question who "owns" a story, never acknowledging that the model has any claim to her own story or to her life in a painting. The model is as dead as a *nature mort* while her authors quarrel over her dead body. The reader becomes a member of the chorus of women mourning Marie at the studio of the painter, telling the story of her gallantry to the crowd at the Rat Mort.

How do we square what we may now read in one sense as a lesbian love story with Nancy Cunard's memories of Moore's coyness about her lesbian friends and his curiosity about their sex lives? What about the sordid scene, a mockery of the ending of *La Bohème*, Mimi's tragic tubercular, romantically triumphant—and purifying—death, in which Marie's deathbed is scattered with money and jewels, as the women gamble and fight, scratching each other's faces, pulling hair? Is the Irishman in Paris learning to tell a story in the naturalist technique of Zola? In the *Confessions* Moore remembers visiting the writer whose entrance hall was lined with Japanese prints of figures engaged in "furious fornication." The technique of Zola is graphic. What is it about "The End of Marie Pellegrin" that makes it part of George Moore's own story? Is it the question it raises about identity as an artist and identity as a model?

Twice in the story the narrator is asked by Marie, the model, to look at her lover's new pictures. He takes the portfolio, but does not comment on the contents, as he does so eloquently on the paintings of Octave Barrès. He can only comment on her looks, insofar as they still resemble her "real" life in Manet's portrait of Olympia. What he sees instead of her paintings is her body—she is a thin woman with red hair and small brown eyes set closely together like little glasses of cognac. The cognac implies an alcoholic demise for Meurent, a myth which took generations to dispel. And the sequel to Olympia, the painting, is Moore's writing a debauched deathbed scene: a crowd of coarse women curse and fight and gamble over the dying body of the model Marie Pellegrin, in a jumble of money, cards, and jewels. The mind's eye recalls *Olympia*. The bold *regard*, the taking up of the painter's brush and the painter's prerogative of sex with his model leads to death in a den of lesbian iniquity.

Was Victorine with Marie when she died, we want to know? Or was she with the survivors, drinking and dancing at the ball? Was "Marie" a real woman? If the story is meant to work in the mode of Zola, the naturalist writer's observation that Victorine looks old and does not wear stays with her old woolen clothes is a comment on the capacity of women to protect each other as life partners or to act as painter and model. Victorine Meurent's canvases deserve less comment than those of one of Manet's students. Marie's story remains in a locket. Moore touches a spring and she appears before him. His memory contains a miniature of the model. Is it by Manet or his student Barrès, or, perhaps, by Victorine Meurent? Is Moore rewriting the story of the Medusa? The model is punished for looking back so boldly at the viewer of *Olympia*. Has her look as a painter corrupted and killed her model?

But there is something more disturbing in "The Story of Marie Pellegrin." It is also a cautionary tale about woman's desire to be an artist and her punishment for wanting to usurp man's place as the "only looker" and interpreter of the world. Olympia, the artist's model who breaks the rules of the gaze by looking back at the viewer of her nakedness, gets up from Manet's picture and puts on a painter's smock. The emancipated white woman chooses as her model the dark Marie, the little blackbird, who lives as a prostitute and gambles away her earnings. Victorine Meurent, the transgressor, suffers the sordid death of her model and lover. Her work as an artist goes unrecognized. The only thing that survives is an image of the olive-skinned Marie in a painting by "Manet's student," Octave Barrès. The narrator tells us she *is* the painting. The model has no life except in the image the male artists makes of her. Once Manet had transformed Victorine into Olympia, she was bound to the role forever.[20] He is determined to associate the woman artist with the death of her subject, to say that a woman can never bring another woman to life.

But the situation becomes even more complicated if we think of George Moore as the model for three paintings by Manet. This is a story about what happens to the model when the painter has moved on. Does Moore see himself as Marie, subject to the fate of one who "sits" for the artist, ending in debauchery, significantly with members of the same sex? He could not resist "the finely cut face," "the closely-cut blonde beard," "the acquiline nose, the clear grey eyes, the decisive voice, the remarkable comeliness of the well-knit figure, scrupulously but simply dressed," that memorable evening when Manet spoke to him in the Nouvelle Athènes café.[21] He was attracted by the painter's looks, confessing that as an art student he had mocked Manet's work. Now that he has met him, sat for him, become the subject of his painting, known what it means to play the role of the model, to be subject to the discipline of the brush, he bursts out with the declaration that "in Manet there is nothing but good painting."[22]

But the role of the model cannot be made heroic for white masculinity. Marie gets her dress and dies. George Moore will go to the dressmaker for her. He will describe the dress he cannot wear. So Moore names himself "the discoverer of Manet," baptizing himself into the role of the critic. He will not be the last of the type—the critic as frustrated cross-dresser. He says that Olympia looks "constipated," that "she might be an illustration for Baudelaire's Les Fleurs du Mal"; yet he has to admit that Rubens and Titian would stop to admire this picture. Olympia is a crude picture, with its "angular, presumptuous and obvious drawing, harsh in its limits and hollow within, the head a sort of convulsive abridgement, the hand void, and the fingers too, if we seek their articulations…"[23] but the pale yellow tones and the Black woman set off "this light of love" to perfection in the only symbolic painting Manet has ever painted:

> [I]n Olympe we find Manet departing from the individual to the universal. The red-headed woman who used to dine at the Ratmort does not lie on a modern bed but on the couch of all time; and she raises herself from among her cushions, setting forth her somewhat meagre nudity as arrogantly and with the same calm certitude of her sovereignty as the eternal Venus whose prey is the flesh of all men born.[24]

A thin, naked redhead was not to Moore's taste. He much preferred one of Manet's signature studies of girls in white dresses. The portrait of Morisot sends him into raptures:

> Never did a white dress play so important or indeed so charming a part in a picture. The dress is the picture—this common white dress, with black spots, *une robe a poix, une pette confection de soixante cinq francs* […] A lady in a white dress with black spots, sitting on a red sofa, a dark chocolate red in the subdued light of her own quiet prosaic apartement […] How well the woman's body is in the dress! there is the bosom, the waist, the hips, the knees, and the white stockinged foot in the low shoe, coming from out the dress.[25]

Moore has created Berthe Morisot in words as Manet did in painting. She is not a painter but a woman, a flirtatious woman in an ordinary dress in an ordinary flat. For her, femininity is not a masquerade, the conversation between men seems to say. This flirt is not a threat. The white stockinged foot peeping out from under the frivolous dress in its revealing shoe displaces any thought of the artist's hand wielding a brush. In naming the parts of Morisot's body as they are revealed by the dress, Moore confirms his claim to the extreme importance of this particular white dress in the history of art. He is congratulating Manet on his ability to banish the thought of serious work from the image of the woman painter. However, Moore was first attracted to Manet by his looks, his extraordinary "comeliness." It seems, however, that one can either be a woman or an artist.[26]

Could one write in this kind of critical voice about the portrait of George Moore? When the 1879 portrait was exhibited in the gallery of La Vie Moderne in 1880, it was ridiculed as a caricature and called the "Dandy of the Batignolles." As he had captured Berthe Morisot in a flirtatious foot and Olympia in a pair of brown eyes like glasses of cognac, Manet renders his friend Moore in a pair of sweet, red, strawberry-colored lips, exposing his weakness, his vulnerability, and the "femininity" that he confesses to in his memoirs. In the catalogue to the 1909 "Homage to Manet" show in Manchester, Moore's final tribute to Manet was to place him in the ranks of those opposed to censorship: "Manet is a sort of Whitman in paint..." He was "unashamed."[27] For the gala party in honor of the opening of a play based on Zola's L'Assommoir, the young dandy writes in Moore's Impressions and Opinions: "Manet had persuaded me to go to the Bal de l'Assommoir dressed as a Parisian workman, for he enjoyed incongruities and the blouse and the casquette, with my appearance and my accent, appealed to his imagination": masculinity as masquerade.[28]

Louisine Havemeyer tells the story of how Mary Cassatt brought her to see, and then to buy, the portrait of George Moore in Paris. It was the object of much discussion and gossip by her guests when she hung it. She was told that it was considered to be "a huge joke on George Moore" that Manet had seen through him to produce a masterpiece "as penetrating as Velasquez: "There was nothing upon the canvas but just the body and soul of George Moore laid bare, divested of all of his self-complacency, of all his effort to produce effect [...] No one ever had such hair."[29] The collector is amused by the joke on the critic. Since he sold it to disown it, she says, and she bought it and gave it to the Metropolitan Museum, "it is forever on view." George Moore *is* his portrait in the way he claims Manet's women models are their portraits, says the collector. "Would the portrait live through George Moore or George Moore through the portrait?" she asks shrewdly. Would it be George Moore's Manet or Manet's George Moore?[30]

Nancy Cunard's decision not to include this portrait of Moore in her memoir is part of this struggle over reputation and representation, which is what Moore's memoirs and stories of artists and models are about. Cunard, for her own purposes as well as for the sake of Moore's reputation, is invested in Moore's masculinity. She removes him from the ignominious position of being subject to Manet as his model by dismissing the picture and replacing it with a later study of the dignified man of letters by an Irish woman artist. Moore is now the owner of Manet's study of the model Alice Lecouvey as a *modèle* for *Le Linge*, the Manet she reproduces in the text and uses to accomplish a reconciliation with her mother, to whom he left the painting, by reading Moore as her mother in the maternal model's exposed breast. Manet's Moore is in another country. Moore's Manet is not one of the painter's masterpieces, but the womanliness of the model is no masquerade.

This cultural displacement, erasing the effeminate image of Manet's Moore and replacing it with Moore's Manet—the sketch or preliminary painting of a laughing, naked model with her hair pinned up, who will appear in *Le Linge* changed utterly, dressed in a smock, domesticated, her face hidden by a poke bonnet, washing small linen with a child holding on to her bucket in a suburban garden—is what I mean by the project of white nostalgia. Belle époque Paris—city of glorious dresses, *flâneurs*, and dandies, the opera, laundresses and ironers, models, painters, and prostitutes—is turned into the green world of a France of "family values," a place, perhaps, to symbolize home during intense colonial expansion. Manet paints a decorous, featureless mother and child washing in a garden full of sunflowers, a quiet, orderly, sunlit, white world for the French soldier to imagine while wandering in the heart of darkness. The scene of washing has been moved from indoors, in the steaming laundries of the city of Paris, crowded with workers, its half-naked washerwomen and *blanchisseuses* painted by Degas especially, forced into prostitution by low wages. Manet was painting a woman of that class demurely enjoying her own housework in her own garden. I suspect he is painting the hope of the bourgeoisie that the working-class women and their comrades in the Commune will give up the common political struggle when they have homes of their own. The fierce women of the Paris Commune are the repressed element in Manet's paintings. They are not part of the discourse of white nympholepsy. But his little laundress is even less of a nymph. The change of subject in this painting is very radical, for it suppresses both work and sex. French dirty linen will no longer be washed in public, but hung privately on a line in the garden by submissive young women dressed in blue cotton.

The erotic maternal of the white woman's breast is part of the past of white nympholepsy, a sketch that Manet kept for himself. It was bought by Moore when Manet died. This portrait Cunard can worship with offerings of wild flowers; she is an icon of another lustier France in their common past for Manet and Moore, their shared white nympholepsy, and for her, the "*torsenuo*" of Alice Lecouvey is an icon of a robust and free "mother country," another England, another mother.

Decorating a Ditch

In *GM: Memories of George Moore* Nancy Cunard tells of taking the visiting Irish writer away from the stately castle of her birth to her secret hiding place as a child of nine or ten. Doubtless one could make a great deal of the daughter of Nevill Holt making her private home in a ditch, foreshadowing Cunard's chosen posture of belligerent homelessness, marking her difference from the "natural" domestic behavior of other women. Her hated mother, she admits, "had a genius for beautifying" and was always moving the furniture, filling rooms with flowers, "creating, transforming, humanizing [...] always at concert-pitch."[31] Lady Cunard's salons were decorated for the leisurely semi-public consumption of art, music, and literature, along with food and sex. Her drawing rooms and her dining rooms at Nevill Holt and in Grosvenor Square encouraged the seduction of artists by rich patrons in an excess of comfort. On her sumptuous sofas, under her glamorous chandeliers, the twentieth-century British moneyed classes, mixed with some Europeans of title and rich Americans, could painlessly consume high culture from late nineteenth-century France or Germany, Wagner and the Impressionists, already guaranteed to become classics and certified by critics like George Moore and conductors like Sir Thomas Beecham.

Nancy wanted her own home from the time she was a small child. And no wonder. Nevill Holt was full of her mother's friends coming and going, and Maud was always "moving the furniture"; and, once she finished, she left it. She spent a fortune redecorating whatever homeliness was left in the old buildings. There was a lot of money in Nancy's mother's world. But there was no stability. Maud Cunard left her husband and home and discreetly set up a London salon with her lover, Thomas Beecham, depriving Nancy of father and the outdoor freedoms of home—as well as herself—and sending her off to be educated in classes in London, then Munich, and finished in Paris. While her mother was "humanizing" away the grandeur and discomfort of the old castle, her daughter was learning to despise the domestic world and the domesticating instinct supposedly characteristic of women.

Little Nancy invited George Moore into her tree house, to share a bottle full of nuts. A mile and a quarter from Holt on the road to Drayton at the top of a steep hill, she shared with her grown-up friend the ditches that so attracted her, where "the land falls away on one side in a great, rolling expanse, a gigantic flank tufted with gorse bushes."[32] She showed him her secret hide-away in a "thickly overhung" hollow in a ditch. He wondered why the odd child wanted such a refuge and accepted her reply that she needed to make things of her own. She wanted to be a wild thing and she needed a wild place in which to be and to make a life and an art for herself, something animal and vegetable, untamed and unframed. Here we see her inventing a space for herself outside of what she felt was the forbidding world of strict govern-esses and her role as hostess in miniature at Holt, where she showed people to their rooms and around the great house with its many wings, discoursing like a museum guide on the history it held. Her "own" house was in a field, and she filled the vases in her mother's guest rooms with branches of trees, wild flowers, and field grasses, her "wild" answer to the orchids and hothouse blooms in the drawing rooms. In the memoir she recites the names of wild flowers from the English Midlands and two landscapes in France as a litany, invoking the blonde radiance of Moore and Maud Cunard at her altar to childhood:

> slender flowering branches of March ... cornelian cherry, pussy-willow and Japanese quince—note how they blend and converse with the blue-green-grey brushstrokes at the bottom of the portrait. Then see this nude, unfinished torso, with tip-tilted nose and round, bright eyes, surmounted by a fringe with a great twist of hair rolled high atop the head, next to a sheaf of French flowers—willow herb and meadowsweet from the stream's edge. And again [...] hips and

haws and spiralling briony curled round its fire red berries from the
Quercy hedgerows [...] the model is nearly alive amid the passing
fronds and festoons [...] now in a pale pinewood frame, the *Etude* is
a dispenser of light. "Oh! sa blondeur!" I say when I open the door
and the whole of my simple country room seems lit by the picture
and I am wishing that Manet and Moore were here to see.[33]

George Moore interfered with the schoolroom too. He actually paid
attention to the girl as a person. In "a paroxysm of indignation" over her being
forced to learn the answers to questions like "What was Leeds famous for?," he
engaged the governess in discussion of Barres's *Les Déracinés* or the meaning
of *Thus Spake Zarathustra*. Nancy Cunard was to grow up to become one of
Maurice Barrès's rootless modern intellectuals (as Moore himself was). If his
painter in the story is based on the figure of the French writer (and right-wing
activist) Barrès, are his portraits of Marie Pellegrin and George Moore to be
read as studies of uprooted cultural misfits, *déracinés*?

"But a house must have contents," Cunard writes of furnishing her ditch,

her "harmless fancy," and these I thought of as "works of art": some
oddly curved root, a stick stripped of its bark, the wood gleaming
with polishing, a few of those fierce sea-green flints stacked by the
road, a beautiful shard of pottery, a small blue, empty medicine
bottle picked up unseen.[34]

So began the work of the Dadaists, Man Ray, and Marcel Duchamp, later to
become her friends, in just such delight in ordinary objects, their shapes and
surfaces bringing a different sort of pleasure than Lady Cunard's remodeling
of gloomy old hunting lodges. Cunard was gifted at using found objects to
grace a space. Her friends tell of full pockets carrying treasures found on
long tramps in hills and woods and fields with Cunard at any age, and her
delighted arrangement of her finds. Part of her love for African objects came
from seeing this purity of natural material and line in ivory, stone, or wood.
Bold sculpture and bright fragments of glass and pottery.

Traveling in England in the fifties, gypsy Nancy would unpack her
portable typewriter and stretch out a piece of African cloth, on which she
set up her altar, her Benin ivory bracelets and some bronzes for "continuity."
Visiting Anthony Thorne in Hungerford in Berkshire, she went for long walks

in "that curious gait of hers, light and springy, the knees flexing easily, rhythmically," like the women he had known in Haiti; "in her chequered cotton
dresses Nancy was sometimes a Negress in all but colour."[35]

Cunard was often to be found by her English friends prowling like a cat
around the local dump, salvaging treasures from the ashes, including, once,
some wildly distorted opalescent bottles, limp like Dalí's molten watches, which
delighted her as much as the blue chemist's bottle she had treasured as a child.[36]
With Charles Burkhart, her young American friend, she rummaged about in
antique shops and provincial junkyards, celebrating their finds with a *grand
vernissage* in their hotel rooms in the evenings on "Nancy's silk squares, a cup
made of horn, a *papier-mâché* snuff box, a model of a pyramid, a ruler made
of various marbles, wooden beads from the South Seas."[37] Sylvia Townsend
Warner remembers her walking over the Downs in Dorset in 1944, "coming
back with such loads of flints in her coat-pockets that silhouetted on a skyline
her slender person gave the impression that panniers had been fastened on a
cheetah."[38] Trust Warner to find an elegant way to describe the rag-picker Nancy
had longed to be as a child, and had eventually, uncannily, become. She would
scrub the flints with a nailbrush, spend hours polishing them and spread them
out for "magpie delighting," that Warner thought "one of her prettiest charms."[39]
She collected beads and shells and "small nonsenses" and made little bags to
keep them in. Her letters to Valentine Ackland, who kept an antique shop, are
full of passionate buying and selling of their little finds, two poets and collectors
amusing each other. When Ackland gave her some mother-of-pearl fish counters in 1953, she responded with a poem, "A Nineteen of Pisces."

Nevill Holt: Theatre of War

Nancy Cunard's ideal "hermitage" was spare, clean-lined, and modernist in
style, and it began in reaction to the Edwardian luxuries of Lady Cunard's
Nevill Holt, with its new paintings, its velvets and silks replacing the dark
Victorian furnishings of the feudal hunting lodge. As her mother filled the
old hall with the warm whites and yellows of French Impressionism, Nancy,
budding Surrealist that she was, reacted violently against the accumulated
history of art, at the same time as she mastered both the details and the names,
dates, schools, and fashions of that history as part of her education in taste,
museum haunting, and gallery going all over Europe and America with her
spendthrift mother.

Nancy was detached from Lady Cunard's remodeling of the estate, except for its historical features, remembering four types of armor in the hall, which she was instructed to inform guests had still been in use in the time of Henry VIII. "A great tapestry concealed a staircase between two of them [men in armor] Cain fleeing from the wrath of God and Abel tumbled at his feet."[40] Cunard says that Nevill Holt cannot rightly be called a castle, but to her it was a castle, and she reproduced the ruined castle as her ideal home twice in her life, converting an old stone house in Normandy, and, after it was pillaged in the war, another "bare ruined choir" in the Dordogne. Both were notable for their lack of the comforts of home—scant of furniture, her mother's domain, isolated, open to nature, and very, very old. Nancy Cunard revelled in the *unheimlich* and the inhospitable. She preferred, like the Surrealists, the uncanny, finding her odd self at home in the strange, the savage, the prehistoric.

She imagined Nevill Holt empty, except for the tapestry and some "smoke brown paintings high up near the roof, possibly the Wars of the Gods and Giants, GM and I said, heavy limbs tusseling upside down in all directions."[41] The castle had a tower from the age of King John and it was there that her father, Sir Bache Cunard, hid from the social whirl below and Lady Cunard's entertainments. He spent his time out of doors, riding, hunting, and, inside, he devoted himself as an artisan to the craft of ironwork, rooting himself in labor as his ancestors had done, the shipbuilders who founded the Cunard Line. This love for a work of one's own he bequeathed to his daughter, who floundered in her mother's world of operas and dinners and dresses and dancing, hit bottom in utter despair and debauchery, and then renewed her spirit in dedication to work. Her father spent a lot of his time in the garden, working on his famous topiary garden of elaborately clipped and shaped hedges. They were perhaps more responsive to this discipline of their natural tendency to grow wild than either his wife or his daughter. Maud responded only to the lavishness of the hothouse and was infuriated by the sight of Sir Bache's homely but vulgar plea "Come Into the Garden, Maud" spelled out in horseshoes on the garden gate. Nancy stuck to her wild flowers.

There were graceful oriel windows from the fifteenth century in the oldest stone parts of the house, which Cunard loved. From its origin as a royal hunting lodge, Nevill Holt had grown into a museum of warfare from other ages, with outcroppings of living quarters added on over the centuries. Instead of a home, one might say that the young Nancy Cunard grew up in a theater of war. Weapons, men in armor, huge scenes of slaughter and killing on a grand scale, among the gods, and on the human, biblical *family* scale, in the tapestry of Cain killing Abel—these were the images that shaped her childhood imagination.

All of Cunard's instincts were against war. Most of her generation of young men were wiped out by World War I, and the horrors of the Spanish Civil War and World War II were at the moral and political center of her life. She did identify with Cain when she named herself and her early volume of poetry *Outlaws*, as the outcast from the family, the wanderer in the desert. As the epitome of the undutiful daughter, she was seen by most people in the class from which she came as if she bore the mark of Cain on her forehead, a psychic scar from her terrible public battle with her mother, fought on as epic a scale as in the old tapestries, a mental and psychological version of the Holt paintings' fleshly struggle. The battle between Nancy Cunard and Lady Cunard was an Old Testament tale, or a Greek tragedy. The figures of mother and daughter were larger than life and the issues at stake were the status of white European culture and woman's role in the salons and great houses where this tradition was fed, groomed, and maintained. They cast enormous shadows on the old castle walls as they struggled in public, Nancy choosing the ditch and the sticks and stones of African cultures, the ancient ritual objects and ivory carvings over the paintings, furniture, and tapestries of her European heritage. To Lady Cunard it must have seemed as if all the suppressed Irish colonial ghosts from her past were rising up in her demon daughter's embrace of the Black, the East, the Other, the prehistoric.

Decorating a ditch was about as far as Nancy Cunard ever got in the way of serious housekeeping, though she furnished Le Puits Carré in Normandy with a stunning collection of African art and ivories, oddly set against paintings and sculptures by her Surrealist friends and great prehistoric stones from the Easter Islands. It is certainly part of her charm that her lovers recall the hideous inconvenience of houses which were constructed around the printing press on which she printed the first thirty *Cantos* of her old lover, Ezra Pound, and other modernist works. Henry Crowder's huffiness at the odd arrangements of her house in Reanville, so that one had to go through all the bedrooms to get to the kitchen (and he had to suffer the indignity of acknowledging the visits of another lover under his nose), is only one way of responding to Cunard's famous inability to generate coziness.

She had grown up a good deal outdoors, riding and hunting with her father at "Slawston and Stockerston, Horninghold, Warley Wood, Beaumont Chase, Stoke End, Cranoe," the place names which enchanted George Moore, and her memoir *GM* is as much about the countryside as it is about Nevill Holt. She told Moore how she loved

> the tramps that came by on the road under the terrace generally at sunset, a bottle and a red wipe sticking out of their pockets—generally dirty, slouchy men with stubbly chins and anger in their eyes. Those tramps excited me and I told G.M. I wanted to run away and be a vagabond.[42]

By the time she wrote this, she could have been taken for the tramp's companion, bottle in hand and scarf around her head, wandering the fields and mountains of the Dordogne and the southern coast of France. She was a great rider and a great walker, exhausting her friends as she explored new terrain, and always on the move. And she remained attracted by dirty working men as boon companions and drinking comrades throughout her life. They were part of Nevill Holt's "forbidden" pleasures. Apparently other upper-class English girls shared the same desire for dirt, as Nancy found much later when her friend Valentine Ackland confessed to the same feelings, and even sent her a story she had written on this peculiar theme.

Cunard's identification with the anger in the eyes of the homeless men lasted a lifetime, and she was always ready to fight for the rights of the downtrodden. Where did her fearlessness come from, her amazing physical and mental courage?

White Father

Nancy Cunard's George Moore is recalled as "an oval white balloon"[43] (her mother's toy or plaything?), a frivolous and available breast, caught in the glare of her childhood's racialized gaze. "[V]ery nice he looked in the narrow, low-ceilinged room, the candle-light all about his whiteness,"[44] she writes of him coming to dinner in her Paris flat, visualizing him set off by a collection of his books, and commenting on the fact that as an art critic he had noticed Manet and Berthe Morisot's use of white paint. She writes of his skin and hair color as an identity and part of her own rejected (racial and national) kinship:

> Ah, that pair of pale eyes on the right of me, facing my own pale eyes when we turned to each other—a "consanguinity" between us because of the Celts and Ireland. At times the mystery of him, the sudden tenderness I felt over his age and whiteness, the great admiration in me for his beautiful "composing" would ... well, that is a sentence that I cannot finish.[45]

She remembered him playing with a large cat called Sarky, "a gorgeous tom [...] rolling in and out of his arms ecstatically," both large and handsome. Moore was Cunard's own personal *grand homme*, an embodiment of European white manhood she could stomach, "G.M. about whom there seemed a sort of frothy white contour, the oval now entirely perfected."[46] For most of her life he advised her to write and rewrite, happy to play the nourishing breast to her starved aesthetic self, Nancy Cunard the modernist poet.

When she published one of Moore's stories, hand-setting the type herself at the Hours Press, he suggested that she write a memoir of her childhood at Nevill Holt as a preface. It is this call that she answers in this memoir, her only record of that privileged, but for her lonely, time, seen through the eyes of Moore, the artist as a gentleman always curious about women and sex, as he describes himself. Seeing her mother's beauty through his eyes and writing about her corsets and elegant dresses, Cunard recalls giving a Christmas dinner for twelve for him "in the upstairs room at the Rotonde" in Paris in the twenties with Brancusi, Dolly Wilde, Tristan Tzara, Iris Tree, Mary Reynolds, and Nina Hamnett, and placing him between two young women deliberately dressed to recall certain paintings and expected to flirt with him during dinner.[47] She was staging with her friends re-enactments of the scenes in her mother's boudoir and Manet's paintings as a form, we can only assume, of *femme camp*.

Moore imagines she was indulging her own fantasies when she recalls

> the singer and *diseuse* Yvonne Georges, with her Eton crop and immense, expressive eyes, and Clotilde Vail, whose long golden hair could be flung to the ground with a single shake [...] Both had dressed themselves to perfection for him [...] One looked like a

> Manet in black and white and something vaguely pink that nestled
> or floated; the other, in blue and green with a touch of yellow was a
> Renoir come to life.[48]

She then imagines him playing "tangle-toe" under the table: "The gentle pressure of a small foot in black velvet on his own, the *soupçon* of a golden slipper feeling its way [...] From which would it have come more acceptably? Who can tell, for both of them played up to him with great brilliance [...],"[49] Cunard says, recalling Moore's notice of the seductiveness of the white stockinged foot in Manet's portrait of Berthe Morisot. What she recalls most vividly is the fall of Clothilde's gorgeous, Gothic, long blonde hair from the one pin which held it up—obviously a reminder of the *fall* of her mother's hair from its period hat, all envisioned through the art critic who "discovered" Manet. "Sa Blondeur!," her exclamation at the sight of the Manet painting left to her at her mother's death, is a cry for her mother and her lost childhood, and for the Celtic racial kinship she had renounced politically.

Cunard describes Moore's body as if it were the national body of Ireland, bathed in the white light of a pure racial type. The whiteness of his body means home and mother to her, mother-country (a little Ireland in Leicestershire), and her own lost innocence and youth. She participates in the same cultural discourse of white nostalgia and white anxiety, the anxiety of empire we might call it, when she uses her talent as a writer and the European rhetoric of radiance to paint him with the same luminescent halo that he used to celebrate Manet's painting, pointing out how it bathes the white body in light.

Now we may ask different questions about the writer and the painter and their celebrations of whiteness at the end of the nineteenth century. And we may wonder why this rhetoric returns when it does to the radical journalist and polemical poet who Nancy Cunard had become. Manet's idealization of a certain type of white femininity and Moore's publicizing the point articulate a European cultural moment when the male gaze was at the height of its proprietary powers. Manet, in *Olympia*, also records the moment when the model looks back at the painter, when the woman boldly looks back at the man who looks at her. That look, Olympia's look, is the look Nancy Cunard wore into the twentieth century. It is the look of a woman who knows her own desires, whose cold boyish sensuality is set off by the maternal reproductive body of her Black servant. This look claims intellectual equality with the painter and the viewer, as Cunard herself did in the famous photographs. Can we read Olympia's unnaturally flat white body as the body of the emancipated European woman? She appears just as Orientalism brings softer, more submissive female bodies of color into the purview of European art. If the picture is usually read as if the Black woman and the black cat are there to set off the odalisque's sexuality, then I suggest we may begin to re-read it as directing the European male gaze to the Black servant's comforting maternal and reproductive sexuality, if that masculinity is intimidated by lack of submission in Olympia's eyes.

White Nympholepsy

The golden glow of the man-about-town in Manet's self-portraits is repeated in the more effeminate face of the portraits of his friend George Moore as a dandy in the 1870s. They are a pair of not-quite-matched sunflower-golden gentlemen-artists in the golden age of bohemian Paris. Manet pays particular attention to his friend's soft and shiny red lips, and something more is betrayed there than the source of the Irish writer's gifted talk. In *Confessions of a Young Man* Moore claims Manet as an Englishman: "Perhaps it was his dress—his clean-cut clothes and figure. That figure! Those square shoulders that swaggered as he went across a room, and the thin waist; and that face, the beard and nose satyr-like shall I say?"[50] The *Confessions* moves from the tale of Moore's first fascination with a "great blond man," an English painter, to other great blond French painters, to his friendship with Manet, the blondest and greatest of them all. He gives up painting for reading and then takes up writing. His narrative is about his education in the observation of women and their clothes, their dazzling white dresses and their exquisite satin slippers. He is not alone with the women and their dresses. He is often in the company of men. The scene is Paris, out of doors. White girls in white dresses. An Impressionist blaze of white light, golden hair a Wagnerian motif of mythical Arayan racial purity. The text bathes his figures in a golden light just as Impressionist paintings do. It is not a coincidence that white writing and white painting should flood Europe at the height of colonialism. Whiteness is the subject of Manet's paintings, the white female body as the continent of culture, Europa. Moore's memoir parades all the clichés about whiteness in a kind of grand display, a foamy fireworks: the odor of gardenias, white kid gloves, snow and lilies, the white glory of Seraphita, milky skin and white cats, white satin dresses and diamonds on waxy bosoms, white fingers playing the Moonlight Sonata on the piano, pearls, white doves, naked youths riding white horses, white northern women with their pure spiritual eyes, the keen blonde passion of poetry … (I simply quote the obvious here).

Moore celebrates the flesh of white women and calls his affliction "nympholepsy"; he says, "I am feminine, morbid, perverse…"[51] "White nympholepsy" we might call the obsession shared by Manet and expressed in his painting, as it is expressed in Moore's *Confessions* and a great deal of other "white writing" in this period. The shared pleasures of "white nympholepsy" are perhaps caught in Manet's portraits of a fellow *flâneur*. Cunard did not like these portraits of her beloved friend in his youth. She thought Manet made him look "much older than his twenty-to-thirty years," "a tall, thin, gangling man," with his face lost in a mass of fair hair.[52] As Victorine Meurent became Olympia when Manet painted her, George Moore became the ultimate dandy, object of the male gaze as well, effeminate, as pale and weak as Olympia is bold and independent, the white male on the wane. He loved posing for Manet:

> Being a fresh-complexioned, fair-haired young man, the type most suitable to Manet's palette, he at once asked me to sit … The portrait did not come right but it gave me every opportunity of studying Manet's method of painting. Strictly speaking, he had no method; painting with him was a pure instinct … the color of my hair never gave me a thought until Manet began to paint it. Then the blonde gold that came up under his brush filled me with admiration … he painted it again and again; every time it came out brighter and fresher every time … Ah! that marvellous hand, those thick fingers holding the brush so firmly—somewhat heavily; how malleable, how obedient that most rebellious material oil-colour, was to his touch. He did with it what he liked … and never did this mysterious power which produces what artists know as "quality" exist in greater abundance in any fingers than it did in the slow thick fingers of Édouard Manet […][53]

Victorine Meurent must have studied those thick fingers too, and their ability to bring his whites and golds up under his brush. She left the model's couch to stand in his place at the easel. George Moore gave up painting. He was better at modeling, better at being looked at than at looking, except when it came to word-painting, and there his whites and golds come up under the pen as brightly as Édouard Manet's. They shared an interest in *commedia del arte*, costume, and the figure of Polichinelle. The period's love for women's clothes, as Bataille says, is evident in Manet's interest, shared by Proust. Stephane Mallarmé wrote a fashion column under the name of "Miss Satin."[54] The dress was the dandy's text. Manet painted it. Berthe Morisot, to the envy of both Manet and Moore, painted the dress and wore it. Moore wrote the text of the dress in the form of the personal essay, inventing an Impressionist style for writing.

Dirty Linen

The opening passage of her memoir of Moore describes different ways in which Nancy Cunard sets off with local wild flowers in France and in England Moore's painting, Manet's *Étude pour Le Linge*, which is now hers, thinking of the model Alice Lecouvey and of Moore's role in the making of Manet's reputation. Her meditation is like that of Eunice Lipton's *Alias Olympia* in the brilliant self-revelation which begins in the search for the life of the model for another of Manet's paintings, *Olympia*—"Remember him,' says his Manet, although I do not need Alice Lecouvey to tell me that..."[55] Lipton's pained search for her mother in *Alias Olympia* is uncannily like Cunard's in *Memories of George Moore*.

The painting inspires description and Cunard's book creates an unforgettable portrait of George Moore as a gorgeous Impressionist breast. Sarah Harrison's portrait of Moore, reproduced at the beginning of the book, is followed by a reproduction of a study of the *modèle* for *Le Linge*, the sensuous maternal breast a metonymy for Moore, the man supposed to have been Cunard's mother's lover and her own romanticized "father." She recalls the "round plump white hands," "those champagne-bottle shoulders [...] that pink-and-white fleshiness of his face [...] those fully rounded dough-like hands that looked incapable of doing up a button or opening a bottle."[56] Her Moore is different from the man in Manet's drawings, and it is his whiteness she recalls most vividly (lividly?): "His moustache, more or less of the walrus kind, hid the baroque fleshiness of his lips, causing those sudden naivetes, those horrid sarcasms and provocative tirades to issue from an oracular and bosky depth," she wrote of the "big pussy cat."[57] But she catches her phallic-motherly Moore also in the figure of a fish; she sees him as "a large distinguished carp."[58]

If the reader has followed me so far, it may be possible to return for a closer look at Cunard's impassioned description of Manet's painting in contrasting colored contexts in England and France; but always "the *Etude* is a dispenser of light. 'Oh! sa blondeur!' I say when I open my door and the whole of my simple country room seems lit by the picture."[59] She is able to describe the historical reality of the woman as model, the genius of Manet's technique and the personal pleasure of the one who gazes at the picture. The study is for one of his most famous paintings, "a portrait of the same young woman at her washing by a wooden bucket, a child holding on to the edge of it," Cunard begins.[60] We may be forgiven for hearing in the voice which cries "Oh! sa blondeur!" a daughter's long-denied love of her mother, bursting out at the sight of mother and child in a "radiant" domestic scene. But the painting is no longer in Lady Cunard's salon, in a domestic space dominated by her taste; the *Étude* is now in Nancy's French mountain hideaway, her unreconstructed, unrestored old castle. On her own territory Cunard can see in Manet's study for his washerwoman, a rosy-cheeked and rosy-breasted young beauty with her hair pinned up and her bodice falling down, a portrait of the mother she loved in the medium she loved, Impressionist painting.

The scene of the painting (not of the *Étude*, which is what Cunard inherited) is the familiar one (though not among Cunard's class) of doing the family wash. Did Cunard hear in her increasing loneliness in the fifties the voices which had chastised her for many years for her public denunciation of her mother, for "washing her family's dirty linen" in public? Did she see in the picture an Irish washerwoman from her own past, that murky American background which suggested that Maud Cunard may not have been too far from the washtub herself, hence her obsession with her "ladyship"? The picture, called *Le Linge*, which translates as "The Laundry" or "The Washing Day" (1875, Barnes Foundation, Philadelphia), occupies an interesting place in the history of Impressionism. Refused by the Salon of 1876, it had a certain cachet along with other famous refused paintings and engendered a lot of commentary about Manet washing dirty linen in public, questions as to what unspeakable piece of underclothing is being washed in front of the child, and arguments about why a woman washing clothes is not a fit subject for painting. The dull figure in *Le Linge* itself could not rouse comparison with Maud Cunard, though it does suggest the washerwomen necessary to keep her in clean linen. Nancy herself was often in the position of the child clinging to the washbucket, left alone with servants as her mother gallivanted. Her mother's maids and their relation to the dirt she loved as a child may have been what she was recalling. Also the scene is outside, in the garden, away from the house where her mother reigned. The smile of the semi-nude in the *Étude* does not suggest a life of toil behind a washtub.

"No link between the two works can exist," Cunard begins her book on Moore. Then she quenches her doubts: "Indubitably it is the same woman's face: 'Modèle, Alice Lecouvey, tante de la petite Lecouvey, de l'Opéra,' says a faded note stuck on the back."[61] Manet must have made it, she tries to convince herself, to learn more about his model's face before painting *Le Linge*. But her doubt remains in the reader's mind. I cannot agree that it is the same woman's face. There are, in fact two paintings of the same nude torso; one is clearly a study for the other. Sotheby's catalogue identifies the George Moore/Lady Cunard/Nancy Cunard picture: "Manet then painted two portraits [after completing *Le Linge*] after Alice Lecouve of which this is the sketch for the earlier painting; both were photographed by Lochard in 1883, nos. 37 and 263."[62] The sale catalogue says that the model for the bust is Alice Lecouve (called Legouve in the 1975 Rouart and Wildenstein Manet catalogue raisonné), a favorite model of Alfred Stevens and the aunt of La Petite Lecouve of the Opéra. The catalogue raisonné claims that Lecouve, "le modele du *Linge*," posed for the torso.[63]

Aside from the fact that there is so little resemblance between the nude and the housewife, there is a letter from Manet to Mallarmé after he showed his "refused" pictures, including *Le Linge*, and suffered the abuse of the public, who wrote their nasty comments about washing dirty linen in his visitors' book, to which he replied, "M. Manet a toujours marqué son linge et jamais demarqué celui des autres." To Mallarmé he wrote: "Si au lieu de peindre Jeanne Lorgnon nettoyant ses hardes, j'ai fait l'imperatrice Josephine lavant son linge sale, quel succès, mes enfants!"[64] Who was Jeanne Lorgnon? Was the nude named Alice Lecouvey and the washerwoman her aunt? Was her aunt named Jeanne Lorgnon? What exactly was the connection between the two torsos and the picture of "washing day"?

In *Modern Painters* George Moore wrote the text of *Le Linge* as the painting of origins, the "germ" of "impressionism and all the other isms of modern French art."[65] His sentimental, nostalgic account of the picture along with the hostility it evoked among viewers has obscured the political import of its anti-metropolitan valorization of petit-bourgeois property values. It could be named *Good Housekeeping*. The critic raves over the originality of

Manet's celebration of the domestic outdoors, its brightness, lightness, and clarity:

> [I]n *Le Linge* no challenge is sent forth to anyone; it is Manet, all Manet and nothing but Manet. In this picture he expresses his love of the gaiety and pleasure of Parisian life. And this bright-faced, simple-minded woman who stands in a garden crowded with the tallest sunflowers, the great flower-crowns drooping above her, her blue cotton dress rolled up to the elbows, her hands plunged in a small washtub in which she is washing some small linen, habit shirts, pocket handkerchiefs, collars, expresses the joy of homely life in the French suburb. Her home is one of good wines, excellent omelettes, soft beds; and the sheets, if they are a little coarse, are spotless, and retain an odour of lavender-scented cupboards. Her little child, about four years old, is with his mother in the garden; he has strayed into the foreground of the picture, just in front of the wash-tub, and he holds a great sunflower in his tiny hand. Beside this picture of bright and happy aspect, the most perfect example of that *genre* known as *la peinture clair*, invented by Manet, and so infamously and absurdly practised by subsequent imitators—beside this picture so limpid, so fresh, so unaffected in its handling, a Courbet would seem heavy and dull...[66]

Moore is wrong about *Le Linge*'s lack of challenge. It does not invoke a classical masterpiece to reinterpret it, that is true. The challenge is in its renunciation of the nude white body of the emancipated woman (*Olympia*) for the dumpily dressed, dimwitted housewife. *Le Linge* is important in the history of art because it *changes the subject* of French art. The *demi-monde* is deserted for the backyard. The electric triangular gaze linking the painter, the model, and the viewer, which was full of challenge, is replaced by the pleasure of looking at the sunlit familiar world—i.e. Impressionism—without having to face the look of the subject looking back at you. The figure of the woman has been suppressed into "service." It is the "maid" or the working wife, not the model (the woman who desires and the woman who sees) who appears in paint. One sees the passive, reproductive, heterosexual woman who puts lavender in the sheets and keeps her eyes on her domestic work. But nature and the child (male to George Moore and the art critics) are now the focus of the picture. Is this "first" Impressionist painting about the birth of the artist? The boy who bedazzles Moore reminds him of himself as well as of Manet, gripping the tub and looking at it with great concentration—as the female figure is completely absorbed in her work. The sunflowers signify the "seeds" of sunlight, the origins of Impressionism's concern with light *en plein air*. The boy holding the sunflower is the artist, the one who sees the light, the "beholder" of beauty. Blinded by the whiteness of the laundry, the child is creating Manet's palette, from flat white to the golden yellow of the sunflower. He is now the subject of his own painting.

In fact, one may see *Le Linge*, with its pastoral suburban garden setting, as a comment on class and working conditions in Paris. Washerwomen and ironers had long been among the most visible of exploited women workers in France, their figures reproduced in photographs and represented by artists half-dressed with bare arms because of the heat of the irons and the stoves. Their wages were so low that prostitution was often necessary to pay the rent. Degas's famous studies of the washerwomen and ironers send conflicting messages about their boredom and drinking, exhaustion and sexual avail-ability. As Eunice Lipton's classic study of the images of laundresses in French culture in this period shows, real work (or the laundresses' participation in the Commune) was not often shown in these pictures, and the *blanchisseuses* were often shown flirting bare-breasted with the viewer of the picture. Lipton argues that the need to depict working women as oversexed rationalized their being overworked, and that Degas was exceptional among the Impression-ists in showing "Paris laundry girls" at work, "unwittingly" capturing their alienation and fatigue.[67] I would add to this analysis that the huge commer-cial enterprise of Paris laundries at the end of the century not only provided people with fresh linen but served a cultural concern with cleanliness which was part of an imperialist discourse about racial purity.

L'Assommoir, Zola's shocking naturalist 1887 novel about a laundress who takes to drink, the model for Moore's story of a woman's descent into alco-holism, *A Mummer's Wife*, re-read with admiration by Cunard as she wrote the memoir, is part of the same discourse of eroticizing and criminalizing women workers that animates the Impressionist portraits of laundresses. "One of the most moving stories ever written," *A Mummer's Wife* impressed Cunard because she knew Moore to be so abstemious that he "could never have got into her skin; masterly is the long decline of Kate, poor Kate in the vicious circle of sherry and jealousy, jealousy and brandy, and, above all, lone-liness." She doubts if Moore was ever drunk in his life:

> The mysterious chemistry in the bodies of all of us said "no" in his case to the enticements of excess. He hated a drunken man, simply hated the sight of one, the accompanying boredom, the ungainliness, the degradation. As for a drunken woman, that was beyond every-thing. And yet, poor Kate.[68]

In this context Manet's *Le Linge* romanticizes the labor of washing clothes by setting the scene in a charming garden. Women's traditional work is more like child's play with the child imaged happily gripping the bucket and the well-dressed (fully clothed) young woman quite possibly the mother of the child. No drudgery is suggested; the woman's face is shaded by a poke bonnet and the scene evokes sensual pleasure. Her lace-trimmed sleeves and bustle imply that this is not hard labor that she is performing; either Manet is romanticizing such work, or seeing it as appropriate and undemanding for the young mother or maid, rather than sending it out to the notorious laundresses in their boiling sweatshops.

But the *Étude* participates in the contemporary French sexual discourse about laundresses, which is entirely absent in Manet's finished painting (if the *Étude* is indeed related to *Le Linge* at all). The woman smiles luxuriously like the yawning and stretching women of Degas and the other painters of the washerwomen. Her pinned-up hair falls in wisps about her cheeks as if she is hot and tired and sexually available. It is very hard to believe that this robust, flirtatious figure is a study for the discreet, bourgeois, even humble figure in *Le Linge* whose face and breasts are hidden from the viewer, whose gaze is drawn to her hands and the linen she is washing as white as the linen hanging on the line. It is in fact the white linen which is the subject of the painting; the features of child and woman are blurred; they are pretty parts of a pleasant garden scene, an Impressionist garden with no evidence of the labor that produced it and no small effort to indicate that household labor is not labor but a woman's pleasure. Demurely her eyes are cast down, looking into the water in the bucket, her gaze directed at the smallclothes of the family circle. Constricted by class, wearing, perhaps, a little maternity smock, she can hardly be connected to the luxuriously sexual creature of the *Étude*.

Somehow Nancy Cunard resolved her lifelong conflict with her mother by writing a memoir of George Moore and using the Manet painting as an *aide-mémoire*. She makes him into a mother-figure in an odd set of substitutions. Her adoration of the Manet painting Moore had given her mother, which was then bequeathed to her, is a belated expression of love in the form of the old triangle of her childhood when she and Moore were both suitors to her mother's beauty. The wild flowers and grasses she sets before the rosy portrait of a woman make an altar before which she may worship unashamedly, and, though she doesn't say so, mourn her mother's death and their long separation. Flowers from the fields replace the formalist informality of the Impressionist bouquet. (One thinks of the artful armful held by the Black maid in Manet's *Olympia*, sent perhaps by a satisfied lover on his way home.) We are closer to the uncultivated found objects of Surrealism, and Cunard's own perverse "taste" for the dark and dirty, rocks and flints and wild things, asserted as a child against the monstrous cultural competence of her mother. The maternal is now distanced as an art object and Cunard can look at the breast without fearing the wrath of the phallic mother, or being turned into one of her prized fossilized stones. The blonde she exclaims over is in Manet's palette as well as in his *modèle*; it is her mother in the guise of the young George Moore, the hairy, sexually ambiguous, blond artist-dandy painted by Manet in the 1870s that Nancy so disliked. That George Moore was the man they all colluded in mythologizing as her father. If we look at Manet's painting of Moore along with Maud Burke's engagement photo, their genders begin to mix; she looks like a very determined young man; he looks like a berry-ripe beauty about to be picked.

I am, of course, deliberately over-reading this complex of images as a form of the Madonna and Child (and the image of the bare maternal breast), as classical signs of Western culture as Manet represents its golden twilight of the white goddesses in his paintings. *Three Women on a Balcony*, which includes a figure of Berthe Morisot, on view in a Grand Palais exhibition in the spring of 1997, is remarkable for the intensity and flatness of the painting of the long, white dresses. Morisot painted a laundry scene quite different from *Le Linge* in its far more exciting, "modern," abstract concentration on the lines of waving sheets, not the figure of the woman washing. Work is implied here, but it is collective work. Cunard, who spent a lifetime rejecting all of these hallowed figures—maternity, a certain chaste erotic of European womanhood, Impressionism, domesticity—tries to make peace with her past. She enters her past as a daughter on a shaft of golden light from Manet's picture.

Nancy Cunard's *Memories of George Moore* is a book about the crisis of white identity. Her own whiteness and its relation to heredity and European culture as represented by Moore's body, his writing, and his relationship to Manet's paintings as a critic, a friend, and an owner, is at stake here. The complicated relationship between Cunard's "English" heritage and its origins in the revolutionary Ireland of Robert Emmett, and her identification with the Irish immigrants to America on both sides who made good and made money and then returned to England, suggest how troubled her personal identity was. She claimed a link to the Cunard Line, the paternal line/lineage of ocean liners, the engines of empire, only when she proved to her own satisfaction that the Cunard ships were never involved in the slave trade, and that her great grandfather had signed an anti-slavery petition.

The sexual interchangeability of the blonde figures of Moore, Manet, his model, and Maud Cunard in a halo of whiteness complicates the mother–daughter plot in many ways. It seems to me that Nancy Cunard's recollection/reconciliation may be read as a composition which could be called white nostalgia, a record of Impressionism's celebration of the feminine body of white European culture (in model, painter, critic, and owner). In it Cunard negotiates a return to her race and a recognition of the limits of her gender after three decades of identification with Africa, its politics, its culture, and its men.

Surrealism, primitivism, communism, and modernism were embraced by Cunard in rebellion against the white nostalgia and the white nympholepsy of European culture as it began to come to terms with its colonialist history of destruction and exploitation of the rest of the world and its peoples. Those others had made their appearances in European and American painting as one of the Three Magi or as servants and slaves, but now their faces and figures were everywhere. And their carvings, masks, and ivory objects were influencing European concepts and methods themselves. The other's way of seeing was being recognized as another way of seeing. Manet's palette of whites and golds and grays, championed by literary critics like George Moore, who understood, however dimly, the cultural importance of what is really a brilliant explosion of racial pride and sadness at the passing of its power, together with his painterly subjects, white girls in white dresses, are part of a *fin-de-siècle* discourse of racial purity. We know this discourse in medicine, psychology, criminology, and most of all in the social sciences. We know it in crude propaganda and the history of the Holocaust. We are only now beginning to see it in the arts. Hitler and the Nazis heard this discourse in Wagner. We may read the discourse of racial purity as well as that of male chastity in the last great wave of cultural expression of the white race's narrative of myths of its own greatness. Nancy Cunard and the Surrealists who rejected the grand narratives of this art for the pleasures of jazz, the blues, and spirituals, for African figurines and Oceanic totemic objects, were making a political point. However much the primitivism of the modernists strikes us today as politically compromised, it is important to see them up against the wall of white culture and its dominating forms. Manet's painting is one of the most seductive and effective examples of white male pleasure in seeing and owning the world.

One cannot help but admire the subtlety of Cunard's pact with history, her uncanny awareness that the *Negro* anthology and her decades of race journalism would be forgotten. But her autobiographical writing between the lines of her memoirs of minor men of letters, constructing the books as closets within closets, would offer a key to the complications of modernism's struggle with race and gender in the imaginary space of what Norman Douglas called "Intellectual Nomadism." "Dordogne," for instance, a poem in the typescript given to Sylvia Townsend Warner, explores the theme of the exile's love of the French countryside where there is no color bar, and where she and her Black lover can work and live.[69]

As a poet, Nancy Cunard wrote in the vernacular voice of the thirties radical realist, as if in answer to the domestication of both work and sex in Impressionism, its depiction of pleasure. The English words come to us haltingly, as if in translation, and French and Spanish, sometimes German and Italian, dot the page with connectives to other cultures, certainly to a united Europe, to the Americas and Africa. She identifies with the old washerwoman putting everything into the same pot: "Si c'est pas *honte* de ne pas envoyer tout ça plus tôt—A perishin' shame on them sending me all that at one go."[70] The *Negro* anthology is like the Old Crepuscular's boiling copper washtub with everything in it, and so was much of Cunard's collective work in publishing poems for Spain and for France, a vigorous resistance to individualism, a "No" to the life of excellent omelets and clean coarse sheets that George Moore read in Manet's *Le Linge*, a "Yes" to the nomad who finds community wherever she goes.

CHAPTER EIGHT

Intellectual Nomads

Norman Douglas, the Desert,
and the Taste for Space

rand Man, Nancy Cunard's 1954 memoir of Norman Douglas,
which includes appreciations by his friends, extracts from his
letters, a bibliography of his writing, and essays on his work as
well as the "Letter to Norman" (her unique form of "personal literature"),
lacks the shared fetishized figure of Lady Cunard that the memoir of George
Moore calls upon to focus its energies. *Grand Man* is instead haunted by
visions of the desert. Apprehensive and rapt by the sight of forbidden territory, Cunard, good Surrealist that she was, records her recurring dream of
effrits and *accidiae*, malicious and invisible gods of the Sahara who tease and
torment her; "natural laws are no more," they whirl away the tent roof and set
her "going further, even further!"[1] Travel, the desert, Africa, dance, music,
and the career of the exiled writer Norman Douglas mix in another hybrid
text of English primitivism to create an atmosphere of exotic sexuality. One
hears echoes of the intrepid Gertrude Bell, writing of her explorations in
Egypt, or Lawrence of Arabia on the emptiness of the desert landscape,
and even the sensual voice of Amelia Edwards, nineteenth-century invader
of Egyptian antiquities, one of the primal voices of female "Orientalist"
primitivism, one eye on the anthropology of racial difference, the other on
real Egyptian bodies and their representations in art. She was a romantic
racialist, participating eagerly in the "scientific" racial discourses of her
time. Edwards, wanting, as much as Cunard did in her *Negro* anthology, to
engage intellectually in the *production of knowledge* about racial difference,

is easy to dismiss as a crank and an amateur. But she, like other outsiders, saw and valued what archeologists did not see. Edwards's ambivalent eye is as entranced by the beauty of the living Other and his/her present culture, not only by ancient monuments, as Cunard's is later about Africa and Africans. They were English eyes, women's eyes. Along with gay men like Douglas, and against the principles of the other white anthropologists, they also sought contact with the eyes and bodies of people of color.[2]

Like Gertrude Stein's modernist classic *Three Lives*, especially the story of Melanctha, in which Stein imagines a Black woman's life in Baltimore, using race to try to understand her own unladylike (or Jewish) penchant for "wandering," her desire for sex, Cunard's hybrid text, her mixed genre memoir, attempts to write the voice of sexual exile and national identity in terms of race. With no gift for fiction, Cunard enlists the memoir form to engage the same questions William James had taught Stein to ask, about the role of genetics and inheritance as well as environment in shaping human character, questions which science was debating hotly at the time. She surrounds her "character" Norman Douglas, the German Scot who made himself into an Italian, an honorary member of the *razza italica* or the exalted race of Mediterranean men, with a set of what can only be called "letters of recommendation" from other marginal men of letters, and quotes him liberally so that the text will "physically" invoke the sound of his voice, defining her author's role as generating "a series of echoes."

Stein's fiction physically and rhythmically echoes the sounds of Black life in Baltimore, its music and its language.[3] Cunard creates the character of the writer as iconoclast in her portrait, out of her own need to find in Douglas a "fellow traveler" in many senses of the phrase, a man as fixated sexually and intellectually on inappropriate objects as she was on the racial other. If Melanctha is the voice of forbidden female desire for the American writer, in a text that also tells stories about what happens to white German women in exile, the Uncle Norman of Cunard's book is a polemicist, author of *What About Europe?* (1929, called in the United States *Goodbye to Western Culture*) as well as *South Wind* and *Siren Land*, and he is a sexual radical, a breaker of taboos.

Back to Africa

Of course, the figure really being recalled by the text is not a white man at all, though Douglas and Moore are among the few in "the race of men" whom Cunard can tolerate for long as friends, but Henry Crowder, her Black musician lover of the late twenties and early thirties. The trip to Tunisia in the late thirties with Douglas was in many ways a belated exercise in nostalgia, doomed to be a disappointment, for Cunard had hoped and planned to go to Africa with Crowder a decade earlier. Now that he was lost to her, Crowder joined the dear dead boys of World War I in her imagination as her one true love.

They never went to Africa together. Quite likely, going to Africa was a fiction that floated their relationship for a time. The problem was real. The stumbling block was "the color bar," the object of Cunard's first forays into the polemics of anti-racism. A white woman and a Black man could not travel together they soon found out, as they tried to get visas and tickets. The British colonies were out, though she and Crowder both wanted to go to Benin. Many an evening was spent in Paris cafés with artist friends from many countries trying to solve the logistics of a trip to Africa. "Could I not learn a good deal in Africa of the Africans themselves, they in their endless diversity? And, again, what of their music? As a pianist and composer, Henry could do good work in that field and bring back something as yet unknown…"[4]

The excitement in Paris was generated by the prospect of the ex-Surrealist Michel Leiris and his colleagues preparing to go on the Djibouti Expedition to collect African art and artifacts, to study African cultures in the field. The expedition was sponsored by the French government as well as by the Trocadero Museum, that, after this major collecting trip, was to become the Musée de l'Homme, the repository of the extraordinarily valuable collection and the research of the anthropologists, and the institution in which Leiris was to work for the rest of his life.

Nancy Cunard, it must be remembered, produced the *Negro* anthology without any funding or institutional backing, still less the army of troops the Djibouti Expedition was given to protect its raids on native villages and thefts of African carvings, masks, religious objects, weapons, and household goods.[5] She, too, dreamed of going to Africa, but she had no academic credentials as an anthroplogist, no national army or institution to fund the work that had to be done, no trained staff to take field notes and extensive photographs. *Negro* was the result of her imaginary trip to Africa, a breathtakingly scholarly, broad, and inclusive piece of work, collectively done by unpaid contributors as a political gesture of solidarity with African peoples everywhere—and her own sheer will and effort. She had no university degree and was self-taught as a scholar and researcher. But the journey to Africa was part of a personal dream she had shared with Crowder, to bring him back to his ancestral roots. They did not go together, and in all her later forays into Africa as a journalist, she never went inland to the heart of Africa, but hovered in its most accessible ports.

Douglas was part of the Paris café discussions in 1930; there was no color bar on French boats to Africa, but Douglas convinced them they weren't safe, so the focus was changed to a German boat to South West Africa, when Douglas suddenly left on his own to visit a friend in Nairobi, then Arusha and Tanganyika. Cunard's annoyance at the thwarting of her voyage "back to Africa" with Crowder was probably a motivating factor in the fury with the English "color bar" expressed in her *Black Man and White Ladyship* pamphlet of 1931, as well as her deliberate flaunting of racial customs by staying in a hotel in Harlem and appearing in public with Black men in New York. If she couldn't go to Africa—and at this point she seems not to have considered going alone—she would make a "collaborative" book on "the Negro race and its affiliations," having sent out a call and collected "half a ton of literary and sociological material for the book."[6] She was off on an intellectual and political adventure that proved to be even more exciting than going to Africa itself.

But in the intense process of travel, study, research, reading, correspondence, editing, and writing, she lost track of her relationship with Henry Crowder, the man who had inspired her to take on such a herculean task. When the *Negro* anthology was published in 1934, dedicated to him, he had already left her and returned to the United States. Taking what she called "the arduous anthological road," Cunard's intellectual voyage to Africa, crossing and re-re-re-crossing the Black Atlantic, held many surprises, she tells Douglas and the eavesdropping reader, not the least of which was the threatening letters she received when she stayed in Harlem. The hate mail was an explosion of one of the "most ornate and roccoco outbursts" of U.S. "race hysteria."[7] Imagine if she and Crowder had gone to Africa together instead of Harlem.

Norman Douglas sent her a peace offering, a letter from Arusha to be published in her anthology, telling her and other would-be travelers to Africa to avoid white officials, learn Swahili, or take a "native" guide. He included a photograph of a Masai girl whose bangles were made of telegraph and telephone wires put in by the British. Regretting his mistake (and Cunard was later to take his advice in the West Indies, Cuba, and Haiti by avoiding the white population altogether) he "invented" a piece for her "monstrous tome," which struck the only humorous note in *Negro*, a wonderful parody of all the primitivist myths about savages.[8]

Dancing in the Desert

Grand Man is a text in which Nancy Cunard examines her own wanderlust by describing Norman Douglas's several exiles, and praises his essay on "Intellectual Nomadism," for in it she finds a description of herself. It is in this book that she tells of her dream of the desert and her vision of herself dancing with Africans. It has none of Douglas's humor, but the dreamwork it does, in the manner of Surrealism, seems to be taking the child's fear of "not having a roof over head" to make a virtue of the nomad's life. There is also a dread of the unpredictable power of something non-human, spirits or gods:

> I wonder now if I ever told you how, when, about six years old, my thoughts began to be drawn towards Africa, and particularly towards the Sahara? Surely I was being taught as much about El Dorado and the North Pole? But there it was: the Desert. The sand, the dunes, the huge spaces, mirages, heat and parchedness—I seemed able to visualize all of this.
>
> Of such were filled several dreams culminating in the great nightmare in which I wandered, repeatedly, the whole of one agonising night, escaping through a series of tents somewhere in the Sahara. Later came extraordinary dreams about black Africa "The Dark Continent"—with Africans dancing and drumming around me, and I one of them, though still white, knowing, mysteriously enough, how to dance in their own manner. Everything was full of movement in these dreams; it was that which enabled me to escape in the end, going further, even further! And all of it was a mixture of apprehension that sometimes turned into joy, and even rapture.[9]

Later, Cunard had a photographic "mental vision" of a desert she had never seen, possibly a "haschish dream," though she swore she knew nothing of hashish.[10] But the imaginary desert she describes hallucinates a landscape haunted by invisible *effrits* and *accidiae*, like the empty space in a Dalí or Magritte painting or the collective vision of the Surrealists, "where something wild and inexplicable would be going on." It is a dance, a "demoniacal ballet," that draws people into it. Both the Libyan desert and African jungle in her dreams are the setting of a primal scene of bodies moving in time to a mysterious rhythm. A man is asleep in a tent, or a "whole company of people." The roof of the tent is blown off in a whirl of sand. It is black noon. What do the spirits want? "Are they angry? [...] Can we come to terms with them?" The sky is electric, "great stretches of sand ruffled with puffs and gusts and blasts of fever-wind." The spirits are "unpredictable, unassuageable by any sacrifice or compromise [...] whimsical [...] and even death-dealing."[11]

The "wicked and wilful" spirits leave the other poor mortals groping in the dark, but Cunard escapes through a series of tents because her body can move like an African's. In the discourse of high imperialist exploration that they share, Cunard tells "Uncle Norman," whose *Fountains in the Sand* (1912) told of his travels in Tunis beginning in 1910, as they travel through Tunisia just after the "troubles" of 1938, aware of the contending forces of many interests, the presence of police and militia, states waiting to pounce and talking to Italian fascists, that she feels that Tunisia is "waiting for something to bring it to life again."[12] This feeling was common among those interested in struggles for freedom in the continent, and it also was part of the "Ethiopia Awakening" discourse of Marcus Garvey's Back to Africa movement.[13] Africa is in chains, degraded and enslaved by the effects of colonialism—a messiah will set her free.

Good Nomads and Bad

Unlike other travel writing about the Arabs, to Cunard at the time Douglas's *Fountains in the Sand* was "ferocious"; it did not try for those "easy *effets de bazar*" of other writers describing "the witchery of Orientalism," Nancy writes in 1954, so entranced, she says, that she is translating his book into French.[14] This is not an innocent remark. It was not very likely that the French reader would be delighted by Douglas's treatment of their travel writing traditions. What she admires is Douglas's analysis of the cultural differences between French and English writing on the Orient, his shrewd claim in the twenties that good travel writing is both "naif and profound," his comparison of the reserve, objectivity, and ruggedness of Charles Doughty's *Arabia Deserta* with the "cloying and tinkling performance" of Pierre Loti's *Le Desert*. The French, including the Frères Tharaud, lack humility and are impervious to foreign languages and ideas; "they are curiously incurious" about other people and other landscapes.[15]

Douglas thinks they are imprisoned in a certain romantic rhetoric by their language. English allows individualism and the culture encourages distrust of authority along with self-respect, so the Englishman abroad can "merge" and "assimilate … He makes a good nomad."[16] Cunard paid careful attention to Douglas's description of fresh independent travel writing. The good observer is not derivative but original, that is, not writing in a tradition of writing about travel as he fears the French writers are. And, interestingly, given the assumption that objective writing is always better than subjective writing, Douglas cheers the opinionated traveler, or the writer most like himself—the perfect traveler is possessed of a strong bias and "the courage to proclaim it and put it to the test."[17] Not only was Uncle Norman a good nomad, but, by his standards, the Nancy Cunard who wrote and edited the *Negro* anthology was a good nomad too—good at wandering, good at observing the other in life and landscape. Somehow, "the good nomad" comes to mean morally admirable as well as born for the geographical life. Cunard and the reader come away connecting Doughty's massive book on Arabia, "the gigantic scale of it all," with Douglas's travel writing and her own *Negro* anthology. Her quote from Harold Acton about Douglas: "His purpose was refreshingly anti-utilitarian, although, in his own words he hoped to add something to the common sum of western knowledge,"[18] reaches back to Doughty and forward to Cunard herself to make a genealogy in which her work can be placed in a tradition of committed English travel writing (which also includes Borrow and Sterne as well as Douglas). Since Cunard's massive text, the *Negro* anthology, has yet to find a generic home, and is not acknowledged either as the classic of pan-Africanism it actually is, nor as the logical continuation of the work of Alain Locke's *The New Negro* or Blaise Cendrars's *Anthologie negre* in the American or French traditions, we might think about the cultural implications of claiming *Negro*, edited by an Englishwoman and published in England by Wishart, as a kind of collective version of a piece of eccentric and political English literature of travel and exploration.

In seeking to place Norman Douglas in history, to create the good nomad as a grand man, Cunard brings herself back to an English tradition, along with her exiled hero. Despite their sexual outrageousness, their lives in France and Italy, their anti-social attacks on their country, the fact that they were good nomads redeems them as English national subjects. The brand of primitivism Douglas and Cunard shared deplores the effects of colonialism on the nomadic peoples and Bedouins they admire. Cunard admires Douglas's desert book: "Ironic, salty and pungent," Fountains proclaims that "'mektoub'—it is written or fatalism" is "the intellectual burnous of the Arab."[19] They both admire the caves of the hermit "Troglodytes," feeling in the desert that they are closer to "pure Islam," the "authentic Arab" culture they are after that appears to them in the figure of "a pure-blooded little Negro of ten or so … the most beautiful child I have ever seen … a very illustration of 'high antiquity.'"[20] This search for pure origins, authenticity, and beauty in the savage lost desert and mountain cultures is a form of primitivism still in effect today. Travel brochures offer images of native children to sell present-day dreams of paradise to jaded metropolitan tourists. Why did those who traveled and most readily mixed with others, intellectually, emotionally, and sexually, speak so romantically about racial purity? Was it only because they were looking for themselves in the land of the Other, and wanted to see their own deep selves as pure rather than corrupt?

Norman Douglas has been accused of pedophilia, and, it seems in defiance of these claims, or perhaps in support of his right to indulge his desires, Cunard's memoir is full of references to his relations with children and photos of him with children.[21] Her memories of his visits always include tales of escapes from the authorities and hopes that his lawyers are settling whatever cases have been brought against him. The cult of the primitive child is shared by them on their desert trip, though Nancy cannot help noticing children eating from the garbage dump and worrying about the burdens of child laborers. "Emaciated children" holding bunches of wild asparagus by the side of the road became to her "one of the national emblems of Tunisia."[22] She affirms Douglas's masculinity in her memoir, as she did with George Moore, so that they appear to be a pair of harmless avuncular characters. Then again, the texts hint at the reputation of both writers for perverse forms of sexuality. It is difficult to know how to read Cunard's retelling of Douglas's story about a previous visit to the hotel in Tozeur where they are staying. An Arab youth had noticed

> how much you seemed to like being with the children at times, talking
> and walking with them, giving them sweets and so on, children of all

ages—and how much they liked you, big and small. "One evening,"
you said, "that very window opened and an arm came in. At the end
of it was a baby, a baby two or three years old, which was gently
deposited on the floor *without a word* … That boy told me later his
idea was that I might like to play with his little sister…"[23]

Were there white cannibals in Norman Douglas's Tunisia, one is tempted to
ask, as in his imaginary Tanganyika? And do they too eat babies on the first
Monday of the month? Colonialism has seen to it that certain young men in
Third World countries came to expect that women like Nancy Cunard wanted
sex and that men like Norman Douglas wanted to play with them or their
sisters. There is nothing new in the much-publicized sex tourism in Thailand.
From their point of view there is probably little difference between good white
"nomads" and bad ones.

Perhaps this is the link Cunard feels with them; they are a company of
outcasts. Sex is a serious subtext in *Grand Man*. An Arab boy offers to make
love to her on their trip, and she says in shock that she is old enough to be
his mother and sends him away. What we know of the rest of her life does
not give credence to this account of things, and in other parts of the text she
boasts about her Venetian gondolier and teasingly mentions the "unprintable"
story of her Italian waiter. The rough passage from Marseilles is made into a
scene of heroic drinking while rolling and flying around the saloon, getting
lost and having the sensation of the boat "ploughing the land" with one of the
engineers, "purposeful conquering thrusts into resisting depths," like something out of Hemingway.[24] The reader is positioned as a voyeur by Cunard.
It is not a pleasant experience. Not only are we reading her letter to Douglas
over her shoulder, as it were, we are sitting opposite her in some café, captives,
as she drunkenly and coyly boasts about her conquests. As in real conversations with drunks, the narrator forgets how much she has told us the night
before and tries to cover her tracks. When we get annoyed with her attitude
toward the "natives," *Voila!* she produces a French colonial who curses the
Arabs as savages and tells stories of disastrous relations between white women
and Arab men.

The text is torn between the desire to tell and the desire to hide the secrets
of her life and the secrets of his. Cunard's own problematic sexuality appears to
be tied up in some way with this dream of the desert. Her white body "knows"
the African dance steps, but she is aware that that knowledge is forbidden.

Her odd friends were also out of step with European cultural norms. Their male bodies know the steps of other forbidden dances. Douglas's account of the Wallawapuplas, the white-faced cannibals who only eat children, and the cutting off of the fingers of artists may have more to do with his own savage world than with Africa.

The "nomadism" they observe in the desert in North Africa and the nomadism they share intellectually is bridged and connected by reading aloud from Isabelle Eberhardt's *Dans l'ombre chaude de l'Islam*. Cunard had admired Douglas's essay, "Intellectual Nomadism" in *Experiments* (1925), on Doughty's *Arabia Deserta* and Isabelle Eberhardt and Marie Bashkirtseff so much that she had typed it out to read on a journey as a model of "thinking straight" and "writing straight."[25] Eberhardt was a Russian journalist brought up as a boy in Geneva, who married an Arab, converted to Islam, and died at age 27 in a sudden flood in the desert. Douglas had read her in 1910 and praised her powers of description and her originality. He thought that being Russian and being able to ride horseback disguised as an Arab youth she could sympathize with the life of nomadic Arabs: "She has what she calls the *goût de l'espace*— the *volupté profond de la vie errant*."[26] Cunard shared her deep pleasure in life on the road, a strong "unfeminine" taste for wide open spaces. Eberhardt was Cunard's heroine and role model. She was at home in the wilderness and she could write. Her writing, said Douglas, was intense and distorted, but "The Arabs of Isabelle are so vital and palpitating that your ordinary ones melt away like phantoms."[27] So *Dans l'ombre chaude d'Islam* and *Notes de route*, the works of a woman who never settled down, became the Bible of another traveling woman. Eberhardt defamiliarized the desert for Europeans, as Cunard sought to defamiliarize African culture. Norman Douglas writes:

> The Sahara used to exist only in its terrifying aspects of desolation and heat and thirst. Then came a generation of men who discovered for us its manifold beauties; this, we said, was the truth and the whole truth, at last: the desert as a mode of art! And now we have Isabelle Eberhardt to whom the desert is no longer a mode of art, but a mode of life. (The Alps have passed through the same three stages.)[28]

Africa had been imagined by the West for a long time in its most savage aspect. This view allowed colonization to take place, empires to be built and expanded. Then the ethnologists and artists began to see the treasures of the tribes as art, the habits of living a "primitive" source for understanding all human activity. Nancy Cunard wanted to take the next step, to demystify African life, to embrace the other as one of "ourselves." This proved harder to do than she had imagined, for in her own mind part of Africa remained "terrifying," and much of it existed as the source of brilliant works of art, new ways of looking at the world spatially, and new musical rhythms, which freed the body.[29] The primitivism that she sought to erase was deeply rooted in her own sexuality. There was an Africa in herself, a far more savage undiscovered territory than the sun-drenched continent itself.

PART IV

Translating Africa:
The *Negro* Anthology

CHAPTER NINE

White Women, Black Books

The *Negro* Anthology and
Sylvia Leith-Ross's *African Women*[1]

In 1934 Nancy Cunard's massive compendium of information about Africa and its cultural diaspora, the *Negro* anthology, a monumental example of the thirties documentary as a collective work of art, appeared in England.[2] No British publisher except the left-wing Wishart would do it; they published it on the condition that she pay for its printing, and all the possible American co-publishers fell through.[3] It was certainly a daunting project. With 385 illustrations, the 855-page volume weighed in at over eight pounds, its heft a measure of the seriousness of the pan-African project of its editor. The anthology was clearly designed to be a secular Bible of African culture, a holy book for the war against racism and fascism. For many Black people all over the world it served as a Bible of revolution and struggle. For others it was a Bible of African culture and artistic achievement.

Holding Nancy Cunard's own leather-bound copy, with the word NEGRO running diagonally across it in deep blood-red, in the Humanities Research Center at the University of Texas, where most of her papers are housed, one is convinced that the *Negro* anthology is more than a book. It was made as a gift in print and visual culture to colonial and postcolonial Africans of oral cultures, to restore (in a small way) their history, making some of that cultural history available to African-descended people of the diaspora, and, most importantly, claiming Africans as peoples of the book, and thus equal to all the other writing cultures of the world. The *Negro* anthology was made to bring Africa (anew) into the written world. The Koran and the Bible, as well

Figure 9.1. Nancy Cunard holding the *Negro* anthology.
Image courtesy Harry Ransom Center, The University of Texas at Austin

as writing, had been brought to Africa much earlier, of course, by Muslim conquerors and Christian missionaries.[4] Some few Africans certainly had spoken and written European languages for many centuries. Cunard believed that evidence of ancient writing would be found once it was looked for.

In terms of modernist book-making, the *Negro* anthology marks a major break with Cunard's previous practice as a coterie publisher of beautiful, hand-set, limited editions on fine paper at her Hours Press, like Ezra Pound's *XXX Cantos* or Louis Aragon's French translation of Lewis Carroll's *The Hunting of the Snark*. It also marks a break with 15 rue Guenegaud, the Paris headquarters of the press, offering "Editions/Imprimerie/Librairie/ Objets Sauvages" to the Surrealists and the avant-garde, a place where European and American artists, exiles and radicals met under the sign of Africa. 15 rue Guenegaud in the 6th arrondissement was now more of an office than a salon, where Cunard could work at her father's big antique desk on collecting the materials for the book she was then calling *Color*. The politics of the precious that Surrealist publishing and book-making became, in the exclusive production of exquisite individualist aesthetic objects of art, ceased to interest her as Cunard embarked on the most grandly ambitious intellectual project of her life.

The mark of French ethnographic Surrealism in its political and satiric vein, however, is clear and unmistakable in the French sections of the anthology. *Le tumulte noir* stirs up the pages of the book, but *Negro* remains in the end very different from those modernist milestones of the thirties in France, *Minotaure*, *Le Surréalisme au service dans la révolution*, *Cahiers d'Art*, or *Documents*. *Negro* looks different from the visually witty and elegant works of ethnographic Surrealism that have survived as modernist works of art, as well as from the images of Cunard and her Black friends and objects of African art that were part of her personal and private life, images that connect Cunard with the primitive and exotic world of Africa as still current icons of high modernist style. The story goes, and as a story it has come to be used against her, that when asked if he knew anything about Africa, Salvador Dalí replied that he knew all about Africa because he knew Nancy Cunard. Dalí's view of her as an embodiment of "Africa as a style of modernist primitivism" was shared by many of her Surrealist admirers. Her ivory-braceleted body in Man Ray's famous photograph was blown up to fill a wall in Aragon's apartment, where it served as a fetish for a number of French intellectuals. To Zora Neale Hurston's biographer, the story is part of a moral narrative about Hurston's abuse by white "patrons"; it excuses Toni Cade Bambara from acknowledging Cunard's role as the publisher of Hurston's many pieces of folklore in *Negro* with the assumption that the relationship between a Black woman and a white woman is always unequal and that the white woman must have been exploiting Hurston. But Nancy Cunard was not a patron of the arts like her mother, Lady Cunard, who supported the opera, symphony, and ballet in London. Nor was she a patron of the arts like the wealthy women in New York who supported Black writers. The assumption that the role of patron was the only role a white woman could play in the Black arts caused mistakes and misunderstandings. Cunard was an artist herself, well known as a poet and publisher, and in the case of *Negro* she saw herself the "maker" or prime mover of a great historical collective work of art.

The *Negro* anthology looks very different from all the other books Cunard herself published. *Negro*'s heaviness in tone and spirit, its anti-style of low modernist documentary, its tremendous textual excess and total visual overload were part of a deliberate effort to command respect. It was meant to overwhelm the reader. Head shots of Black intellectuals in suits alternate with visual evidence of oppression and slavery, images of Blacks at work, and photographs and drawings of African art that Tyrus Miller argues are static in comparison with their use in other French Surrealist publications of the time.[5] They are indeed static and perhaps were meant to suggest a stability they had not yet received as art objects in museums. I believe that the reverent and solemn treatment of the African objects in Cunard's book was a deliberate effort to confer the status of art on pieces that were usually exhibited as anthropological evidence in museums of natural history for a large audience that had never seen them except in an ethnographical context. The Surrealists who were part of the circle at 15 rue Guenegaud shared her views but they did not expect their journals to appeal to a mixed audience of the kind Cunard envisioned. Her work in *Negro* may more profitably be compared with the still controversial work of the Barnes Collection in Pennsylvania as a deliberate attempt to place African works in the same category as the most highly prized European paintings. In fact the contributions of Barnes as a collector and Cunard as an anthologist to the recognition of African culture may be seen as similar kinds of cultural work.

Africa had been written about, fantasized, and translated to the rest of the world for centuries. Its exotic jungles, unusual flora and fauna, its magnificent mineral treasures, gold, diamonds, oil, and its splendid peoples whose bodies had been sold into slavery for centuries, then used as forced labor, often worse than slavery, by colonial rulers in the Belgian Congo, for example—these images enlivened tales of conquest and exploration, creating a continent that was a stage set for European adventure narratives. But things were changing. Africa in the thirties was now being written in the black books of white women, as ethnography and as culture. Africa was being translated to the West, and to future native readers of its own cultures in terms of what remained of its social structures, often by admiring observers who saw in these "primitive" peoples the childhood of the whole human race. What do we make of these "translations" now?

In that same year, 1934, another white Englishwoman for whom Africa was an intellectual passion, Sylvia Leith-Ross (1883–1980), went out to Nigeria officially on the first of two government-funded Leverhulme fellowships. She was not the first Englishwoman to write about Nigeria, but her visits and memoirs over most of a century give us a very good example of what an enlightened Englishwoman of Nancy Cunard's class thought about Africa. Leith-Ross became an "expert" on Africa by living in Nigeria. In the spirit of the British colonial attitude, she cheerfully records that Nigeria was then called The White Man's Grave. And Leith-Ross certainly saw herself as a white man. She had first been out to the British colony in 1907 where her husband of one year died in his post. His grave was her altar and fetish in Africa for seventy years.

Her report from the field, *African Women: A Study of the Ibo of Nigeria* (Faber, 1939), collects specific information on the women who had organized the Women's War. Called the "Aba Riots" by the British, anxious to defuse the memory of the rebellion of 10,000 women who took over 6,000 miles of territory with a population of two million people in 1929 with a name that would give history no clue to the fact that African women had made war on their British occupiers—the name indicates a town, not a gender.[6] The Igbo[7] women refused to speak and answered the ethnographer's questions with questions of their own—they accused Leith-Ross of stealing their words to put in a government book to be used in a war against them. But her wildest fantasies always include a scene of native recognition of the importance of her work and her book, as in this passage from *Beyond the Niger* (1951) about her precious notebook getting wet in a storm. It is prefaced by the assertion that all illiterate peoples regard the book as sacred:

> Each seized the notebook in turn, blew on it, sat on it, rubbed it, waved it up and down, but all in vain. Then cook's wife, ignorant, illiterate, haphazard, slapdash cook's wife, pushed them aside, took the book, knelt by the table and dried it page by page in the light of the oil lamp. Patiently, reverently, she knelt there, delicately turning over the leaves, her eyes alight, breathing fast. In some dim recess of her brain she knew that at that moment she was a colleague, a contributor to that shining edifice of knowledge that men [sic] build up bit by bit. She had not the faintest idea what that edifice was, but she knew she was a collaborator in something bigger than herself, bigger than her own work, bigger than the world itself...[8]

Sylvia Leith-Ross should have taken up fiction. There are similar scenes in *African Women*. In one memorable passage Leith-Ross describes her native translators (they were called Mary and Salome) having an epiphany over measurement, a fantasy in which she, unconsciously of course, plays the part of the intrepid lady explorer Mary Kingsley, who earlier had measured everything and every person she encountered in Africa.[9] Such scenes are the cultural equivalent of Sir Frederick Lugard's taxation of the tribes to pay for their own colonization, scenes in which the natives rejoice in being part of the big picture of British colonization. In his novel about the Women's War, *I Saw the Sky Catch Fire* (1992), T. Obinkaram Echewa, obviously using Leith-Ross's *African Women* as a source, invents the character of Elizabeth Ashby-Jones, an anthropologist taken hostage during the *Ogu Umunwanyi* or Women's War, whose notebook pages, along with a strand of light hair and a pearl, are kept by Ajuzia's grandmother Nne-nne as a talisman to keep alive the African women's version of the story of their war, material evidence of their own attempts to understand the other.[10] The fictional Ashby-Jones's notebooks record her frustration at the way her questions are answered with other questions; she does not speak the language and pays no attention to facial expressions; she counts everything and dismisses the proverbs, essential to the culture (those of many different African and diasporic cultures are included in *Negro*) as "only marginally meaningful":

> What the African ceremoniously disguises as deep thinking is to genuinely deep and complex thought what a baby's babblings are to a great poem. (N.B. This probably sounds harsher than I intended and possibly reflects the frustration I feel at this moment. Generally I have a kindly disposition towards these people, especially the women, and believe there is something "noble" in the very simplicity of their lives, but...)[11]

Leith-Ross's confidence that she was writing in the big book of world history, alas, was not misplaced. Later in this chapter we shall discuss the survival of comparative truths of memoir, interview, ethnography, and fiction regarding the Women's War. With the *imprimatur* of an introduction by Lord Lugard, the colonial policymaker who had established what was called indirect rule in the British territories in Africa,[12] Leith-Ross's *African Women* became an instant classic in anthropology, often reprinted. (The edition I use here from 1966 is from a Praeger series called *Books That Matter*, but there are later editions as well.) *African Women*, unlike the lost or bowdlerized *Negro* anthology, has not ceased to matter as a factual sourcebook after independence and beyond, and is quoted as an authority by Salome Nnoromele in *Life Among the Ibo Women of Nigeria* (1998).

Leith-Ross returned to Nigeria many times for official projects, mostly in education after initial work that produced a Fulani grammar. In the course of that work she studied with Maurice Delafosse in Paris, but seems to have confined her acquisition of knowledge to the language itself, not the enlightened attitudes of the French professor toward African cultures. As "translation" *African Women* has a major weakness. Igbo was a difficult "tone" language and she did not speak or understand it. All of Leith-Ross's researches were carried out through interpreters. In old age she collected and catalogued Igbo pottery when new local museums began to collect in Africa what little material culture had not been looted or taken abroad, presumably having changed her definitive opinion in *African Women* that the people she had studied earlier produced no art whatsoever. She had noticed pottery on earlier visits but, again, it did not fall into her category of what art is. The last story in her memoir records her effort on what she thought was to be her last night in Africa, "when I was able to guess what she was doing," to help Binta, the Jarawa potter, fire fifty pots at Jos: "This was not work, it was rather a collaboration between the woman and the elements."[13] Only nine small pots greeted the puzzled potter in the morning and these she gave to Leith-Ross, who writes that they had no idea where the "bad medicine" came from that destroyed the potter's magnificent work.[14] The end of the British Protectorate and the end of Leith-Ross's life in Nigeria coincided, she notes. Some part of her seems to acknowledge, dimly, in this anecdote, that she did not always protect the African women in her care.

For Nancy Cunard and other modernist artists and collectors, African pottery was not a product of guesswork or some magical confluence of moon, fire, and woman. It was made by an artist. In her childhood in the English Midlands, Cunard's encounter with a blind potter in the hills was marked with elemental awe at the creative instinct. To her this is what linked human beings across cultures and over centuries, the desire to make. When she "made" the *Negro* anthology or any of her other books, she was most fully human.

Sylvia Leith-Ross's views, shockingly retrograde to the contemporary reader (though there are those, I am sure, who will find pleasure in a certain nostalgia for the empire, particularly in the descriptions of dressing for dinner on a canoe in the Niger), may be traced in a series of books and the posthumous *Stepping-Stones: Memoirs of Colonial Nigeria 1907–1960*, edited by Michael Crowder.[15] The historian of Nigeria presents the memoirs without comment, but does allow himself a comparison not often made in colonial studies because, for him, the memoirs of the wives have given a different view of life in Nigeria from the administrators and district officers:

> We are fortunate to have this lively and penetrating account of the passage of a British protectorate from colonialism to independence. No Roman matron, as far as we know, joined her husband just after her countrymen had occupied Britain and then, despite his death from a chill while building roads across some East Anglian fen, returned again to the land she now loved though it had claimed her husband's life. Or, if she did, she left no record of her travels in that far-off isle, or of her reaction to its peoples and to her fellow Romans who ruled them.[16]

As a British education did not dwell on the period of slavery to the Romans, so Nigerian education did not teach the great periods of African history before colonization, but began with slavery, describing the British invasions as the pursuit of the slavers. How different the process would have been had the British in Africa described themselves as a former colony of the Romans or described Africa itself in Roman times.

In *African Women*, Leith-Ross chides the patriarchal administrators for not having sent women in earlier to study African women, and hints that if Igbo women had been given some of the power they were used to wielding in their traditional societies, violence could have been avoided. The British had set up individual men as "chiefs," disrupting local community organization, and they had usurped the role of the women by setting up courts of English law to settle disputes that had been handled by women's age groups. Leith-Ross could have, one thinks, insisted then, while the militant women were still alive, on the return of the Igbo social structure to its original democracy. But she did not. Neither did she take responsibility for the loss of Nigerian women's power under an English-style patriarchy, allowing herself to believe on one level that her work was of the utmost importance and, on another, that she could not really affect policy. Leith-Ross was involved with women's education from the beginning and its failure must in part be laid at her door. She jokes that the education of women was always on the agenda of the board of education but never discussed. In her lifetime the Igbo women warriors were reduced to ignorant dependents on their men, exactly like women in

England. Their punishment for rebelling was to become playthings of two patriarchies. The agent of this punishment was a woman.

As independence approached, Leith-Ross made a last (and failed) effort to run a finishing school for the wives of those who would rule the new state in the market town of Onitsha where she had lived earlier. Ironically, Onitsha was the home of the African nationalist Dr. B. N. Azikiwe. Leith-Ross was suspicious of the young men who had been educated in the West and then became the leaders of the drive for independence. She was outraged by the Igbo press's attempt to make a hero out of Azikiwe in a story that compared the young man's being sent to school at Calabar "to the Hegira or Flight into Egypt"; she blanched at the assertion that "Zik is a teacher showing light to his countrymen to find the way out of the horrors of British rule."[17] The Igbo were seduced by Azikiwe's oratorical skills, she writes in her memoir, on the eve of his election in the fifties: "From his first quiet words to the last, almost hysterical shriek, his contact with the crowd was like a fine-drawn wire, quivering at every breath."[18] Azikiwe's speaking skills were acquired in his local culture, of course, where oratory was cultivated and warmly appreciated.

But there was another way a white woman could express her concern for the future of Africa. Azikiwe and other Africans and Indians from the colonies were encouraged by intellectuals like Nancy Cunard, who nurtured them and introduced them to others who shared their politics for decades in radical circles in London, Paris, New York, and the West Indies. Big Brother was watching them, of course. From the U.S. Embassy in London (Department of Eastern European Affairs) in January 1934 came a memo: "Information has been received that George Padmore has given to Nancy Cunard the address of Professor B.N. Azikiwe, Lincoln University, Chester County, Pennsylvania, U.S.A. He thinks this individual may be able to help her in her negro propaganda." The informer was right, but it gives one a chill to think of who used the information and for what purposes. Moscow, Washington, and London were watching as Black and white intellectuals met to plan the future of Africa. White women did have a place in Africa, but representing English values, not fomenting the revolutions to come. The credentials of Azikiwe and Cunard were suspect compared to the relationships established with local chiefs by colonial "experts" like Leith-Ross.

Leith-Ross's authority as an investigator is established on the title page of *African Women* by the line "Sometime Leverhulme Research Fellow," and

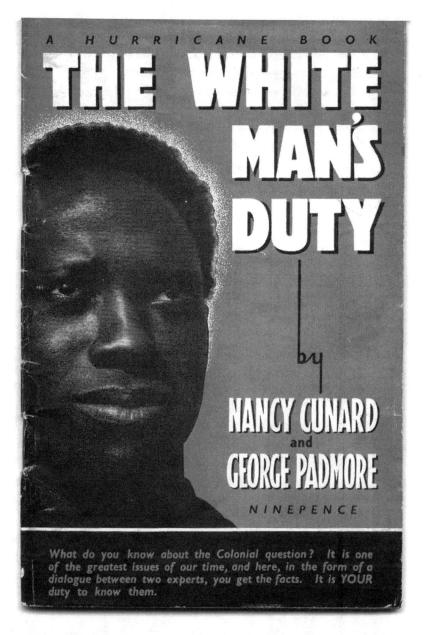

Figure 9.2. Cover of Nancy Cunard and George Padmore, *The White Man's Duty* (1943). Padmore, a leading pan-Africanist, journalist, and author, published *How Britain Rules Africa* with the help of Cunard in 1936.

by Lord Lugard's name in boldface followed by the details of his honors: "G.C.M.G., C.B., D.S.O." But Leith-Ross makes clear that she knows she was asked to do this work, despite her lack of training and academic qualifications, because of her family's long service to the empire in naval battles as colonial governors and district officers: "Nigeria has always been part of my life," she writes. Her grandfather had been in command of the sloop *Pandora* as it captured the last Portuguese slave ship. That narrative, that the British were in West Africa to end the slave trade run by the Portuguese and the Fulanis, is another story. Because she has taken on this difficult assignment out of patriotic duty, she is particularly frustrated at the Igbo women's lack of respect for the British Empire and what she regards as its gift of schools, roads, railways, and English culture and "civilization."

Furious at her subjects for addressing her as "Government," and asking her over and over again wherever she went why England had bought whale oil to reduce the price of palm oil, she absolves herself and her work from implication in England's manipulation of the world market. The Igbo women clearly have a global sense of economics, and in their way are telling her that the rebellion was based on a refusal to pay taxes to a government that did not have their economic interests at heart. The rebellion was about taxation without representation. The Igbo knew that their livelihood depended on palm oil. If Britain did not protect its pricing, her African subjects saw no point in paying taxes. Lugard's policy of getting the colonized to pay for their own colonization did not work among the Nigerian tribal women whose public role was to be responsible for their people's welfare. The local women had an analysis of the situation that was correct. Such an economic analysis of their own activities was made by the ruling sector of the colonial administration, but it is clear from their writing that those in the field believed in their own and England's benevolence.

Brought up in a class and culture that sought to separate women from trade and money as a sign of superior femininity, Leith-Ross's distaste equates the values of the African women traders with those of Jews, and her descriptions of the Nguru, for example, suggest that they live in slums that remind her of the East End of London. (Echewa's characters remark that the British named them with "Jewish" names.) Her own fear of finance—a taboo for upper-class women in her own society, far removed from the origins of their wealth, however violent its accumulation, and taught to believe that open discussion of the amassing of wealth was vulgar and even immoral—causes her to see their activity as un-sexing, and her praise of the Igbo's "abstract sense of justice" is tempered by its closeness to a similar stereotype of Jews.[19]

Indignant that she should be taken for an official surveillance officer, Leith-Ross claims an independence and objectivity that exposes for the contemporary reader the government's manipulation of her patriotic belief in a "just" imperialism. Leith-Ross acted for British Nigeria as an English native informant; in their eyes her gender was equivalent to the race of her African native informants, a guarantee of her sincerity. Feminist critiques of white women's work in the colonies and their contributions of knowledge to imperialism often fail to see the idealism and false sense of agency with which women like Leith-Ross undertook their tasks, ideologically committed to male colonial administrations that exploited them.[20] In the field of anthropology as well, her work does not have the status of that of another Leverhulme Fellow, E. E. Evans-Pritchard, whose study of the Nuer (1940) is highly respected despite his similar idiosyncrasies.[21] Evans-Pritchard dismisses the thought of studying gender relations among his subjects with evident distaste. But, of course, gender indeed would have been his topic if the Nuer women had made war on their conquerors like the Igbo, and he did eventually write about women in "primitive societies."

It had so happened that Leith-Ross's brother, Upton Fitzherbert Ruxton, was the luckless officer from the North who had brought Lugard's taxation policy to Iboland, and, in effect, stirred up the women's rebellion. Was he also the officer who shot and killed the unarmed women rebels? In searching out the African women's motives, Leith-Ross's family honor was at stake, her own (to use her own oddly repeated phrasing) white manhood was to be satisfied.

One might say, in the spirit of the psychological explanation to which she finally reverts in her discussion of three different groups of women, that Leith-Ross acted out her ethnography of African women in (repressed) revenge for the death and defeat of certain white Englishmen. She was supposed to discover how the women had communicated with each other so fast over so large a territory to mobilize for war so quickly, and to figure out the symbolism of the palm leaf the women warriors carried. She failed. Inadvertently she remarks that the women wore small drums with sticks attached on their wrists. But she only hears the drums as musical instruments and does not know that they are used to communicate. I cannot resist the picture of the Igbo women filing off to market with their "primitive" cell phones, like women on Wall Street, traders like themselves, bargaining for a good price for palm kernels or palm oil, occasionally sending a message home to the children, telling them to get dinner started. What is interesting about *African Women* is that it invites such readings. Leith-Ross was observant. She did, like her predecessor, Mary Kingsley, count and measure. Her ultimate frustration was at never achieving a woman-to-woman cross-cultural, cross-racial connection, undermined as her work was by her own subject position as a woman under British patriarchy, by the imperialist demands of the state, and by her own ideas of racial superiority.

Unauthorized, Unfunded, and Surveilled: Cunard and the Collective Work of *Negro* Anthology

The *Negro* anthology and its £1500 printing costs were paid for by British newspapers that Nancy Cunard had sued for racist libel and slander. These were articles published while she was doing research for a book that was to give Black people all over the world overwhelming evidence for pride in the achievements of Africa and its cultural diaspora. More than 800 pages of texts, drawings, and photographs, the anthology is a rare volume worth thousands of dollars, available to scholars in a limited number of libraries (not, insignificantly, the Library of Congress). The contemporary reader might judge this encyclopedic work to have been a government-sponsored project, so wide-ranging is it in expertise and scope. It is still hard to imagine how Cunard collected and edited this huge mass of material on her own without any subvention from government agencies, universities, or museums.

Hugh Ford edited and reprinted about one third of the volume in the 1970s at the height of the Black Power movement in the U.S., and that bowdlerized version has recently been reprinted in the United States. The African section alone, 271 pages (584 to 855 in *Negro*), is reduced in Ford to 102 pages. Eighty-four pages of plates of West African and Congo sculpture are reduced to twenty-one. The *Negro* anthology's final essay is not included in Ford, Raymond Michelet's thirty-three-page history of colonization, "The White Man is Killing Africa," an indictment of Western civilization and, arguably, the signature piece of the volume, its primary political statement.[22]

> I have ended the book with this—I cannot say: I have ended it on this *note*, for the chord of oppression, struggle and protest rings, trumpet-like or muffled, but always insistent throughout. In this

present day it is not possible to write otherwise of the Negro, and write with truth.[23]

Because Michelet was a student working closely with Cunard, the essay may be read as a collaboration reflecting her views as well. The book that Nancy Cunard *made*, and that is her word, emphasizing the hands-on effort of collecting, sorting, illustrating, revising, setting up and designing the pages, proofreading and overseeing the printing, binding, and collating of the volume, with the help of her "chief collaborator, Raymond Michelet" in writing, editing, and drawing masks and maps, and Edgell Rickword in production and proofreading—that book has not mattered enough to be kept in circulation.

Or, perhaps one should say that the *Negro* anthology is a book that mattered too much to those who did not want its message about the historical power and living vitality of African arts and culture around the world to be widely disseminated, not to mention its revolutionary politics. The book was banned in British colonies and protectorates, clearly because of the hard-hitting analyses of British colonialism by a whole generation of African and African-identified intellectuals, including T. K. Utchay, H. Kwesi Oku, Lapido Odunsi, Kobina Sekyi, Ben N. Azikiwe, Johnstone (Jomo) Kenyatta, George Padmore, and E. T. Mofutsanyana.[24] Cunard's association in Paris with M. Perez-Medina, who wrote on the position of the negro in Cuba, was duly noted for the file. The State Department copy of the proofs of the table of contents with corrections in Cunard's hand crosses out Wallace Johnson's name as the author of "Letter from Nigeria," leaving it anonymous, possibly for fear of reprisals. In his essay in *Negro* called "African Exploration," Arthur Schomburg writes, "Africa has been for centuries a closed book."[25] Clearly there were strong interests in keeping that book closed. Raymond Michelet's "African Empires and Civilizations," later reprinted as a separate pamphlet, does more, perhaps, to open that book than any other contribution to the volume, providing as it does a history of African civilizations before the Europeans came.[26]

The title page reads *NEGRO / Anthology Made By / Nancy Cunard / 1931– 1933*, humbly stressing her role as merely assembler or collager of evidence of ancient and thriving artistic cultures in Africa and the diaspora. Cunard had established herself as a maker of small beautiful books at the Hours Press, a maker in the mold of her one-time mentor, Ezra Pound, whose tribute to the scholar Frobenius appears in *Negro*. Fulminating against academics for not translating Frobenius, Pound quotes a passage that might have been useful to Sylvia Leith-Ross about an artist leaving his drawing paper behind on an expedition in 1903, and the European's amazement at the speed of the signal drum to send for it. Frobenius also mentions a tribe that uses little flutes for communication with a vocabulary as large as a language.

Now Nancy Cunard was making a very big book, not by herself, but in collaboration with a huge collective of authors. She did not ask for a dispensation from Lord Lugard or any other authority. The collection was to generate its own authority as a socialist text. Her volume, too, had a signature, a photograph of a Black worker's head in a cap in profile titled "An American Beast of Burden," and captioned "Photo by Howard Lester, New York, courtesy of the artist." Lord Lugard would not have approved, though Sylvia Leith-Ross also thought of the Black man as a laborer—her image of the Black man in a torn white singlet recurs throughout her writing, though it is his muscular buttocks that recur in the drawings that accompany her memoirs. The African dockworker or proud rower of canoes in the Niger inspired the imperialist as well as the revolutionary. Cunard makes him a man by picturing his head; Leith-Ross makes him a savage by picturing his naked body at work.

Leith-Ross comments several times on the fact that these people produce no art. Yet while she was there the magnificent Ife heads were found, thought to be some of the most beautiful works of African art in existence. The *Negro* anthology is a treasure-house of African art, including what had come to be seen as the signature of Cunard's personal style, magnificent ivory bracelets and anklets from Nigeria, particularly those worn by the Igbo, photographed for *Negro* by Raoul (Rolf) Ubach from Cunard's extensive collection. The ivory bracelets and other African pieces owned by Cunard were vandalized and destroyed when the Nazis occupied her house outside of Paris. Leith-Ross does not mention the Igbo women's ivory bracelets, earned at puberty and signatures of status, according to Basden, an omission that seems very odd indeed. They appear only in her portrait of Madam Naomi, a rich trader who wears them with her rose velvet costume, rolling from side to side as she walks, sitting with her legs wide apart and drinking neat whiskey, one of Leith-Ross's persistent examples of the Igbo equation of "good" with "rich."[27]

It is instructive that it is over the figure of the African intellectual Ben N. Azikiwe that the two women writers we are discussing here actually meet. As a young radical, Azikiwe wrote "Liberia: Slave or Free" for *Negro* in 1934 and then, as Dr. Nnamdi Azikiwe, returned from the U.S. in 1937, he founded the *West African Pilot*, and was the N.C.N.C. Party candidate in 1956, in the election that led eventually to Nigerian independence. The symbol to Leith-Ross of the communist Antichrist, whose "hysterical" election speech and "bribery" at the polls she recalls in *Stepping-Stones*, Azikiwe became first governor-general, then president of Nigeria. Nina Emma Mba reports that when taxation of women was introduced again in the region in 1956 there was a protest demonstration in Aba of over a thousand market women, and that Azikiwe promised a delegation that if elected he would exempt women from tax.[28] It would be ironic if the speech that Leith-Ross "heard," although she did not speak the language, gave women's rights as part of his platform. As in England the qualification for the vote was tied to the ownership of property and its taxation, so the franchise for women was limited and differed from region to region. Azikiwe was considered to be the strongest male supporter of women's rights in Nigeria by all the women interviewed by Mba.[29]

To *Negro*'s visual signature of the Black working class in the United States was added a textual signature, a poem by Langston Hughes, "I, Too." What Cunard calls upon to authorize her production of *Negro* is the beauty of "the darker brother" in body and in work. African cultural production on the continent and abroad is called up in a European/Russian primitivist communist discourse, shared by fellow travelers Cunard and Hughes, that sees Black workers simultaneously as "beasts of burden," their plight symbolizing the plight of all the workers of the world, and as unspoiled Adams and Eves in a pure African garden of Eden where all humanity can be seen "as it was in the beginning." Their strength derives from bodies not yet degenerate from industrial toil in cities and at machines. Cunard somehow expected her white metropolitan readers to see what she (and Hughes) saw in the African body, the natural strength and beauty of all mankind's origins, an inspiration to those whose physical and spiritual freedom was lost in centuries of "civilization." Langston Hughes contributed five other poems to the anthology, "Florida Road Workers," "House in the World," "To Certain Negro Leaders," "Always the Same," and "Goodbye Christ," along with the rabble-rousing "People Without Shoes" for the section on Haiti:

> Hayti is a land of people without shoes—black people, whose bare feet tread the dusty roads to market in the early morning, or pad softly on the bare floors of hotels, serving foreign guests. These barefooted

ones care for the rice and the cane fields under the hot sun. They climb high mountains picking coffee beans, and wade through surf to fishing boats in the blue sea. All of the work that keeps Hayti alive, pays for the American occupation, and enriches foreign traders— that vast and basic work—is done by Negroes without shoes ... Yet shoes are things of great importance in Hayti. Everyone of any social or business position must wear them. To be seen in the streets bare-footed marks one as a low-caste person ... What then, pray, have the dignified native citizens with shoes been doing all the while ...? Hayti today: a fruit tree for Wall Street, a mango for the occupation, coffee for foreign cups, and poverty for its own black workers and peasants.[30]

An international multicultural future is imagined in Cunard's utopian project with a faith she shared with Hughes for the next three decades. They were satellites to the Communist Party who often found themselves in the same orbit. Doubtless the Party found them problematic in the same ways, in their unconventional and changing sexualities and their insistence on the primacy of the race issue in the class struggle. Regarded as naive loose cannons, whose public utterances could not be controlled, Langston Hughes and Nancy Cunard remained revolutionaries on the race question when the Party changed its position over and over again. Hughes wrote to Cunard faithfully and sent her every book he published, even when she was destroyed from illness and drink.

How could white people in the face of so much evidence of Black creativity and excellence, so much proof of injustice, torture, and enslavement, fail to be, as Langston Hughes put it in the diction of the American schoolroom, ashamed of themselves? Cunard deliberately designed and printed the anthology as a compendium whose size and thin paper resembles the Bible. She meant it to do the cultural work of anti-racism as a (left-wing) Bible of racial brotherhood, to shame whites and to encourage Black pride. That *Negro* did not and could not fulfill such dreams is a measure, not of Cunard's effort or her commitment to the struggle for racial freedom, but of the systems of publication, circulation, and reviewing that pitched it into the dustbin of history.

Why is it that *African Women* became a book that mattered and the *Negro* anthology did not? Both Nancy Cunard and Sylvia Leith-Ross worked in anger. Leith-Ross wanted respect from the African women as "a fellow woman." They withheld that respect because she was gathering information that might be used against them. Wounded in her womanhood, and envious of African women's freedom and independence in comparison with Englishwomen, Leith-Ross retaliated by characterizing her subjects as utterly materialistic, lacking ethics or spiritual values as she sees them. This justifies her anger at being treated like an Englishman.

Evans-Pritchard found the legendary hostility and obstinacy of the Nuer a challenge to his manhood. He befriended a group of young men while hunting and fishing who convinced their elders to accept him. They were so uncooperative that he was "driven crazy," and he jokes that a few weeks of living with the Nuer produced the "symptoms of Nuerosis" in "the most patient ethnologist." He concludes that "Nuer social organization is simple and their culture bare," but he does not take their opposition to his questioning personally.[31] He understands their perception of him as the enemy. In fact, he knows he is the enemy. Leith-Ross projects her discomfort onto the women she is studying and she describes the Nguru women as suffering from "arrested development" and living a "mass neurosis"[32] as a result of the Women's War:

> [E]ach time my memory goes back to them I invariably find myself caught up in the unreal, super-sensitive, egocentric atmosphere of a vast concourse of neurasthenics, I invariably hear the illogical arguments, the exaggerated reiterations and see the tense faces, the thin bodies and slightly glaring eyes [...] the real texture of their lives was made up of suspicion and fear, self-pity and self-justification, a sense of frustration and a sense of guilt [...] Their voices were shrill with anxiety, their bodies ready poised to dive off the deep end [...] they were both servile and truculent. And their cupidity knew no bounds.[33]

Leith-Ross takes a novelist's liberty here, inventing a story perhaps more appropriate to the emotional lives of the downtrodden women of her own culture. In fact it is her experience with European mental patients that she projects onto her subjects. This is how myths are made. When Mrs. Leith-Ross first came to Africa as a young wife in 1907, she lived in the North. She carried a book and was looked on as a wise woman by the Muslims and treated very deferentially.

The failure of the Igbo (called pagans by the British) to accord her the status of priestess offends her particularly because she admires their courage. To them she is doubtless a failure as a woman because she is doing the work of the government men, the work of counting, of collecting information that goes to the rulers and ends in the destruction of their palm-oil economy. In her country few women concerned themselves with such economic problems and her hopes for a cozy chat over the fire about domestic issues were dashed.

Gender was not at stake in Nancy Cunard's work. She behaved like a man in the sense that, assuming authority and control of her project and taking full responsibility for every aspect of its production from the broadest philosophy of intent and politics to the layout of its pages, she was in charge. Cunard's anger at injustice was the force that drove her to complete such an enormous task. Anger became the chief aspect of her personality at some points, much to the chagrin of her friends. But it fueled her work for the cause and she was very productive and very effective. Her anger was never directed at Blacks, and the *Negro* anthology is amazingly free from personal anger. But the book is a monument to the fury of Black intellectuals and their white supporters at imperialism and colonialism in Africa. *Negro* bristles with righteous anger at white southern lynch gangs in the United States, the Ku Klux Klan, white police in South Africa, and even dated Communist Party anger at bourgeois Black institutions, seen for a brief period as obstructing the path of the revolution of the Black working class in the United States. The text is marked visually as a documentary in its typefaces, margins, headlines, illustrations, drawings, and photographs. *Negro* is a factual encyclopedia for change, a textbook for revolution, a book that proved that Africa and Africans were everywhere, makers of spiritual philosophies and great art forms. *Negro* contains no element of defensive autobiography; Nancy Cunard, the woman with the famous face is faceless here. *African Women* tells us as much about English women as it does about Leith-Ross's Igbo women. The reader's attention is directed to the plight of the author, struggling alone in the jungle with uncooperative Africans. But *Negro* gives us more information than we can process about African culture and none about its editor. Hundreds of different voices speak; Cunard's unmistakable tones are heard when one of her contributors failed to complete a piece or when a translator fell through. She produces the play and stays behind the scenes.

The *Negro* anthology, despite what those few critics who have seen it have made of it, is not about Nancy Cunard. It is about Africa and its cultures in diaspora. *Negro* is not about white people, though they contribute to its building of a knowledge base. The labor of white intellectuals certainly gives weight to the volume. There are no white faces authorizing the text. The only white faces in the book are those of a lynch mob leering at a Black man's body hanging from a tree.[34] This fact cannot be emphasized strongly enough, given that much of the criticism of the book is based on readers' response to images of Cunard herself. Hugh Ford tried to make his bowdlerized edition of the anthology a success by filling it with icons and images of Nancy Cunard, the celebrity, a violation of every principle of the book's organization. She would have been horrified. The reprint's back cover quotes Julius Lester in the *New York Times*: "The most ambitious anthology on Blacks ever attempted and a mirror of a fascinating woman." The *Negro* anthology is not in any sense a mirror of its editor's looks or likes. It has no touch of the fascinating woman about it, though many other parts of her life did. For some readers indeed her poem "Southern Sheriff" and her Scottsboro piece's rush to judgment make her look far more foolish than "fascinating." Cunard's signature appears on seven pieces in the anthology as well as several translations, though the major presence in the volume of Samuel Beckett's many translations from the French indicates the origins of the project in Paris, and one may assume that many unsigned pieces include her efforts. Ford's use of her face to sell the book is an unforgivable act, a betrayal on top of so many other betrayals of Cunard's respect for Black culture and hope for the revolution.

Official and Unofficial Knowledges

Reading the two texts together, the *Negro* anthology and *African Women*, one may note certain differences between the production of official and unofficial knowledges about Africa for various publics in the thirties and after. The disciplines and discourses in which the volumes participated or did not participate provide a useful cultural setting in which to view the work of translating Africa (here we shall be looking specifically at British Nigeria) undertaken by European and American intellectuals in the thirties, as well as African intellectuals and political activists who wrote for the *Negro* anthology. Memoirs and fiction about the period by former white colonial officers like Joyce Cary, and novels by Africans recreating the period, may be read against anthropological and historical texts by Africans themselves as well as the British. Knowledges are produced and reproduced. Is it possible that a novel, the kind of fiction Cunard excluded from *Negro* because she feared it would contaminate the truth-value of her text, could, in the end, be the better bearer of knowledge about Africa?

Because Nancy Cunard and Sylvia Leith-Ross shared common race, gender, class, and cultural backgrounds, as well as, and perhaps most importantly, English national identity, during a critical period for colonialism, this reading of *Negro* historicizes the production and reception of the text in a way that accounts for the gender, race, class, and nationality of the editor in relation to the world from which she came. Contextualization with Leith-Ross's officially sanctioned ethnographical study makes clear how completely Cunard had to break with her culture and its values to embark on the primary intellectual work of her life, the translation of Africa to the West. Her radical world-view comes into focus beside Leith-Ross's liberal humanist, maternalistic imperialism, a view that was decidedly enlightened compared to that of most white Europeans and North Americans. Stripping herself of English national identity, Cunard became in the course of her research work a pan-Africanist, a member of a multiracial international group of left intellectuals. Leith-Ross got caught in the folds of the Union Jack as it flew over Nigeria. Infantilized as a woman in her own culture, she treated the haughty and dignified Igbo women like naughty children or mental patients (her own comparison), but it is clear that on one level she envies their independence and their power to act politically in the world outside their yam fields. Reading her now at some distance we may perhaps see that she is an agent of the state punishing the Igbo women for making war by bringing them, like Western women, into the experience of patriarchy and powerlessness.

The extent to which one may call *African Women* official knowledge is itself problematic, as it seems to have functioned on several different levels: first, as a detailed analysis for colonial administrators after the Aba Riots/ Women's War of the power structures of women's lives that had been ignored; second, as a straightforward scientific textbook in the field for many years and; third, later, as an example for a new generation of professional anthropologists of collusion between government and anthropology. To these readers *African Women* was simply a "paternalistic and extremely ethnocentric" memoir or "travel diary" lacking academic anthropological "analysis."[35]

If we see the *Negro* anthology and *African Women* as forms of unofficial and semi-official knowledge production, the fact that the writer-researchers were women is important. Gender was not an essential component of Nancy

Cunard's identity, and she established her credentials on the left in a pamphlet called *Black Man and White Ladyship*, denouncing her mother and her mother-country as racist and imperialist, sacrificing all future claim to white ladyship and allying herself with the Black man and his struggle against her own people. The publication of the hard-hitting attack on family and culture and her bold public appearances with Henry Crowder in public places in London to challenge the "color bar" disinherited her both as Lady Cunard's daughter and as an Englishwoman, and in some primal shattering of European taboos, seems to have un-gendered her, so that journalists felt no qualms in printing the most scurrilous and unfounded stories about her. Cunard's class allowed people, particularly Americans, to dismiss her work in advance as merely a lady's scrapbook, while her race and class drew upon her the accusation that she was a thrill-seeker in search of Black men.

No one accused Leith-Ross of sleeping with Igbo men. She traveled long distances alone with African porters and servants without the slightest fear. Helen Calloway writes that generations of white women traveled alone in West Africa without fear of African men, who kept their distance, that there was no African interest in sex with whites.[36] Leith-Ross's admiration for Igbo women was directly the result of a feminist realization that they had had far more power and dignity in their lives and more public political responsibility and freedom than any European women. I don't imagine that this knowledge made her work any easier.

Such a feminist attitude based on a fierce independence and an insistence on agency would have been natural in a woman of Nancy Cunard's personality and political background. That she was not a feminist in any active sense, however, differentiates her from most other politically active white women of her era. Race and class came first for her. Cunard certainly had sex with Black men who were her comrades in political struggle and intellectual action, much as men in similar circumstances did. And she was harshly judged for it. There would obviously have been far less of an outcry if her book had been called *Negro Women*. Had she traveled to Harlem alone or with another woman, or concentrated her work on negro women alone, Cunard would properly have been following in the footsteps of those redoubtable British lady-travelers, who were, in fact the predecessors of Sylvia Leith-Ross: Mary Kingsley, who set the tone for future ethnographers in her passion for measurement, and Gertrude Bell, the formidable explorer of the desert. It has been suggested that Cunard neglected the cause of African women. However advanced African women were in their own societies, the two patriarchies set them back, and they were not among the generation of young intellectuals sent abroad to study; so, of course, they were not befriended by Cunard. The alliance then forged between African male intellectuals and white women abroad was set up by the fact that African women were not educated to go abroad with their men—which brings us back to Sylvia Leith-Ross and that belated finishing school in Onitsha in the fifties. Colonialism produced the difference in education between African men and women. But the anthology does include the work of Black women, and whites as well, among them, aside from the major contributions of folklorist Zora Neale Hurston, Gladdis Berry Robinson whose "Three Great Negro Women" gave biographies of Phyllis Wheatley, Sojourner Truth, and Harriet Tubman; Heba Jannath on "America's Changing Color Line"; Pauli Murray's "Three Thousand Miles on a Dime" on a ten-day hobo train ride across the U.S.; Dr. Sarah Frances Chenault's furious indictment "The Ku Klux Klan in Indiana"; Josephine Herbst's "Lynching in the Quiet Manner"; Maud Cuney Hare's "Folk Music of the Creoles" and "Negro Music in Porto Rico"; Carrie W. Clifford's "The Black Draftee from Dixie"; Black poet Georgia D. Johnson's "Old Black Men" and "Celibacy," and white poet Florence Ungar's "Elevator Men"; Beatrice Hastings on "The Young Race of the Veld"; Grace Hutchins on "Hayti"; Hazel Ballance Eady on "Virgin Island Negroes"; and Olga Comma on "Folklore in Trinidad." Altogether, with Cunard's own contributions, the presence of women in the *Negro* anthology is certainly stronger than it is in any other collection from the time.

Sylvia Leith-Ross could be dismissed as daughter, widow, and sister of colonial officers by a government that was embarrassed by or no longer needed her services, when, in fact, her very lack of objectivity was the qualification that brought her the fellowship to begin with. She had internalized British imperialist ideology so completely and was so politically and historically naive that her challenge to the government as a feminist was weak and ineffective. She saw Igbo women as "ambitious, courageous, self-reliant, hardworking and independent," but she agreed with her predecessor, Margery Perham, that the Igbo were "one of the least disciplined, and least intelligible" of African peoples.[37] She found that traditionally the women lived in full equality with men and were often the dominant partners in a social structure based on an exogamous family; they were responsible for the economic well-being of the community and she admired their "highly-developed" business instincts. But she recommended that they not be given back the power that had been theirs before the Women's War in the native courts, but rather that, like women in England, they run "borough councils" and handle issues like housing, markets, hygiene, and cleanliness. The government should establish the post of "Woman Secretary of Women's Affairs." The Ibo women reminded her of French businesswomen, reveling in their power to organize and deal with money on a large scale:

> There would be no confining these women within the conventional bounds of home life, not unless we wished to atrophy, to waste their vigour and their special savour [...] If we want them to be ladies they will cease to be women; if we expect them to be womanly, they will merely become weak.[38]

The Igbo women's self-assurance and lack of reverence or respect for white people frightened her, Leith-Ross admitted: "True democrats, no one was better than themselves but yet they were better than anyone else."[39] Trying to obey the precepts of the new anthropological methods that take account of the investigator's attitude, she confesses that "I would be deeply distressed if, because I have no great liking for a people so entirely dominated [...], I had not perceived their qualities nor helped others to appreciate them."[40]

Both books participate in the production of knowledge about Africa in the West. As a personal account of ethnographic fieldwork, Leith-Ross's study follows Gregory Bateson's dictate, new in the thirties, that the ethnographer admit her own biases and explain her values in relation to those of her subjects, the Igbo, already identified by previous observers on whom she relies as simultaneously the most forward-looking of African peoples and the most "primitive." Following Margery Perham's *Native Administration in Nigeria*, Leith-Ross openly acknowledges her goal of discovering how women's rights and responsibilities are perceived among the Igbo in order to understand the Women's War. Clearly her work is a form of government surveillance, undercover work as it were, in which it is imagined that the Igbo women will bond with the anthropologist in their common femaleness and reveal the secrets of their power to organize quickly when threatened. They don't. Her efforts to discover the symbolism of the palm branches passed from one woman to another, according to Perham's account of the call to arms in the Women's War, is fruitless. Her contribution is to psychoanalyze what she sees as the anxiety and guilt of the natives.

Nancy Cunard's function as editor of an enormous collection of essays, ethnographies, photographs, music, poetry, stories, folklore, and studies of African art and politics in African countries and in the African diaspora allows many voices to speak, most of them the voices of Black people in English and in translation. The effect is to celebrate and record difference and debate. Leith-Ross calls her book *African Women*, generalizing from the particular Igbo villages she researches to gender in the continent, assuming similarity. The *Negro* anthology acknowledges that its collection of knowledges about Africa is partial and contradictory.

The two Englishwomen were self-educated. Were they inspired amateurs or untrained interlopers when they sought to discover and disseminate information about Africa? Cunard herself was an autodidact in metropolitan Paris and London, imagining Africa from afar, prevented by the color bar from traveling to the colonized countries with her Afro-American companion, Henry Crowder. Leith-Ross was a colonial insider and, unlike Cunard, who maintained a continual critique of British colonialism, she was shocked at the refusal of Africans to acknowledge the moral and ethical justice she thought imperialism had brought to Africa.

Leith-Ross first went out to Northern Nigeria as the bride of the Chief Transport Officer in 1907. As a young widow she was asked to make a study of the Fulani language by Sir Frederick Lugard; later she toured the country for the colonial Education Department, returning again to Ilorin to study the possibility of "educating Mohammedan girls," and later to Kano to start a school for girls. Leith-Ross's "credentials" consist of her relation to various Englishmen who conquered and ruled Nigeria. Despite the fact that her brother "served," as she puts it, first with the Royal Niger Company, then as Resident and Lieutenant-Governor of the Southern Provinces, she believed that the empire was good for Africa and that England's primary interest in Africa was the spread of its ethics and morals. She had imbibed these views not with her mother's milk but with her father's first poetry lesson, "the grim old sailor's rhyme: The Bight of Benin—the Bight of Benin, Few come out though many go in," casting the British imperialist attackers as victims of African geography—a bight is a bay between headlands—as Conrad and others had described the heart of darkness as a devouring female cave—and obscuring the fact that the British raids on the ancient city looted the magnificent Benin bronzes now in the British Museum. "He was in command of a sloop at the taking of Lagos," Leith-Ross writes proudly.[41] In that kind of historical narrative we could say that later she was in command, metaphorically speaking, of Britain's revenge for the Women's War, passively overseeing the subjection of the once-proud Igbo women to a new patriarchal social structure that would ensure their obedience. Leith-Ross was the natural choice of investigator when the government belatedly wanted to know why the Women's War had happened, and she set off to study the women to discover the secret of their power of instant communication.

Two other women-led rebellions had occurred in 1925 and 1927, called the Spirit Movement and the Dancing Women, and they are analyzed from the point of view of interviews with African women in Nina Emma Mba's *Nigerian Women Mobilized*. Mba also gives a different view of the Women's War through the memories of African women. Despite his denial, all of the African movements were fictionalized by Joyce Cary from the perspective of the British colonial officer. Caricatures of Sylvia Leith-Ross and other women anthropologists and missionaries, as well as portraits of the wives and sisters of the British officers, appear in his books alongside the characters of African and British men and doubly demonized African women. Cary's novels *Aissa Saved* (1932), *An American Visitor* (1933), *The African Witch* (1936), and *Mister Johnson* (1939) in fact may be seen as the most widely disseminated version of the story of the struggle between the natives and the British in Nigeria. Cary's African novels create a semi-official discourse about colonialism that is then rewritten by the Africans Chinua Achebe in *Things Fall Apart* (1958), Kole Omotoso in *Just Before Dawn* (1988), and T. Obinkaram Echewa in *I Saw the Sky Catch Fire* (1992).[42] British cultural knowledge about Africa in this period exists on many levels: the official reports of the district administrators, and in the case of the Women's War, the results of two commissions of inquiry; administrative and ethnographic studies by women like Perham and Leith-Ross, funded specifically to discover the causes of the Women's War, although Leith-Ross was not aware of her "official" position; works of white male anthropologists; the diaries of missionaries; shows of major collections of African art and artifacts in museums as art and as "natural history" in dioramas for ethnographic museums; and reproductions in living color, as it were, of African village life in Colonial Exhibitions in London and Paris with real Africans on view. The story of the African women warriors from their own point of view exists in Mba's oral history and, perhaps, in a cross-reading of their responses/resistance to the questions of English investigators like Leith-Ross.

Negro: A Scottsboro Book—Du Bois, the Communist Party, and the Struggle for Black Power

There are, of course, many ways to read the *Negro* anthology, for example for its production of knowledge for an international audience of Black readers, its place in the history of the form of the documentary, its participation in communist ideology, its powerful dynamic as a work of visual culture. But at the moment I want to put it in a context that challenges its recent reception in American Studies and African Diaspora Studies. The rare volume has been ransacked for material from Zora Neale Hurston, for instance, without crediting Cunard for discovering or publishing Hurston's anthropological essays or mentioning *Negro* as their source.[43] In their recovery of the lost writer, African-American feminists first focused on the fiction, particularly *Their Eyes Were Watching God*. The third American section of the anthology contains the first publication of Hurston's brilliant ethnological studies "Characteristics of Negro Expression," "Conversions and Visions," "Shouting," "The Sermon," "Mother Catherine," and "Uncle Monday,"[44] and "Spirituals and Neo-Spirituals" appears in the American chapter of the music section.[45] This other Zora Neale Hurston was a Ph.D. student of Franz Boas at Columbia, an extraordinary field worker from a family not so far from physical work in the fields. Hurston and Cunard were very much alike as bold, taboo-breaking women of powerful intellect, political conviction, and transgressive sexuality. Self-made women of genius, they were both personally flamboyant figures and serious intellectuals who lived hard, fought for their (very different) beliefs, made trouble and enemies, and were forgotten, figures who died hard into obscurity. Both were vilified, Hurston most notably by Richard Wright for her politics, as well as by those who thought that her celebration of Black dialect writing and speaking was regressive; and Cunard by barrages of racist hate mail, slanderous newspaper articles publicly accusing her of criminal sexual relations with Black men, and, now, as a scapegoat for the modernist avant-garde's supposed exploitation of the arts of Africans and Afro-Americans. In Cunard's case the vilification continues.

The pan-African construct of the Black Atlantic, perhaps the most important intellectual contribution of Cunard's project, its evidence of an African cultural diaspora, has been put forward as a new idea without reference to one of its major sources.[46] Arthur Schomburg's essay calling for a university chair in African History has provided historians and editors with full lists of slave narratives and a bibliography of works about Africa and Africans and by Africans and people of African descent for six decades. It's time to own up to the origins of such discoveries in the pages of a forgotten book.

Negro has been unfavorably compared to other American anthologies of Black literature, not models Cunard looked to, though their editors were asked to contribute and she commented favorably on their common work. The *Negro* anthology was "inspired," though that is a difficult concept, more basically, I think, by Blaise Cendrars's *L'anthologie negre*, a collection of African folk tales, as well as by the popular passion for African art and Afro-American jazz in which Cunard was caught up with her close colleagues, the Surrealists in France, the *tumulte noir*. It was in Paris that her racial ideology and identity was radically reshaped. When she came twice to do research in Harlem, she had heard all about it from the jazz musicians and Black boxers who were part of her world in Paris, as well as her writer friends like Claude McKay.

Alain Locke's *The New Negro* has been canonized as the collection that matters, despite his praise for Cunard's anthology:

> I congratulate you, almost enviously, on the finest anthology in every sense of the word ever compiled on the Negro. When I saw the announcements, I feared a scrapbook, but by a miracle of arrangement, you have built up a unity of effect and a subtle accu-mulative force of enlightenment that is beyond all contradiction and evasion [...] The serious analyses of Jazz by Antheil and Goffin are path breaking. You will have endless vindications in the years to come.[47]

The fact that such vindications did not come forth is as much a challenge to the historian of today as it was a disappointment to Cunard at the time. One of the reasons they do not appear now is that very few people have actually seen the *Negro* anthology. Another is that critics repeat a later disparaging comment by Locke in a move that is calculated to nationalize the work of knowledge production then and now in Afro-America, specifically Harlem, and in the field of American Studies, avoiding the international context of thirties poli-tics and focusing on the twenties and the Harlem Renaissance as a separate development. Of course, the reprinting of *Negro* would contribute much to that discourse as well. Cunard's own essay on Harlem is very interesting. It would be more productive of dialogue on the issues to try to understand why

Locke might have changed his mind. Was he pressured by Du Bois and the N.A.A.C.P. to do so? Claude McKay scholars have done the same thing in distancing him from the research for the anthology, for which he was a major source, on the basis of a much later comment in his memoir. Locke praised *Negro*'s "miracle of arrangement," and that unique gift for organizing intellectuals to write for a cause that had been Cunard's trademark ever since she had worked with Edith Sitwell, her brothers and other poets to protest World War I in the anthologies called *Wheels*. She practically invented the collective documentary of the thirties. It was a form of protest. Driven by its explosive content, the anthology was meant to stir things up. The U.S. publications had a different goal, to prove the Black man to be the intellectual equal of the white. For Cunard that was already a given, and she concentrated on radical content, and did publish writers just because they were Black.

Cunard's decision not to include fiction, concentrating on music, folklore, poetry, ethnography, history, journalism, and essay, was an attempt to keep the anthology on a higher plane. She didn't often read fiction, she didn't write fiction, and she didn't like fiction. She was particularly uncomfortable with fictions that were based on real people and real events. One may speculate that one of the attractions of African art was that it contained no stories about her or people like her.

Sensationalized into the kind of stories about her that Cunard was trying to escape in producing her most important life's work, current estimates of the anthology ignore its content. Illustrated with provocative photographs of Cunard as a fashion icon of the twenties from other contexts, this kind of slanderous "scholarship" implies that the *Negro* anthology itself contains such images. But all the images in *Negro* are of Blacks, and there are thousands of them. It was Cunard's stated policy not to include photos of the white contributors or herself. She knew the power of those photographs to affect her reputation as an intellectual. But her detractors have had a field day with her image in order to discredit her ideas. Why fetishize the face of an author when she has deliberately excluded that face from her documentary work? The book Nancy Cunard made created a whole world of Black people of all classes and conditions. It made connections between African peoples and their artwork, between history, slavery, and present conditions of African-American workers. It was visually stunning in its impact and totally unprecedented. *Negro* was a treasury of beautiful Black faces, faces of writers, dancers, anthropologists, historians, college presidents, men in suits, workers with their tools, intellectuals and politicians, actors and jazz musicians. The Black bodies in the *Negro* anthology are not the naked savages from the *National Geographic* or books of travel, adventure, exploration, or ethnography. The effect is of an enormous range of cultural difference, a difference that white readers would read as likeness to them, while Blacks would find in such a broad range of differences a sense of Black presence in the world that was not to be found in the daily newspapers.

Because the *Negro* anthology has been demonized by certain critics in American Studies, it seems all the more necessary to republish the volume and study its place in the cultural work of translating Africa.[48] Who benefits, we may ask, when Cunard is constructed as a brainless sexual predator and scapegoated as a particularly virulent kind of racist, a white woman who identifies with Black people? Why is it represented as ethically more incorrect to identify with the struggles of the oppressed than to ignore them? *Negro* has also been disappeared from Black British Studies, a discourse in which it deserves a major place, as well as from French intellectual history, though it is arguably a major document in the study of the Surrealist left. Had histories of the left in Europe, America, the West Indies, etc. claimed *Negro* as part of the struggle to build international connections across race and class lines, its reputation may have survived.

National tensions about race and class issues were clearly stronger than the utopian identification with the politics of the Black workers of the world that Cunard's collection demanded of its readers. The contradictions of the many conflicting political views expressed in the book, along with the presence of American Communist Party propaganda, practically insured its demise as a crucial document in the U.S. narratives of Black history as a specifically U.S. history that sought to erase the Party's importance and to stress instead the cultural importance of the twenties Harlem Renaissance over the political activism of the thirties. These narratives, perhaps suspicious of all international connections as communist, sought to gather up figures like Claude McKay into a story of Blacks as an American ethnic group. His Jamaican origins and his long sojourns in Europe and Africa, the things that made him a global figure as a Black intellectual, and certainly one of the most important influences on the making of *Negro*, are ignored in favor of a parochial view of McKay as a writer of fiction and a few poems.

Such narratives have also created a Black U.S. history with heroes and villains, starring W. E. B. Du Bois and dismissing people and movements like

Marcus Garvey's United Negro Improvement Association, certainly the most important Black political mass movement in America before the Black Power movement. The *Negro* anthology gave space to all the leaders and movements of the time. Typical of what Alain Locke calls "the miracle of arrangement" in the volume's organization is the placement of Pauli Murray's "Three Thousand Miles on a Dime" next to William Carlos Williams's "The Colored Girls of Passenack," or Kenneth Macpherson's plea for "A Negro Film Union" in the same section as the memoirs of the champion boxers, Bob Scanlon and Jack Taylor.

Cunard's editorial comments about Du Bois are omitted from Hugh Ford's 1970 reprint of the anthology, as well as her attack on his "bourgeois" journal *The Crisis*, and his organization, the N.A.A.C.P., over the Scottsboro Case. Du Bois supported the policy of counting as lynching only those cases that had been investigated, rather than the number reported. For Cunard and the International Labor Defense, it was vital to organize around the Scottsboro Case, because there were so many other Scottsboros or instances of lynching that never came to trial. In a sense one may see the *Negro* anthology as a victim of the battle between the N.A.A.C.P. and the I.L.D. for control of the Scottsboro Case. Historians have recorded these battles over Scottsboro, its lawyers and lawsuits and its publicity campaigns to rally support all over the world, as a struggle in which the cause was not well served by internal divisions on the left.

In challenging Du Bois, *The Crisis* and the N.A.A.C.P. in print, Cunard did not foresee the power of Du Bois's mainstream Black circles to boycott the *Negro* anthology and to see that it was not reviewed in the Black press in the United States. Their silence was deafening and Cunard never understood what had alienated her book from the good offices of Black intellectuals in the U.S. Surely the omission was calculated by Ford to enhance Cunard's reputation with an audience of Black nationalist readers in the seventies for whom Du Bois, who by this time had moved far to the left, was a hero.

"Black America," the article Du Bois wrote for *Negro*, is not listed in bibliographies of his work, nor are the article or Cunard and her critique mentioned by his biographers. Is it too bold to suggest that Du Bois's appearance in this international volume, situating his politics on the conservative side among many different radicals, may have irked him and initiated or contributed to his move to the left? Is it too bold to suggest that for some writers Du Bois's place as the most important Black American thinker as well as his central place in the mainstream of Afro-American history might have seemed threatened by the existence of this book in which he is only one of many voices? Seen in an international context in 1934, Du Bois is not the radical he became. This is perhaps embarrassing to those invested in a particular narrative of his life. Should we revise our estimate of his politics and imagine a scenario in which Nancy Cunard is an important factor in pushing Du Bois to the left? Whose interest does it serve to leave this incident in the life of a Black intellectual out of his biography?

Cunard's race may well be as much of a reason for the failure of her documentary to appear in histories of African-American thought, except as an example of misguided enthusiasm. There are certainly those who think that, like Leith-Ross's unconscious work for the British government, Cunard's position as a fellow traveler in the Communist Party made her necessarily their dupe. The Labour Party socialist Leonard Woolf, a long-time friend of Cunard's, saw her as so pure and single-minded on the subject of the revolution that she reminded him of a Russian "simple." But gender counts as well. That both self-made Africanists were women is important here. In re-reading their work we may want to take into account the fact that neither woman had the credentials usually necessary for such important undertakings, and both could easily be discredited because of their status as amateurs in fields that had now earned academic and institutional status, if their findings displeased the experts. Certainly, Cunard's failed trip to the Soviet Union, during which it became clear that the proposed translation and publication of *Negro* in Russian had fallen through, is an example of such a scenario, though further investigation would reveal, I think, a change of policy on the part of the Party regarding the centrality of race in its U.S. operations.

The *Negro* anthology got caught in a web of conflict between Black intellectuals and political activists over the Scottsboro Case. As the Soviet Union's policies toward the negro struggle in the U.S. changed often during the thirties, her book had gone to press with many writers denouncing the N.A.A.C.P. and moderate Black leaders as traitors when that was the Party line.[49] By the time it came to be reviewed, a United Front policy was in effect and writers like Eugene Gordon, who had joined the editor in attacking Du Bois and *The Crisis* for their cautious positions on lynching, were embarrassed by their fulminations. Consequently, there is a section of *Negro* on Blacks in the U.S. that is marked inescapably by a brief moment in history when the Communist Party's hopes were pinned on the Black workers whose signature stamps the volume to make a revolution without the help of bourgeois intellectuals. The Party had underestimated the ways in which Black Americans were Americans and were shaped by an American class structure and American values.

As a guide to race politics in the thirties, the *Negro* anthology is a truly remarkable document. When scholars begin to study it, there is no doubt that many established narratives will be called into question. It is so steeped in its moment, so suffused with socialist rhetorics and racial pride, so dated by the fierce languages of communist invective and denunciation, that we may begin to see it as the ultimate in the production of the documentary form of the thirties, as extreme in its insistence on the class components of racial consciousness as other classic monuments of Black Marxism by Richard Wright or Malcolm X.

PART V

Reporting War: The Journalism

CHAPTER TEN

Nanción's Canciós
Nancy Cunard and the Spanish Civil War

Nancy Cunard was a woman of action, physically brave, psychologically fearless, and morally intrepid. She was the female counterpart to *los intellectuals*, the writers and artists of the International Brigades who became the romantic heroes of the Spanish Civil War. Cunard's startling looks and "intrepid" white-girl-reporter braveries would have made her a popular figure in today's visual journalism, though she would doubtless encounter the usual macho battlefield critics like the jealous Hemingway, who is reported to have accused Cunard and her photographer-comrade John Banting of being "war-tourists" in Spain.[1] Writers accusing other writers of being war-tourists is a subtext of the work in anthologies of Spanish war writing, reminding the reader of the *angst* felt by writers about heroism in the field and their conflicting desires about being men of action.

Cunard's usurpation of the manhood of that role was disconcerting to her fellow reporters, especially when her trusty sidekick at the Front and in prison camps was a gay man. War enforces rigid gender categories. Stephen Spender's reports from Spain, for example, are mostly concerned with describing his personal experience of heroic masculinity as it appeared in the bodies of foreign intellectuals. Spender's anxiety, not to say panic, over his own masculinity appears in his writing as obsessive, guilty breast-beating about bringing his working-class lover, Jimmy, into left politics and inciting him to volunteer for Spain.

The Communist Party is constructed in Spender's writing as a monstrous lesbian matriarch controlling the war in Spain: "[a] Communist lady writer, and her friend, a lady poet," obviously the other English delegates to the Writers' Congress in 1937, Sylvia Townsend Warner and Valentine Ackland, the word "lady" a clue to his class panic at their presence in dangerous Spain. In a maneuver worthy of a generalissimo of propaganda, Spender manages to blame the home front or suburban middle-class Englishwomen (from whom heroes like himself and Auden must escape) for the deaths of beautiful young men in the Spanish war. Republican Spain turns into "a tea party" presided over by the "graciously forbidding" Warner acting like a "secretly superior [...] vicar's wife," her "shovel hat" a sign of allegiance to the murderous Party: "She insisted—rather cruelly, I thought—on calling everyone 'comrade,' and to me her sentences usually began, 'Wouldn't it be less selfish, comrade' ..." Spender reacts to the couple's presence at the writers' congress with several overlapping states of panic—about his masculinity, his homosexuality, his class and national status, all of which are threatened by these figures of middle-class British manners, who are really the commissars in disguise. They seem to represent both a smothering mother-country and a politics of suppressed violence and control.

Spender cannot bear to hear females use the word comrade, a word that in his world has a sexual subtext in its call to brotherhood, and he mocks the "Communist lady" writers for calling each other "comrade darling" and fussing over each other's tiredness. The term selfishness recurs in the passage, making clear Spender's psychic creation of his relation to the Communist Party as a child who is punished by a stern and forbidding Nanny. His figure works so that the reader will equate Warner and Ackland's committed antifascist writing with a ferocious female dogmatism that crushes the genuine uncommitted male writer like himself.[2] The taint of passages like these still clings to the writing of women comrades, whether in or out of the Party. Exposing its source in gender and class panic may allow us to re-read poets like Cunard, Ackland, and Warner with more pleasure. It is certainly ironic to recover a body of women's war writing that has been dismissed because it was too factual, too angry, too impersonal. The hesitancy and narcissism of the canonical poems has been construed after the fact as a real form of heroism in resistance to communism.

But gender was not one of Cunard's interests. Being a woman was not a source of her identity and it did not emerge in her brilliant war reportage for the Associated Negro Press International, the *Manchester Guardian* and hundreds of other wire services, newspapers, newsletters, and journals like the *Left Review*. Her gift to modern (and modernist) public discourse was the shaping, if not the invention, of the *form* of collective protest most characteristic of the century, the anthology of writing for a cause, the now ubiquitous pamphlet or newspaper advertisement bearing the signatures of intellectuals to demand the release of political prisoners, or an end to war or repression, often in some remote part of the world. Certain British writers and critics have never been able to come to terms with such protest forms as art. Cunard's hybrid writing, race-centered local color reportage that gets Black voices out on the news wires, or journalistic poetry that is as full of facts as feeling, is essentially a thirties documentary form.

The *Negro* anthology as well as Cunard's many political pamphlets, her multilingual editions of poems "for Spain" and later "for France," her powerful manifesto, *Authors Take Sides on the Spanish War*, a survey she sent out, compiling the replies for the *Left Review* when no other publisher would print it, organized intellectuals into publishing collectively their individual responses to fascism and racism. What is remarkable about that? the reader may ask. Her private practice of going public with the issues has become common practice.

Then and now the collective manifesto created and maintained international networks of like-minded people. The protest, bringing far-flung names together for a cause, functions like a political wire service. The multi-voiced political pamphlet is as heteroglossic as Bakhtin claims the historical novel is. It also creates a world, however fictional, of international solidarity. Cunard did not identify as a feminist. But the intense, lifelong political effort of connecting people and groups to one another, gathering them for intellectual action, publishing and translating radical poems and introducing revolutionary writers to their counterparts from all over the world was, I believe, the feminist element in her anarcho-communism.[3]

What I want to argue here, however, is that Cunard and her comrades produced an international and multiracial cross-class culture of protest against fascism in journalism, multilingual propaganda in poetry, theater, poster art, film, radio, collage, and pamphlets in the thirties. That culture's anti-national and mixed-race solidarities have been so systematically erased or buried by scholars of the period that the work of recovery has of necessity become oppositional to an established nationalist and elitist (male) canon.

The effect of the cultivation of Auden and Spender as *the* poets of the Spanish War, succeeding Owen and Sassoon as *the* poets of World War I, has been to deprive readers of color, women, the working classes, and lesbians and gay men who were not part of the Oxbridge poetry scene of the various literatures and cultures of their own that flourished during these wars. Worse, it has assumed that international subcultures of these groups did not exist. Nancy Cunard was at the center of many of these subcultures, wired like a wireless news service for world communication. As we recover these stories, it is well to remember that a generation before us lost or "disappeared" the racial and international stories that interest us today.

Cunard's energetic efforts, bringing together poets and intellectuals for Spain or rallying writers against racism from all over the world (Langston Hughes went to Spain at the bidding of a telegram from her), were, as some of her critics have argued, a political extension of Lady Cunard's salon. The friendships she forged between Langston Hughes and Nicolás Guillén, for example, or Louis Aragon and Pablo Neruda, or Samuel Beckett and Henry Crowder, were part of a political strategy of collectivity and connectedness that we associate with feminism. It is doubtless her gender, however, that allows scholars to continue to attribute *Writers Take Sides on the Spanish War* to the editors of *Left Review*, or to Louis Aragon, one of the signatories Cunard obtained for her introductory call.

It is not clear whether it was gender that caused Valentine Cunningham to deliberately undo the effect of Cunard's collective pamphlet in his *Spanish Front: Writers on the Spanish Civil War* (1986) by segregating the women in his "Taking Sides" sections.[4] Actually, only men are included in his "Authors Take Sides," a category that ought to be called "famous upper- and middle-class British male writers assimilating Eliot and Pound," and the women from Cunard's survey are included in a separate section called, defiantly, as if to make some kind of feminist statement, "Women Write Spain." Nancy Cunard's name is not among the women, nor does it appear in Cunningham's index, despite the fact that her survey forms the basis of his book. He even reprints Auden's "Spain," with a note saying it was first published as a pamphlet in 1937, but not that Cunard was the pamphlet's publisher, as well as the publisher of series of six leaflets of poems for Spain beginning in 1936, *Les Poètes du monde défendent le peuple espagnol*. The poems were in English, French, and Spanish, and Cunard set the type herself at Le Puits Carré in Reanville, Normandy, on the Hours Press machine with the one case of type she had kept after giving up the press. She had the help of Louis Aragon and Tristan Tzara (who also contributed poems), the ever-faithful John Banting, and one of her other favorite class renegades, Brian Howard, who contributed a satirical poem called "For Those With Investments in Spain," and also arranged a meeting in Paris between Cunard and Auden. There were poems by Lorca, Vicente Aleixandre, Gonzales Tunon, and Rafael Alberti in the series. Pablo Neruda, poet, lover, and comrade from the Spanish Front, recalled the snowstorm that raged as he clumsily tried to set type for the first time.

> I printed p's upside down and they turned into d's [...] A line in which the word "parpados" (eyelids) appeared twice ended up with two darpados. For years afterward, Nancy punished me by calling me that. "My dear Darpado..." she would begin her letters from London.[5]

In 1939 Geoffrey Faber and T. S. Eliot rejected the Cuban poet Nicolás Guillén's "España" because its message did not "fit in as an essential part of our programme." Faber found the poem a "vigorous [...] parallel [...] to Auden's *Spain*" and Cunard's translation "very good," but in the end its politics represented "too much of a side-turning off our own carefully planned route."[6] The agenda of the Faber and Faber poetry series was not disturbed. It was the aesthetic equivalent of the policy of non-intervention in Spain. Guillén's "Spain—a Poem in 4 Anguishes and 1 Hope" was an elegy and lament for the war in Spain. He joined the Communist Party in the same year, was a delegate to the anti-fascist Second International Congress of Writers for the Defense of Culture, and in addition to writing on Black issues, also began "to embrace the cause of the poor masses of Cuba and the world."[7]

Read Orwell or Hemingway if you want the Spanish Civil War with nostalgia, regret, atmosphere, or local color.[8] Read Cunard (or Martha Gellhorn) for unmitigated partisan politics.[9] Cunard also wrote for Charles Duff's *Spanish Newsletter*, *Spain at War*, and *Voices of Spain*. She published an essay called "Three Negro Poets" in the *Left Review* (which also circulated as an ANP dispatch) to call the attention of white European readers to the anti-fascist writing of Guillén, Langston Hughes, and the Haitian poet and "romantic personality" Jacques Roumain, and to publish parts of their speeches at the Paris Writers' Congress.[10] There is a certain primitivism about her description of Guillén's "dominant and masculine" poetry, "surging along through the hot panoramas of man's daily toil [...] full of hard rich image and the Black peasant's sonorous emphasis and vernacular [...] resonant with the Afro-Cuban drum-beat," a poetry that expressed "the secular mating of Africa and Spain in an oppressed exotic island."[11]

To Nancy Cunard the chief struggle against fascism in Spain and beyond was always tied to fascism's primary endorsement of racial and colonial oppression. She advocated violent action and revolt in Africa and revolution against Franco in Spain until she died, in contrast to that other English public intellectual who had abandoned her class, the Virginia Woolf of *Three Guineas*, written in the same year, for whom the origins of fascism were to be found in gender oppression and the patriarchal family, as she recommitted herself to her early pacifism. Neither the relationship of fascism to the oppression of women and children nor the relation of fascism to the oppression of people of color has received much scholarly attention, as fascism continues to be studied in relation to certain nationalisms and certain class constructions, efforts that, of course, disallow the possibility of any universal applications of the lessons of the thirties.[12]

"Writing is my fighting," wrote Woolf. "Writing," Cunard declared in the *Left Review*, "to all those who have a true sense of life [...] perforce rhymes with fighting," invoking the call to activism of the German writers at the Front with the People's Army, Gustav Regler and Ludwig Renn, "to make history" not stories. To the militant poets of color, she wrote, fascism "is an attempt to reinstitute, to prolong, slavery," and it was "a familiar enemy since birth—for what else are imperialism, race prejudice, and the myriad brutalities of the dominant white?"[13] Langston Hughes, caught in the anti-communism of the fifties, recalled his pride as a Black man, as Cunard was as a woman, of having earned his living as a writer for five years: "In the Civil War in Spain I am a writer, not a fighter. But that is what I want to be, a writer, recording what I see," he temporized in *I Wonder as I Wander* in 1956, though he makes clear that he had outgrown the Harlem and American identities that had shaped him and now wanted to speak to "all the colored peoples of the world."[14]

The credentials of Guillén, Hughes, and Roumain as revolutionary writers included the youth and beauty and heroism that Spender noticed in his foreign comrades—all were in their thirties and all had been to jail—but their color was deeper than the bronze of his "affectionate" Mexicans at the Spanish Writers' Congress. Cunard printed excerpts from Hughes's speech "Too Much of Race," and praised his combination of "resilient determination" and "ease—both of manner and of mind," so different from her own impatience, as he handled "that strange mixture of ferocity, ignorance and, more recently, appreciation of talent" that faces the negro intellectual in the U.S.[15] She admired his "grace and tact," virtues she had never possessed, and Roumain reminded her that he never forgot a friend. The speech was dynamite. Hughes's inflammatory message was that the 15 million poor Blacks in the United States "knew fascism in action" at home in the "theories of Nordic supremacy and suppression" that produced Jim Crow segregation in education and social life, race riots, lynchings, the denial of the right to vote and of entry to schools and colleges.[16] Hitler's

> abolition of labour unions, his tyranny over the Jews and the sterilisation of the Negro children of Cologne: Mussolini in Italy with his banning of Negroes on the theatrical stages, and his expedition of slaughter in Ethiopia: the Military Party in Japan with their little maps of how they'll conquer the whole world and their savage treatment of the Koreans and Chinese; Battista and Vincent, the little American-made tyrants of Cuba and Haiti; and now Franco with his absurd cry of "Viva España" at the hands of Italians, Moors and Germans invited to help him achieve "Spanish Unity."[17] (532)

Stephen Spender's Introduction to his 1939 edition *Poems for Spain* (with John Lehmann) is included in Cunningham's widely circulated anthology, and so the myth continues that this was the place where Auden's poem "Spain" first appeared.[18] A canon of Spanish Civil War writing is thus established that not only erases the major role played by one particular Englishwoman, but actually silently dismantles the political work done by Cunard's *Authors Take Sides*. She had mixed men and women, of course, as she had included right-wingers and pacifists; Beckett replied Irishly "Up the Republic!," G. B. Shaw offered a Stop Press growl, and Sean O'Faolain "contemptuously" refused to choose.[19] Also surveyed in Cunard's manifesto were writers of color like Ghanaian intellectual George Padmore, the political analyst C. L. R. James, the Indian novelist Mulk Raj Anand, and the West Indian political leader Marcus Garvey. It is a major sin of historical omission to expunge this fact from contemporary British discussions of responses to the civil war in Spain. The main feature of the survey was its lack of parochialism. Cunard's list was integrated by gender and race and it was also integrated by class—William

Forrest was included among many working-class writers, as was James Hanley, whose novel *Boy* (1931) was dedicated to Cunard.[20] What does it mean now, especially for Black British readers, working-class readers of all races, and women, to reconstruct the response to the Spanish war and the rise of fascism as white, male, and upper-class, while denying the presence of African, West Indian, and Asian postcolonial intellectuals in anti-fascism? It would be natural to assume that such issues were not of interest to those groups, when the opposite was the case, as the popularity of Nancy Cunard's journalism for Black readers was to prove.[21]

There were university professors and publishers and editors of papers, scientists and journalists, anthropologists and trade union leaders whose words were included.[22] The left-wing former suffragette Sylvia Pankhurst was there, as was Christina Stead, the Australian novelist. There were playwrights and Party hacks, and the reporter David Scott, who had just resigned as Paris correspondent of *The Times* to devote himself to the struggle against fascism. But Cunningham's notion of what constitutes an author is considerably narrower than Nancy Cunard's, so their responses are not in his book, with the result that his canon of Spanish Civil War writing is not only ethnocentric and masculinist, but elitist in class terms and outrageously provincial.[23] He boasts of his bizarre re-segregation of women by declaring their stories "newly tellable" with one hand, while with the other he takes many out of the story altogether. He makes individual heroines out of Nan Green, Felicia Browne, Sylvia Townsend Warner, and Valentine Ackland, all of whom would have been furious at their segregation in a women's section as well as for being singled out of the international collective, a vision they shared with Nancy Cunard as activist women intellectuals.[24] (Cunningham's *British Writers of the Thirties* remains uncomfortable about women; he prides himself on an occasional reference to aid some future segregated study;[25] Ackland and Warner get points for their "modesty"; Warner, the "mediocre" poet, surprises him by writing serious novels.) Cunningham has reduced a major thirties strategic weapon, *Writers Take Sides on the Spanish War*, to a pathetic parochial piece of English propaganda, when, in fact, Cunard's cross-race, cross-class, cross-gender effort was the pioneer version of the "Whose Side Are You On?" questionnaires that are now a democratic journalistic commonplace. By reinstating the old hierarchies, Cunningham's anthology is a dishonest picture of the cause and those who fought for it.[26] It forces one to ask Cunard's question to scholars who erase her authorship and her activism and replace her ungendered, multiracial, and cross-class text, a many-voiced narrative of protest, with a bland, British, single-tongued substitute, one story instead of many: "contemporaries, what have you done?"

Cunard's rebuke to her own contemporaries and the prediction of her subsequent career as an itinerant public intellectual animates *Parallax*. The long—and long neglected—poem published in 1925 at the Hogarth Press by her friends Leonard and Virginia Woolf,[27] left intellectuals as rooted as she was *déracinée*, echoes across the years as a caution against the stresses of the activist life. "[C]ontemporaries, what have you done?" strikes one now as a good question to have asked of modernism's writers and artists. *Parallax* was dismissed by critics at the time as an imitation of *The Waste Land*, but might now fruitfully be re-read with the modernist classic along with the "Fresca" section, supposedly based on Eliot's anger at her ability to get published as well as her sexuality, and wisely edited out by Pound. Cunard was addressing her peers, Eliot, Pound, Edith Sitwell, Aldous Huxley, Wyndham Lewis, most of whom rejected (left) public activism and political commitment as inconsistent with their idea of the intellectual life, though their letters reveal a good deal of private lobbying for their own causes. If the bitterness of *The Waste Land* was partly produced by the author's rage at Cunard's flamboyant flaunting of her sexuality and her rejection of English class and family values, it becomes both a more personal poem and one more rooted in the gendered political debates of the period. Eliot's *The Waste Land* is, to a certain extent, Western culture destroyed by women artists.[28]

Cunard's passionate, finger-pointing demand "contemporaries, what have you done?" was, of course, most severely addressed to herself. The question, so unlike the inward-looking Russian question "What is to be done?" that has inspired so many modern political debates, resonates with its origins in the uncompromisingly violent single-mindedness of a self-taught "outlaw," a member of that "other breed," the political *woman*, the autodidact, self-educated, and like the Virginia Woolf of *Three Guineas*, a renegade from her class. There was no hand-wringing, hesitation, or holding back. Nancy Cunard's question as an avant-garde modernist poet in 1925, "most surely at the beginning yet," was a version of the "Which Side Are You On?" moral debates that still characterize our times. It was a question about doing rather than being, about creating a life of useful intellectual labor, a work of "one's own," until the full break could be made with family and class and country, when the work for the cause shared out collectively would become *our* work.

Much of her journalism and publishing efforts during this time has little in common with the voices of the Spanish Civil War as they have been collected and marketed as history. Her most important subjects, the sellout of Ethiopia, the price of non-intervention in Spain, the concentration camps in France holding Spanish refugees, fascism's driving force as racial fanaticism, modern European war as a battle between colonized Blacks—these are not the topics objective enough to survive in the textbooks.

Nancy Cunard had become, instead, the "vagrant" she decided to be in her 1925 poem *Parallax*. She had indeed "gone further," was "lost." She tried to bury or disguise everything in her voice that was white, privileged, female, or European. She was unable to do it, but in the process she developed an international, interracial poetic that served her political purposes, and she also gained the courage to take up reportage as a serious writing career.

CHAPTER ELEVEN

Race on the Wire

Nancy Cunard's War Stories[1]

Question: What's black and white and red all over?

Answer: Nancy Cunard's journalism.

On October 12, 1936, Claude A. Barnett (1889–1967), the director of the Associated Negro Press, a Chicago-based U.S. wire service with some international outposts, wrote to his reporter Nancy Cunard, care of Lloyd's of London's Paris office, that he was relieved to get her latest dispatch from the Spanish Civil War even though the censors had opened it. "We were tremendously alarmed," he wrote, "when we read that a woman journalist had been killed"[2] in Spain, thinking of what a loss to his enormous Black readership it would be if the dead reporter were indeed the white Englishwoman who had been supplying him with news of Black troops on both sides of the war, interviews with Black soldiers and prisoners, and stories of the recruitment of North African "Moors" to fight for Franco. The Spanish Civil War is not often viewed as the racial battleground it was for European imperial powers. But race and empire shadowed the civil war story of this war, the anarchist-communist story, and the romantic stories of the volunteer Lincoln Brigade and the sacrifice of the passionate young intellectuals, poets, and artists who died struggling against fascism. The journalistic backstory of the nurses from Harlem Hospital working at the Front, the story of how the Black volunteers from the United States fought and died, the scare tactics of the armies massing troops from Africa to fight in Spain—these were the stories Cunard set out to write.

Nancy Cunard may not have been the only woman reporting from the battlefronts of Spain in 1936, but surely, she was the only woman reporting for the Associated Negro Press. To single her out like this, however, as the only white or the only woman to do something, is to challenge Cunard's politics in fundamental ways. For whatever she did after her conversion to left intellectual life, it was always for and with a collective cause. After Mussolini invaded Abyssinia in 1935, Cunard had begun her impassioned pro-African, anti-fascist, and anti-imperialist reporting for the ANP with the story of Haile Selassie's negotiations for sanctions against Italy with the League of Nations in Geneva. The cynical "breaking of their own clauses and covenants" by the League's members shocked and dismayed her as much as the harmful "neutrality" of England and France during the Spanish Civil War; she wrote day and night: "Everything but reporting was out of the question for me during those strenuous days."[3]

It seems likely that her introduction to the Associated Negro Press may have come from the Afro-American reporter Eugene Gordon, who was now writing for the Moscow *Daily News*. She had questioned him on her visit to the Soviet Union in 1935 as a comrade and contributor to her *Negro* anthology, about the revolutionary volume's failure to rouse support among either the Black workers in the U.S. to whom it was addressed, or in the journals of the American left. Gordon told her that her rash statement (among many rash statements) in the book that the Black press was its own worst enemy was taken to mean that it was worse than the oppression of whites, and that both sections of the press retaliated by not reviewing the book.[4]

Certainly, Claude Barnett's letters indicate that he was impressed with the information she had gathered for the *Negro* anthology without his help or the help of the ANP's files on her visits to the United States in the early thirties.[5] Whether she became a race reporter out of penance for her past sins against the Black press or because of the rejection of her film and publishing projects by the comrades in Moscow, Cunard was typecast for the role of intrepid reporter. Her biographer apologizes for Cunard's devoted commitment and enthusiasm for her work, embarrassed perhaps by the self-educated woman's prose which shouts against fascism and her slanted dispatches, commenting that she made "no attempt at all at objective reporting."[6] But the press had tormented her ever since she began to travel with Black men to do research on African cultures for *Negro*. Her lawsuits against their libels and slanders of her character had paid for the printing of the expensive 800-page volume with its thousands of pictures. Nancy Cunard had been created as what is now called a celebrity personality, a dangerous diva, by the London society and fashion press in the drawings and photographs of Cecil Beaton, Wyndham Lewis, Curtis Moffat, Eugene McCown, and Alvaro Guevara, as well as in the paintings and sculpture of French Surrealist avant-garde artists from Brancusi to Man Ray and Tristan Tzara, and as the vamp in the popular romantic novels of Michael Arlen and Aldous Huxley. She had posed for *Vogue* in Sonia Delaunay's modernist multicolored collage costumes, and in furs and feathers, with mirrors and bracelets, in veils, on tiger skins, and in the dark spaces of *film noir* in Barbara Ker-Seymer's disturbing photo solarizations.

The press hounded Cunard and she exploited them. That was her history. To join the ranks of the journalists as one of them, a subject looking for a story not the story itself, she had to find an angle outside of herself, her face, her clothes, her body, her family name. Race turned out be the right angle for her byline—as indeed race and race reversals are the essence of the power of the photographs and drawings that fetishize her image as the lady vagrant, modernism's icon of the Jazz Age. She had remade her English rose debutante face first into the mask of the white negress who dazzled the Surrealists in Paris. Then she turned that mask into the pose of a Medusa whose stony stare accused friends and enemies alike. What have you done for social justice? What have you done for Black freedom? Nancy Cunard the radical activist accused from behind the piercing blue eyes, her shield a "bright armor of belief," as John Banting called it, a look withering to her enemies and sometimes a trial to her friends. His portrait of her emphasizes the mask-like stillness of the white face and kohl-ringed eyes compared to the movement of the black hands and strong braceleted arms, suggesting a woman of action. Cunard's hands are not black with the ink that Leonard and Virginia Woolf warned their old friend would blacken the hands of the hand-press publisher, for she was always meticulous; they are meant to mark her as a race woman, a worker for racial justice.

As her comrade in the making of *Negro*, organizing demonstrations for the release of the Scottsboro Boys and for the cause of anti-fascism in Spain, Banting, a gay white artist and photographer, enabled her activism. He tells of Cunard's bravery in fending off the hostile press in Harlem—sick with

Figure 11.1. Nancy Cunard with the artist John Banting and the writer
Taylor Gordon, in front of the Grampian Hotel in Harlem, her home
at the time, May 3, 1943.
Photo courtesy *NY Daily News* / Hulton Archive via Getty Images

horror but impressed by her capacity to survive attacks "in the gutter press": "she stood up to the barrage smilingly in her bright armor of belief and her quick wit."[7] Although they quarreled at the end of her life, Banting was both as independent and as committed to the struggle for freedom as she was. He had done what she had done and has disappeared from the art world even more thoroughly than she disappeared from the world of letters. Banting's term brilliantly captures Cunard's Amazonian attitude. "Her bright armor of belief" is a perfect description of the transformation of Cunard's image from celebrity bad girl of the twenties into an icon of thirties' vampire political modernism, the woman activist whose story, to use Valentine Cunningham's phrase about women intellectuals of the thirties, has only recently moved into the realm of "the tellable." The choice of race as her subject was a shrewd one, though Cunard was not often anywhere near as shrewd in her decisions. Perhaps it is because her reports from Spain for the next three years were about Black and brown races, Arabs and Africans, that Nancy Cunard has disappeared so thoroughly from that history, watered down as it has been by very limited scholars like Cunningham to the tragic story of a few fair-skinned, privileged, English poets who went to the Spanish war and lost their lives or later changed their minds.

Cunard the journalist emerges from her biography in this English atmosphere of untellability. She is portrayed as hard-working, "useful" (an odd word, suggesting that she was a communist dupe), and fatally, problematically, committed to her cause, every impassioned dispatch evoking the oft-repeated rebuke "she made no effort at all to be detached and keep her opinions out of her reports," as if her tragedy were somehow related to her belief in the cause of freedom.[8] Cunard's journalism was "useful" to Black readers of the newspapers served by the Associated Negro Press because it provided practically the only source of news about Black people and race issues in a war where colonial troops from Africa fought each other and died by the thousands for a European cause. Was it useful to the Communist Party? Probably, at least for as long as the Party made African freedom struggles and American anti-lynching and anti-racism work one of its priorities.

But it is hard to dispel the myth that such a thing as objective journalism exists at all, and whether one would know it if one saw it. "She had the reporter's instinct to find out for herself what was going on and convey as directly as possible what she saw and learned," Chisholm concedes.[9] But this is not the reason Nancy Cunard's journalism was "useful," effective, or important. She was an eyewitness, but she reported the facts according to her belief in the Republican cause against Franco. Her ideological stance made no concession to an ideal of impartiality. Is there ever such a thing as an impartial news report? To my mind, there is often partisanship in what is called objective. And Cunard's pieces have no such false modesty; they were certain to stimulate argument and debate as they raged and cursed across the wires, accusatory and inflammatory. They were a real response to the civil war's daily tragedies, large and small, as well as to the smugness of non-intervention. They were meant to be read by Black workers, but the clippings suggest that those strong headlines reached out to other readers as well. Cunard's story is tellable now in terms of several discourses on gender, race, and the left, postcolonial studies and whiteness studies that allow us to see her outside of the categories of eccentricity and exploitation and their limited explanatory power.

From the Associated Negro Press's offices on Chicago's South Side, an urban ghetto overflowing still with Black workers from the South as the Great Migration met the Great Depression, Barnett sent his odd reporter, the errant Cunard person who didn't want to use her title, a money order for $5 for postage and a batch of clippings from papers that had used her stories as they went out on the wire service. He hoped she would be able to write more freely of her experiences once she was out of Spain and expressed his admiration for her "courage and sacrifice in serving our group," as he referred to his Black audience, and the "splendid work" she was doing "without recompense." He sent on Langston Hughes's thanks for her dispatch on his speech at the International Writers' Congress in Paris, emphasizing the presence of the Black intellectuals Jacques Roumain and Nicolás Guillén. This fact is not recorded in standard histories because the story had appeared in the Black press wherever he went. Cunard's article called Hughes "the travelling star of coloured America, the leader of the younger intellectuals." Her stories about him for the wire services certainly helped to build his worldwide reputation.[10]

Like most of the other reporters for the Associated Negro Press, Cunard was simply glad to get her clippings and some expenses paid. The credentials she carried from the ANP often got her into places she could never have entered otherwise, and she made a little money from other papers, enough to keep her going. She described to her Irish friend, Charles Duff, sheltering refugees from the war in Spain in her house in France, surviving "on the smell of an oil rag" from her hand press.[11] Duff attributes the force of Cunard's unwaveringly radical politics and her great-heartedness to her Irish genes, her family relationship through her mother to the revolutionary Robert Emmett, an analysis quite as racially romantic as her own embrace of African cultures. He found her both "transparently clear and still full of baffling contradictions. She could be highly intuitive and at the same time coldly rational. She was, of course, an intellectual, but with that went the instincts of a cat: she was aware of a potential friend or enemy at a glance."[12] Though she appeared to be frail, Cunard could stand up to fatigue and stress better than many strong men, Duff declared, absolute necessities for the wartime journalist; and he, too, like many who knew her, praises, and wonders at, her fierce courage, the famous Nancy Cunard fearlessness.

While money didn't matter to Cunard, authorship did, and she needed to see her words in print. The ANP's stories appeared in 70 American papers (and in African and Caribbean papers somewhat later with the World News Service in the fifties and sixties), as Barnett told her in the same letter, from the *Pittsburgh Courier* to the *Norfolk Journal and Guide*, the Baltimore *Afro-American*, the *New York Age*, the *Amsterdam News*, the Houston *Informer*, the *Black Dispatch* in Oklahoma City, the *Kansas City Call*, and the *Atlanta World*. The Associated Negro Press served many Black papers (with the exception of the independent Chicago *Defender*) from 1919 to 1964, sending two or three mailings a week for a modest fee.

A graduate of Tuskegee Institute, Barnett was an entrepreneur who kept the wire service alive in the thirties by exchanging its dispatches for "white space" in the local papers to advertise cosmetics. His mother was housekeeper to wealthy Chicago families, and young Claude had worked as a houseboy for Richard Sears of Sears, Roebuck while attending high school in Oak Park, Illinois, an apprenticeship that taught him a great deal. "I Reach the Negro" was the slogan of Barnett's advertising agency, and he made money from Nile Queen Cosmetics before serving on the boards of many Black institutions as well as becoming a national figure in the Republican Party. There was a fortune to be made in skin-lightening and hair-straightening among the assimilating Black masses, hungry for jobs as well as news.

What an odd pair they are to contemplate, Barnett the self-made American businessman and Cunard the "Lady" journalist who had frizzed and marcelled her hair and posed for solarized photographs to make her skin look black. Arms covered with African ivory bracelets, her white primitivism preserved by modernist image-makers like Man Ray and Brancusi, Cunard aspired to an African look as powerfully as Barnett's customers aspired to an Egyptian look. Labeled a "negrophiliac" by the society press that hounded her, Cunard joined the radical press in the thirties without giving up her image, the face and the walk of the *Vogue* model and columnist of the twenties. Those kohl-ringed eyes saw bombs fall and frontiers close. An eyewitness report is an eyewitness report, whether or not the eyes that saw action wore mascara. A Black wire service sent out news about Black people, no matter who gathered it (at least for a while), despite the fact that it was funded by face creams. The Black capitalist man and the white anti-capitalist woman were united by a desire to inform the Black masses. They were an unbeatable team.

Most of the reporters for the Associated Negro Press were volunteers, and that seems to have been the businessman's greatest coup, to amass an enormous team of talented writers who were grateful to get into print. Nancy Cunard was in very good company; Alvin E. White was their full-time Washington reporter; William Pickens, field secretary of the N.A.A.C.P., wrote a regular column; Charles S. Johnson, the president of Fisk University, wrote a column called "Minority View." The masthead sported a dark goddess with a book and a torch and six Black *putti* playing around with the symbols of truth and justice. Ralph Dunbar was listed as London reporter and there was a special correspondent for radio as well as a sportswriter. In 1947 Alice Dunnigan of the ANP was the first Black reporter regularly accredited by the White House in Washington, D.C.; Emmanuel Racine reported from Haiti, John C. Robinson from Ethiopia, J. V. Clinton from Nigeria, and Henry B. Cole from Ghana.[13]

At the offices of the Associated Negro Press, 3507 South Parkway in Chicago, Nancy Cunard's name inspired editors over the years with delusions of grandeur, and they claimed that "Lady" Cunard was sending them dispatches from North Africa or from prison camps in France. The title, as well as her sensational stories, were obviously a great selling point. The shipping heiress, they assured their readers, was the ANP's own correspondent with the African troops in France. Periodically, Cunard implored Barnett to discard the title, only to see the baronetcy bounce back in her face in the next batch of press clippings. A copy of an ANP wire from January 20, 1937, however, is headed by this pacifying editor's note:

> Miss Nancy Cunard, intrepid young woman journalist [she was 41], writing for the Associated Negro Press, has covered many important

news points, the most recent being the Spanish revolution. Miss Cunard visited Madrid and wrote of governmental activities retailing the racial angle present. Returning to Paris she has embarked for Morocco and this week gives a picture of the situation in northern Africa where the Fascist rebels fighting in Spain have secured much of their man power [*sic*].[14]

The three-page wire itself is dated Tangier, December 20, and it begins with a little geography lesson:

Tangier—northernmost tip of Africa—and, like British-owned Gibraltar just across the straights [*sic*], strategic key to the Mediterranean and to the vast colonial possessions of England and France—Tangier, fourfold international zone, held by Spanish, French, British, and since some five years, also by Italian interests, aptly described now as "the ring-side seat of events in Spain"— Tangier, racially Arab, with a visible twenty per cent of Negro and mixed Negro and Arab in its population.[15]

That telltale phrase "since some five years" marks the wire as authentic vintage Nancy Cunard, and it turns up everywhere in her prose. She goes on to say that the provocative violence of the Italian sailors has eased a bit and the situation is less tense.

An "important" government official, that ubiquitous stock character in the drama of news reporting, is quoted as saying that

The rebel fascist generals in Morocco used every means, from bribery to force, to raise Moorish troops to fight for them in Spain … each native who enlisted was given 500 francs, an important sum to any colored worker, kept as he is in direst poverty by imperialism.[16]

Were the Moroccans aware of the role they were playing in Spain? she asked. They were promised independence, he says. "Of what interest is this colony to fascism? At present it is a reservoir from which to draw soldiers … The losses among them are enormous because they are always put in the front lines of every attack."[17] The Loyalists in Spain believe that Franco's forces have 30,000 Moroccans fighting in Spain she tells him, and the dialogue continues, ending with a plea to remember the "appalling poverty" in which the masses of Moroccans live, that Franco pays well, and they have been taught to fear the "impious reds" who will destroy Islam and burn down the mosques. The interviewer asks a local authority to explain why Black soldiers from North Africa are fighting on what for herself and her Black readers in the U.S. and the Caribbean is the "wrong side."[18]

Nancy Cunard's journalism is often conducted as a conversation or interview with the people whose lives are affected by the story—a representative citizen or soldier, war nurse, refugee, or prisoner—and it rings with the sounds of many voices. Her "I" is there but submerged in the dialogic *heteroglossia* of a journalism that wants to tell the people's story. Cunard's voice as a journalist attempts the same kind of collective dialogue as her *Negro* anthology, the quintessential thirties' documentary heteroglossic text. Her role (as editor or journalist) is to ask questions, summarize the situation, publish and disseminate the results. The voice of the text was supposed to be that of the *vox populi*, but there were times when Cunard's individual blessings and curses escape from the common cry to make a point of their own.

The news report to go on the wire and then into newspapers across the world and even to be broadcast on the radio was often bigger than today's CNN or BBC sound bite, but it served the same purpose, putting the reader/listener/viewer at the scene of the breaking news. Cunard practiced a journalism of political human interest. That Cunard byline still brings recognition from Blacks because Black newspapers printed her stories for decades. Nancy Cunard's readers were Black, and as she grew older, the people who came to visit the old radical were Blacks from Africa and the diaspora who had read her in their local papers, and old comrades from the Spanish struggle, a cause which she never gave up.

Cunard's lively reports from Spain and North Africa and then from the refugee camps at Perpignan in France went not only to the Associated Negro Press but to the independent Black papers in the United States that paid her directly, as well as the London *News Chronicle*, the French *Regards*, Sylvia Pankhurst's *New Times and Ethiopia News*, and the General News Service that went to the British colonies, India, and the Far East. Cunard's name as a journalist among white European readers was made when the *Manchester Guardian* published "The Exodus from Spain," "The Refugees from Perpignan," "The Soldiers Leave their Battlefields Behind," and "At a Refugee Camp" in February, 1938, calling attention to the plight of the refugees, helping to raise

money for ships to carry the Spanish anti-fascists to South America, to organize relief efforts of clothing and blankets and food, as she was to do later for
war-torn France.

Nancy Cunard wrote no fiction, no autobiography. For her, journalism
and poetry were pursuits worthy of a public intellectual, genres close to each
other, not opposites. Poems belonged in newspapers; journalism circulated
in broadsides at public meetings and demonstrations. She had a distinctly
un-postmodern vision of truth. We may observe that all of these forms practice fiction, but Cunard, fearing, I think, the return of her repressed class
background, or falling into a certain English mode common to women of
her class of memoir or highbrow fiction, professed allegiance to the voice of
reportage and the voice of verse as suitable sources of political truth. In that
she shared an ideology with her friends from the Harlem Renaissance and
away from formal modernisms.

Travel writing was another vehicle in which truth might safely ride, or
art criticism, narratives of exploration, ethnographies, and other efforts at
writing anthropology that we now read as self-serving fictions, making myths
and building empires, as well as the novels and epics she and her fellow fellow
travelers found so full of lies and evasions. One cannot help imagining what
would have happened if Cunard had established her own column in *Vogue*
as a counterpart to Janet Flanner's in the *New Yorker*. But she found her real
milieu in dispatches to the Associated Negro Press, the *Manchester Guardian*
or left papers like Sylvia Pankhurst's *New Times and Ethiopian News*. If Flanner's journalism is what we mean by modernist reportage by women, or
Djuna Barnes's quirky pieces, Cunard's writing does not fit, except insofar as
all three "do" the police—or the roving dentist, or the society murderess, or
the Moroccan shepherd in a Spanish prison—in many voices, ventriloquizing
human character, reproducing voices rather than pontificating with authority
about their subjects.

Cunard's Spanish Civil War journalism included human interest stories
about Salaria Kee (or Kea), a Black nurse who had organized the nurses at
Harlem Hospital, on duty with the second American medical unit. Cunard
interviewed her several times, and stories about the brave nurse who married
an Irishman from the International Brigade crackled across the wires of
the Associated Negro Press. Barnett was thrilled with Cunard's reports and
wrote to her in Moscow in 1935 to ask for reports on Soviet society. "It will
be influential with our group too because your name has become exceedingly

well-known among them," he wrote, thanking her for her story on Langston Hughes being named a future U.S. representative at the Paris Conference for the Defence of Culture in July. Cunard replied enthusiastically that her first priority was "the filming of the immense scenario I am at present writing on Negro History (Slavery and America)," but that she would continue to write for him if only he would stop calling her Lady Cunard—"I have no title of any kind. That was an invention of the Hearst Press..."[19]

Among Cunard's papers are hundreds of clippings from a wire she sent from ANP in 1939 that "the French Expect a Million-Man African Army" from Senegal alone. The intent was to frighten the Germans, but she seems to have spread havoc elsewhere as well. The million-man army of fierce Black warriors was being held in reserve, she declared in her next report. It was not yet marching through France. The legions of African and colonial troops being mustered on both sides of this European war, and used against each other in the front lines, became her topic later. But she began by calling for Black volunteers for a war against Hitler's racism, delighting her readers yet again with stories of the heroics of Black soldiers. War reporting, from the race angle and the refugee angle, made her name as a journalist. But it was that same experience of war reporting that made Cunard into a peace poet.

Homelessness was the signature of Nancy Cunard's writing and her life. From dreary hotel rooms as she typed her reports for the wire services and the Associated Negro Press from the battlefields of the Spanish Civil War, the refugee camps in France and the recruitment points, the barracks and the prisons of Black troops in France and North Africa, her dispatches were a form of white woman's blues, a song with a sad refrain—"Sometimes I feel like a motherless child."

Cunard's voice as a reporter was certainly invented as an act of cross-racial ventriloquism, a form of blackface minstrelsy performed by a white lady. We know that voice and its register of comradeship from the songs of the Lincoln Brigade of the Spanish Civil War, or Pete Seeger singing a South African freedom song. Hemingway and Josephine Herbst found human interest in the war in Spain. Cunard saw the tragedy in racial terms and forged on that front a vocal weapon for the defense of Black soldiers and prisoners on all sides, a voice that called attention to their plight in racial terms and then found its first fame reporting on the refugees from Spain in French camps at the end of the war in a series of remarkable pieces for the *Manchester Guardian*.

Cunard's name and the name of the *Negro* anthology mean a great deal to African freedom fighters and their comrades in the Black Atlantic, in South America and the Caribbean. Her byline—"Nancy Cunard, Barcelona ANP," or Valencia, Toulouse, Zurich, Moscow, Senegal, Barbados, Mexico City— brought her name and her stories about Blacks fighting Blacks in European wars or heroic American nurses in the Spanish Civil War to thousands of readers all over the world. She was a "race woman" and she was white. As a traveling journalist, Cunard wrote stories about people of color for people of color. Her stories were progressive in politics, frankly propagandistic dispatches from sites of struggle all over the world. She was not the only reporter dedicated to sending strong words about race crackling across the wires and into the newspapers. But for three decades in the middle of a war-torn century, Nancy Cunard made a place for race in the world news.

End Notes: An Afterword

In a way, our relationship began on an End Note. Or two. Which is fitting, because it was in the endnotes to *Perfect Stranger* that I was reminded of the sheer intellectual pleasure it was to have a conversation with Jane Marcus. The endnotes, as they are meant to do in any given text, give one both the gift of closure, and paradoxically an open door. For it is within the endnotes, I discovered, that we, as Clarissa Dalloway might say, "kindle and illuminate"; we pose further questions, build on ideas suggested there, and continue a multitude of other conversations, some initiated by false starts and disappointments, others by new research and intellectual possibilities.

I first met Jane in the fall of 2001 over discussions about a poem that Virginia Woolf chose and hand-set for the Hogarth Press in 1919, and described as "very obscure, indecent, and brilliant."[1] Jane and another leading figure in feminist modernist studies, Julia Briggs (1943–2007), were involved in recovering *Paris: A Poem* by Hope Mirrlees as a modernist masterpiece for their seminars. In it, a female speaker walks around Paris, as dignitaries and superpowers descend upon the city to carve up the world and sign 1919's Treaty of Versailles, a document even its contemporaries regarded as a punitive peace. Briggs would go on to republish the original version of the poem with commentary in Bonnie Kime Scott's *Gender in Modernism: New Geographies, Complex Intersections* in 2007. The poem was distinctive, not only for its literary value (Virginia Woolf was right—it's brilliant), but for its many similarities to T. S. Eliot's *The Waste Land*, which it pre-dated by two years.

Mirrlees and Eliot were also close friends. Like *The Waste Land*, *Paris* took place in spring in a single day; its speaker toured a hellish postwar urban landscape; like Eliot's poem, *Paris* relied on found objects, musical allusions, historical, biblical, mythological, and religious references; it made use of dialect, colloquialisms, vernacular, non-standard language and diction, and slang. Both poems ended with a blessing. And *Paris*, too, like the later *Waste Land*, in yet another modernist signature often attributed to Eliot's poem as a first, had endnotes.

The endnotes raised more questions about the poem than they answered. They sent our seminar into the archive at Jane's insistence and direction. One note, keyed to the line, "The first of May, there is no lily of the valley," a line which typographically replicates the stem of the flower, informed us that "On May 1, the *Mois de Marie*, lily of the valley is normally sold in all the streets of Paris; but on May 1, 1919, the day of the general strike, no lily of the valley was offered for sale." From the endnotes, we sprang into action. We learned about the general strike, about the thousands of tents stretched out across the Bois de Boulogne, where war veterans camped out hoping to be paid their wages, about the city's bread rationing, unemployment, inflation, and how the strike paralyzed the city by July 1919; from Paris, Jane sent us to China and the mass student protests against the terms of the peace treaty; from China, to the workers' revolts in the Ruhr in 1920. Her methods as an educator were intimately tied up not only with the excitement of her own research but with the research process itself. She loved the archive, and she instilled that love, and its significance, in each of us.

Having studied *The Waste Land* with Christopher Ricks while briefly at Trinity College, Oxford, as an undergraduate, and over fifteen years before I encountered *Paris* in Jane's seminar in 2001, I was immediately struck not only by the poems' similarities, but also by the fact that I had never heard of it before. It was not taught, not respected, not read. It was in these half-measures of history, amid a literary landscape of lost art, and an intellectual and cultural narrative that was as remarkable for what it ignored as for what it celebrated, that I also began to share Jane's interests in the politics of representation and reputation; how issues of gender, race, and class are used to determine who gets to say, how it is said, and who will be allowed to hear it became part of our conversations as she guided each of us in our individual research projects. In the archive and library collections, she insisted we work with primary sources, the letters, diaries, and family albums of erased history, in order to correct and reshape the public record. She mentored me, as I went on to defend and then publish on the importance of intellectual mentorship between women scholars and thinkers, in this case on Jane Ellen Harrison, one of the first professional women scholars to graduate from Newnham College, Cambridge, and Virginia Woolf. My work on Harrison also arrived by way of my discussions with Jane about *Paris*, as Harrison and Mirrlees had an eleven-year relationship, and her research into linguistics and the feminist foundations of Greek rituals is inscribed in nearly every line.

Jane and I went on to become colleagues and friends. When she passed away in May 2015, she joined a number of feminist scholars of her generation whose intellectual absence was acutely felt in the constellation of fields in which they worked: Adrienne Rich, Lillian Robinson, and Julia Briggs, among others. When her husband, Michael Marcus, asked me to help him organize her papers, I agreed as a friend. But when I began to read through the many chapters she had written on Nancy Cunard and the boxes upon boxes of research she had compiled over the course of more than a decade, I tried to move through the process as the scholar and critic she had trained me to be. Her networks of friends and colleagues all knew she was working on Cunard, but that her progress was being intermittently interrupted by health concerns. As I combed through the manuscript, I became convinced of its merits, its argument, the quality of the research and, of course, Jane's unmistakable writing style. Even her parentheticals in the body of the manuscript were inventive, thrilling sometimes ("I will boldly enter her consciousness here," for example). Without a doubt, it was a gift to me, on a personal and emotional level, to have the chance to read her work so soon after her death, to be intellectually close to her again, to be engaged in the pursuit of her inquiry, carried on, as Jane Harrison once wrote, "For love of an idea"; but on a professional level, I became determined to see the manuscript through to publication.

I hope that readers will agree that *Nancy Cunard: Perfect Stranger* makes a significant contribution to our understanding of Cunard as well as to the many fields with which it intersects. I consider Jane's critiques of the narratives of Cunard's progress as a poet, her activism against fascism, and advocacy on behalf of African-American and African diasporic literature and culture to be unique and insightful, as well as current and relevant to today's political and academic trends across disciplines.

But my plea, here, in the Afterword, is that we will also pay heed to the endnotes. I was initially concerned that these might be dated. The references, of course, are linked to earlier decades of feminist research and scholarship, but as I read through them, across the distance of time, a different narrative emerged that I thought worth preserving: it's the story of a woman's mind at work, a scholar following multiple threads and intellectual possibilities within the frame of an explicit argument that she has constructed, supported, and advanced, herself. Her endnotes are inclusive and collaborative, as she acknowledges networks of colleagues, scholars from around the world, her students and former students, and the institutes and their staffs which had supported her research. The erudite bibliophile Anthony Hobson, who was, at the time, the head of Nancy Cunard's literary estate, makes an appearance, as does Bloomsbury's Dadie Rylands, as in "Dadie Rylands told me ..." but also the anonymous opera singer and piano player from the Manhattan School of Music, who played *Henry-Music* for her one evening in Carmago, where she was writing large portions of the text. Her former students will recognize her nods not only to them, but also to her friends and colleagues, the Marxist-feminist critic Lillian Robinson, and lesbian feminist scholar Gay Wachman. In the paratexts you see the importance of the conferences, the seminars, and informal gatherings of scholars and students to the arguments as she developed her ideas.

The endnotes to *Perfect Stranger*, far from operating as static, sentence-ending punctuation, instead challenged my notions of time, even death. The endnotes housed both the beginning and end of her research (the process itself, the excitement of her inquiries); they were connections to the past, but also potential pathways for new research, different questions, leads to follow up on for future and succeeding generations of readers and scholars. But in addition to the work, the endnotes marked both the beginning and the end of our relationship.

In a recent issue of *Aperture*, a journal of fine art photography, the actress Tilda Swinton, who curated the issue, bringing visual artists into conversation with Virginia Woolf's novel *Orlando* (a role that Swinton memorably played on film in 1991) wrote of searching for a citrine ring she wore in the film. As a kind of visual coda to the issue, the editors agreed with Swinton that they wanted to include a picture of that ring. She had no idea, however, where to find it, after "over twenty-five years of a fully lived life, after children, and multiple relocations." She began searching "deep into those boxes in the shadows and under the eaves in which the past crouches with its intoxicating combination of emotional turmoil and treasure." Even though the ring was of no consequence to the plot of the film—as endnotes are sometimes deemed in relation to a book, skipped over, given a cursory glance—Swinton wore it every day during the shoot, and she began to identify it with "the soul of Orlando," as a "reliable personal talisman of this life's long—seemingly never-ending—journey." When she finally found the ring, "this beautiful bright thing," she writes of experiencing an "unparalleled existential exhilaration." Her life felt less disorganized; she felt "more buttressed by the past and all that [she] cherish[ed] there, material and not." It was as if the ring, she writes, was waiting there for "its close-up" and she wonders, "Was it for this moment now, decades in the future, that it was made?"[2]

Such, I believe, is the function of endnotes, to challenge temporality, to give us the freedom to oscillate, destabilize the plot, digress, or flash forward. The endnotes are generative. The story is never finished. And I think of my conversations with Jane as having occurred, and as occurring.

Accord, NY
October 2019

Notes

Editor's Introduction: Scholarship's Afterlife: The Return of Rage

1   Both essays have resonances with themes raised throughout *Perfect Stranger*, but are more specifically tied to issues of race in relation to British imperialism and totalitarianism. "Laying Down the White Woman's Burden: Michael Arlen's *The Green Hat* and Mulk Raj Anand's *Coolie*" deals with the figure of Cunard as she is represented in popular fiction, as well as offering an incisive reading of *Coolie* next to E. M. Forster's more frequently studied and respected *A Passage to India*.

2   A version of this essay was published in the conference proceedings of *Work in Progress at CUNY on the African Diaspora: An Interdisciplinary Conference* in 1998, and is reprinted here with permission.

3   See Urmila Seshagiri, "Mind the Gap! Modernism and Feminist Praxis," *Modernism/Modernity* 2, no. 2 (2017), https://modernismmodernity.org/forums/modernism-and-feminist-praxis.

4   Cassandra Laity, "Editor's Introduction: Toward Feminist Modernisms," *Feminist Modernist Studies* 2 (2018): 1.

5   Laity, "Editor's Introduction," 3.

6   Its call for papers tellingly opens with the declaration: "Feminists are raging." The issue considers "our rage as a global, complex phenomenon that mandates interdisciplinary and intersectional analysis."

7   See Margot Kotler, "After Anger: Negative Affect and Feminist Politics in Virginia Woolf's *Three Guineas*," *Woolf Studies Annual* 24 (2018): 41.

8   Nancy Cunard, ed., *Negro: An Anthology* (London: Wishart, 1934), iii.

9   Sandeep Parmar, "Introduction," in *Nancy Cunard: Selected Poems* (Manchester: Carcanet, 2016), xv. Parmar's introduction is somewhat

dismissive, in my view, of decades of feminist scholarship recovering obscure or forgotten women writers, as she seems to be suggesting that such an act of recovery required some sort of sleight of hand, or "deft manoeuvring" that "inevitably fails" as it attempts to place these writers "into an imagined, evaluative male space" (xi). Is it "imagined"? Have all of feminist literary acts of reclamation failed? Marcus's manuscript, in documenting "the making of a woman artist as a perfect stranger," not only recovers Cunard, but exposes the very real consequences of any kind of challenge to or rejection of that very explicitly experienced "evaluative male space." The introduction then turns on an "and yet," but the opening salvo flies in the face of innumerable examples of feminist literary criticism upon whose shoulders we all stand. Why frame it in terms of failure, with no examples given for support, unless failure itself will be examined, perhaps, as it has been quite productively, through a queer theoretical lens, as a point of possibility and opportunity for different forms of knowledge construction. As it is, it reads, instead, like a micro-aggression.

10   See Jane Marcus, *Hearts of Darkness: White Women Write Race* (New Brunswick, NJ: Rutgers University Press), 169–70.

11   See Anna Girling, "More than a Muse," *The Times Literary Supplement*, January 8, 2019, as well as the short story, as evidence of a successful act of recovery by a feminist literary critic in the twenty-first century.

Introduction to the Original Text

1   This section, previously chapter 5 of the manuscript, was published in 2004 in Jane Marcus, *Hearts of Darkness: White Women Write Race*, as "Laying Down the White Woman's Burden: Michael Arlen's *The Green Hat* and Mulk Raj Anand's *Coolie*," 150–78. Please refer to that text for a discussion of Arlen and Anand, as this material was dropped from the final version of *Perfect Stranger*. However, Marcus extends this discussion with new material in "Women of Affairs: Lempicka, Garbo, and Cunard," a subsection of Chapter 2 below, "The Artist as Antichrist: Thamar, the Demon Lover." Another section to which Marcus sometimes refers in the paratexts of *Perfect Stranger*, "Bonding and Bondage: Nancy Cunard and the Making of the *Negro* Anthology," is also not reprinted here, as it was previously published in Mae Henderson's Harvard English Institute volume *Borders, Boundaries, and Frames: Essays in Cultural Criticism and Cultural Studies* (New York: Routledge, 1995) and reprinted in *Hearts of Darkness*. The section on Cunard and the making of the *Negro* anthology, Chapter 9 below, "White Women, Black Books," is new material, previously unpublished.

Chapter One: The Cunard Line: A Poet's Progress, 1925

1   Vernon Lee, *Satan the Waster. A Philosophic War Trilogy with Notes and Introduction* (London: John Lane, the Bodley Head, 1920). See also *The Ballet of the Nations. With Pictorial Commentary by Maxwell Armfield* (London: Chatto and Windus, 1915), dedicated to Romain Rolland "fraternellement." My thanks to Gay Wachman for a copy of this.

2   Darius Milhaud, *La Création du monde*, op. 81a (1922–23), libretto by Blaise Cendrars, premiered October 25, 1923, at Theatre des Champs-Elysées in Paris.

3   From Edith Sitwell, *Clowns' Houses* (Oxford: Blackwell, 1918).

4   "A Parallel," *New Statesman*, June 20, 1925, 290, also reviews *Adriatica and Other Poems* by Ferenc Becassy, a Hungarian educated at Cambridge who died in 1915, also published by the Hogarth Press. Clare Smith, archivist at the *New Statesman*, confirms that the review was written by M. K. Wardle. An M. K. Wardle, DSO Leicestershire Regiment, was the author of *Foundations of Soldiering* (1936).

5   *Times Literary Supplement*, May 28, 1925, 364.

6   Charles Hobday, *Edgell Rickword: A Poet at War* (Manchester: Carcanet, 1989).

7   Hobday, *Edgell Rickword: A Poet at War*, 145.

8   Edgell Rickword, *Essays and Opinions 1921–31*, ed. Alan Young (Manchester: Carcanet, 1974).

9   Rickword, *Essays and Opinions*, 38.

10 Rickword, *Essays and Opinions*, 39.

11 Hobday, *Edgell Rickword: A Poet at War*, 145.

12 Hobday, *Edgell Rickword: A Poet at War*, 150.

13 Hobday, *Edgell Rickword: A Poet at War*, 150.

14 Hobday, *Edgell Rickword: A Poet at War*, 150.

15 *New Statesman*, March 10, 1934, 252; Hobday, *Edgell Rickword: A Poet at War*, 151.

16 Hobday, *Edgell Rickword: A Poet at War*, 151.

17 Edgell Rickword, *Collected Poems* (London: John Lane, the Bodley Head, 1947).

18 Rickword, *Collected Poems*, 9, 11.

19 Rickword, *Collected Poems*, 57.

20 Rickword, *Essays and Opinions*, 170–75.

21 Rickword, *Collected Poems*, 77.

22 Hugh Ford, *A Poet's War: British Poets and the Spanish Civil War* (Oxford: Oxford University Press, 1965), 142–45.

23 Letter from Gerald Berners to Diana Cooper from Rome, 1925, describing Maud Cunard's anger with her daughter in Venice over the alleged homosexual character of her friends. Cooper papers, Eton College.

24   Hobday, *Edgell Rickword: A Poet at War*, 273.

25   Nancy Cunard, *Henry-Music* (Paris: The Hours Press, 1930), 3–4.

26   Cunard, ed., *Negro: An Anthology*, 75.

27   Donna Ford Grover made an excellent analysis of the demonization of white women by the left in my first CUNY seminar on the *Negro* anthology and presented a paper on it in the Scottsboro panel at MLA, 1999.

28   Samuel Putnam, *Paris Was Our Mistress: Memoirs of a Lost and Found Generation* (Carbondale, IL: Southern Illinois University Press, 1947), 23.

29   Cunard, ed., *Negro: An Anthology*, 432.

30   Cunard, ed., *Negro: An Anthology*, 174–76.

31   See Alan Friedman's important study, *Beckett in Black and Red: Samuel Beckett's Translations for Nancy Cunard's Negro (1934)* (Louisville, KY: University of Kentucky Press, 2000).

Chapter Two: The Artist as Antichrist: Thamar the Demon Lover

1   Part of this chapter was given as a paper at the Women Writers Between the Wars conference in Oxford in March 1998. My thanks to Nicola Luckhurst, Julia Briggs, David Bradshaw, and the organizers and participants for their lively and helpful responses. Desley Deacon's groundbreaking intellectual biography *Elsie Clews Parsons: Inventing Modern Life* (Chicago: University of Chicago Press, 1997) helped me to rethink the problem of Nancy Cunard's relation to the artists of modernism in London during World War I.

2   Shari Benstock, *Women of the Left Bank* (Austin, TX: University of Texas Press, 1986). This pioneering work recuperates the figure of Nancy Cunard as publisher at the Hours Press in Paris, noting that she was one of the few modernist poet-publishers who did not publish her own work, but encouraged other avant-garde writers in close collaboration and a spirit of cooperation. Benstock notes that Cunard's work as a publisher led to a highly productive period for her own writing and editing of the *Negro* anthology. Richard Aldington worked with her on the press and was disappointed when she gave up the project as only an apprenticeship for her work as an anti-racist journalist. Both Benstock and Cunard's biographer, Anne Chisholm, attribute Cunard's disappearance from the scene of modernism and the vilification of her reputation to "reactions against her liberal politics, her insistence on sexual freedom, and her outspoken denouncement of the English upper class" (Benstock, *Women of the Left Bank*, 395), led by Aldington's publication of a vicious portrait of her in "Now She Lies There" in his 1932 volume of stories, *Soft Answers*. Chisholm comments on Aldington's "hysterical relish": "His revenge was to turn every aspect of her character into a nightmare caricature, not allowing her any taste, brains or passion, not allowing her lovers or protégés any success or distinction, not granting her any generosity of mind or body. He painted a vicious portrait of a rich, useless erratic girl

in rebellion against her family and class for want of anything better to be" (Anne Chisholm, *Nancy Cunard* [New York: Knopf, 1979], 253–54, quoted in Benstock, *Women of the Left Bank*, 393). Benstock attributes Aldington's response to racism in reaction to Cunard's attachment to Henry Crowder. She also points out that criticism of modernist women based on their class and money has affected the reputations of Gertrude Stein, Natalie Barney, Zelda Fitzgerald, Mabel Dodge Luhan, Winifred Ellerman (Bryher), Djuna Barnes, and Caresse Crosby. One might also add Edith Sitwell, Virginia Woolf, and Peggy Guggenheim to this list.

3   Nancy Cunard, *Outlaws* (London: Elkin Mathews, 1921), 41.

4   Mikhail Lermontov, *Major Poetical Works*, trans. Anatoly Liberman (Minneapolis, MN: University of Minnesota Press, 1983), 562. In "The Demon," the devil is excited by Thamar's virgin beauty and kills her bridegroom; he torments her for her entire life in a convent, then kills her with a kiss in a struggle with her guardian angel over her soul.

5   Thamar or Tamar appears in the Bible in the books of Genesis and Samuel. There are also two historical queens called Thamar, a flying virgin from Georgia and a Byzantine one who appears in an icon. I have no reason to suppose that Cunard knew the American Robinson Jeffers' poem, but his unruly Tamar is a figure of female desire associated with horses. Cunard was a rider as a girl and cared for horses. Wyndham Lewis caricatures her and her affair with a stableboy in *The Roaring Queen*.

6   Nancy Cunard, *Grand Man: Memories of Norman Douglas* (London: Secker and Warburg, 1954), 140.

7   Cunard, "1917," in *Outlaws*, 32.

8   Cunard, "Thamar," in *Outlaws*, 63.

9   Robinson Jeffers, *Tamar and Other Poems* [1924] (New York: Random House, 1959), 29.

10   Lermontov, *Major Poetical Works*, 562.

11   Laura Claridge, *Tamara de Lempicka: A Life of Deco and Decadence* (New York: Clarkson Potter, 1999). A full catalogue raisonné of Lempicka's work by Alain Blondel appeared in 2004 to accompany the first exhibition of her work in Britain held at London's Royal Academy of Arts.

12   Katharine Cornell, *I Wanted to Be an Actress* (New York: Random House, 1938), 76.

13   Betsy Erkkila, "Greta Garbo: Sailing Beyond the Frame," *Critical Inquiry* 11, no. 4 (1985): 595–619.

14   Tallulah Bankhead, *My Autobiography* (New York: Harper and Bros, 1952), 168.

15   Lee Israel, *Miss Tallulah Bankhead* (New York: Putnam's, 1972), 104–7.

16   Brendan Gill, *Tallulah* (New York: Holt, Rinehart and Winston, 1972), 43–44.

17   Kiernan Tunney, *Tallulah: Darling of the Gods* (New York: E. P. Dutton, 1973), 185.

18   Gill, *Tallulah*, 44.

19   Cornell, *I Wanted to Be an Actress*, 78.

20   Cornell, *I Wanted to Be an Actress*, 223.

21   Cornell, *I Wanted to Be an Actress*, 225.

22   Nancy Cunard, "The Knave of Spades," in *Outlaws*, 37.

23   John Rodker, a young English poet and publisher of Ovid Books and Casanova Editions, once married to Mary Butts, a friend of Ezra Pound, went on a walking tour of Provence with Cunard in 1924, and visited Pound at Rapallo with her in 1925. His *Collected Poems* was to be her last publishing project at the Hours Press. Printed in England by Curwen Press for Cunard, Rodker's poems were seen through the press by the author. When Cunard returned to her Norman house and printing press after the German occupation she found the "once green vellum covers of John Rodker's large and beautiful edition of Pound's *Cantos* ... nailed firmly to a window in lieu of glass" (Chisholm, *Nancy Cunard*, 276). According to Hugh Ford, Rodker published a fourth edition of Gertrude Stein's *Three Lives*. Self-critical and introspective, Rodker was called a poet of despair. Cunard said he made one believe that "even utter blackness may be a thing of beauty"; Hugh Ford, *Published in Paris: American and British Writers, Printers and Publishers in Paris, 1920–1939* (New York: Macmillan, 1975), 280.

24   See Shari Benstock's groundbreaking exploration of this phenomenon in *Women of the Left Bank*.

25   Peter Makin, *Provence and Pound* (Berkeley, CA: University of California Press, 1978), 1–2.

26   Quoted in Makin, *Provence and Pound*, 99.

27   "From Afar" was collected in *Sublunary* (1923).

28   Postcard in Scrapbook from Nancy Cunard to Ezra Pound, possibly September 1922, Harry Ransom Center, University of Texas, Austin.

29   Chisholm, *Nancy Cunard*, 85. The reviews in the *TLS* and the *Nation* were very good and in the *New Statesman*, Edgell Rickword placed her work with Charlotte Mew and Robert Graves as "an original mind." The reviewers found her strange and full of intellectual dignity.

30   John Lucas, *The Radical Twenties: Writing, Politics, Culture* (Nottingham: Five Leaves, 1997), 210. Lucas regards H.D. as "boring," and explains Cunard's desire to be a poet as an aspect of her radical politics.

31   Rickword, *Essays and Opinions*, 39, quoted in Lucas, *The Radical Twenties*, 210.

32   Daphne Fielding, *Emerald and Nancy* (London: Eyre and Spottiswoode, 1968). Daphne Fielding's letters to Solita Solano in the Solano–Janet Flanner papers at the Library of Congress tell quite a different story from the published book.

33   Pound's letter is quoted in Chisholm, *Nancy Cunard*, 86–87. Chisholm appears to have looked at the scrapbook itself. Now its contents are dispersed

throughout the collections of the Harry Ransom Humanities Research Center, and I have not actually seen this letter.

34   Cunard, "Answer to a Reproof," in *Outlaws*, 57–59.

35   The reprover may well have been John Rodker, another of her intellectual companion lovers from the twenties. She told Solita Solano that he was "rather sneering, and sneer a lot he did at me for not knowing 'Oh western wind, when wilt thou blow.'" Janet Flanner and Solita Solano papers, Manuscript Division, Library of Congress, Series 1, General Correspondence.

Chapter Three: Between Men: Eliot, Pound, and Fresca

1   Nancy Cunard's letters to John Hayward are in King's College Library, Cambridge. She wrote to him first as editor of *The Book Collector* in 1964 regarding details in her article on the Hours Press (XIII, Winter, 1964) and thanking him for corrections and offprints. Her "letter" of condolence was a poem. Later, on January 11, wanting to know what he thought of it, she wrote to ask if she might send copies to a few friends. Hayward said no, that the letter/poem was private, and asked her about her relationship with Eliot. "I assure you nor Eliot nor I—surely—could be described as 'bright young things,'" she replied of the "odious expression" that only fit Elizabeth Ponsonby. "As for the personal element in my 'Letter' to you, I meant it that way. So you understood. I wondered, thinking you would," she wrote, agreeing to privacy and signing herself "Sorrowing," sympathizing— "Indeed 12 years is good and long to live together, and 40 is ... what word to use?" She wrote again, "I did not ever know exactly, but thought I was right in thinking you were one of Eliot's closest friends ..." She was in a clinic in Nice, having fallen and broken her thigh, and died a terrible death in Paris that March.

2   Cunard's poem is in the John Hayward papers, King's College, Cambridge.

3   Letter to the author from Dadie Rylands. There is a typo in the text, p. 7, in the word reiterative which is spelled "reiter(er)ative." The copy of *Parallax* in the Berg Collection of the New York Public Library was given by Cunard to W. E. B. Du Bois and sent by a librarian from the Schomburg in 1981 who wrote "It seems difficult to relate to people of African descent, although Miss Cunard befriended many people of African descent, it seems difficult to determine if this particular poem covers the subject or not. It seems to be written about a man, possibly a Black Musician." The poem was written well before Cunard met Henry Crowder but the note makes clear how the fact of their relationship determined many people's attitude to her.

4   Nancy Cunard, *Parallax* (London: Hogarth Press, 1925), 11.

5   Laura Riding and Robert Graves, *A Survey of Modernist Poetry* (Garden City, NY: Doubleday, Daran, and Co., 1928), 39.

6   Quoted in Chisholm, *Nancy Cunard*, 98–99.

7   Chisholm, *Nancy Cunard*, 331.

8   See *The Letters of T. S. Eliot*, vol. I, ed. Valerie Eliot (London: Faber and Faber, 1988); Peter Ackroyd, *T. S. Eliot: A Life* (New York: Simon and Schuster, 1984); Lois Cuddy and David Hirsch, *Critical Essays on T. S. Eliot's The Waste Land* (Boston: G. K. Hall, 1991); and Humphrey Carpenter, *A Serious Character: The Life of Ezra Pound* (Boston: Houghton Mifflin, 1988).

9   Cunard, *Grand Man*, 140.

10   For two strong arguments about this issue, see Rachel Blau DuPlessis, "'Hoo, Hoo, Hoo': Some Episodes in the Construction of Modern Whiteness," *American Literature* 67, no. 4 (1995): 667-700; and Michael North, *The Dialect of Modernism; Race, Language, and Twentieth-Century Literature* (New York: Oxford University Press, 1994). DuPlessis reads Hoo as full of meaning, while North calls it a "purely phatic sound ... associated with cultures outside of Europe."

11   Letter from Pound to Eliot, 24 December 1921, in *The Letters of T. S. Eliot*, vol. I, 498.

12   Lyndall Gordon, *Eliot's Early Years* (Oxford: Oxford University Press, 1977), 76.

13   Gordon, *Eliot's Early Years*, 67.

14   Wayne Koestenbaum, *Double Talk: The Erotics of Male Literary Collaboration* (New York: Routledge, 1989).

15   Quoted in Ackroyd, *T. S. Eliot: A Life*, 87. He points out that anxiety about going to war produced Eliot's sense of being "paralysed" or numbed, without feeling. What Septimus Smith in Woolf's *Mrs. Dalloway* condemns in himself is the inability to feel. Eliot's response could be seen as a form of shell shock on the home front. Readers' strong responses to this dead or numb feeling expressed in *The Waste Land* might be due to the war.

16   T. S. Eliot, *The Waste Land: A Facsimile and Transcript of the Original Drafts*, ed. Valerie Eliot with Ezra Pound's annotations (London: Faber and Faber, 1971), 23. Pound edited the poem drastically and well. He saved Eliot from alienating both Lady Cunard, a source of money and support for many of his artist friends, and Nancy, with whom Pound had an affair. She went on walking tours of the Dordogne with him and did research in Provencal sources. She also published *XXX Cantos* at the Hours Press.

17   *The Waste Land: A Facsimile and Transcript*, ed. Eliot, 27.

18   Ackroyd, *T. S. Eliot: A Life*, 97.

19   *The Waste Land: A Facsimile and Transcript*, ed. Eliot, 27.

20   *The Waste Land: A Facsimile and Transcript*, ed. Eliot, 29.

21   *The Criterion* 2, no. 7 (1924).

22   Carpenter, *A Serious Character*, 475.

23   *The Waste Land: A Facsimile and Transcript*, ed. Eliot, 1.

24   See Nancy Berke's 1997 CUNY dissertation on the radical poets Lola Ridge, Genevieve Taggart, and Margaret Walker.

25   Henry Crowder, *Henry-Music. A set of six Piano Pieces. In photographic covers on boards from a series of photographs by Man Ray* (Paris: The Hours Press, 1930).

26   Louise Morgan (Theis) 1925, quoted in Chisholm, *Nancy Cunard*, 99.

27   See Walter Lowenfels, *Sonnets of Love and Liberty* (New York: The Blue Heron Press, 1955); and Brian Daldorph, "The Politics of His Poetry: Walter Lowenfels' Poetic Response to United States v. Kuzma (1953–54): His Smith Act Trial," *Left History* 2, no. 1 (1994): 51–66. I am indebted to Nancy Berke for these references.

28   *Times Literary Supplement*, January 1, 1931, 8.

29   See Friedman, *Beckett in Black and Red*. Friedman makes clear that this set of translations is Beckett's largest body of work and it deserves to be taken seriously as evidence of his considerable skills as a translator, Cunard's field of expertise as well, and his concern for the radical race issues expressed in the essays for *Negro*, as well as his friendship for Henry Crowder and contribution of a poem to be set to music for *Henry-Music*. He sent her copies of his plays with love and wrote in 1956 that *Godot* was to re-open on Broadway (September 1956) "with an ALL NEGRO CAST."

Chapter Four: The Rites of Spring

1   Bengt Hager, *Ballets suédois* (London: Thames and Hudson, 1990), 189–209. My thanks to Maureen Flanagan for discussions of these designs and performances at Camargo in the fall of 1996.

2   Modris Eksteins, *The Rites of Spring: The Great War and the Birth of the Modern Age* (New York: Anchor Books, 1989). Despite the fact that it does not take into account any economic reasons for the war or any imperialist motives, this is a powerful analysis.

3   Gillian Beer, "The Dissidence of Vernon Lee: *Satan the Waster* and the Will to Believe," in *Women's Fiction and the Great War*, ed. Suzanne Raitt and Trudi Tate (Oxford: Clarendon Press, 1997), 107–31.

4   Eksteins, *The Rites of Spring*, xiv.

5   Osbert Sitwell, "London," in *Wheels: A Second Cycle* (Oxford: Blackwell, 1917), 18–22. Eliot claimed to have written his satires before Sitwell, in a letter to John Quinn 26 March 1920, qtd. in Ackroyd, *T. S. Eliot*, 99.

6   Sherard Vines, "New Saints," in *Wheels, Fourth Cycle* (Oxford: B. H. Blackwell, 1919), 74.

7   Sherard Vines, "War Strike," in *Wheels, Third Cycle* (Oxford: B. H. Blackwell, 1918), 80; Edith Sitwell, "Singerie," in *Wheels, Third Cycle*, 1918, 81.

8   Osbert Sitwell, "At the House of Mrs. Kinfoot," in *Wheels, Fifth Cycle* (London: Leonard Parsons, 1920), 22.

9   Osbert Sitwell, "Mrs. Freudenthal Consults the Witch of Endor," in *Wheels, Fifth Cycle* (London: Leonard Parsons, 1920), 30.

10   Osbert Sitwell, "De Luxe," in *Wheels, Fifth Cycle* (London: Leonard Parsons, 1920), 20.

11   Ackroyd quotes a letter from Eliot to Wyndham Lewis on his refusal to associate with groups of poets like those who wrote for *Wheels*, and comments on his "extraordinary caution" in protecting his reputation (Ackroyd, *T. S. Eliot: A Life*, 89).

12   Aldous Huxley, "Nero in the Circus," in *Wheels, Sixth Cycle* (London: C. W. Daniel, 1921), 10.

13   Edith Sitwell, "From the Balcony," in *Wheels, Second Cycle*, 1917, 77; Osbert Sitwell, "Rag-Time," in *Wheels, Second Cycle*, 1917, 14.

14   Osbert Sitwell, "This Generation," in *Wheels, Third Cycle*, 1918, 15.

15   Aldous Huxley, "Beauty V," in *Wheels, Third Cycle*, 1918, 25.

16   Aldous Huxley, "Evening Party," in *Wheels, Third Cycle*, 1918, 24.

17   Aldous Huxley, "Siesta Thoughts," in *Wheels: A Second Cycle* (Oxford: B. H. Blackwell, 1917), 28.

18   Victoria Glendinning, *Edith Sitwell: A Unicorn Among Lions* [1981] (London: Phoenix, 1993), 58.

19   The English painter and modernist intellectual Nina Hamnett remembered sharing with her friend Nancy Lady Cunard's gorgeous cast-off designer gowns as another "dissipated bacchante" who was also a serious artist. The mistress of Modigliani and other painters in Paris in the twenties, Hamnett helped Gaudier-Brzeska steal the piece of marble from which he sculpted her torso. A bohemian in London and Paris, who died an alcoholic's death in 1956, she has not had the recognition she deserves. Nina Hamnett, *Laughing Torso* (1932) (London: Virago, 1984), 98.

20   Nancy Cunard, "Wheels," in *Wheels: An Anthology of Verse* (Oxford: B. H. Blackwell, 1916), 9–10.

21   Alvaro Guevara's portrait of Cunard is in the National Portrait Gallery, Australia, and the portrait of Edith Sitwell is in the National Portrait Gallery, London.

22   Geoffrey Elborn, *Edith Sitwell: A Biography* (Garden City, NY: Doubleday, 1981), 24, 26.

23   See *Wheels, A Second Cycle*, 1917, 110.

24   Virginia Woolf, *A Room of One's Own* (1929), ed. Susan Gubar (Orlando, FL: Harvest/Harcourt, 2005), 12.

25   Maxwell Bodenheim, "The Decorative Straight-Jacket: Rhymed Verse," *Little Review* 1 (December 1914): 22–23.

26   Celeste Schenck, "Exiled by Genre: Modernism, Canonicity and the Politics of Exclusion," in *Women's Writing in Exile*, ed. Mary Lynn Broe and Angela Ingram (Chapel Hill, NC: University of North Carolina Press, 1989), 227.

27   Schenck, "Exiled by Genre," 227.

28   *The Observer* objected to "piling towers of rich imagery to describe squalor." The *Wheels* poets gloried in the inappropriate. Edith Sitwell's work was

read as part of a program of deliberate provocation of public taste. In "Fetes Galantes and perverted nursery rhymes," the critics hated the harlequinades that were part of the anthology's brilliant and morbid war dance. (qtd. in Press Cuttings, *Wheels, Third Cycle* [Oxford: B.H. Blackwell, 1918], 99–101). Reading the poems now is like hearing the haunting notes of the pipe and drum dancing dirge in the Basel Carnival.

29   Nancy Cunard, "Remorse," in *Wheels, First Cycle*, 1916, 34.

30   *Wheels, First Cycle*, 1916, 33.

31   See Angela Ingram, "Un/Reproductions: Estates of Banishment in English Fiction after the Great War," in Broe and Ingram, eds., *Women's Writing in Exile*, 325–48.

32   Ackroyd, *T. S. Eliot: A Life*, 85 n23.

33   From a "Letter" composed upon hearing the news of Eliot's death on January 7, 1965 sent privately to John Hayward, Harry Ransom Humanities Research Center, University of Texas, Austin.

34   "In Bad Taste," in *Wheels: An Anthology of Verse* (2nd ed., 1917), v.

35   Roberts's jackets and endpapers of 1919 and 1921 are the most visually exciting; the baby carriage led to bicycles with Lawrence Atkinson's "The Sky Pilot" on the jacket of *Wheels* for 1918. The 1920 cover of a classical figure playing a harp is by Severini.

36   See Richard Cork, *A Bitter Truth: Avant-Garde Art and the Great War* (New Haven, CT: Yale University Press, 1994), for more on William Roberts's war paintings. He did two drawings for the War Number of Wyndham Lewis's *Blast* and, like Lewis, produced remarkable canvases on commission for the Canadian government while on active duty at the Front. *The First German Gas Attack at Ypres 1918* is in the National Gallery of Canada, Ottowa; a pen and ink sketch, *The Gas Chamber*, is in the Imperial War Museum, London; Roberts's *4.5 Howitzer Gunner RFA 1916–1918: Memories of the War to End War 1914–1918* (The William Roberts Society, 1974 Exhibition, Estate of John David Roberts, Tate) reveals his fury and despair at the brutality of the mass killings. Lawrence Binyon was astonished at the twenty-three-year-old's *Gas Attack* with its "torrent of Turcos and Zouaves pouring headlong down the canvas, convulsed, grimacing and sick." The khaki uniforms of the Canadians mixed with the wild colors of the French made the battlefield look like a bed of tulips (Cork, *A Bitter Truth*, 213).

37   Quoted in Cork, *A Bitter Truth*, 320.

38   Cunard, "New Coasts," in *Nancy Cunard: Selected Poems*, 67–68.

39   Cunard, "Destruction," in *Wheels: An Anthology of Verse*, First cycle 1, 1916, 32.

Chapter Five: Girlfriends, Boyfriends, and Bright Young Things

1   Iris Tree, "III," in *Wheels: An Anthology of Verse*, Cycle 1, 1916, 63; "Black Velvet," in *Wheels, Second Cycle*, 1917, 54.

2   Iris Tree, "Revision," in *Wheels, Third Cycle*, 1918, 62.

3   See Daphne Fielding, *The Rainbow Picnic: A Portrait of Iris Tree* (London: Eyre Methuen, 1974).

4   Iris Tree, "Return," in *Wheels, Third Cycle*, 1918, 66.

5   Fielding, *The Rainbow Picnic*, 53.

6   Chisholm, *Nancy Cunard*, 38.

7   Lucas, *The Radical Twenties*, 87.

8   Wyndham Lewis, *The Roaring Queen* (New York: Liveright, 1973). Scheduled to be published by Cape in 1936, the book was withdrawn in proof for fear of libel. Arnold Bennett, the writer and reviewer satirized as Shodbutt, had been dead for five years, but Rhoda Hyman (Virginia Woolf) was alive and still smarting from Lewis's charge in *Men Without Art* that *Mrs. Dalloway* was a "pathetic crib" of *Ulysses*, a "sort of undergraduate imitation" of Joyce's masterpiece. Mrs. Lewis, Gladys Anne Hoskins, "Froanna" (1900–79), told the editor of the Liveright edition that Baby Bucktrout was based on Nancy Cunard, who had wanted to publish *The Roaring Queen* at the Hours Press after it was censored, despite the satire on herself, her friend Brian Howard (the "Roaring Queen" himself), and her friend and the publisher of her poems, Virginia Woolf—but he needed an advance which she couldn't supply.

9   Wyndham Lewis, *Blasting and Bombardiering: Autobiography (1914–1926)* (London: Eyre & Spottiswoode, 1937), 237. Lewis painted her in Venice and recalled her "extensive experience" of beautiful stammering society "boys." Interestingly, he accepted her contradictions, reporting that at the time of his writing she retained these attributes, and admiringly recalling that she "has been on the Aragon Front helping the Catalans to repel the attack of the Rebels."

10 Nancy Cunard, *These Were the Hours: Memories of My Hours Press, Reanville and Paris 1928–1931*, ed. Hugh Ford (Carbondale, IL: Southern Illinois University Press, 1969), 187. Cunard admired Ellis's book on Spain and he signed her petition against Franco in *Authors Take Sides* in 1937. She quotes Bob Brown's *Gems: A Censored Anthology* about *Studies in the Psychology of Sex*: "The first two volumes may only be sold to Rabbis, Ministers, Parson, Lawyers, librarians, and people over the Climacteric and Menopause stages…" (*These Were the Hours*, 188).

11 Michel Leiris, *L'Afrique Fantôme* (Paris: Editions Gallimard, 1934).

12 Cunard, *These Were the Hours*, 189.

13 Ellis, *Revaluation of Obscenity*, qtd. in Cunard, *These Were the Hours*, 190, 192.

14 Cunard, *These Were the Hours*, 191, 192.

15 John Banting's unpublished memoirs are in the Tate Gallery Archives. My thanks to Jennifer Booth and her helpful colleagues for their guidance to this collection as well as to the uncatalogued Barbara Ker-Seymer papers.

16 The photographs of the Bright Young Things are in the Barbara Ker-Seymer papers in the Tate Gallery Archive. Some are published in biographies of Brian Howard and Frederick Ashton, and in David Garnett's memoirs. The filmmaker and editor of *Close-Up*, Kenneth Macpherson, husband of Bryher, the writer and companion-lover of the poet H.D., appears in many pictures with his Black lover, Jimmie Daniels. Brian Guinness, Eddie Sackville-West, Stephen Tomlin, Eddie Gawthorne-Hardy, and Julia Strachey are among those cavorting on the beach in poses not quite "off the scene," in Havelock Ellis's terms, and rather openly shown on the stage of life.

17 "Tanning" in Hemingway's fiction and the relationship of race crossing to gender crossing is explored in a dissertation by my student Ira Elliott, CUNY English Department, 1995, and I am indebted to him for discussion of these issues in modernism.

18 Henry Crowder, *As Wonderful as All That? Henry Crowder's Memoir of his Affair with Nancy Cunard 1928–1935*, with the assistance of Hugo Speck (Navarro, CA: Wildtrees Press, 1987). For discussion of the posthumous publication of this "as-told-to" document now in the possession of the Harry Ransom Humanities Research Center, University of Texas, see Marcus, "Bonding and Bondage: Nancy Cunard and the Making of the *Negro* Anthology," repr. in *Hearts of Darkness*, 196–97 n4.

19 See Aldous Huxley, *Point Counter Point* (1928) (London: Penguin, 1955), 297. Huxley's biographer, Sybille Bedford, believes that Lucy is not based on his affair with Cunard, "but any stylized siren of the 20s," although she quotes D. H. Lawrence's assurance that Lucy was, and that his wife was upset. Maria Huxley was typing *Lady Chatterley's Lover* as Huxley was finishing *Point Counter Point*, and, when the censorship problems with the novel began, Lawrence wrote to Huxley to ask for Nancy Cunard's address so that he could ask her to publish it at the Hours Press (Sybille Bedford, *Aldous Huxley: A Biography, Volume One, 1894–1939* [London: Chatto and Windus/William Collins, 1973], 202, 207). Huxley and Lawrence were very close at the time; Lawrence said that *Point Counter Point* was "disgusting," that Huxley could only "thrill to murder, suicide and rape," but that it took "a fine courage" to tell the truth about himself and his generation.

20 Huxley, *Point Counter Point*, 337, 323–24.

21 Huxley, *Point Counter Point*, 358.

22 Huxley, *Point Counter Point*, 358–59.

23 Huxley, *Point Counter Point*, 57.

24 Huxley, *Point Counter Point*, 137.

25 Richard Dyer, *The Matter of Images: Essays on Representations* (London: Routledge, 2002), 55.

26   Dyer, *The Matter of Images*, 55.
27   Dyer, *The Matter of Images*, 55.
28   Huxley, *Point Counter Point*, 49.
29   Huxley, *Point Counter Point*, 86.
30   Huxley, *Point Counter Point*, 95.
31   Dyer, *The Matter of Images*, 145.
32   Huxley, *Point Counter Point*, 1.
33   Wyndham Lewis, *Men Without Art* (1934), ed. Seamus Cooney (Santa Rosa, CA: Black Sparrow Press, 1987), 242–43.
34   Huxley, *Point Counter Point*, 74–75.
35   Huxley, *Point Counter Point*, 76.
36   Huxley, *Point Counter Point*, 78.
37   Huxley, *Point Counter Point*, 85.
38   Huxley, *Point Counter Point*, 107.
39   Bedford, *Aldous Huxley: A Biography*, vol. I, 213.
40   Aldous Huxley, "The Horrors of Society: The Unutterable Boredom Involved in the 'Diversions of the Leisured Classes,'" *Vanity Fair*, June 1925, 46.
41   Huxley, "The Horrors of Society," 94.
42   Nancy Cunard, "Letter from Paris," *Vogue*, late May 1926, 75, 108.
43   Cunard also reports on the replacing of *transition* by a review with musical extracts from George Antheil, a bullfight story by Hemingway, some Joyce and Pound's *Cantos*, William Carlos Williams and Kay Boyle and a suffragette memoir by Ethel Moorehead, though she doesn't care for the editorials.
44   The ballet *La Création du monde* was performed in Paris by the Ballet suédois.
45   This show at the Gallerie Surréaliste in the rue Jacques Callot, Paris, in March 1926, under the auspices of the still-friendly André Breton and Louis Aragon—described by Cunard as "among the most discussed personalities of Paris, not only as the insurgents of the 'Surréalisme' movement, but individually as brilliant young writers and poets whose erudition is as solid as their outlook and their way of writing is new"—was quite possibly the first to show "primitive" art from Africa and Oceania with modern pieces, in this case by Man Ray. Of course, the pieces were together in the artists' studios, but the juxtaposition was novel.
46   See William Rubin, ed., *Primitivism in 20th Century Art: Affinity of the Tribal and the Modern*, exhibition catalogue (New York: Museum of Modern Art, 1984), published to accompany the exhibition of the same name, September 1984–January 1985, Museum of Modern Art, New York.
47   Cunard, "Letter from Paris," late May 1926, 75.
48   Cunard, ed., *Negro: An Anthology*, 329.
49   René Crevel was a French Surrealist and contributor to the *Negro* anthology of "The Negress in the Brothel," which was removed by the censor from the volume, before being printed elsewhere by Cunard and tipped in during the binding process. It is not listed in the table of contents, making the book

unusual in the history of publishing. Brian Howard overdosed after the sudden accidental death of his lover Sam Langford (1926–58).

50   Letter from Nancy Cunard to Janet Flanner, Late Autumn 1925, the Janet Flanner and Solita Solano Papers. The Library of Congress. Manuscript Division. Also, qtd. in Chisholm, *Nancy Cunard*, 99–100.

51   Louis Aragon, *Irene's Cunt* (published anonymously by René Bonnel in 1928), trans. Alexis Lykiard (London: Creation Books, 1996), 84. René Bonnel, who also published erotic works by Jarry, Apollinaire, Pierre Louys and Raymond Radiguet, produced George Bataille's *Histoire de l' Oeil* in the same year. The edition of 150 copies had five illustrations by André Masson. The 1968 L'Or du Temps edition "by Albert de Routisie" was seized by the Brigade Mondaine (Vice Squad), but it again served to confirm the French Communist Party leader's virility. A very long review in the *Times Literary Supplement* (March, 1968) praised the mysterious work of "genius" that Aragon never openly acknowledged as "a lyrically urgent evocation of the mystical core of true sexual carnality." His other adventures in the genre include *1929* with Benjamin Peret and Man Ray and a preface to Apollinaire's *Les Onze Mille Verges*.

52   Nancy Cunard's complicated reputation among white American historians and cultural critics is discussed elsewhere. Her place in the history of African liberation politics and to Afro-Americans as a reporter for three decades for the wire service, United Negro Press International, is adumbrated in this book, but there is much more work to be done.

53   Issue 4, 1931.

54   André Thirion, *Revolutionaries Without Revolution* (1972) (New York: Macmillan, 1975), 308.

55   See Thirion, *Revolutionaries Without Revolution*, 316.

56   The Man Ray photograph appeared in the August 15, 1929 issue of *Variétés*. It was paired with a photograph of Kiki de Montparnasse. They are facing each other, Kiki's heavily made-up eyes looking pensively down over her bare shoulder, straight dark hair cut short in a fringed bob, an earring dangling beneath the curve of her hair. Cunard, whose marcelled hair emerges into provocative kiss curls on her cheek, looks out from under her darkly outlined eyes at Kiki, ringed hands folded rather demurely under her chin, exposing her braceleted arms in a V-shape, like an arrow pointed at the other woman. Kiki looks like the archetype of the mysterious woman from the East—a paisley shawl is just visible beneath the famous round white shoulder and curved back. Cunard looks like a tiger about to pounce. The round ivory bracelets echo the circle of Kiki's earring and the half-circles of eyebrows and ears, lips and curls of hair suggest that the images belong together or to each other; each is one half of the perfect woman, or they are the same woman in different moods.

57   Thirion, *Revolutionaries Without Revolution*, 89.

Chapter Six: Closet Autobiography: Bones and Stones

1   Nancy Cunard, *GM: Memories of George Moore* (London: Rupert Hart-Davis, 1956); Cunard, *Grand Man: Memories of Norman Douglas*. Irish man of letters George Moore, who died in 1933, began as a painter in Paris in the 1870s, giving it up for criticism, and producing a lifetime of essays on culture, memoirs such as *Confessions of a Young Man* (1886) and brilliant Zola-esque novels (though he denied their social vision) such as *Esther Waters* and *A Mummer's Wife*. He used to be credited with making the reputation of his friend Manet, who painted his portrait at least twice, and the Impressionists, in the influential *Modern Painters* and *Manet and the Impressionists*, and so he described himself. He met the American heiress Maud Burke as she was being rejected by a titled fiancé, upon which she abruptly married Sir Bache Cunard. Rumor, to which he, Maud, and Nancy appear to have contributed, each for their own purposes, casts him as Nancy's real father, while he also had a reputation for being impotent, and as a boaster about liaisons with women, which he invented. He spent a great deal of time at Nevill Holt as one of Lady Cunard's admirers, writing, explaining Wagner's music, and supporting the Irish Literary Revival. He befriended Nancy as she was learning to read and encouraged her intellectual work and her writing until he died.

     Norman Douglas (1868–1952), born in Austria to Scottish and German parents, is always associated with the Isle of Capri, where he built a villa, planted trees, encouraged what we now call ecology, and about whose English colony he wrote a successful romantic novel called *South Wind* in 1917; he published scientific papers on herpetology, exposed child labor conditions in the stone industry on the Lipari Islands, and worked for the Foreign Service for many years. Author of *Siren Land, Old Calabria, Fountains in the Sand, London Street Games* and several other books including a memoir called *Looking Back*, he was married in 1898, had two children, and divorced in 1903. He and Nancy took a trip to Tunisia together.

2   See Jane Marcus, "Invincible Mediocrity: The Private Lives of Public Women," in *The Private Self: Theory and Practice of Women's Autobiography*, ed. Shari Benstock (Chapel Hill, NC: University of North Carolina Press, 1988).

3   George Moore, *Confessions of a Young Man* (1886) (London: Heinemann, 1928), 95.

4   Moore, *Confessions of a Young Man*, 124.

5   Eve Kosofsky Sedgwick, *The Epistemology of the Closet* (Berkeley, CA: University of California Press, 1990).

6   Cunard, *These Were the Hours*, 115–17. John Sullivan was the singer, and Beecham did hear him sing. Joyce "dropped more than a hint that if Sullivan were engaged, well, some piece of work suitable to the Hours might come my way," Cunard writes, remembering the "bargain" with some distaste. She was startled by Joyce's unannounced visit to her hotel room. She was ill and

they had never met. She found him, aside from his insistence on it being her "duty" to use her influence with her mother—and he refused to believe she had no influence with her mother—"very conventional and rather difficult to talk to."

7   Cunard, *GM: Memories of George Moore*, 11.

8   Moore, *Confessions of a Young Man*, 7–8. In his preface to the 1928 edition, Moore announces that "The end of the Nineteenth Century cannot brag of a more original book than *The Confessions of a Young Man*," citing Pater's comment on his "audacious" book, which is the "genesis" of everything else he wrote, from *Esther Waters* to eulogies of Manet, Degas, Whistler, Monet, and Pissaro. "At the time of writing them I knew nothing of Jean Jacques Rousseau. It is barely creditable that I could have lived into early manhood without having heard of him, but *The Confessions of a Young Man* testifies that I never read him; a page of Jean Jacques would have made the book I am prefacing an impossibility ... I wrote without a model, Jean Jacques, too, wrote without a model, but he wrote at the end of his life..." (*Confessions of a Young Man*, viii).

9   Moore, *Confessions of a Young Man*, 1.

10   Cunard remembered often having tea with Moore "under the plaster plaque of my great grand-uncle, Robert Emmett, the Irish patriot," in the oldest part of Nevill Holt, the Cloisters. Robert Emmett was hanged for his part in an insurrection. Lady Maud Cunard was an Irish-American from San Francisco. Anne Chisholm relates that rumor had it that her father was not James Burke, but was actually William O'Brien, the Great Bonanza Mine millionaire, who left her a fortune. Her mother's protector after Burke's death, real estate magnate Horace Carpentier, was expected to give Maud two million dollars on her marriage to Sir Bache Cunard. She had remained his ward when her mother remarried, and he began to educate her in literature and the arts and often took her to Europe from the age of twelve. The upwardly mobile Lady Cunard quite naturally repressed her Irish background in England after her marriage. Sir Bache Cunard was the grandson of Samuel Cunard, the Philadelphia-born engineer who founded the steamship line in Halifax, Nova Scotia, in 1840. He was made a baronet on settling in England after the *Britannia* cut 15 days off the sailing time from Boston to Liverpool. Bache and his brothers were educated at Rugby, and it is hard to imagine him at Trinity College, Cambridge, given his future life as an eccentric English country gentleman, fishing, hunting, and making topiaries in the gardens on the 13,000-acre property. He worked as a craftsman in his Tower, using a forge on a nearby farm, making metalwork weathervanes for Holt and Medbourne churches in the nearest town. Cunard said little about her father, though she cherished the silver fox she inherited after he died, given him by the members of his Hunt. It is clear from her career at the Hours Press and her joy in hand-setting type that she also inherited his Irish-American love of

craftsmanship, as well as the revolutionary Irish spirit of Robert Emmett and the great will to live of the immigrant prospecting Burkes of California.

11 Cunard, *Grand Man*, 71.

12 Christopher Hassall, *Edward Marsh, Patron of the Arts* (London: Longman, 1959), 453, quoted in Chisholm, *Nancy Cunard*, 38.

13 Cunard, *GM: Memories of George Moore*, 168.

14 Cunard, *GM: Memories of George Moore*, 168.

15 *George Moore: Letters 1895–1933 to Lady Cunard*, ed. Rupert Hart-Davies (London: Rupert Hart-Davies, 1957), 140. Cunard's copy is in the Harry Ransom Center. Moore left his pictures to Lady Cunard; she died at 75 in 1948. Lavery's portrait of Lady Cunard and George Moore is owned by Lord Semphill and Lady Diana Cooper.

16 Moore, *Confessions of a Young Man*, 196–97.

17 Cunard, *GM: Memories of George Moore*, 35–36.

18 Cunard, *GM: Memories of George Moore*, 32–33.

19 Cunard, *GM: Memories of George Moore*, 178.

Chapter Seven: White Nympholepsy: George Moore, Manet, and the Modern

1 George Moore, *The Collected Works of George Moore: Volume X, Memoirs of My Dead Life* (1906), The Carra Edition (London: Boni and Liveright, 1923), 29–30.

2 Wilhelm Uhde, *The Impressionists* (Vienna, 1937), 6–7.

3 Moore, *Memoirs of My Dead Life*, 244.

4 Moore, *Memoirs of My Dead Life*, 57.

5 Moore's portrait was painted several times by Manet; he describes one portrait in his memoirs and says it was destroyed. The one I refer to here is in the Metropolitan Museum, New York. His *Confessions* is dedicated to Jacques Emile Blanche.

6 Moore, *Memoirs of My Dead Life*, 38.

7 Moore, *Memoirs of My Dead Life*, 40.

8 Moore, *Memoirs of My Dead Life*, 40.

9 Moore, *Memoirs of My Dead Life*, 42.

10 Moore, *Memoirs of My Dead Life*, 43.

11 Moore, *Memoirs of My Dead Life*, 44.

12 Moore, *Memoirs of My Dead Life*, 44–45.

13 Moore, *Memoirs of My Dead Life*, 230.

14 Moore, *Memoirs of My Dead Life*, 46.

15 Moore, *Memoirs of My Dead Life*, 50.

16 Moore, *Memoirs of My Dead Life*, 50.

17 Moore, *Memoirs of My Dead Life*, 52–53. At times it appears as if Moore is recording the themes and plots of French popular culture of the day. At a performance of Charpentier's *Louise* in Toulouse that I attended in 1996, the

audience wept and was deeply moved by scenes that were so sentimental that they reduced Americans to laughter.

18 Cunard in her memoir of Moore remarks that in Jacques Emile Blanche's memoir he is described as a wicked critic; Maurice Barrès, the writer and leader of Action Française, is said never to have forgiven his attacks (*GM: Memories of George Moore*, 31).

19 Moore, *Memoirs of My Dead Life*, 57.

20 Moore, *Memoirs of My Dead Life*, 57–58.

21 George Moore, *Modern Painters* (1893) (New York: Scribner's, 1906), 30. This and the other quotations from Moore's *Modern Painters* are taken from Edith Sitwell's copy in the Harry Ransom Humanities Research Center, University of Texas.

22 Moore, *Modern Painters*, 24.

23 Moore, *Modern Painters*, 35.

24 Moore, *Modern Painters*, 34.

25 Moore, *Modern Painters*, 43.

26 See Eunice Lipton's influential *Alias Olympia: A Woman's Search for Manet's Notorious Model and Her Own Desire* (New York: Scribners, 1992). Victorine Meurent exhibited paintings in the salons of 1876, 1879, 1885, and 1904. Lipton's book is a landmark in its conception of a "life" in terms of desire, rather than a record of achievments. It is in this spirit that I am attempting to capture something of the passionate desire for justice that drove Nancy Cunard.

27 Cunard tells the story (*GM: Memories of George Moore*, 161–63) of bringing Janet Flanner to tea with Moore in Ebury Street and the discussion of his paintings. He owned two Manets, the *Étude pour Le Linge* and a portrait of Manet's mother. Also hanging in his flat were a David, a Constable, a Guillaumin, some Mark Fishers, a Steer, a Degas pastel, and pictures by Conder and Orpen. The Manet portrait had been bought for Lord Grimthorpe, who then changed his mind. Flanner was interested in his two Berthe Morisots, *Le Leçon de couture* and *La Femme à la tasse à thé*, done in the same blue, green, and yellow of his Monet of willows in a submerged meadow. Cunard found the Morisots "full of grace" (*GM: Memories of George Moore*, 98) and Moore said she was "perhaps the best of all the women painters" because of "how wonderfully she used white in her pictures; no one ever made such a fine use of white" (*GM: Memories of George Moore*, 162), the very words he had used to praise Manet and not at all evident in the Morisots he owned—and because of the influence of Manet. He used the word *chien*—a dressmaker's word—to describe the "arrogant provocative dash" of the ballet girls drawn by Degas. And he told them that *Ulysses* was not a novel because there wasn't a tree in it. Cunard remembered the occasion because "G. M. wore an absolutely 'white' look concerning all subjects and persons and he was being rather formal" (*GM: Memories of George Moore*, 162).

28 George Moore, *Impressions and Opinions* (New York: Brentanos, 1894), 66.

29 Quoted in Alice Cooney Frelinghuysen, *Splendid Legacy: The Havemeyer Collection* (New York: Metropolitan Museum of Art, 1993) 27.

30 Louisine Havemeyer, "On Collecting Manet," n.d., Tate Gallery Library.

31 Cunard, *GM: Memories of George Moore*, 34.

32 Cunard, *GM: Memories of George Moore*, 67.

33 Cunard, *GM: Memories of George Moore*, 9–10.

34 Cunard, *GM: Memories of George Moore*, 67.

35 Anthony Thorne, "A Share of Nancy," in Ford, *Nancy Cunard: Brave Poet*, 299.

36 Thorne, "A Share of Nancy," 300.

37 Charles Burkhart, in Ford, *Nancy Cunard: Brave Poet*, 330.

38 Sylvia Townsend Warner, in Ford, *Nancy Cunard: Brave Poet*, 228.

39 Warner, in Ford, *Nancy Cunard: Brave Poet*, 228.

40 Cunard, *GM: Memories of George Moore*, 21.

41 Cunard, *GM: Memories of George Moore*, 21.

42 Cunard, *GM: Memories of George Moore*, 40.

43 Cunard, *GM: Memories of George Moore*, 64.

44 Cunard, *GM: Memories of George Moore*, 183.

45 Cunard, *GM: Memories of George Moore*, 183.

46 Cunard, *GM: Memories of George Moore*, 189.

47 Cunard, *GM: Memories of George Moore*, 149.

48 Cunard, *GM: Memories of George Moore*, 151.

49 Cunard, *GM: Memories of George Moore*, 151.

50 Moore, *Confessions of a Young Man*, 89.

51 Moore, *Confessions of a Young Man*, 48.

52 Cunard, *GM: Memories of George Moore*, 25.

53 Moore, *Modern Painters*, 31–33.

54 See Theodor Duret, *Histoire du Édouard Manet et son oeuvre* (Paris: Bernheim-Jeune, 1919), 149, *Le Modèle du Linge*, 262, *Le Linge*; Moore, *Modern Painting*, 25–44. For a discussion of Mallarmé, see Claire Lyu, "Stéphane Mallarmé as Miss Satin: The Texture of Fashion and Poetry," *L'Esprit Créateur* 40, no. 3 (2000): 61–71, https://www.jstor.org/stable/26288349.

55 Cunard, *GM: Memories of George Moore*, 11.

56 Cunard, *GM: Memories of George Moore*, 23, 25.

57 Cunard, *GM: Memories of George Moore*, 26.

58 Cunard, *GM: Memories of George Moore*, 27.

59 Cunard, *GM: Memories of George Moore*, 11.

60 Cunard, *GM: Memories of George Moore*, 10.

61 Cunard, *GM: Memories of George Moore*, 9.

62 Sale catalogue, Sotheby's, July 4, 1962.

63 My thanks to Kate Garmeson, archivist of Impressionist and Modern Art at Sotheby's, who supplied their records showing the sale of Cunard's Manet painting—the study for a more finished nude torso, which disappeared from

Paris during the German Occupation—three times in the 1960s; to Cunard's friend Schrieber in 1962 for £12,000, to P. Pochin in 1963 for £9,000, and to Shriver in 1966 for £16,000; then to E. V. Thaw & Co., New York; Stephen Hahn, New York; Dr. Arthur Sackler, New York. The catalogue raisonné states that "Alice Lecouve, the model for *Le Linge*, posed for this bust." Denis Rouart and Daniel Wildenstein, *Edouard Manet catalogue raisonné*, vol. 11 (Lausanne: La Biblioteque des Arts, 1975). I still find little to connect the open face in the nude torso with the face hidden in *Le Linge*. A letter to Solita Solano (July, 1964?, Library of Congress) says "Sotheby have been VILE with me—finis Sotheby—they dare charge me £600 for not selling Manet. I've paid half."

64   Rouart and Wildenstein, *Edouard Manet catalogue raisonné*, vol. 11.

65   Moore, *Modern Painters*, 38.

66   Moore, *Modern Painters*, 39.

67   T. A. Gronberg, *Manet Retrospective* (New York: Hugh Lauter Levin, 1988); Eunice Lipton, "The Laundress in Late Ninetenth-Century French Culture: Imagery, Ideology and Edgar Degas," *Art History* 3, no. 3 (1980): 295–313.

68   Cunard, *GM: Memories of George Moore*, 182–83.

69   Cunard's typescript is in the Sylvia Townsend Warner papers, Dorset County Library.

70   Nancy Cunard, "Dordogne," in *Nancy Cunard: Selected Poems*, 169–70.

Chapter Eight: Intellectual Nomads: Norman Douglas, the Desert, and the Taste for Space

1   Cunard, *Grand Man*, 140.

2   See *Gertrude Bell: The Arabian Diaries, 1913–1914*, ed. Rosemary O'Brien (Syracuse, NY: Syracuse University Press, 2000); and on Amelia Edwards, Ruth Jenkins, "More Usefully Employed: Amelia B. Edwards, Writer, Traveler, and Campaigner for Ancient Egypt," *Victorian Studies* 49 (2007): 365–67.

3   See Carla Peterson, *"Doers of the Word": African-American Women Speakers and Writers in the North (1830–1880)* (New Brunswick, NJ: Rutgers University Press, 1998).

4   Cunard, *Grand Man*, 91–97. Crowder felt that Douglas had just been humoring them and had no intention of going to Africa with an interracial couple.

5   Leiris, *L'Afrique Fantôme*.

6   Cunard, *Grand Man*, 97.

7   Cunard, *Grand Man*, 99.

8   Cunard, *Grand Man*, 97; Norman Douglas, "Letter about Arusha," in Cunard, ed., *Negro: An Anthology*, 645.

9   Cunard, *Grand Man*, 140.

10   Many of the memoirs of Cunard in Hugh Ford's *Nancy Cunard: Brave Poet* suggest a drug habit at different points in her life. Anne Chisholm does not discount the possibility. In *Grand Man* (84), Cunard tells of a fancy dress ball

she gave in Venice at the time she first met Henry Crowder. Dressed like a Velasquez dwarf, one of her guests searched madly for his lost jeweled box containing cocaine. Her gondolier, who was neither young not handsome, complained about being "amiably solicited." Crowder's "memoir," for what it is worth, tells a version of this story in which he is being solicited and offered cocaine in Venice by one of Cunard's gay men friends whose eyelashes are painted silver.

11 Cunard, *Grand Man*, 140–41.
12 Cunard, *Grand Man*, 147.
13 See also B. Steiner Ifekwe, "Rastafarianism in Jamaica as a Pan-African Protest Movement," *Journal of the Historical Society of Nigeria* 17 (2008): 106–22.
14 Cunard, *Grand Man*, 277.
15 Cunard, *Grand Man*, 45.
16 Cunard, *Grand Man*, 44–46.
17 Cunard, *Grand Man*, 44–45.
18 Cunard, *Grand Man*, 45.
19 Cunard, *Grand Man*, 276.
20 Cunard, *Grand Man*, 147.
21 See Richard Aldington, *Pinorman: Recollections of Norman Douglas, Pino Orioli, and Charles Prentice* (London: Heinemann, 1954), 113, 118.
22 Cunard, *Grand Man*, 122.
23 Cunard, *Grand Man*, 138.
24 Cunard, *Grand Man*, 117.
25 Cunard, *Grand Man*, 284.
26 Cunard, *Grand Man*, 151.
27 Cunard, *Grand Man*, 151.
28 Cunard, *Grand Man*, 152–53.
29 See, for instance, the typescript of "Whose Desert?," one of the poems made at Montacute in Somerset in April 1944, in the Sylvia Townsend Warner papers at the Dorset County Library. The typescript includes a note on the wars that afflicted Spanish Morocco in the first decades of the twentieth century. Both poem and note appear in *Nancy Cunard: Selected Poems*, the poem on p. 168, the note on p. 253.

Chapter Nine: White Women, Black Books: The *Negro* Anthology and Sylvia Leith-Ross's *African Women*

1   Much of this chapter had its origin in many years of discussion with Molara Ogundipe-Leslie, Joshua Leslie, Sterling Stuckey, and Michael Marcus. Our animated informal seminar discussions on "Benito Cereno" and the history of slavery, as well as on the intersections of race and class, and the concept of gender in Africa and the West Indies, when Molara and I were in graduate

school at Northwestern and the men were colleagues of my husband on the faculty, were far more formative of my ideas than any formal classes I ever took. This book is in many ways a tribute to our spirited debates in the 1970s.

2   Nancy Cunard, *Negro: Anthology Made by Nancy Cunard 1931–33* (London: Wishart, 1934), 855+ pages, 250 pieces, lavishly illustrated with photographs, drawings, maps, illustrations, musical notations, etc. 315 pages on Africa, 60 on Europe and the rest on the U.S.A. The volume is a large royal quarto, 12 inches by 10 inches. Cunard paid £1500 to print it, exactly the sum she earned in libel costs from British newspapers for their attacks on her relations with Henry Crowder and other people of color, a fact she noted as "poetic justice." She had already put more than £350 into gathering the materials. The contributors were not paid, though it is consistent with her record to believe that she paid Samuel Beckett for his many translations from the French in order to support him. Claude McKay claimed that he didn't know that contributors would not be paid and so dropped out in the end, leaving Cunard to write the Jamaica section herself, based on interviews with his brother, photographed on a banana farm. Much has been made of a remark to this effect in his memoirs, obscuring McKay's major contribution to the volume in introducing Cunard to his friends and relatives, other writers, and so on. When *Negro* was published on February 15, 1934, Cunard celebrated by going out "to meet the English hunger marchers on the Midland Road." The price was a steep £2 2s., and while hopes for a cheaper American edition never materialized, contributors, libraries, and the press were sent free copies. Hugh Ford published a much-reduced version of *Negro* in 1970 with an introduction, and this Ungar/Continuum edition has been reprinted (1996). For details on what was omitted, see Bonnie Kime Scott's review, "Limited Edition," *The Women's Review of Books* 14, no. 10/11 (1997): 41–42, www.jstor.org/stable/4022738.

3   From Cunard's State Department file we learn that the spy who sent proofs of the table of contents and the foreword from the US Embassy in London (January 23, 1934) expected an American edition by Covici, Friede, and later (March 30) reported that Little, Brown had turned it down.

4   "Hausa Writing," in Cunard, ed., *Negro: An Anthology*, 642–44.

5   Tyrus Miller, paper delivered at the 1996 MLA "*Negro* Anthology" panel chaired by Lillian Robinson; also Carole Sweeney's "Le 'tumulte noir:' Negro, Negrophilia and Modernist Anthropology," given at the same meeting.

6   Sylvia Leith-Ross, *African Women: A Study of the Ibo in Nigeria*, foreword by Lord Lugard (1938) (New York: Praeger, 1966).

7   Ibo is an Anglicized spelling and incorrect; there being no phonetic representation for the sound "gb" in the Igbo language, it was dropped, but there is no word "Ibo" in the Igbo language.

8   Sylvia Leith-Ross, *Beyond the Niger* (London: Lutterworth, 1951), 107. In this scene Leith-Ross establishes herself as an expert. She is eyewitness to

a scene where "primitive people" recognize something "more important than themselves." Such monumental self-aggrandizement at the expense of a people she despised for their vulgar concern with trade would never have occurred to Nancy Cunard.

9   See Karen Lawrence, *Penelope Voyages: Women and Travel in the British Literary Tradition* (Ithaca, NY: Cornell University Press, 1994).

10   T. Obinkaram Echewa, *I Saw the Sky Catch Fire* (New York: Dutton, 1992). See also Bella Brodski, "History, Cultural Memory, and the Tasks of Translation in T. Obinkaram Echewa's *I Saw the Sky Catch Fire*," *PMLA* 114, no. 2 (1999): 207–20. Leith-Ross was not in Igboland until after the war, so she was not the actual historical source for the figure of Ashby-Jones, as the article suggests, but part of a composite of several women in the field. Her text, *African Women*, is, however, a direct source for the novel, as Echewa has exactly caught the trick of Leith-Ross's style—negative descriptions of the women followed by a plea to the reader hoping she has not caused one to think ill of the Igbo.

11   Echewa, *I Saw the Sky Catch Fire*, 109–10.

12   Leith-Ross points out that indirect rule did not work as well in Southern Nigeria as it did in the North because the Igbo were "too democratic" in their social structures, and Lugard agreed. Indirect rule meant that the British colonizers were to work with existing social structures among the natives. The policy worked in the North where the people had already been conquered and subjugated by the Arabs and emirs, and chiefs ruled and mediated for the British in a patriarchal and hierarchical system that was familiar to them. The Igbo groups studied by Leith-Ross had no leaders and functioned in complex collectives that shared decision making. Women were very powerful and independent in these groups. They farmed and went to markets far away from home, leaving their children with older children, and they were the source of economic power in their communities. The British appointed as chiefs men who had no status and they were resented by the people. Since women's courts had settled most of the local problems, they particularly disliked the imposition of English law and its foreign system of punishment.

13   Sylvia Leith-Ross, *Stepping-Stones: Memoirs of Colonial Nigeria 1907–1960*, ed. Michael Crowder (London: Peter Owen, 1983), 172.

14   Leith-Ross, *Stepping-Stones*, 172–73.

15   With her sister-in-law Genevieve Ruxton, Leith-Ross also produced *Practical West African Cookery* (Zungeru, 1908, and Ibi, 1910), which was used by generations of colonials, encouraging them to eat local produce and fish. Her other publications include the *Fulani Grammar* (Lagos, n.d.), *African Women* (1939), *African Conversation Piece* (1943), *Cocks in the Dawn* (1944), *Beyond the Niger* (1951), and *Nigerian Pottery* (Ibadan, 1970). The edition of her memoirs edited by Crowder, along with Salome Nnoromele's *Life Among*

the Ibo Women, are examples of the making of official knowledge about the history of Africa. Leith-Ross and her work are revered. They matter. They matter to the people most likely, one would think, to be outraged by the effects her reports had on the dismantling of local social structures, and the repression in particular of women's institutions for maintaining power.

16   Leith-Ross, *Stepping-Stones*, 13.

17   Leith-Ross, *Stepping-Stones*, 126.

18   Leith-Ross, *Stepping-Stones*, 140.

19   Thanks to Lillian Robinson for a useful conversation on this topic.

20   See Helen Calloway, *Gender, Culture, Empire: European Women in Colonial Nigeria* (Urbana, IL: University of Illinois Press, 1987).

21   Evans-Pritchard's work earned him a professorship at Oxford, not a likely option for a woman, who would remain an amateur in England no matter what her status was in Africa. In his introduction Evans-Pritchard also mentions the "suspicion and obstinate resistance" of his subjects, "a difficult people in adverse circumstances." E. E. Evans-Pritchard, *The Nuer: A Description of the Modes of Livelihood and Political Institutions of a Nilotic People* (Oxford: Clarendon Press, 1940), 14.

22   Michelet's maps are not in Ford. Nor is J. J. Rabearivelo's piece on Madagascar, Westermarck's "Negro Influence in Morocco," Melville Herskovits's "The Best Friend in Dahomey," Tete Kwesi Orgle's "Pre-British Gold Coast," "Hausa Writing" or "Baronga Proverbs." Also missing are Charles Ratton's "The Ancient Bronzes of Black Africa," Henri Lavachery on Congo statuary, Michelet's drawings of masks from the Tervueren Museum, Cunard's list of collections of African art, B. P. Feuilloley's "Magic and Initiation in the Ubangi-Shari," and another major piece by Raymond Michelet, "Primitive Life and Mentality," a critique of the principles of French anthropology. Very few essays from the third section on Africa in the original *Negro* anthology are included. Missing are Lapido Odunsi's "Britain and the Africans," George Schuyler's "Black Civilisation and White," "Under King Leopold's Domination," "Experience of a Black Man with the Missionaries," "Letter From Nigeria," "Letter From a Worker in South Africa," "Letter on South Africa by Ivan Navarro, "Extracts from a Pamphlet circulating in Belgian Congo," E. Stiers's "A Negro Empire: Belgium," G. Citerne and F. Jourdain, "French Imperialism at Work in Madagascar," George Padmore's "Pass Laws in South Africa and "How Britain Governs the Blacks," and E. T. Mofutsanyana's "Imperialist Terror in South Africa."

23   Cunard, ed., *Negro: An Anthology*, iv.

24   Cunard's State Department file has a copy of the ban from Trinidad; publisher Wishart's press clipping from *West Africa*, April 20, 1935, cites *Negro* as banned from the Gambia on the grounds of sedition under the Criminal Code.

25   Arthur Schomburg, "African Exploration," in Cunard, ed., *Negro: An Anthology*, 604.

26 Raymond Michelet, "African Empires and Civilizations," in Cunard, ed., *Negro: An Anthology*, 585–603.

27 Leith-Ross, *Stepping-Stones*, 96–97. Precisely at this juncture in the book is a portrait of the thin, ageing, sharp-featured Leith-Ross, legs crossed in a ladylike pose, white hair in a net, wearing a modest string of pearls. In her culture, her own and her family's considerable wealth are well hidden.

28 Nina Emma Mba, *Nigerian Women Mobilized: Women's Political Activity in Southern Nigeria 1900–1965* (Berkeley, CA: University of California, Institute of International Studies, 1982), 102.

29 Mba, *Nigerian Women Mobilized*, 241.

30 Langston Hughes, "People Without Shoes," in Cunard, ed., *Negro: An Anthology*, 468–69.

31 Evans-Pritchard, *The Nuer*, 9.

32 Leith-Ross, *African Women*, 175.

33 Leith-Ross, *African Women*, 174–75. She imagines that "glint of madness" in thousands of eyes in "the Riots" [*sic*]. They believed that the trade depression that had reduced them to poverty was the British punishment for the Women's War. Leith-Ross regarded this belief as entirely irrational. How stubborn they must have found her.

34 A sharp-eyed reader will note that there is another white woman in the text, in full evening dress with an Indian prince. Lady Cunard, object of her daughter's scorn for refusing to meet Black people socially, was punished eternally by having her photograph in print as a racist in the *Negro* anthology long after she has been forgotten as a society hostess.

35 Helen Lackner, "Colonial Administration and Social Anthropology: Eastern Nigeria, 1920–1940," in *Anthropology and the Colonial Encounter*, ed. Talal Asad (Atlantic Highlands, NJ: Humanities Press, 1988), 123–51. Lackner points out that Leith-Ross's friend, M. Green, who went with her to Nigeria also on a Leverhulme Fellowship, produced a more professional piece of work in *Ibo Village Affairs* (1947), but that both were part of British colonialism's use of anthropology for its own purposes to solve particular problems. Lackner cites a critique by Gerard Leclerc in *Anthropologie et Colonialisme*, attributing the origins of functionalism in British anthropology to this relationship, arguing that in France other theories developed because there was no government interference. This is not true, as we shall see in the discussion of Michel Leiris and French anthropology.

36 Helen Calloway, *Gender, Culture and Empire: European Women in Colonial Nigeria* (Urbana, IL: University of Illinois Press, 1987). She quotes Leith-Ross at length on the way dressing for dinner in the bush and observing strict rules of decorum was equivalent to maintaining moral superiority, self-respect, and British identity.

37 Leith-Ross, *African Women*, 38.

38 Leith-Ross, *African Women*, 352.

39   Leith-Ross, *African Women*, 357.

40   Leith-Ross, *African Women*, 365.

41   Leith-Ross, *Stepping-Stones*, 41.

42   The introduction to *The African Witch* (1936) includes Cary's warning: "Incidents of the women's war described in it [the novel] must not be taken to refer in any way to the women's wars in Southern Nigeria in the last ten years." Such a signal alerts the reader.

43   This point is made in detail in Holly McSpadden's dissertation on Cunard. Alain Locke claimed to have introduced Hurston to Cunard, and wrote to thank her for giving Hurston so much space in the book. See correspondence at the Harry Ransom Humanities Research Center.

44   Cunard, ed., *Negro: An Anthology*, 39–61.

45   Cunard, ed., *Negro: An Anthology*, 359–61.

46   Paul Gilroy, *The Black Atlantic: Modernity and Double Consciousness* (Cambridge, MA: Harvard University Press, 1993).

47   Letter from Locke to Cunard, dated April 14, 1934.

48   See Michael North, *The Dialectic of Modernism* (New York: Oxford, 1994); Ann Douglas, *Terrible Honesty: Mongrel Manhattan in the 1920s* (New York: Farrar, Straus and Giroux, 1995) (see also Marianne DeKoven's important review of Douglas in *The Women's Review of Books* XIII, no. 1 [1995], 5); Susan Gubar, *Racechanges: White Skin, Black Face in American Culture* (New York: Oxford University Press, 1977) (and see the review by Karen Lehrman, "Against Appropriation: A Feminist Takes on the Color Line and its White Transgressors," *New York Times*, October 26, 1997, 43). Many of Gubar's illustrations of white political incorrectness in identifying with Blacks involve Nancy Cunard, obviously not a figure in "American culture," but useful in terms of Gubar's mockery of her sexuality as from "a classy brothel," and for characterizing her left politics as "sinister," a tactic that allows Americans to continue to dismiss the local power of communism in the Black community and to brand its bearer as a foreign, white, sex maniac.

49   See Wilson Record, *The Negro and the Communist Party* (New York: Atheneum, 1971). My thanks to Norah Chase for lending me her copy of this book and for sharing her important work on women and the Communist Party in the Women's Biography Seminar.

Chapter Ten: Nanción's Cancións: Nancy Cunard and the Spanish Civil War

1   Actually Hemingway was resting in the Hotel Florida in Madrid according to Banting, who joined Cunard on her second trip to Spain. Hemingway thought their nasty-smelling cigarettes were marijuana and that they were just too late to be characters in his play about "war-tourists," and he annoyed them by talking about the "stimulation" of fighting (Ford, *Nancy Cunard: Brave Poet*, 183).

2   Stephen Spender, *World Within World* (London: Hamish Hamilton, 1951), 244–47.

3   See Maroula Joannou, "Nancy Cunard's English Journey," *Feminist Review* 78 (2004): 141–63.

4   Valentine Cunningham, ed., *Spanish Front: Writers on the Spanish Civil War* (New York: Oxford University Press, 1986).

5   Pablo Neruda, *Memoirs* (New York: Farrar, Straus and Giroux, 1976).

6   Cunard met Guillén in Cuba in 1932 while researching the *Negro* anthology; his contributions were translated by Langston Hughes, along with those of Jacques Roumain and Regino Pedroso, and later in Paris, Guillén and Hughes spent time with Aragon and Cunard. GCF to NC 4 January 1939 (in response to her letter to him 16 October 1938, Harry Ransom Center, UT, Austin; also cited in *Letters of T.S. Eliot Volume 8: 1936-1938*).

7   Nicolás Guillén and Teresa Labarta De Chaves, "Poems," *Latin American Literary Review* 2, no. 3 (1973): 114, www.jstor.org/stable/20118902.

8   George Orwell, *Homage to Catalonia* (1938) (New York: Harcourt Brace, 1969).

9   Martha Gellhorn, *The Face of War* (New York: Simon and Schuster, 1959). Another fine piece of writing about Spain is Josephine Herbst, *The Starched Blue Sky of Spain* (New York: Harper Collins, 1991). Gellhorn's *The Face of War* has been updated to include Vietnam. She met Hemingway (and later briefly married him) while reporting on Spain for *Collier's*; her reports were about children and the wounded, her politics of outrage much like Cunard's; she reported on Vietnam for the *Guardian*, but the *St. Louis Post-Dispatch* in the U.S. only published two of her five reports because of her criticism of U.S. policy. "We were guilty of the dishonest abandonment of Spain and the quick cheap betrayal of Czechoslovakia," she wrote. "We niggled and refused asylum to doomed Jews. We inspected and rejected anti-Fascists fleeing for their lives from Hitler. We were full of shame and ugly expediencies." Julia Edwards, *Women of the World: Great Foreign Correspondents* (Boston: Houghton Mifflin, 1988), 132. Her social consciousness is evident in four novellas about the Depression published in 1936 as *The Trouble I've Seen*, the result of her investigation into whether the Federal Emergency Relief Program really worked. *The Novellas of Martha Gellhorn* (New York: Knopf, 1992).

10   "Three Negro Poets" first came to my attention when I was working on Leonard Woolf in the Monks House papers at the University of Sussex. The always helpful curator Bet Inglis introduced me to the Rosey Pool papers, also catalogued by her. The Dutch poet and translator who had been Anne Frank's teacher and was imprisoned, escaped, and worked in the Resistance, devoted herself like Cunard to the cause of Black art internationally and produced several anthologies of Black poets in Dutch and English.

11   Nancy Cunard, "Three Negro Poets," *The Left Review* 3, no. 9 (October 1937): 536.

12 Cunningham notes that thirties writing attacks the family, but does not see the source of the argument made by Woolf (that the origins of fascism are in the patriarchal family) in the international socialist feminisms that flourished before and after World War I. See Valentine Cunningham, *British Writers of the Thirties* (Oxford: Oxford University Press, 1988), 14–16.

13 Cunard, "Three Negro Poets," 529–30.

14 Langston Hughes, *I Wonder as I Wander* (1965) (New York: Hill & Wang, 1993), 400. For Hughes in Spain, see vol. I of Arnold Rampersad, *The Life of Langston Hughes* (New York: Oxford University Press, 1988); Michel Fabre, *From Harlem to Paris: Black American Writers in Paris, 1840–1980* (Urbana, IL: University of Illinois Press, 1991); and Faith Berry, ed., *Good Morning, Revolution: Uncollected Writings of Social Protest* (New York: Lawrence Hill, 1973). In Langston Hughes, *Collected Poems*, ed. Arnold Rampersad (New York: Knopf, 1994), are versions of "Song of Spain," "Letter from Spain," and "Postcard From Spain," and "Air Raid: Barcelona"; these should, like Auden's poems, be compared for later revisions with their original publication. Hughes's "A Song of Spain" was first published in one of Cunard's pamphlets with a poem by Federico García Lorca, *Les Poètes du monde defendent le peuple espagnol*. Cunard's letters to Hughes are at Yale; his to her in Texas.

15 Cunard, "Three Negro Poets," 532.

16 Cunard, "Three Negro Poets," 532.

17 Cunard, "Three Negro Poets," 532.

18 The original manuscript of Auden's poem is in Cunard's papers at Texas. The errors in her typescript show that she had trouble with Auden's handwriting. They were corrected in Spender and Lehmann's anthology. But to cite that collection as its first publication erases the history of Cunard's handpress production of multilingual editions of poetry for the people, circulating among a wide audience of non-intellectuals, the errors a mark of their production in the haste of wartime. In this war as in World War I, poetry had a life like journalism, in rabble-rousing and in consoling the people. Spender's anthology is engaged in the opposite kind of cultural work—it selects out an elite of poets for an elite of readers. Brian Howard, Cunard's gay poet friend, had introduced Auden, and it is odd to think of Cunard as midwife to the controversial poem that came to signify the relation between intellectuals and fascism. Auden recanted and later deleted the stanza with the line "The conscious acceptance of guilt in the necessary murder," when he could no longer support the responsibilities of activism, but lines such as "To-morrow for the young poets exploding like bombs ... But today the struggle" have come to characterize the narcissistic English response to the war in measuring the cost to the self rather than concern for the people of Spain.

19 The call to take sides was dated Paris, June 1937; the French origin of the effort was also lost in Cunningham's transmission. The signatories were Louis Aragon, W. H. Auden, Jose Bergamin, Jean Richard Bloch, Nancy Cunard,

Brian Howard, Heinrich Mann, Ivor Montagu, Pablo Neruda, Ramon Sender, Stephen Spender, and Tristan Tzara, and Cunard's signature is under the typed list of authors.

20   Thanks to Claire Tylee for pointing this out.

21   The gay and lesbian presence in anti-fascist movements also deserves more attention than the valorizing (and, for once, this is the correct word) of Spender and Auden has allowed. John Banting and Brian Howard, among the gay men in Nancy Cunard's international left circle, introduced her to Auden. She introduced them to Langston Hughes and to gay French, Spanish, Latin American, and Caribbean writers on the left who came from many different races. The gay and lesbian left, though clearly present in European intellectual life during World War I, especially in the pacifist movement, first begins to make its historical presence known in the anti-racist and anti-fascist movements of the thirties. The repression of homosexuality demanded by the Communist Party and war's insistence on extremely polarized sex roles not only did not erase the powerful effect on left movements of gays and lesbians, but perhaps enhanced the erotic elements in the politics of international brother- and sisterhood.

22   *Authors Take Sides on the Spanish War* was published as a sixpenny pamphlet by the *Left Review* in 1937, with a note that many more responses on the side of the government had been received than could be printed but that the proportions correctly reflected the authors' views for or against.

23   In an odd Francophobic section of Cunningham's *British Writers of the Thirties*, 346, on Paris, Cunard surfaces for a second to get "the signatures of Auden and Spender, Brian Howard and Ivor Montagu for the circular letter that resulted in the pamphlet *Authors Take Sides*." Her name has crept into the text, but only as a messenger girl in a foreign land; no agency as author, editor, political thinker, publisher, reporter, poet, translator is allowed, though Cunard was the producer, in fact, at all levels, of the pamphlet. *Authors Take Sides* is a major subject of discussion in this book too, and Cunningham again segregates women writers in a separate category that Cunard and her comrades had dissolved in thirties culture, and he does not mention the Black contributors. Admitting that the pamphlet introduced a "broader picture" of left sympathy for the Republican cause, he nevertheless insists on seeing it as Communist Party propaganda produced by the CP journal, *Left Review*, as "its survey." That Cunard was not a member of the CP might spoil the argument that "manifestoes of the *Authors Take Sides*" kind were "generally instigated by Communist Party Front committees and organizations" (*British Writers of the Thirties*, 29).

24   Their inclusion is undercut by the reprinting of Stephen Spender's nasty dismissal of Sylvia Townsend Warner at the Writers' Congress in Spain in 1937 (Cunningham, ed., *Spanish Front*, 86). The reputations of Warner and Ackland were seriously damaged by Spender's attacks in left journals at the time and

then in his memoirs, and only now are they being taken seriously as public intellectuals. Cunard was a close friend of the couple and their correspondence is itself an astonishing record of the times. Spender's piece is transparently envious of their presence as a lesbian couple; he mocks Warner misogynistically for "dragging one of the Mexicans forward" as an excuse to ask for a night's rest because she was "dead tired," though his own heroic male "tiredness" while traveling through war-torn Spain is a major point of the essay, stressing, as his and Auden's work does, their personal pain rather than the suffering of the Spanish people. The rest of the essay consists of physical descriptions of the bodies of men of action, presumably the type who never got tired— "magnificently bronzed," "massively built," "jet-eyed," as the Mexican delegation was, to Malraux's disappointment, not the mad cowboys he expected, carrying whips and shooting revolvers. This writing is war tourism for a gay readership; its racist erotic primitivism derides "reckless" Spanish driving as one of the "serious defects of the Spanish character," while lingering over descriptions of foreign bodies: "Malraux, with his youthful appearance, his close-set greenish eyes, pale looming face, with one lock of hair overhanging his forehead, his hands in the pockets of his rough tweed suit, his rather slouching walk, and, at intervals his long nervous sniff, had the air of being a senior, if not altogether respectable boy" (Cunningham, ed., *Spanish Front*, 86).

25   The section on Cunard in Jane Dowson's *Women's Poetry of the 1930s* (New York: Routledge, 1996), with its hopelessly confused source notes, reprints a poem whose "filmic quality" and "journalistic economy" she admires, "To Eat To-day" (from the *New Statesman and Nation*, October 1938; also anthologized in *The Penguin Book of Spanish Civil War Verse*, ed. Valentine Cunningham [London: Penguin, 1996]). "The inclusion of Spanish phrases," Dowson writes, "is an important strategy in disorienting the English reader who might otherwise have some psychological immunity to the images of the suffering peasants whose home has been bombed" (Dowson, *Women's Poetry of the 1930s*, 53). But Cunard is not being simply bilingual. The poem actually speaks in many languages—German, Italian, French, Spanish, and cockney English—to illustrate the international structure of the battle against fascism. Nor is she addressing only English-speaking readers. The bombers are Italian and German supporters of Franco; the victims a Spanish mother and child, and a pregnant cat. Cunard names the voice of the bombs as another language invented by war—"codicils, dashes along the great Maniac speech." Janet Montefiore in *Men and Women Writers of the 1930s: The Dangerous Flood of History* (New York: Routledge, 1996), 118, notes that Cunard's Spanish War poem, "To Eat To-day," and her translations of Pablo Neruda's poems, for example, "Almeria" (*Left Review*, August 1937, 407; also reprinted in Cunningham's Penguin volume, 379), refer to "inhuman feasts": "A dish for the bishop ... A dish for the banker ... A dish of smashed axles, a dish of heads trampled on, / A black dish, a tray of blood for him..." Montefiore admires

Cunard's thirties poetry for its "syncopated rhythms and vernacular English" learned from jazz, attributing the energy of the poems to Cunard's "political anger" and her "ear for spoken voices." Unlike Susan Gubar in *Racechanges*, 150, who attributes sinister motives of "schizophrenic self-loathing" to what she describes as Cunard's appropriation of "the language of the Other" in her "Glossaries of Negro Slang" in *Negro* and elsewhere, Montefiore claims Cunard's dramatic monologue "Southern Sheriff," a lynching poem that she quotes from the *Negro* anthology, as "a vigorous, angry satire" in a short list of public poetry of "distinction" of the thirties (Montefiore, *Men and Women Writers of the 1930s*, 116–17).

26   See also Jim Fyrth and Sally Alexander's collection *Women's Voices From the Spanish Civil War* (London: Lawrence and Wishart, 1991), a laudable attempt to put women back into Spanish Civil War history, though without examining the process by which they were initially excluded. Cunard is represented by one of her *Manchester Guardian* pieces on the refugee camps in France. The editors note: "Some of the writers in this anthology refer to the 'Moors' and condemn the use of Black troops by Franco, or the use of Islamic troops in what purported to be a Christian crusade. This refers to Franco's use of North African mercenaries, part of the Spanish Army of Africa, and reflects a degree of racism, even among left-wing and other progressive people, which would be unacceptable today." They state that this *reconquista* "offended the Republic and its supporters" (Fyrth and Alexander, eds., *Women's Voices From the Spanish Civil War*, 31). A piece by Salaria Kea (origin unidentified), the Black nurse from Harlem who was the subject of Nancy Cunard's dispatches, is headed "Doing Christ's Duty," and her photograph appears in the text. Cunard's pursuit of the "race angle" in this context could very easily be misinterpreted.

27   Dadie Rylands told me that he set the type for Cunard's poem.

28   See the discussion of "Fresca" in Anne Chisholm's biography of Cunard, Valerie Eliot's edition of *The Waste Land*, and the section on the erotics of the Pound–Eliot collaboration in Koestenbaum's *Double Talk*, 112–39.

Chapter Eleven: Race on the Wire: Nancy Cunard's War Stories

1   A brief version of this chapter was read at the 1997 MLA in Toronto in a session on radical women writers sponsored by the Division of Non-Fiction Prose, and a version was later published as part of IRADAC's conference proceedings *Work in Progress at CUNY on the African Diaspora: An Interdisciplinary Conference* (New York: IRADAC & CAAN, 1998). My thanks to panelists Lillian Robinson, Robin Hackett, Carla Kaplan, and Gay Wachman, whose work on the letters and journalism of women public intellectuals Sylvia Townsend Warner, Valentine Ackland, and Zora Neale Hurston connects Cunard to the left tradition.

As I have noted above, Cunard's 800-page *Negro* anthology has yet to be republished. A bowdlerized version edited by Hugh Ford is in print but falsifies the collective project by its omissions. Critical work includes Patricia Clements's excellent "Transmuting Nancy Cunard," *Dalhousie Review* 66, nos. 1–2 (1986), 187–214, and my "Bonding and Bondage: Nancy Cunard and the Making of the *Negro* Anthology." Note that Susan Stanford Friedman's section on Cunard in Bonnie K. Scott's *The Gender of Modernism* (Bloomington, IN: Indiana University Press, 1990) reprints a bowdlerized version of the controversial pamphlet of 1931, *Black Man and White Ladyship*, from Ford, ed., *Nancy Cunard: Brave Poet*, 103–09. Copies of the original exist in the Harry Ransom Humanities Research Center, the Schomburg Library in New York, the Bienecke Library, Yale University, and other collections of modern manuscripts. This 1931 broadside is Nancy Cunard's modernist manifesto, connecting the greed of London art collectors in high society and the exploitation of people of color. The misreading of the edited text of *Black Man and White Ladyship* as merely a pathological mother–daughter scene acted out in public has perhaps led to the major misinterpretations of Cunard and her relationship to Black culture expressed in North, *The Dialectic of Modernism*; Douglas, *Terrible Honesty*; and Gubar, *Racechanges*.

2   Claude Barnett and the Associated Negro Press, Indiana online archive, Call no. 76-068.

3   Claude A. Barnett papers 1918–1967, Chicago History Museum, Research Center.

4   Reported in Chisholm, *Nancy Cunard*, 230–31.

5   Claude A. Barnett papers, Chicago History Museum.

6   Chisholm, *Nancy Cunard*, 231.

7   Ford, *Nancy Cunard: Brave Poet*, 182.

8   Chisholm, *Nancy Cunard*, 234.

9   Chisholm, *Nancy Cunard*, 234.

10 This letter is in the Cunard papers at the Harry Ransom Humanities Research Center; a carbon is in the Claude A. Barnett papers at the Chicago History Museum, which contain the records of the Associated Negro Press from the 1920s to the 1960s. Information on Barnett is taken from the description of the archive by curator Linda J. Evans. See also Lawrence D. Hogan, *A Black National News Service: The Associated Negro Press and Claude Barnett, 1919–1945* (Rutherford, NJ: Fairleigh Dickinson University Press, 1984).

11 Charles Duff, "Nancy Cunard: The Enigma of a Personality," in Ford, *Nancy Cunard: Brave Poet*, 186–90; he says she worked for a pittance for the Free French in London during World War II, but left when an accountant tried to cheat her out of her tiny wages (wages that she gave back to DeGaulle in any case); he insists that she was not really a communist but that her genius was in her spirit. Duff argues that Cunard's projects were always hugely ambitious politically and intellectually, that she worked tirelessly on the details but

never lost sight of the big picture—fascism, racism, etc. Her work, whether poetry, propaganda, publishing at the Hours Press, or editing the massive *Negro* anthology, was always "built up in flashes," a "vast panorama much of which is made up of items and minutiae of an often seemingly disparate nature" (Ford, *Nancy Cunard: Brave Poet*, 190).

12   Duff in Ford, *Nancy Cunard: Brave Poet*, 190.

13   Linda Evans, catalogue of the Barnett papers, Chicago History Museum.

14   Claude A. Barnett papers, Chicago History Museum.

15   Claude A. Barnett papers, Chicago History Museum.

16   Claude A. Barnett papers, Chicago History Museum.

17   Claude A. Barnett papers, Chicago History Museum.

18   Claude A. Barnett papers, Chicago History Museum.

19   Claude A. Barnett papers, Chicago History Museum.

End Notes: An Afterword

1   *The Letters of Virginia Woolf, Volume Two, 1912–1922*, ed. Nigel Nicolson and Joanne Trautman (New York: Houghton Mifflin, 1978), 384–85.

2   Tilda Swinton, "Object Lessons," *Aperture* 235 (summer 2019): 144, special issue on *Orlando*.

Index